# SOURCE BOOK OF THE HISTORY OF EDUCATION
## FOR THE GREEK AND ROMAN PERIOD

# SOURCE BOOK
## OF THE
# HISTORY OF EDUCATION
## FOR THE
# GREEK AND ROMAN PERIOD

BY

**PAUL MONROE, PH.D.**
ADJUNCT PROFESSOR OF THE HISTORY OF EDUCATION,
TEACHERS COLLEGE, COLUMBIA UNIVERSITY

GYAN

*Published by*

GYAN

Gyan Publishing House
5, Ansari Road
Daryaganj, New Delhi-110002
Phone: 011-47034999, 9811692060
E-mail: books@gyanbooks.com

*Distribution Network*
gyanbooks.com
India, USA, Canada, UK, Australia, Francc



ISBN : 978-81-212-6296-5 (PB)
First Published, 1902

2nd Impression 2022

*Printed at:* Gyan Press, Delhi.



**SOURCE BOOK OF THE HISTORY OF EDUCATION FOR THE GREEK AND ROMAN PERIOD**
Author: PAUL MONROE

# SOURCE BOOK

OF THE

# HISTORY OF EDUCATION

FOR THE

## GREEK AND ROMAN PERIOD

BY

PAUL MONROE, Ph.D.

ADJUNCT PROFESSOR OF THE HISTORY OF EDUCATION,
TEACHERS COLLEGE, COLUMBIA UNIVERSITY

1902

# PREFACE

SINCE neither history nor education has a meaning of universal acceptation, the "History of Education" presents for solution a problem containing two variable quantities. Without attempt at definition of either term, the following selections from the literary sources are presented as an aid to the exposition of education in its historic aspect. For the most part, these relate to education in the accepted historic meaning of the term, — that of a definitely organized institutional attempt to realize in individuals the ideals controlling a given people. In the early historic period of any people such efforts are not exerted through an institution specially organized for the one purpose; hence the earlier sources are quite general in their nature, relating more to the aims and ideals of education than to its organization. The great majority of the selections, however, deal with education as the work of a specific institution, for thus it is found to be as soon as a people comes into a consciousness of its own ends and of ways of attaining them. With the Greeks a third type of sources is essential to an understanding of their educational thought and practices. These are the philosophical discussions of education, both as to its proper function and as to its theoretically perfect means.

It is not to be understood that all such sources for the Greek and Roman people are here presented; for it would be a difficult, if not impossible, task to indicate the limits of the literature that might be used as historical evidence. Nevertheless, this volume includes most of the important discussions of organized educational efforts that are to be found in classical literature. There exist other sources, such as inscriptions, vase and mural paintings, and other art works, which possess no less value as sources than the literary monuments of the past, and which offer corroborative evidence for the use of the historian.

The purpose of this volume is to render accessible to the student with limited time and limited library facilities, the ideas of the Greeks and Romans concerning education, and such descriptions of their educational systems as are given in their own literature. In lieu of such available material the student has hitherto been restricted to secondary or more remote discussions, which in many cases are not even based upon a study of the sources. It is believed that by such direct study there will result, not only a more correct idea of the education of the classical period, but also a better apprehension of the meaning of education in its historical and contemporary aspects. This volume is designed as a text; hence the sources are classified into periods, in order to afford the student aid in their interpretation, and each group of sources is accompanied by a brief introductory sketch indicating the general setting of the period to which it belongs and the main principles of interpretation to be followed. These introductory chapters furnish little more than a syllabus for study; the interpretation is purposely left in a large degree to the student. The brief connecting links between the various periods under which the sources are classified secure for the student a connected text, and do away with a serious limitation to the usefulness of many source books.

As far as possible, all questions of controverted historical interpretation and all textual criticism have been avoided. There has been no effort at original translation, since with one or two minor exceptions standard versions are available, and the greater need is for selection and classification. Wherever possible, selections have been made from such translations as are most readily accessible in complete form. The passages from the Dialogues of Plato are from the second Jowett edition, those from Aristotle and Thucydides are from the first Jowett editions, and most other passages from the Bohn Library editions. Where other translations have been used, due credit has been given. At the expense of no little variety, it has seemed best to preserve the punctuation and spelling of the translations used. Where, in deference to modern standards of taste, it has been necessary to expunge passages or phrases, the omission has been indicated by asterisks. This necessity is regrettable, for in the passages expunged are very frequently indicated some of the most characteristic aspects of ancient education; but in a text for general use such omissions cannot well be avoided.

The scope of the book does not include any specific account of Roman education after the Christianization of the Empire. As being more vitally connected with early

Christian and mediæval education, the presentation of such sources is reserved for a future volume.

The author desires to express his obligation to Messrs. Bell and Sons, publishers of the *Bohn Library* series, for the privilege of making very liberal use of their publications; to Messrs. Little, Brown and Company for the privilege of using the selection from Professor Goodwin's edition of Plutarch's *Morals;* to Messrs. Butterworth and Company for the privilege of using the selection from their publication on Roman Law; and to Messrs. Macmillan and Company for the privilege of using the extract from Jebb's *Attic Orator:* also to Professor Franklin T. Baker and Mr. Theodore C. Mitchill for assistance in the revision of the text, and to Mr. Rudolph I. Coffee for the preparation of the Index.

PAUL MONROE.

NEW YORK,
September 26, 1901.

# CONTENTS

## PART I

### *GREEK EDUCATION*

### CHAPTER I

#### Old Greek Education



### CHAPTER II

#### Education of Women in Greece

## CHAPTER III

### The New Greek Education



## CHAPTER IV

### Greek Educational Theorists: The Historical View



## CHAPTER V

### Greek Educational Theorists: The Philosophical View

## CHAPTER VI

### Greek Educational Theorists: The Scientific View



## CHAPTER VII

### The Later Cosmopolitan Greek Education



# PART II

## *ROMAN EDUCATION*

## CHAPTER I

### Early Roman Education in General

## CHAPTER II

### THE SECOND PERIOD OF EARLY ROMAN EDUCATION



## CHAPTER III

### CONTRAST BETWEEN THE EARLIER AND THE LATER PERIODS OF ROMAN EDUCATION



## CHAPTER IV

### SURVIVAL OF EARLY ROMAN EDUCATIONAL IDEALS IN THE LATER PERIOD

## CHAPTER V

### The Third Period: The Hellenized Roman Education



## CHAPTER VI

### The Orator as the Ideal of Roman Education



## CHAPTER VII

### Scientific Exposition of Roman Education

# PART I

## GREEK EDUCATION

### I. OLD GREEK EDUCATION

**The Periods of Greek Education** may be characterized as that of the Old Greek Education and that of the New Greek Education. The Periclean Age, or the middle of the fifth century B.C., forms the dividing line. However, the characteristic changes marking the transition from the old to the new are not simply political, but are manifold, and can be understood in respect to education only by a study of such sources as those presented in the third section of this book. Each of these general periods may be subdivided. The earlier one includes, first, the Homeric period, and second, the historic period down to the middle of the fifth century. The second general period includes, first, the period of transition in educational, religious, and moral ideas, this being the time of philosophical activity and of development of formal education. The second of these special periods may be dated from the Macedonian conquest toward the close of the fourth century B.C. By the opening of this last period the philosophical schools have become definitely formulated, and during the period are organized into the University of Athens. In her intellectual life Greece now becomes cosmopolitan, and ceases to have distinctive characteristics aside from the philosophical schools.

**The Education of the Homeric Period** was that of a primitive people. It was an education that had little or no place for definite instruction of a literary character, but was essentially a training process in definite practical activities. Though noble youths are spoken of as having been given a course of instruction in arms and martial exercises, and Achilles as having had instruction in music, the healing art, and even in rhetoric (*Iliad*, IX. 414), this instruction amounted to little more than a direct training by imitation, into which entered little or no instruction, as later distinguished by the Greeks. The education of this period, as with all primitive peoples, consisted in that practical training which prepared for the immediate duties of life. Such training was given in the home for the humbler needs of life, — those connected with the securing of food, clothing, and shelter. The remainder of their education was the training received in council, wars, and marauding expeditions, for the more general public services demanded. This constituted the higher aspect of their education. The Homeric poems are a fertile source of information on this topic, though only in a very general way. In the Homeric period educational institutions were not distinct; the council and the camp furnished all higher education. The ideal of education was twofold: the man of valor, typified by Achilles; the man of wisdom, by Odysseus. The characteristics of these ideals are found throughout the narratives of the *Iliad* and the *Odyssey*, though these passages are so general and so remote in character from education, as technically understood, that it is impossible to make brief selections that would be to the present purpose. The following selections, giving descriptions of council, or battle, or of the man of bravery, or man of wisdom, may, nevertheless, be found helpful as an introduction to the further study of the historic type of Old Greek education: the *Iliad*, I. 52–302; II. 35–380, 445–482; IX. 50–180; X. 335–579; XI. 617–804; XVIII. 245–318; XIX. 40–275.

**The Character and Organization of Old Greek Education** is determined by the city state. This institution furnished the basis and ideals of education, as did the family with the Chinese and the theocracy with the Hebrews. Even in the Homeric period there were evidences of the fundamental importance of the city state, though it had not completely taken shape at that time (*Iliad*, XVIII. 490). In the historic period, on the other hand, it furnished the key to the understanding of the educational development of the Hellenic people. The city state grew up by the successive amalgamation of patriarchal families into village communities, of village communities into phratries or brotherhoods, of phratries into tribes, and of tribes into cities. The bond which held the family together was dominantly that of blood relationship. The village depended more on economic interests; the phratry, upon religious ties; the tribe, upon the communal ownership of land. So too the city state in its beginning as a union of tribes was held together by this descent from the old families and by possession of land. This "ancient wealth and worth" constituted the nobility of the Grecian citizen. Citizenship was confined at first to the heads of these noble families, but in time expanded until inclusive of all freemen. Though economic independence and free birth were always essential, this ideal of nobility came in time to consist less and less of wealth and noble birth, and more and more of certain traits of character that could be produced by education. Nobility now became virtue or worth. The Grecian idea of virtue underwent development, and this development constituted the basis of the historic growth of these educational ideals and practices. Virtue consisted at first almost wholly of physical bravery and a subordination of individual motives to the social welfare or demands. But in time it became spiritualized and intellectualized, and this growing intellectuality produced the literary element in education. With the transition to the period of new Greek education the literary element became supreme, at least with the Ionic Greeks; yet, whether small or great, it formed but a part of the Greek ideal of virtue or nobility. This idea of nobility is, then, the basis of their fundamental social institution, the city state. The possession of nobility was the prerequisite to membership in that institution. The dominant purpose of every prospective Grecian citizen was to attain this nobility or virtue. While economic independence, or wealth, and membership in the old families, or birth, were essential, all these could, in the later periods, be acquired. The intellectual and spiritual elements, the latter consisting largely of æsthetic appreciation, could be obtained only by education. Nobility or virtue, whatever was the stage of its development, constituted the basis of social organization, and at the same time the ideal of achievement of every citizen or prospective citizen. This idea of virtue, or nobility, then, constituted the aim or purpose of education. The development of the organization, means, and method of education followed the evolution of this idea of nobility or virtue and that of the city state. This development constitutes the history of Greek education.

**The Sources relating to the Historic Period of Old Greek**

**Education** are rather meagre if the selection be limited to direct discussion of education in a technical sense. The fullest are those which relate to Spartan education. This is owing to the fact that the old education was characteristic of Sparta throughout its history, for Sparta never accepted the new educational ideas or tolerated the new practices. Hence there are many authorities on the old education as found at Sparta, but comparatively few detailed discussions of the same period at Athens. Sparta, however, offers the best type of the old education, though of a much more extreme type than that found anywhere else in Greece, unless Crete be an exception. The account of Spartan education is from Plutarch's *Life of Lycurgus*, that being the fullest description of these educational institutions. It could be supplemented by passages drawn from the *Morals* of Plutarch, as well as by briefer references from Herodotus, Thucydides, Xenophon, Plato, and Aristotle. Plutarch was a citizen of Bœotia, and lived about 50 to 120 A.D. His *Parallel Lives* were written during the first years of the second Christian century. Plutarch was a moralist rather than a historian, and was more concerned in emphasizing the morals of an incident or life than in the accuracy of his facts. Hence his value as a historian depends upon the sources which he uses. In the *Life of Lycurgus* these are chiefly subsequent to Aristotle; Plato, Xenophon, and three of the minor poets are his only earlier authorities. His best authority is Aristotle.

However, the errors in the *Life of Lycurgus* relate to statements that are not essential to the discussion of education. They are for the most part connected with the question of the character of Lycurgus and the division of the land. The question whether Lycurgus was an historical personage does not affect the value of the present narrative. There is no agreement on this point among modern historians. On the other hand, there is quite general agreement that Plutarch's account of the division of the land is without historic basis. But there is no question as to the characteristic social and educational institutions. The testimony from ancient authorities on these points is uniform and voluminous. As to the time of the introduction of these educational institutions, there is also substantial agreement. Though the writers make no mention of Lycurgus as the author of these changes which were responsible for the characteristic Spartan institutions, both Thucydides and Herodotus refer to these changes, as having taken place in the ninth century B.C. This is the period to which Lycurgus is assigned by other writers, including Plutarch.

The educational and social institutions of Sparta were peculiarly her own, for, while they form the best type of the old Greek education, they were not a common possession even among the Dorians. The nearest approach to them was in Crete; but here they were more communistic and of but brief duration. At Sparta, on the other hand, this education was coincident with Spartan political power. While there was evidently a marked decline in these institutions by the time of Aristotle, they were yet characteristic and influential. By the third century B.C., they had fallen into decay, when Agis (244–240 B.C.) and Cleomenes (236–222 B.C.) attempted their restoration. With the coming of the Roman power these old ideals ceased to have any influence whatever, and the old institutions became obsolete.

It is the new Greek education that was typical of

Athenian life, hence the references to the old education as it existed at Athens are not so numerous or detailed. As the literary age was essentially that of the new education, the sources referring to the old period are from writers that lived in the new. The best complete description of the old education is the brief passage from the *Protagoras* of Plato. The *Protagoras* belongs in the early group of Plato's writings, dating probably from the first decade of the fourth century B.C. The scene is supposed to have been laid about 425 B.C. Protagoras was the first of the Sophists at Athens, where he began to teach about the middle of the fifth century B.C. The passage given is merely incidental to the main trend of the argument in the dialogue. The discussion between Socrates and Protagoras is concerning virtue. The substance of Socrates' argument is that virtue is unified because it reduces to a common principle, that common principle being knowledge. If this is true, then virtue is teachable. In regard to this last point, the position taken by disputants in the earlier part of the dialogue is reversed. The passage given is taken from a lengthy speech of Protagoras, in which he argues that virtue is teachable. One evidence he cites is this general account of old Athenian education, the aim of which was substantially the inculcation of virtue. The account is very concise and covers the entire scope of early education. This account can be supplemented by passages found in selections relating to later periods, notably the contest between the old and new education in the *Clouds* of Aristophanes, in the ideal education advocated in the *Republic*, and in the scientific exposition of the *Politics* of Aristotle.

The latest period of education mentioned in the *Protag-*

*oras* is that devoted to the service of the state. The ideal of this education is given in the oath which the Ephebes were required to take, here given as the second selection. The third selection is the famous funeral oration of Pericles written by Thucydides. This is one of the best presentations of the ideal governing the Athenian people, and indicates quite clearly the spirit and purpose of their education. Both Pericles and Thucydides were among the earlier products of the new Greek education — at least, both were profoundly influenced by it. The speeches of Pericles, especially those reported by Thucydides, are clear samples of the results of the new education, showing evidently the influence of the rhetorical schools. But while the form of the speech is a product of new conditions, its content is one of the best presentations of the ideals of the old. The lives and deeds celebrated in the panegyric were the product of the old education. The passage is especially valuable as giving an analysis of those conditions which made possible the growth of the new type of education. Even under the old régime there was a place for the individuality of the citizen at Athens as there had not been elsewhere in Greece; and while this individualism was wholly subject to the interests of the city state, it at least had a place under conditions which provided for its development. Thucydides was born about 471 B.C. and lived until the opening of the next century. He received rhetorical training from some of the earliest Sophists, Gorgias among others, but in the severity and conservatism of his ideas he belonged to the earlier period. The oration given is most probably his own work and not that of Pericles; if of Pericles, it is rather the compilation of a number of speeches. Though it may be designed for the reader of the history, rather than for the audience of occasion, it reflects accurately the spirit of such occasions and the character of the times. While Pericles, both in his training and in his life, was more clearly than Thucydides a product of the newer education, it would not be inconsistent that on such an occasion he should express the dominant characteristics of the old. Irrespective of its authorship, this oration can be taken as an exposition of the ideals and results of the old education.

**Spartan Education** was almost identical with Spartan life in general. Sparta was practically a military camp organized for the training of warriors. The Spartans were a small group of conquerors among a large subject population. Their national existence depended upon the military excellence of their citizens, and their whole life was organized to this end. The home was practically abolished, and for it was substituted the camp or school. While there was no definite school, all of childhood was a schooling, definitely systematized for educational purposes; and the chief occupation of the adults, aside from their military life, was the education of the younger generation. This education was almost wholly physical and moral. It was narrow but intense, producing the highest and most permanent results that have ever been attained along these restricted lines. Above all, it meant the production of individuals wholly subject to the state. Next to this idea of the complete subordination of the welfare of the individual to that of the community, came the Spartan ideal of physical bravery, power, and endurance. Patriotism and sacrifice of the individual to the common welfare were inculcated throughout life and in every incident and interest in life. The physical results were obtained through the definite training that was a substitute for all school work. This rigid discipline began from the day of birth, but for the first seven years the boy remained in the charge of the mother. Thereafter he was in the charge of selected state officials that were responsible for his physical and moral education. The boys were trained in companies, lived in public barracks, and ate at common tables. These companies were under immediate command of boys of an older age, though the general supervision of adults was never absent. The training consisted of a definite system of exercises and games, of a more military character after the age of twelve, and wholly so from the eighteenth or twentieth year, during which time the youth lived in barracks or was engaged in actual military service. In time of peace this service was in the nature of police or garrison duties. Only at the thirtieth year were the youths admitted into full citizenship. The moral training aimed to produce self-control in action and speech, endurance, reverence, a spirit of patriotic self-sacrifice, dignity of action, and subjection of all emotional expression. Such results were obtained by a constant association with others of the same age under the close supervision of the elders at their meals, at their games, in public dances of military character, in religious services of choral character, in their sports, especially hunting, and in their barrack life. After the age of twelve, boys were trained to provide for their own wants through the obligation resting upon them of contributing to the common mess and to the few comforts allowed in their sleeping quarters. In this elaborate state education there was little provision for the intellectual element save as it was incidental in the physical and moral training indicated above. There was practically no literary instruction. In the later centuries, however, it was customary, or at least not unusual, for reading and writing to be taught, though aside from the state education. Otherwise the intellectual training was received in committing to memory and mastering the Laws of Lycurgus, — these being handed down from one generation to another through several centuries in the verbal form, — the national hymns and choruses, and later the poems of the few native writers held in repute.

As with all the Greeks the content of Spartan education was included in music, gymnastic, and dancing. But music was a much narrower term than it came to be elsewhere, and never contained more than the rudiments of a literary education.

The details of this system of education are given in full in the selection from Plutarch. This education, introduced in the ninth century B.C. was largely responsible for the military power of Sparta. It lost much of its rigidity after the Peloponnesian War, and ceased to have any force by the opening of the second century B.C.

**Athenian Education** of the old period was similar to the Spartan education in its simplicity of aim and narrowness of content, but not in its organization or in its stationary character. While the details of Spartan education were quite full, the sources on early Athenian education leave much to be desired. The selections from the speech of Protagoras give a general outline, but few details. Education was public only in so far as it was subject to close state supervision of the general results to be expected of home training or individual private institutions. It could be given in the home, but was more commonly obtained in private schools. In contradistinction to the general authority and responsibility of adults at Sparta, a law of Solon forbade any adult save teachers and pedagogues entering the school. There was not the training in large groups as at Sparta, though the ability to act in common and the community sentiment were developed to some extent through the religious chorus, dance, and procession. Athenian education was neither so severe nor so prolonged as that at Sparta, and, after the fifteenth or sixteenth year, it permitted much greater freedom.

As elsewhere in Greece, formal education included music and gymnastic, perhaps with dancing as a third branch, though it was but a combination of the other two. Gymnastic was less important and less military in character than at Sparta. The purpose of gymnastic was the development of a sound and beautiful physique, not simply the making of a warrior. Beauty and grace, quite as well as power of endurance, entered into the aims. The exercises were less rigid and more varied, consisting in running, discus throwing, javelin casting, and wrestling, to which should be added dancing as a culmination and combination of the other phases of their training. By these exercises there were to be obtained health and strength, beauty and grace, and, in addition, the self-possession and dignity of bearing that were but the outward manifestations of the moral results of this physical training. Music included the remainder of their formal education. But even in this early period music was a much broader term than at Sparta. It always included the literary element, at least reading, writing, and the mastery of the Homeric writings. Later, other national literature was introduced, so that this literary education would mean a familiarity with national myths, religious customs, and laws. While music was a term applicable to all the interests of the nine muses, it meant music in the restricted sense as well. Along with reading went instruction in playing the lyre and in singing, for the three were combined to a considerable extent. It is not until the later period that the literary element becomes the prominent factor, and that the use of musical instruments other than the simple one for accompanying the voice was introduced. The method of these schools was little more than simple training through imitation. Of elaborate literary instruction there was none. The work in literature consisted in memorizing the Homeric poems and in repeating them with appropriate musical accompaniments. At fifteen and sixteen the boy devoted the greater part of his time to gymnastic, and passed from the palæstra into the gymnasium for advanced physical training, association with adults in the agora being substituted for the music school. At eighteen the ephebic stage was reached, when the oath given in the selections (p. 33) was administered, and the youth entered on the last stage of apprenticeship for citizenship. This period included a two years' military service in guard and police duty, mostly in the rural regions. At twenty he was admitted to full citizenship.

While this education was more literary in character than the Spartan, its dominant motive was moral and social. Its whole purpose was preparation for active Athenian citizenship, but a citizenship which demanded political as well as military services. The influence of these political obligations upon the character of the youth and the citizen is emphasized in the oration of Pericles. The dominant moral purpose of the musical and literary training is emphasized in the argument of Protagoras. The intellectual or rational element had little place. The old myths and legends formed the basis of the work of the music schools, and the inculcation of reverence for them gave the chief reason for the existence of these schools. It was not intellectual power, but reverence, loyalty, and temperance in word and deed, that constituted the educational aim. That these results were to be obtained, not by complete suppression of the individual but by his development, is the key-note to the oration of Pericles. But it was in no sense the individualism of the later age in the dawn of which Pericles himself lived; it was an individualism gained through participation in all social activities, political, religious, and military, and always under the dominance of a rigid public opinion upholding the traditional social morality. The freedom of the individual did *not* consist in the liberty to determine his moral standards, his religious ideas, or his civic or social activities. In respect to the means for attaining to these recognized and approved standards there was also freedom, as we have already seen. Hence the wide divergence from Sparta in the organization and rigidity of detail in education.

Though the old education passed into the new practically with the beginning of the literary period at Athens, the general nature of the elementary education remained much the same. Hence in the selections from the later period there is much evidence relating to the earlier. In Aristophanes the old is set over in contrast against the new. Aristotle writes, not as an idealist, but as a scientist, explaining the nature of and the reason for many of the old practices. For this reason there is in his discussion a clear exposition of certain phases of the old practices. In these respects the later selections will, therefore, furnish additional material relating to the simple education of this early period.

## *Selections from the Life of Lycurgus by Plutarch*[1]

. . . It was not left to the father to rear what children he pleased, but he was obliged to carry the child to a place called Lesche,[2] to be examined by the most ancient men of the tribe who were assembled there. If it were strong and well proportioned, they gave orders for its education, and assigned it one of the nine thousand shares of land; but if it were weakly and deformed, they ordered it to be thrown into the place called Apothetæ, which is a deep cavern near the mountain Taygetus, concluding that its life could be no advantage either to itself or to the public, since nature had not given it at first any strength or goodness of constitution. For the same reason the women did not wash their new-born infants with water, but with wine, thus making some trial of their habit of body — imagining that sickly and epileptic children sink and die under the experiment, while healthy become more vigorous and hardy. Great care and art were also exerted by the nurses; for, as they never swathed the infants, their limbs had a freer turn and their countenances a more liberal air; besides, they used them to any sort of meat, to have no terrors in the dark, nor to be afraid of being alone, and to leave all ill-humour and unmanly crying. . . . The Spartan children were not in that manner under tutors purchased or hired with money, nor were the parents at liberty to educate them as they pleased; but as soon as they were seven years old, Lycurgus ordered them to be enrolled in companies, where they were all kept under the same order and discipline, and had their exercises and recreations in common. He who showed the most conduct and courage amongst them was made captain of the company. The rest kept their eyes upon him, obeyed his orders, and bore

**Care of infants.**

**Training of the Spartan boy.**

[1] The *Langhorne* translation. [2] Place of public conversation.

with patience the punishments he inflicted; so that their whole education was an exercise of obedience. The old men were present at their diversions, and often suggested some occasion of dispute or quarrel that they might observe with exactness the spirit of each and their firmness in battle.

As for learning, they had just what was absolutely necessary. All the rest of their education was calculated to make them subject to command, to endure labour, to fight and conquer. They added, therefore, to their discipline as they advanced in age — cutting their hair very close, making them go barefoot, and play, for the most part, quite naked. At twelve years of age their undergarment was taken away, and one upper one a year allowed them. Hence, they were necessarily dirty in their persons, and not indulged the great favour of baths and oil except on some particular days of the year. They slept in companies, on beds made of the tops of reeds which they gathered with their own hands, without knives, and brought from the banks of the Eurotas.[1] In winter they were permitted to add a little thistle-down, as that seemed to have some warmth in it.

**How the boy lived after his twelfth year.**

At this age the most distinguished amongst them became the favourite companions of the elder; and the old men attended more constantly their places of exercise, observing their trials of strength and wit, not slightly and in a cursory manner, but as their fathers, guardians, and governors; so that there was neither time nor place where persons were wanting to instruct and chastise them. One of the best and ablest men in the city was, moreover, appointed inspector of the youth, and he gave the command of each company to the discreetest and most spirited of those, called Irens. An Iren was one that had been two years out of the class of boys; a Melliren, one of the oldest lads. This Iren then, a youth twenty years old, gives orders to those under his command in their little battles, and has them to serve him at his house. He sends the oldest of them to fetch wood, and the younger to gather pot-herbs; these they steal where they can find them, either slily getting into gardens, or else craftily and warily creeping to the common

[1] Chief river of Laconia, on which Sparta was situated.

tables. But if any one be caught, he is severely flogged for negligence or want of dexterity. They steal, too, whatever victuals they possibly can, ingeniously contriving to do it when persons are asleep or keep but indifferent watch. If they are discovered, they are punished not only with whipping, but with hunger; indeed, their supper is but slight at all times, that, to fence against want, they may be forced to exercise their courage and address. This is the first intention of their spare diet; a subordinate one is to make them grow tall. For when the animal spirits are not too much oppressed by a great quantity of food, which stretches itself out in breadth and thickness, they mount upwards by their natural lightness, and the body easily and freely shoots up in height. This also contributes to make them handsome; for thin and slender habits yield more freely to nature, which then gives a fine proportion to the limbs, whilst the heavy and gross resist her by their weight. . . .

The boys steal with so much caution, that one of them, having conveyed a young fox under his garment, suffered the creature to tear out his bowels with his teeth and claws, choosing rather to die than be detected. Nor does this appear incredible, if we consider what their young men can endure to this day; for we have seen many of them expire under the lash at the altar of Diana Orthia.

The Iren, reposing himself after supper, used to order some of the boys to sing a song; to another he put some question which required a judicious answer, for example: "Who was the best man in the city?" or, "What he thought of such an action?" This accustomed them from their childhood to judge of the virtues, to enter into the affairs of their countrymen. For if one of them was asked, "Who is a good citizen, or who an infamous one?" and hesitated in his answer, he was considered as a boy of slow parts, and of a soul that would not aspire to honour. The answer was likewise to have a reason assigned for it, and proof conceived in few words. He whose account of the matter was wrong, by way of punishment had his thumb bit by the Iren. The old men and magistrates often attended these little trials, to see whether the Iren exercised his authority in a rational and proper manner. He was

**Methods of instruction.**

permitted, indeed, to inflict the penalties; but when the boys were gone, he was to be chastised himself if he had punished them either with too much severity or remissness.

Relation of inspirer and boy.

The adopters of favourites also shared both in the honour and disgrace of their boys: and one of them is said to have been mulcted by the magistrates because the boy whom he had taken into his affections let some ungenerous word or cry escape him as he was fighting. This love was so honourable and in so much esteem, that the virgins, too, had their lovers amongst the most virtuous matrons. A competition of affection caused no misunderstanding, but rather a mutual friendship between those that had fixed their regards upon the same youth, and a united endeavour to make him as accomplished as possible.

The boys were also taught to use sharp repartee, seasoned with humour, and whatever they said was to be concise and pithy. For Lycurgus, as we have before observed, fixed but a small value on a considerable quantity of his iron money; but, on the contrary, the worth of speech was to consist of its being comprised in a few plain words, pregnant with a great deal of sense; and he contrived that by long silence they might learn to be sententious and acute in their replies. As debauchery often causes weakness and sterility in the body, so the intemperance of the tongue makes conversation empty and insipid. King Agis,[1] therefore, when a certain Athenian laughed at the Lacedæmonian short swords, and said, "The jugglers would swallow them with ease upon the stage," answered in his laconic way, "And yet we can reach our enemies' hearts with them." Indeed, to me there seems to be something in this concise manner of speaking, which immediately reaches the object aimed at, and forcibly strikes the mind of the hearer. Lycurgus himself was short and sententious in his discourse, if we may judge by some of his answers which are recorded; that, for instance, concerning the constitution. When one advised him to establish a popular government in Lacedæmon, "Go," said he,

Importance of brief answers.

[1] Reigned 244–240 B.C. In his attempt to reinstate the policy of these early laws, he was defeated by Leonidas II., thrown into prison, and killed.

"and first make a trial of it in thine own family." That, again, concerning sacrifices to the Deity, when he was asked why he appointed them so trifling and of so little value, "That we may never be in want," said he, "of something to offer him." Once more, when they inquired of him what sort of martial exercises he allowed of, he answered, "All except those in which you stretch out your hands." Several such-like replies of his are said to be taken from the letters which he wrote to his countrymen: as to their question, "How shall we best guard against the invasion of an enemy?" "By continuing poor, and not desiring in your possessions to be one above another." And to the question, whether they should enclose Sparta with walls, "That city is well fortified which has a wall of men instead of brick." Whether these and some other letters ascribed to him are genuine or not, is no easy matter to determine. However, that they hated long speeches, the following apophthegms are a farther proof. King Leonidas[1] said to one who discoursed at an improper time about affairs of some concern, "My friend, you should not talk so much to the purpose of what it is not now to the purpose to talk of." Charilaus, the nephew of Lycurgus, being asked why his uncle had made so few laws, answered, "To men of few words, few laws are sufficient." Some people finding fault with Hecatæus the sophist, because when admitted to one of the public repasts he said nothing all the time, Archidamidas replied, "He who knows how to speak, knows also when to speak." . . .

This was the manner of their apophthegms: so that it has been justly enough observed that the term lakonizein (to act the Lacedæmonian) is to be referred rather to the exercises of the mind than those of the body.

Education in poetry and music.

Nor were poetry and music less cultivated among them than a concise dignity of expression. Their songs had a spirit which could rouse the soul, and impel it in an enthusiastic manner to action. The language was plain and manly, the subject serious and moral. For they consisted chiefly of the praises of heroes that had died for Sparta, or

[1] Succeeded Areus on the throne of Sparta, 257 B.C. For a time compelled to resign by his colleague Agis. Died 230 B.C.

else of expressions of detestation for such wretches as had declined the glorious opportunity, and rather chose to drag on life in misery and contempt. Nor did they forget to express an ambition for glory suitable to their respective ages. . . .

And the king always offered sacrifice to the muses before a battle, putting his troops in mind, I suppose, of their early education, and of the judgment that would be passed upon them, as well as that those divinities might teach them to despise danger, while they performed some exploit fit for them to celebrate.

On those occasions they relaxed the severity of their discipline, permitting their men to be curious in dressing their hair, and elegant in their arms and apparel, while they expressed their alacrity, like horses full of fire and neighing for the race. They let their hair, therefore, grow from their youth, but took more particular care when they expected an action to have it well combed and shining; remembering a saying of Lycurgus, that a large head of hair made the handsome more graceful, and the ugly more terrible. The exercises, too, of the young men during the campaigns were more moderate, their diet not so hard, and their whole treatment more indulgent: so that they were the only people in the world with whom military discipline wore in time of war a gentler face than usual. When the army was drawn up, and the enemy near, the king sacrificed a goat, and commanded them all to set garlands upon their heads, and the musicians to play Castor's march, while himself began the *pæan*, which was the signal to advance. It was at once a solemn and dreadful sight to see them measuring their steps to the sound of music, and without the least disorder in their ranks or tumult of spirits, moving forward cheerfully and composedly, with harmony, to battle. Neither fear nor rashness was likely to approve men so disposed, possessed as they were of a firm presence of mind, with courage and confidence of success, as under the conduct of heaven. When the king advanced against the enemy he had always with him some one that had been crowned in the public games of Greece. And they tell us that a Lacedæmonian, when large sums were offered him on condition that he would not enter the

**Spartans were less severe when on campaigns.**

Olympic lists, refused them: having with much difficulty thrown his antagonist, one put this question to him—"Spartan, what will you get by this victory?" He answered with a smile, "I shall have the honour to fight foremost in the ranks before my prince." When they had routed the enemy, they continued the pursuit till they were assured of the victory; after that they immediately desisted, deeming it neither generous nor worthy of a Grecian to destroy those who made no farther resistance. This was not only a proof of magnanimity, but of great service to their cause. For when their adversaries found that they killed such as stood it out, but spared the fugitives, they concluded that it was better to fly than to meet their fate upon the spot. . . .

**Wherein Spartan honor consisted.**

The discipline of the Lacedæmonians continued after they were arrived at years of maturity. For no man was at liberty to live as he pleased; the city being like one great camp, where all had their stated allowance, and knew their public charge, each man concluding that he was born, not for himself, but for his country. Hence, if they had no particular orders, they employed themselves in inspecting the boys, and teaching them something useful, or in learning of those that were older than themselves. One of the greatest privileges that Lycurgus procured his countrymen, was the enjoyment of leisure, the consequence of his forbidding them to exercise any mechanic trade. It was not worth their while to take great pains to raise a fortune, since riches were of no account: and the Helotes,[1] who tilled the ground, were answerable for the produce above-mentioned. To this purpose we have a story of a Lacedæmonian, who, happening to be at Athens while the court sat, was informed of a man who was fined for idleness; and when the poor fellow was returning home in great dejection, attended by his condoling friends, he desired the company to show him the person that was condemned for keeping up his dignity. So much beneath them they reckoned all attention to mechanic arts and all desire of riches! . . .

**Occupation of the men.**

[1] Spartan serfs, the original owners of the land. They cultivated the lands for the Spartans.

Upon the whole, he taught his citizens to think nothing more disagreeable than to live by (or for) themselves. Like bees, they acted with one impulse for the public good, and always assembled about their prince. They were possessed with a thirst of honour, an enthusiasm bordering upon insanity, and had not a wish but for their country. These sentiments are confirmed by some of their aphorisms. When Pædaretus lost his election for one of the three hundred, he went away rejoicing that there were three hundred better men than himself found in the city. Pisistratidas going with some others, ambassador to the king of Persia's lieutenants, was asked whether they came with a public commission, or on their own account; to which he answered, "If successful, for the public; if unsuccessful, for ourselves." . . .

**Their disdain of being for one's self.**

Thus far, then, we can perceive no vestiges of a disregard to right and wrong, which is the fault some people find with the laws of Lycurgus, allowing them well enough calculated to produce valour, but not to promote justice. Perhaps it was the Cryptia,[1] as they called it, or ambuscade, if that was really one of this lawgiver's institutions, as Aristotle says it was, which gave Plato so bad an impression both of Lycurgus and his laws. The governors of the youth ordered the shrewdest of them from time to time to disperse themselves in the country, provided only with daggers and some necessary provisions. In the daytime they hid themselves and rested in the most private places they could find, but at night they sallied out into the roads and killed all the Helotes they could meet with. Nay, sometimes by day they fell upon them in the fields, and murdered the ablest and strongest of them. Thucydides relates in his history of the Peloponnesian War, that the Spartans selected such of them as were distinguished for their courage, to the number of two thousand or more, declared them free, crowned them with garlands, and conducted them to the temples of the gods; but soon after they all disappeared, and no one could, either then or since, give account in what manner they were destroyed.

**Attacks on Lycurgus are unwarranted.**

[1] A custom which permitted the ephors at night to fall upon the Helots and kill them. Its purpose was military training for the Spartan youths.

Aristotle particularly says, that the ephori,[1] as soon as they were invested in their office, declared war against the Helotes, that they might be massacred under pretence of law. In other respects they treated them with great inhumanity; sometimes they made them drink until they were intoxicated, and in that condition led them into the public halls, to show the young men what drunkenness was. They ordered them to sing mean songs, and to dance ridiculous dances, but not to meddle with any that were genteel and graceful. Thus they tell us that when the Thebans afterwards invaded Laconia, and took a great number of the Helotes prisoners, they ordered them to sing the odes of Terpander, Alcman,[2] or Spendon the Lacedæmonian, but they excused themselves, alleging that it was forbidden by their masters. Those who say that a freeman in Sparta was most a freeman, and a slave most a slave, seem well to have considered the difference of states. But in my opinion, it was in after-times that these cruelties took place among the Lacedæmonians; chiefly after the great earthquake, when, as history informs us, the Helotes joining the Messenians, attacked them, did infinite damage to the country, and brought the city to the greatest extremity. I can never ascribe to Lycurgus so abominable an act as that of the ambuscade. I would judge in this case by the mildness and justice which appeared in the rest of his conduct, to which also the gods gave their sanction. . . .

Cruelty of the ephori.

It was not, however, the principal design of Lycurgus that this city should govern many others, but he considered its happiness, like that of a private man, as flowing from virtue and self-consistency; he therefore so ordered and disposed it, that by the freedom and sobriety of its inhabitants, and their having a sufficiency within themselves, its continuance might be the more secure. Plato, Diogenes, Zeno, and other writers upon government, have taken Lycurgus for their model; and these have attained great praise, though they left only an idea of something excellent. Yet he who not in idea and in words, but in fact,

Principles established by Lycurgus.

[1] Five magistrates whose powers in Sparta corresponded to the Roman tribune.

[2] Chief poet of Sparta. Flourished about 630 B.C.

produced a most inimitable form of government, and by showing a whole city of philosophers, confounded those who imagine that the so much talked of strictness of a philosophic life is impracticable; he, I say, stands in the rank of glory far before the founders of all the other Grecian states.

### *The Funeral Oration of Pericles, from Thucydides* [1]

The basis of the traditional funeral ceremonies.

'Most of those who have spoken here before me have commended the lawgiver who added this oration to our other funeral customs;[2] it seemed to them a worthy thing that such an honour should be given at their burial to the dead who have fallen on the field of battle. But I should have preferred that, when men's deeds have been brave, they should be honoured in deed only, and with such an honour as this public funeral, which you are now witnessing. Then the reputation of many would not have been imperilled on the eloquence or want of eloquence of one, and their virtues believed or not as he spoke well or ill. For it is difficult to say neither too little nor too much; and even moderation is apt not to give the impression of truthfulness. The friend of the dead who knows the facts

[1] Thucydides, Book II. par. 35–47. Jowett translation.

[2] It was the custom of the Athenians to give public burial to those who fell in battle. Thucydides describes these ceremonies as follows: —

"Three days before the celebration they erect a tent in which the bones of the dead are laid out, and every one brings to his own dead any offering which he pleases. At the time of the funeral the bones are placed in chests of cypress wood, which are conveyed on hearses; there is one chest for each tribe. They also carry a single empty litter decked with a pall for all whose bodies are missing, and cannot be recovered after the battle. The procession is accompanied by any one who chooses, whether citizen or stranger, and the female relatives of the deceased are present at the place of interment and make lamentation. The public sepulchre is situated in the most beautiful spot outside the walls; there they always bury those who fall in war; only after the battle of Marathon the dead, in recognition of their preëminent valour, were interred on the field. When the remains have been laid in the earth, some man of known ability and high reputation, chosen by the city, delivers a suitable oration over them; after which the people depart."

is likely to think that the words of the speaker fall short of his knowledge and of his wishes; another who is not so well informed, when he hears of anything which surpasses his own powers, will be envious and will suspect exaggeration. Mankind are tolerant of the praises of others so long as each hearer thinks that he can do as well or nearly as well himself, but, when the speaker rises above him, jealousy is aroused and he begins to be incredulous. However, since our ancestors have set the seal of their approval upon the practice, I must obey, and to the utmost of my power shall endeavour to satisfy the wishes and beliefs of all who hear me.

'I will speak first of our ancestors, for it is right and becoming that now, when we are lamenting the dead, a tribute should be paid to their memory. There has never been a time when they did not inhabit this land, which by their valour they have handed down from generation to generation, and we have received from them a free state. But if they are worthy of praise, still more were our fathers, who added to their inheritance, and after many a struggle transmitted to us, their sons, this great empire. And we ourselves assembled here to-day, who are still most of us in the vigour of life, have chiefly done the work of improvement, and have richly endowed our city with all things, so that she is sufficient for herself both in peace and war. Of the military exploits by which our various possessions were acquired, or of the energy with which we or our fathers drove back the tide of war, Hellenic or Barbarian, I will not speak; for the tale would be long and is familiar to you. But before I praise the dead, I should like to point out by what principles of action we rose to power, and under what institutions and through what manner of life our empire became great. For I conceive that such thoughts are not unsuited to the occasion, and that this numerous assembly of citizens and strangers may profitably listen to them.

**The greatness of Athens due to the character of her citizens and of her institutions.**

'Our form of government does not enter into rivalry with the institutions of others. We do not copy our neighbours, but are an example to them. It is true that we are called a democracy, for the administration is in the hands of the many and not of the few. But while the law secures

**The government is a democracy which rewards merit.**

equal justice to all alike in their private disputes, the claim of excellence is also recognised; and when a citizen is in any way distinguished, he is preferred to the public service, not as a matter of privilege, but as the reward of merit. Neither is poverty a bar, but a man may benefit his country whatever be the obscurity of his condition. There is no exclusiveness in our public life, and in our private intercourse we are not suspicious of one another, nor angry with our neighbour if he does what he likes; we do not put on sour looks at him which, though harmless, are not pleasant. While we are thus unconstrained in our private intercourse, a spirit of reverence pervades our public acts; we are prevented from doing wrong by respect for authority and for the laws, having an especial regard to those which are ordained for the protection of the injured as well as to those unwritten laws which bring upon the transgressor of them the reprobation of the general sentiment.

Their enjoyment of life.

'And we have not forgotten to provide for our weary spirits many relaxations from toil; we have regular games and sacrifices throughout the year; at home the style of our life is refined; and the delight which we daily feel in all these things helps to banish melancholy. Because of the greatness of our city the fruits of the whole earth flow in upon us; so that we enjoy the goods of other countries as freely as of our own.

Their military powers not gained by tyranny or isolation.

'Then, again, our military training is in many respects superior to that of our adversaries. Our city is thrown open to the world, and we never expel a foreigner or prevent him from seeing or learning anything of which the secret if revealed to an enemy might profit him. We rely not upon management or trickery, but upon our own hearts and hands. And in the matter of education, whereas they from early youth are always undergoing laborious exercises which are to make them brave, we live at ease, and yet are equally ready to face the perils which they face. And here is the proof. The Lacedæmonians come into Attica not by themselves, but with their whole Confederacy following; we go alone into a neighbour's country; and although our opponents are fighting for their homes and we on a foreign soil, we have seldom any difficulty in overcoming them. Our enemics have never yet felt our united strength; the care of a navy divides our attention, and on land we are obliged to send our own citizens everywhere. But they, if they meet and defeat a part of our army, are as proud as if they had routed us all, and when defeated they pretend to have been vanquished by us all.

**The free development, not the repression of the individual, the basis of their strength.**

'If then we prefer to meet danger with a light heart but without laborious training, and with a courage which is gained by habit and not enforced by law, are we not greatly the gainers? Since we do not anticipate the pain, although, when the hour comes, we can be as brave as those who never allow themselves to rest; and thus too our city is equally admirable in peace and in war. For we are lovers of the beautiful, yet simple in our tastes, and we cultivate the mind without loss of manliness. Wealth we employ, not for talk and ostentation, but when there is a real use for it. To avow poverty with us is no disgrace; the true disgrace is in doing nothing to avoid it. An Athenian citizen does not neglect the state because he takes care of his own household; and even those of us who are engaged in business have a very fair idea of politics. We alone regard a man who takes no interest in public affairs, not as a harmless, but as a useless character; and if few of us are originators, we are all sound judges of a policy. The great impediment to action is, in our opinion, not discussion, but the want of that knowledge which is gained by discussion preparatory to action. For we have a peculiar power of thinking before we act and of acting too, whereas other men are courageous from ignorance but hesitate upon reflection. And they are surely to be esteemed the bravest spirits who, having the clearest sense both of the pains and pleasures of life, do not on that account shrink from danger. In doing good, again, we are unlike others; we make our friends by conferring, not by receiving favours. Now he who confers a favour is the firmer friend, because he would fain by kindness keep alive the memory of an obligation; but the recipient is colder in his feelings, because he knows that in requiting another's generosity he will not be winning gratitude but only paying a debt. We alone do good to our neighbours not upon a calculation of interest, but in the confidence of freedom and in a frank and fearless spirit. To sum up: I say that Athens is the school of Hellas, and that the individual Athenian in his own person seems to have the power of adapting himself to the most varied forms of action with the utmost versatility and grace. This is no passing and idle word, but truth and fact; and the assertion is verified by the position to which these qualities have raised the state. For in the hour of trial Athens alone among her contemporaries is superior to the report of her. No enemy who comes against her is indignant at the reverses which he sustains at the hands of such a city; no subject complains that his masters are unworthy of him. And we shall assuredly not be without witnesses; there are mighty monuments of our power which will make us the wonder of this and of succeeding ages; we shall not need the praises of Homer or of any other panegyrist whose poetry may please for the moment, although his representation of the facts will not bear the light of day. For we have compelled every land and every sea to open a path for our valour, and have everywhere planted eternal memorials of our friendship and of our enmity. Such is the city for whose sake these men nobly fought and died; they could not bear the thought that she might be taken from them; and every one of us who survive should gladly toil on her behalf.

The resulting versatility of the Athenians.

'I have dwelt upon the greatness of Athens because I want to show you that we are contending for a higher prize than those who enjoy none of these privileges, and to establish by manifest proof the merits of these men whom I am now commemorating. Their loftiest praise has been already spoken. For in magnifying the city I have magnified them, and men like them whose virtues made her glorious. And of how few Hellenes can it be said as of them, that their deeds when weighed in the balance have been found equal to their fame! Methinks that a death such as theirs has been gives the true measure of a man's worth; it may be the first revelation of his virtues, but is at any rate their final seal. For even those who come short in other ways may justly plead the valour with which they have fought for their country; they have

The praise of Athens is the praise of each Athenian citizen.

blotted out the evil with the good, and have benefited the state more by their public services than they have injured her by their private actions. None of these men were enervated by wealth or hesitated to resign the pleasures of life; none of them put off the evil day in the hope, natural to poverty, that a man, though poor, may one day become rich. But, deeming that the punishment of their enemies was sweeter than any of these things, and that they could fall in no nobler cause, they determined at the hazard of their lives to be honourably avenged, and to leave the rest. They resigned to hope their unknown chance of happiness; but in the face of death they resolved to rely upon themselves alone. And when the moment came they were minded to resist and suffer, rather than to fly and save their lives; they ran away from the word of dishonour, but on the battle-field their feet stood fast, and in an instant, at the height of their fortune, they passed away from the scene, not of their fear, but of their glory.

**All have preferred death to dishonor.**

'Such was the end of these men; they were worthy of Athens, and the living need not desire to have a more heroic spirit, although they may pray for a less fatal issue. The value of such a spirit is not to be expressed in words. Any one can discourse to you for ever about the advantages of a brave defence which you know already. But instead of listening to him I would have you day by day fix your eyes upon the greatness of Athens, until you become filled with the love of her; and when you are impressed by the spectacle of her glory, reflect that this empire has been acquired by men who knew their duty and had the courage to do it, who in the hour of conflict had the fear of dishonour always present to them, and who, if ever they failed in an enterprize, would not allow their virtues to be lost to their country, but freely gave their lives to her as the fairest offering which they could present at her feast. The sacrifice which they collectively made was individually repaid to them; for they received again each one for himself a praise which grows not old, and the noblest of all sepulchres — I speak not of that in which their remains are laid, but of that in which their glory survives, and is proclaimed always and on every

**The memory and influence of the martyr dead.**

fitting occasion both in word and deed. For the whole earth is the sepulchre of famous men; not only are they commemorated by columns and inscriptions in their own country, but in foreign lands there dwells also an unwritten memorial of them, graven not on stone but in the hearts of men. Make them your examples, and, esteeming courage to be freedom and freedom to be happiness, do not weigh too nicely the perils of war. The unfortunate who has no hope of a change for the better has less reason to throw away his life than the prosperous who, if he survive, is always liable to a change for the worse, and to whom any accidental fall makes the most serious difference. To a man of spirit, cowardice and disaster coming together are far more bitter than death striking him unperceived at a time when he is full of courage and animated by the general hope.

Consolation for the parents of the dead.

'Wherefore I do not now commiserate the parents of the dead who stand here; I would rather comfort them. You know that your life has been passed amid manifold vicissitudes; and that they may be deemed fortunate who have gained most honour, whether an honourable death like theirs, or an honourable sorrow like yours, and whose days have been so ordered that the term of their happiness is likewise the term of their life. I know how hard it is to make you feel this, when the good fortune of others will too often remind you of the gladness which once lightened your hearts. And sorrow is felt at the want of those blessings, not which a man never knew, but which were a part of his life before they were taken from him. Some of you are of an age at which they may hope to have other children, and they ought to bear their sorrow better; not only will the children who may hereafter be born make them forget their own lost ones, but the city will be doubly a gainer. She will not be left desolate, and she will be safer. For a man's counsel cannot have equal weight or worth, when he alone has no children to risk in the general danger. To those of you who have passed their prime, I say: "Congratulate yourselves that you have been happy during the greater part of your days; remember that your life of sorrow will not last long, and be comforted by the glory of those who are gone. For the love of honour alone is ever young, and not riches, as some say, but honour is the delight of men when they are old and useless."

'To you who are the sons and brothers of the departed, I see that the struggle to emulate them will be an arduous one. For all men praise the dead, and, however preeminent your virtue may be, hardly will you be thought, I do not say to equal, but even to approach them. The living have their rivals and detractors, but when a man is out of the way, the honour and good-will which he receives is unalloyed. And, if I am to speak of womanly virtues to those of you who will henceforth be widows, let me sum them up in one short admonition: To a woman not to show more weakness than is natural to her sex is a great glory, and not to be talked about for good or for evil among men.

**Examples for imitation.**

'I have paid the required tribute, in obedience to the law, making use of such fitting words as I had. The tribute of deeds has been paid in part; for the dead have been honourably interred, and it remains only that their children should be maintained at the public charge until they are grown up: this is the solid prize with which, as with a garland, Athens crowns her sons living and dead, after a struggle like theirs. For where the rewards of virtue are greatest, there the noblest citizens are enlisted in the service of the state. And now, when you have duly lamented, every one his own dead, you may depart.'

**Athens' tribute to the fallen.**

## *Speech of Protagoras on "Teaching of Morals," from the Protagoras of Plato*

325 C–326 D. Education and admonition commence in the first years of childhood, and last to the very end of life. Mother and nurse and father and tutor are quarrelling about the improvement of the child as soon as ever he is able to understand them: he cannot say or do anything without their setting forth to him that this is just and that is unjust; this is honourable, that is dishonourable; this is holy, that is unholy; do this and abstain from that. And if he obeys, well and good; if not, he is straightened by threats and

**The scope and character of education.**

blows, like a piece of warped wood. At a later stage they send him to teachers, and enjoin them to see to his manners even more than to his reading and music; and the teachers do as they are desired. And when the boy has learned his letters and is beginning to understand what is written, as before he understood only what was spoken, they put into his hands the works of great poets, which he reads at school; in these are contained many admonitions, and many tales, and praises, and encomia of ancient famous men, which he is required to learn by heart, in order that he may imitate or emulate them and desire to become like them. Then, again, the teachers of the lyre take similar care that their young disciple is temperate and gets into no mischief; and when they have taught him the use of the lyre, they introduce him to the poems of other excellent poets, who are the lyric poets; and these they set to music, and make their harmonies and rhythms quite familiar to the children's souls, in order that they may learn to be more gentle, and harmonious, and rhythmical, and so more fitted for speech and action; for the life of man in every part has need of harmony and rhythm. Then they send them to the master of gymnastic, in order that their bodies may better minister to the virtuous mind, and that they may not be compelled through bodily weakness to play the coward in war or on any other occasion. This is what is done by those who have the means, and those who have the means are the rich; their children begin education soonest and leave off latest. When they have done with masters, the state again compels them to learn the laws, and live after the pattern which they furnish, and not after their own fancies; and just as in learning to write, the writing-master first draws lines with a style for the use of the young beginner, and gives him the tablet and makes him follow the lines, so the city draws the laws, which were the invention of good law-givers who were of old time; these are given to the young man, in order to guide him in his conduct whether as ruler or ruled; and he who transgresses them is to be corrected, or, in other words, called to account, which is a term used not only in your country, but also in many others. Now when there is all this care about virtue private and public, why, Socrates, do you still wonder and doubt whether virtue

The music school.

The school of gymnastic.

Public education of the ephebes.

can be taught? Cease to wonder, for the opposite would be far more surprising.

### *Oath of the Athenian Ephebes*

I will never disgrace these sacred arms, nor desert my companion in the ranks. I will fight for temples and public property, both alone and with many. I will transmit my fatherland, not only not less, but greater and better, than it was transmitted to me. I will obey the magistrates who may at any time be in power. I will observe both the existing laws and those which the people may unanimously hereafter make, and, if any person seek to annul the laws or to set them at nought, I will do my best to prevent him, and will defend them both alone and with many. I will honor the religion of my fathers. And I call to witness Agraulos,[1] Enyalios,[2] Ares,[3] Zeus, Thallo,[4] and Auxo,[5] and Hegemone.[5]

[1] Daughter of Cecrops and Angraulos. She threw herself from the Acropolis because an oracle had declared that the Athenians would conquer if some one would sacrifice himself for his country.

[2] A surname frequently given to Mars in the *Iliad*, and corresponding with the name Enyo given to Bellona.

[3] The Greek god of war, called Mars by the Romans.

[4] Daughter of Zeus and Themis. Guarded and promoted the order of nature in the springtime.

[5] Auxo (increase) and Hegemone (queen) were the two graces worshipped at Athens. When the Athenian youth received his weapons of war he swore by them.

## II. EDUCATION OF WOMEN IN GREECE

**Period and Source.** — The social revolution of the fifth and fourth centuries B.C. affected the position of women as well as other aspects of Greek society, but the changes in the education of women were in no wise so profound as those affecting the education of men. It is true that there was a demand for greater freedom for women. Evidences of this are to be found in the teachings of Socrates and the writings of Plato. The latter held that the women possessed the same faculties as men, only in a lesser degree, and were entitled to a similar education. In this respect he approved the practices of the Spartans. A distinct cult relating to the greater freedom and higher education of women seems to have centred about Apasia. But so far as these changes concern the status of married women, they appear to have been limited to greater freedom and responsibility in the home. Literary education and intellectual pursuits belonged only to those who were without the home circle, the *hetæræ*, and in such privileges they were placed in sharp opposition to the position of the wife. The approved education of the women in the home during the later period did not differ materially from that of the earlier period. There was permissible a greater attention to dress and the toilet, somewhat greater freedom in the home, and a greater responsibility in its management. But as a rule the sphere of woman's activities and the scope of her education were still very limited. Hence the description of woman's education is essentially the same for the two periods of Grecian education that include the historic portion of independent existence of the nation.

The description here given is taken from the *Economics* of Xenophon. Xenophon lived during the last quarter of the fifth century and the first half of the fourth, though the dates of his birth and of his death are unknown. Some authorities make the period of his life a quarter of a century earlier. However that may be, he writes from well within the period of the new practices. It has been suggested that this selection is but another evidence of a campaign for the rights of the "new woman," and as such is a source belonging to education of the later period only. But Xenophon was a conservative in almost every respect, and was an advocate of the old education for men, as will be seen in a later selection (p. 122). Moreover, the education here advocated for women is essentially the old education. It contains no intellectual training whatever, but is essentially a training in domestic duties. There is nothing to indicate that the education advocated for the woman in the home should approximate in its freedom and intellectuality that allowed to the *hetæræ*. It is, therefore, correct to take this passage as descriptive of the approved education of the Athenian woman in the earlier as well as in the later period, though as described by Xenophon this education is systematized and somewhat elaborated.

The *Economics* is one of the so-called "Socratic" writings of Xenophon, and treats of the management of the household. But it is rather an exposition of his own ideas than of those of his master, for concerning such practical affairs Xenophon was more of an authority than Socrates.

While in many respects Xenophon was a cosmopolitan in his treatment of this subject, in the main he is well within the old conservative Grecian practices. The description given is of an Athenian girl brought up in total ignorance of practical affairs, and, though kept in seclusion according to the old ideas, yet trained in some of the frivolous practices of the more degenerate times. The girl, thus neglected in her earlier training, is educated by her husband as she should have been by her parents. This is one of the most striking and detailed accounts relating to education to be found in Greek literature.

**The Education of Women in Greece**, as described in this passage from the *Economics*, relates specifically to Athens but is typically Grecian. References in the Homeric poems are indicative of the same practices in an earlier stage of development. . At Sparta a widely divergent type of education was found. There girls received an education similar to the boys, even in respect to gymnastic and rudimentary military training. Boys and girls were not educated together, but girls were under the discipline of women, as boys were of the men. These statements are made by Plutarch and others, though few details are given. There was, of course, this general difference in principle: men were educated with the sole idea of becoming warriors; women with the sole idea of becoming mothers of warriors. At Athens, women were educated for the home, hence their education was essentially a training in domestic duties. The ideal of this education receives a clear statement in the passage in Pericles' *Funeral Oration:* ". . . to a woman not to show more weakness than is natural to her sex is a great glory, and not to be talked about for good or evil among men." Such an education could be given only in the home. The literary and gymnastic schools were for boys. Woman's education was in the performance of household duties, and in the attainment of domestic virtues. In the later period, when the old moral, religious, and social ideas had lost much of their binding force, many Greek women did, to be sure, receive a literary education, but in so doing lost their place as the head of the household and the reverence that had been given them as such. The Grecian woman was never on an equality with her husband, as was true in many respects at Rome; and when she attained or aspired to intellectual equality, it was at the sacrifice of the position in the home that she had, up to that time, held securely. The dialogue from the *Economics* gives an account of the approved education with as much detail as one could otherwise secure by a reconstruction from a great variety of isolated passages. In addition to supplying the details, it gives also the philosophy of this restricted education as it appeared to a keen, observing, conservative Greek of the period, when both old and new could yet be compared.

## *Selections from the Economics of Xenophon*

### CHAPTER VII. THE EDUCATION OF WOMEN

1. "Observing him[1] therefore sitting one day in the portico of the temple of Jupiter Eleutherius,[2] I went towards him, and as he seemed to me to be at leisure, sat down near him, and said, 'Why are you, Ischomachus,

[1] Ischomachus, a friend of Socrates, called *fair* and *good;* these terms indicate the ideal educated man.

[2] The temple of Zeus, "the Deliverer." After the battle of Platæa, 479 B.C., a special feast of liberty was instituted in honor of "the Deliverer."

Why called "fair and good."

who are not accustomed to be idle, sitting thus? for in general I see you either doing something, or certainly not altogether wasting your time, in the market-place.' 2. 'Nor would you now see me quite unoccupied, Socrates,' said Ischomachus, 'if I had not made an appointment to wait here for some strangers.' 'But when you have no such engagements,' said I, 'where, in the name of heaven, do you spend your time, and how do you employ yourself? for I have the strongest desire to learn from you what it is you do that you are called *fair* and *good;* since you certainly do not pass your life indoors, nor does your complexion look like that of a man who does so.' 3. Ischomachus, smiling at my inquiry, *what do you do to be called* FAIR *and* GOOD, and being pleased at it, as it seemed to me, replied, 'Whether people, when they talk together about me, give me that appellation, I do not know; but certainly when they call upon me as to the *antidosis*[1] of the duties of a trierarch[2] or choragus,[3] no one summons me by the name of FAIR and GOOD, but they designate me plainly as Ischomachus, distinguishing me by the name of my father; and as to what you ask me besides, Socrates, I assuredly do not spend my life indoors; for,' added he, 'my wife is quite capable herself of managing what is to be done in my house.' 4. 'But,' said I, 'Ischomachus, I would very gladly be permitted to ask you whether you instructed your wife yourself, so that she might be qualified as she ought to be, or whether, when you received her from her father and mother, she was possessed of sufficient knowledge to manage what belongs to her.' 5. 'And how, my dear Socrates,' said he, 'could she have had sufficient knowledge when I took her, since she came to my house when she was not fifteen years old, and had spent the preceding part of her life under the strictest restraint, in

Training of the girl.

[1] An Athenian law which specified that if any person was called upon to take the duty of any public office, and could point out any person richer than himself, who ought to have been called upon instead of himself, he might summon that citizen to take the office or to exchange properties.

[2] Commander of a ship of war.

[3] The person who supplied a properly trained choir in the production of the tragedies or comedies.

order that she might see as little, hear as little, and ask as few questions as possible? 6. Does it not appear to you to be quite sufficient, if she did but know, when she came, how to take wool and make a garment, and had seen how to apportion the tasks of spinning among the maid-servants? for as to what concerns the appetite, Socrates,' added he, 'which seems to me a most important part of instruction both for a man and for a woman, she came to me extremely well instructed.' 7. 'But as to other things, Ischomachus,' said I, 'did you yourself instruct your wife, so that she should be qualified to attend to the affairs belonging to her?' 'Not, indeed,' replied Ischomachus, 'until I had offered sacrifice, and prayed that it might be my fortune to teach, and hers to learn, what would be best for both of us.' 8. 'Did your wife, then,' said I, 'join with you in offering sacrifice, and in praying for these blessings?' 'Certainly,' answered Ischomachus, 'and she made many vows to the gods that she would be such as she ought to be, and showed plainly that she was not likely to disregard what was taught her.' 9. 'In the name of the gods, Ischomachus, tell me,' said I, 'what you began to teach her first; for I shall have more pleasure in hearing you give this account, than if you were to give me a description of the finest gymnastic or equestrian games.' 10. 'Well, then, Socrates,' returned Ischomachus, 'when she grew familiarized and domesticated with me, so that we conversed freely together, I began to question her in some such way as this: "Tell me, my dear wife, have you ever considered with what view I married you, and with what object your parents gave you to me? 11. For that there was no want of other persons with whom we might have shared our respective beds must, I am sure, be evident to you as well as to me. But when I considered for myself, and your parents for you, whom we might select as the best partner for a house and children, I preferred you, and your parents, as it appears, preferred me, out of those who were possible objects of choice. 12. If, then, the gods should ever grant children to be born to us, we shall then consult together, with regard to them, how we may bring them up as well as possible; for it will be a common advantage to both of us to find them

**Instruction of wife by husband.**

of the utmost service as supporters and maintainers of our old age. 13. At present, however, this is our common household; for I deposit all that I have as in common between us, and you put everything that you have brought into our common stock. Nor is it necessary to consider which of the two has contributed the greater share; but we ought to feel assured that whichsoever of us is the better manager of our common fortune will give the more valuable service." 14. To these remarks, Socrates, my wife replied, "In what respect could I coöperate with you? What power have I? Everything lies with you. My duty, my mother told me, was to conduct myself discreetly." 15. "Yes, by Jupiter, my dear wife," replied I, "and my father told me the same. But it is the part of discreet people, as well husbands as wives, to act in such a manner that their property may be in the best possible condition, and that as large additions as possible may be made to it by honourable and just means." 16. "And what do you see," said my wife, "that I can do to assist in increasing our property?" "Endeavor by all means," answered I, "to do in the best possible manner those duties which the gods have qualified you to do, and which custom approves." 17. "And what are they?" asked she. "I consider," replied I, "that they are duties of no small importance, unless indeed the queen bee in a hive is appointed for purposes of small importance. 18. For to me,"' continued he, '"the gods, my dear wife," said I, "seem certainly to have united that pair of beings, which is called male and female, with the greatest judgment, that they may be in the highest degree serviceable to each other in their connexion. 19. In the first place, the pair are brought together to produce offspring, that the races of animals may not become extinct; and to human beings, at least, it is granted to have supporters for their old age from this union. 20. For human beings, also, their mode of life is not, like that of cattle, in the open air; but they have need, we see, of houses. It is accordingly necessary for those who would have something to bring into their houses to have people to perform the requisite employments in the open air; for tilling, and sowing, and planting, and pasturage are all employments for the open air;

**As to their common interests.**

**Duties of a wife in care of the household;**

and from these employments the necessaries of life are procured. 21. But when these necessaries have been brought into the house, there is need of some one to take care of them, and to do whatever duties require to be done under shelter. The rearing of young children also demands shelter, as well as the preparation of food from the fruits of the earth, and the making of clothes from wool. 22. And as both these sorts of employments, alike those without doors, and those within, require labour and care, the gods, as it seems to me," said I, "have plainly adapted the nature of the woman for works and duties within doors, and that of the man for works and duties without doors. 23. For the divinity has fitted the body and mind of the man to be better able to bear cold, and heat, and travelling, and military exercises, so that he has imposed upon him the work without doors; and by having formed the body of the woman to be less able to bear such exertions, he appears to me to have laid upon her," said I, "the duties within doors. 24. But knowing that he had given the woman by nature, and laid upon her, the office of rearing young children, he has also bestowed upon her a greater portion of love for her newly-born offspring than on the man. 25. Since, too, the divinity has laid upon the woman the duty of guarding what is brought into the house, he, knowing that the mind, by being timid, is not less adapted for guarding, has given a larger share of timidity to the woman than to the man; and knowing also that if any one injures him who is engaged in the occupations without, he must defend himself, he has on that account given a greater portion of boldness to the man. 26. But as it is necessary for both alike to give and to receive, he has bestowed memory and the power of attention upon both impartially, so that you cannot distinguish whether the female or the male has the larger portion of them. 27. The power of being temperate also in what is necessary he has conferred in equal measure upon both, and has allowed that whichsoever of the two is superior in this virtue, whether the man or the woman, shall receive a greater portion of the benefit arising from it. 28. But as the nature of both is not fully adapted for all these requirements, they in consequence stand in greater need

and in care of children.

of aid from one another, and the pair are of greater service to each other, when the one is able to do those things in which the other is deficient. 29. As we know, then, my dear wife," continued I, "what is appointed to each of us by Providence, it is incumbent on us to discharge as well as we can that which each of us has to do.

Duties imposed upon the wife by divine, civil, and natural law.

30. "'"The law, too," I told her,' he proceeded, '"gives its approbation to these arrangements, by uniting the man and the woman; and as the divinity has made them partners, as it were, in their offspring, so the law ordains them to be sharers in household affairs. The law also shows that those things are more becoming to each which the divinity has qualified each to do with greater facility; for it is more becoming for the woman to stay within doors than to roam abroad, but to the man it is less creditable to remain at home than to attend to things out of doors. 31. And if any one acts contrary to what the divinity has fitted him to do, he will, while he violates the order of things, possibly not escape the notice of the gods, and will pay the penalty whether of neglecting his own duties or of interfering with those of his wife. 32. The queen of the bees," I added, "appears to me to discharge such duties as are appointed to her by the divinity." "And what duties," inquired my wife, "has the queen bee to perform, that she should be made an example for the business which I have to do?" 33. "She, remaining within the hive," answered I, "does not allow the bees to be idle, but sends out to their duty those who ought to work abroad; and whatever each of them brings in, she takes cognizance of it and receives it, and watches over the store until there is occasion to use it; and when the time for using it is come, she dispenses to each bee its just due. 34. She also presides over the construction of the cells within, that they may be formed beautifully and expeditiously. She attends, too, to the rising progeny, that they may be properly reared; and when the young bees are grown up, and are fit for work, she sends out a colony of them under some leader taken from among the younger bees." 35. "Will it then be necessary for me," said my wife, "to do such things?" "It will certainly be necessary for you," said I, "to remain at home, and to send out such of the labourers

as have to work abroad, to their duties; and over such as have business to do in the house you must exercise a watchful superintendence. 36. Whatever is brought into the house, you must take charge of it; whatever portion of it is required for use you must give it out; and whatever should be laid by, you must take account of it and keep it safe, so that the provision stored up for a year, for example, may not be expended in a month. Whenever wool is brought home to you, you must take care that garments be made for those who want them. You must also be careful that the dried provisions may be in a proper condition for eating. 37. One of your duties, however," I added, "will perhaps appear somewhat disagreeable, namely, that whoever of all the servants may fall sick, you must take charge of him, that he may be recovered." 38. "Nay, assuredly," returned my wife, "that will be a most agreeable office, if such as receive good treatment are likely to make a grateful return, and to become more attached to me than before." Delighted with her answer,' continued Ischomachus, 'I said to her, "Are not the bees, my dear wife, in consequence of some such care on the part of the queen of the hive, so affected toward her, that, when she quits the hive, no one of them thinks of deserting her, but all follow in her train?" 39. "I should wonder, however," answered my wife, "if the duties of leader do not rather belong to you than to me; for my guardianship of what is in the house, and distribution of it, would appear rather ridiculous, I think, if you did not take care that something might be brought in from out of doors." 40. "And on the other hand," returned I, "my bringing in would appear ridiculous, unless there were somebody to take care of what is brought in. Do you not see," said I, "how those who are said to draw water in a bucket full of holes are pitied, as they evidently labour in vain?" "Certainly," replied my wife, "for they are indeed wretched, if they are thus employed."

**Instruction of servants by the wife.**

41. "'"Some other of your occupations, my dear wife," continued I, "will be pleasing to you. For instance, when you take a young woman who does not know how to spin, and make her skilful at it, and she thus becomes of twice as much value to you. Or when you take one who is igno-

rant of the duties of a housekeeper or servant, and, having made her accomplished, trustworthy, and handy, render her of the highest value. Or when it is in your power to do services to such of your attendants as are steady and useful, while, if any one is found transgressing, you can inflict punishment. 42. But you will experience the greatest of pleasures, if you show yourself superior to me, and render me your servant, and have no cause to fear that, as life advances, you may become less respected in your household, but may trust that, while you grow older, the better consort you prove to me, and the more faithful guardian of your house for your children, so much the more will you be esteemed by your family. 43. For what is good and honourable," I added, "gains increase of respect, not from beauty of person, but from merits directed to the benefit of human life." Such were the subjects, Socrates, on which, as far as I remember, I first conversed seriously with my wife.'

## Chapter VIII

**Results of previous training.**

1. "'Did you then observe, Ischomachus,' said I, 'that your wife was at all the more incited to carefulness by your remarks?' 'Indeed I did,' replied Ischomachus, 'and I saw her on one occasion greatly concerned and put to the blush, because, when I asked for something that had been brought into the house, she was unable to give it me. 2. Perceiving that she was in great trouble, however, I said, "Do not be cast down, my dear wife, because you cannot give me what I am asking you for. It is indeed pure poverty not to have a thing to use when you need it; but our present want—not to be able to find a thing when you seek it—is of a less serious nature than not to seek it at all, knowing that it is not in your possession. However," added I, "you are not in fault on the present occasion, but I, as I did not direct you, when I gave you the articles, where each of them ought to be deposited, so that you might know how you ought to

**Importance of order in the household.**

arrange them and whence to take them. 3. There is indeed nothing, my dear wife, more useful or more creditable to people than order. A chorus of singers and dancers, for instance, consists of a number of persons; but when they do whatever each of them happens to fancy, all appears confusion, and disagreeable to behold; but when they act and speak in concert, the same persons prove themselves worthy of being seen and heard. . . ."

11. "'I once saw, I think, the most beautiful and accurate arrangement of implements possible, Socrates, when I went on board that large Phœnician vessel to look over it; for I beheld a vast number of articles severally arranged in an extremely small space. 12. For the ship,' continued he, 'is brought into harbour and taken out again by means of various instruments of wood and tow; it pursues its voyage with the aid of much that is called suspended tackle; it is equipped with many machines to oppose hostile vessels; it carries about in it many weapons for the men; it conveys all the utensils, such as people use in a house, for each company that take their meals together; and, in addition to all this, it is freighted with merchandise, which the owner of the ship transports in it for the purpose of profit. 13. And all the things of which I am speaking,' continued he, 'were stowed in a space not much larger than is contained in a room that holds half a score dinner-couches. Yet I observed that they were severally arranged in such a manner that they were not in the way of one another, nor required anybody to seek for them, nor were unprepared for use, nor difficult to remove from their places, so as to cause any delay when it was necessary to employ them suddenly. 14. The pilot's officer, too, who is called the man of the prow, I found so well acquainted with the location of them all, that he could tell, even when out of sight of them, where each severally lay, and how many there were, not less readily than a man who knows his letters can tell how many there are in the name Socrates, and where each of them stands. 15. I saw,' pursued Ischomachus, 'this very man inspecting, at his leisure, all the implements that it is necessary to use in a ship, and, wondering at his minute examination, I asked him what he was doing. "I am examining, stranger," said he, "in case anything should happen, in what state everything in the vessel is, and whether anything is wanting, or is placed so as to be inconvenient for use. 16. For," said he, "there is no time, when heaven sends a storm over the sea, either

to seek for what may be wanting, or to hand out what may be difficult to use; for the gods threaten and punish the negligent; and if they but forbear from destroying those who do nothing wrong, we must be very well content; while, if they preserve even those that attend to everything quite properly, much gratitude is due to them." 17. I, therefore, having observed the accuracy of this arrangement, said to my wife, that it would be extremely stupid in us, if people in ships, which are comparatively small places, find room for their things, and, though they are violently tossed about, nevertheless keep them in order, and, even in the greatest alarm, still find out how to get what they want; and if we, who have large separate repositories in our house for everything, and our house firmly planted on the ground, should not discover excellent and easily-found places for our several articles;—how could this, I say, be anything but extreme stupidity in us?

The beauty of order.

18. "'"How excellent a thing a regular arrangement of articles is, and how easy it is to find, in a house, a place such as is suitable to put everything, I have sufficiently shown. 19. But how beautiful an appearance it has, too, when shoes, for instance, of whatever kind they are, are arranged in order; how beautiful it is to see garments, of whatever kind, deposited in their several places; how beautiful it is to see bed-clothes, and brazen vessels, and table furniture, so arranged; and (what, most of all, a person might laugh at, not indeed a grave person, but a jester), I say, that pots have a graceful appearance when they are placed in regular order. 20. Other articles somehow appear, too, when regularly arranged, more beautiful in consequence; for the several sorts of vessels seem like so many choral bands; and the space that is between them pleases the eye, when every sort of vessel is set clear of it; just as a body of singers and dancers, moving in a circle, is not only in itself a beautiful sight, but the space in the middle of it, being open and clear, is agreeable to the eye. 21. Whether what I say is true, my dear wife," said I, "we may make trial, without suffering any loss, or taking any extraordinary trouble. Nor ought we at all to labour under the apprehension that it will be difficult to find a person who will learn the places for every article, and remember how

to keep each of them separate; 22. for we know very well that the whole city contains ten thousand times as much as our house, and yet, whichsoever of the servants you order to buy anything and bring it to you from the market-place, not one of them will be in perplexity, but every one will show that he knows whither he must go to fetch any article. For this," added I, "there is no other reason than that each article is deposited in its appointed place. 23. But if you should seek for a person, and sometimes even for one who is on his part seeking you, you would often give up the search in despair before you find him; and for this there is no other cause, than that it is not appointed where the particular person is to await you." Such was the conversation that I had with my wife, as far as I remember, concerning the arrangement and distinction of articles.'

## Chapter IX

The instruction of the wife concerning the apartments of the household.

1. "'And what was the result,' said I, 'my dear Ischomachus? Did your wife appear to attend to any of the matters which you took so much pains to impress upon her?' 'What else did she do but promise that she would attend to what I said, and manifest the greatest pleasure, as if she had found relief from perplexity? and she requested me to arrange the various articles, as soon as I could, in the manner which I had proposed.' 2. 'And how, Ischomachus,' said I, 'did you arrange them for her?' 'What else could I do but determine upon showing her, in the first place, the capacity of the house? For it is not adorned with decorations, but the apartments in it are constructed with such a view that they may be as convenient receptacles as possible for the things that are to be placed in them; so that they themselves invite whatever is adapted for them respectively. 3. Thus the inner chamber, being in a secure part of the house, calls for the most valuable couch coverings and vessels; the dry parts of the building for the corn; the cool places for the wine; and the well-lighted portions for such articles of workmanship, and vases, as require a clear light. 4. I pointed out to her, too, that the apartments for people to live in, which are well ornamented, are cool in the summer and exposed

to the sun in winter; and I made her notice as to the whole house how it lies open to the south, so that it is plain it has plenty of sun in winter, and plenty of shade in summer. . . . 6. When we had gone through these places,' he continued, 'we then proceeded to classify our goods. We began by collecting, first of all, whatever we use for offering sacrifices; after this, we arranged the dresses for women, such as are suited for festival days; and then the equipments for men, as well for festivities as for warfare; and next the bed-covering in the women's apartments, the bed-coverings in the men's apartments, the shoes for the women and the shoes for the men. 7. Of utensils there were distinct collections, one of instruments for spinning, another of those for preparing corn, another of those for cooking, another of those for the bath, another of those for kneading bread, another of those for the table. These in general we divided into two sorts, such as we have to use constantly, and such as are required only at festal entertainments. 8. We also made one assortment of what would be used in a month, and another of what was computed to last for a year; for in this way it is less likely to escape our knowledge how particular things are expended. When we had thus distinguished all our goods into classes, we conveyed them severally to the places best suited for them. 9. Afterwards, whatever utensils the servants require daily, such as those for preparing corn, for cooking, for spinning, and any others of that sort, we pointed out to those who use them, the places where they were to put them, and then committed them to their keeping, charging them to keep them safely; 10. but such as we use only for festival days, for entertaining guests, or only occasionally at long intervals, we committed, after pointing out the places for them, and numbering and making lists of them, to the housekeeper, and told her to give out any of them to whatever servant needed them, to bear in mind to which of them she gave any one, and, after receiving them back, to deposit them respectively in the places from which she took them.

Duties of the wife in caring for household furnishings.

11. "'Of the housekeeper we made choice after considering which of the female servants appeared to have

most self-restraint in eating, and wine, and sleep, and converse with the male sex; and, in addition to this, which seemed to have the best memory, and which appeared to have forethought, that she might not incur punishment from us for neglect, and to consider how, by gratifying us, she might gain some mark of approbation in return. 12. We formed her to entertain feelings of affection toward us, giving her a share in our pleasure when we had an occasion of rejoicing, and consulting her, if anything troublesome occurred, with reference to it. We also led her to become desirous of increasing our property, by stimulating her to take accounts of it, and making her in some degree partaker of our prosperity. 13. We also excited in her a love of honesty, by paying more respect to the well-principled than to the unprincipled, and showing her that they lived in greater plenty and in better style. We then installed her in her appointment. 14. But in addition to all this, Socrates,' said he, 'I told my wife that there would be no profit in all these arrangements, unless she herself took care that the appointed order for everything should be preserved. I also instructed her that in the best-regulated political communities it is not thought sufficient by the citizens merely to make good laws, but that they also appoint guardians of the laws, who, overlooking the state, commend him who acts in conformity with the laws, and, if any one transgresses the laws, punish him. 15. I accordingly desired my wife,' continued he, 'to consider herself the guardian of the laws established in the house, and to inspect the household furniture, whenever she thought proper, as the commander of a garrison inspects his sentinels; to signify her approbation if everything was in good condition, as the senate signifies its approval of the horses and horse-soldiers; to praise and honour the deserving like a queen, according to her means, and to rebuke and disgrace any one that required such treatment. 16. But I moreover admonished her,' added he, 'that she would have no reason to be displeased, if I imposed on her more trouble with regard to our property than I laid on the servants; remarking to her, that servants have only so far a concern with their master's property as to carry it, or keep it in order, or

**Training of the wife as guardian of the household.**

take care of it; but that no servant has any power of using it unless his master puts it into his hands, while it belongs all to the master himself, so that he may use any portion of it for whatever purpose he pleases. 17. To him therefore that receives the greatest benefit from its preservation, and suffers the greatest loss by its destruction, I showed her that the greatest interest in its safety must belong.'

18. "'Well then, Ischomachus,' said I, 'how did your wife, on hearing these instructions, show herself disposed to comply with your wishes?' 'She assured me, Socrates,' replied he, 'that I did not judge rightly of her, if I thought that I was imposing on her what was disagreeable, in telling her that she must take care of the property; for she remarked,' said he, 'that it would have been more disagreeable to her if I had charged her to neglect her property, than if she were required to take care of the household goods. 19. For it seems to be a provision of nature,' concluded he, 'that as it is easier for a well-disposed woman to take care of her children than to neglect them, so it is more pleasing (as he thought, he said), for a right-minded woman to attend to her property, which, as being her own, affords her gratification, than to be neglectful of it.'

## Chapter x

"On hearing that his wife had made him such a reply," proceeded Socrates, "I said, 'By Juno, Ischomachus, you show us that your wife is possessed of a manly understanding.' 'And accordingly,' returned Ischomachus, 'I wish to give you other instances of her extreme nobleness of mind, in matters in which she complied with my wishes after hearing them only once.' 'Of what nature were they?' said I; 'pray tell us: for it is a far greater pleasure to hear of the merit of a living woman, than if Zeuxis were to exhibit to me the most beautiful representation of a woman in a painting.' . . .

## III. THE NEW GREEK EDUCATION

**The Period.** — The introduction of new educational ideas and practices was, of course, gradual, and no definite date can be assigned for the beginning of the period. But the transition that took place in Greek society, in the fifth century, particularly at Athens, was comparatively rapid. Athens, hereafter the centre of Greek life, was the centre of this change, though similar changes, less pronounced in character, occurred elsewhere. The discussion of the new education is, however, directly applicable only to Athens. The change may be said to have occurred in the period of Athenian political supremacy, between the close of the Persian Wars (479 B.C.) and the outbreak of the Peloponnesian War in 431 B.C. While the new ideas and practices became dominant, it was not without a struggle with the old, which had many worthy adherents throughout the fifth and the fourth centuries. The dominant educational characteristic of this period, then, was the conflict itself, in which the new practices always held the stronger position. The sources given in this section relate to this conflict.

The new eductional ideas and practices were not limited to the fifth and fourth centuries, but were characteristic of Greek life thereafter. Yet this period of strife was distinct from the period beginning with the Macedonian era, when the new education had become thoroughly established, and tended to become cosmopolitan as Greece extended her sway in the world of intellect and art both to the east and the west.

This period of the fifth and the fourth centuries had certain well-defined characteristics which may be included in the one, the growth of individualism. Foremost among these characteristics is the fact that Athens had now become thoroughly democratic in its political constitution and practices. The reforms of Pericles had completed the democratization begun earlier by Solon and Clisthenes. Every citizen was now qualified to hold office, and each was required to render political as well as military service. Upon the dicasts, or popular juries, six thousand citizens served each year. The functions of these dicasts were in private cases judicial; but their decisions in public affairs became not only judicial, but legislative. During this period Athens converted her leadership in the Delian league into an imperial control. This, while of but short duration, demanded an extension of political and diplomatic activities and a broadening of political and social ideas. It called for a wholly new type of ability, a versatility unknown and foreign to the earlier times. This leadership was gained and held by intellectual supremacy rather than by military power. Though the political leadership was lost, the intellectual supremacy was retained. Along with the political development went a commercial expansion and a massing of wealth through an industrial growth that gave a means of fostering intellectual and artistic activities. While there yet remained many evidences of intolerance of the democracy, as seen in the cases of Themistocles, Aristides, Socrates, Thucydides, and others, there went along with the political and commercial expansion a tolerance in ideas that had not been characteristic of early

Athens. This tolerance extended to opinions as well as to actions, and as a result there developed a radical change in religious and ethical ideas. The period became one of scepticism, and the old religious myths and legends lost their social and religious value. With many there resulted simply the popular atheism of the times; with others, an attempt at constructive ethical and religious thought. In this respect, Socrates was undoubtedly guilty of the popular charge of corrupting the youth. The destructive and critical tendency was popularly represented by the Sophists. In another respect the constructive effort constituted the most striking characteristic of the times, the change in the character of Grecian philosophy. Hitherto the interest had been in various interpretations of the material universe. The earlier systems of Grecian philosophy were attempts at such interpretations. Now the interest became subjective; attention was turned inward. Such questions were raised as the nature of knowledge, of opinion, of virtue, of justice. The centre of interest was man, not nature. This movement in its beginning was, in other words, more largely negative than positive; it was a disbelief in the previous course of inquiry into the nature of the universe, even in the possibility of such knowledge at all. This general skepticism, which extended to religious as well as to intellectual affairs, was one of the conditions that aroused against the Sophists the bitter antagonism of the more conservative. One further characteristic of the period was the change in literature. The sixth and the first half of the fifth centuries were included in the great period of the tragic drama, which dealt with mythical and heroic characters and with ethical themes. These dramas were religious ceremonies in themselves, and were religious and ethical in their nature and influence. In the middle of the fifth century the comedy was introduced, in which the characters were representations of real personages drawn from contemporary life and treated with the greatest license. The comedy was essentially a comment on everyday life in Athens, but a comment made with the greatest freedom. In it were permitted the most scurrilous attacks on the character of citizens, on religion, on civic institutions. In respect to individuals greater freedom of speech was allowed at Athens than would be tolerated in any modern time. This freedom was undoubtedly abused, and hence arises the difficulty in using such sources. The last half of the fifth century was the period of the old comedy; the fourth century includes the period of the middle comedy, — the two practically constituting the period under discussion.

Such profound changes as those indicated could not take place without affecting education in every aspect. These changes constitute the transition to the new education.

**The Sources.** — The classic reference to this change is the *Clouds* of Aristophanes, and in the passage which contains the contest between the Just and the Unjust Causes there is the best presentation of this conflict from the conservative point of view that is to be found. It is, however, so obviously a presentation from one point of view that its interpretation is subject to many difficulties. The general view presented is undoubtedly that of the conservatives who held to the old practices. In some respects it expresses also the views held by the masses at that time (423 B.C.) in regard to the new teachers. The representation of Socrates had much to do with the hostile attitude of the populace toward him, though his death was not decreed until twenty-four years later.

Aristophanes lived from 444 to 381 B.C., practically the period of this transition. He is considered the greatest writer of Greek comedies. The *Clouds* is usually considered to be his greatest work, though when presented in 423 B.C. it received only third prize. Aristophanes was considered by the Greeks, by Plato among the rest, as one of their greatest men. His general attitude is one of highest patriotism and of regard for civic uprightness and decency. While a comedian in the form of his art, he was a moralist in purpose and influence. The great number of passages in his writings that are utterly unworthy, according to modern criteria of taste, are to be explained, not only by the general character of his age, which in matters of morality was much below the standard of modern times, but also by the license of the comedy and of the Dionysiac festivals. Aristophanes' intensity of purpose and conservatism of view, together with the license of the occasions on which his comedy was presented, gives rise to the difficulties of interpretation. It is readily seen that his view of Socrates is but partial, though in selecting him as a type of those who were undermining old ideas and practices his judgment was correct. The question as to how far his view of the new educational ideas and their influences is in a similar way partial, is much more difficult to answer. The following principles of interpretation are suggested: His analysis of the old education, narrow and intense, but productive of great results, may be accepted. His view of the new education may be taken as essentially that of the conservative element in society, backed by the prejudices of the thoughtless multitude. His presentation of the character of the Sophists and of Socrates is a biased one — a presentation based on a clear comprehension of the negative results of their teachings, but at the same time showing no comprehension of the fact that positive advance could come only through a preceding critical movement. His misrepresentations of the Sophists are no more erroneous than those of Plato are now seen to be, though from a wholly different point of view. As to the superficial results of the new education, his presentation may be taken as indicative of existing conditions, though even here there are evidently exaggerations. As a contrast between the long-tried results of the old education and the superficial tendencies of the new, his views may be accepted as essentially correct. His indictment can be accepted even concerning the disintegrating political effects and the demoralizing and irreligious social effects of the new education on the large portion of the populace that accepted the teachings. But in this connection it must be borne in mind that there is no correct presentation of the essential intellectual characteristics of the new education, or of the permanent ethical and religious advances that were to result therefrom; and that, on the contrary, Aristophanes might be taken simply as a representative of the enemies of enlightenment and progress, though he was correct in assuming that the progress was to be gained only by the destruction of the old religion and of national existence.

Two other selections relating to this educational transition are from the orations of Isocrates, himself a type of the Sophists of the second generation when their educational work was definitely formulated into schools. Isocrates was born 436 B.C., and was instructed by Prodicus,

Protagoras, Gorgias, and the other Sophists. In 392 B.C. he established a school in Athens, though he had taught elsewhere for twelve years. This school was largely attended by Athenians and other Grecians, and brought him wealth and great reputation. His influence was exerted, not through participation in actual public activities, but by means of orations prepared for circulation throughout Greece rather than for delivery on special occasions.

The first of the selections here given is the oration *Against the Sophists*, written about 390 B.C., when Isocrates was just beginning his work at Athens. In this oration he declares the principles underlying his work by protesting against the practices adopted by other members of the teaching profession. Isocrates was a Sophist, and so calls himself; but from his point of view there were many unworthy members of the craft. The first class of teachers criticised are those who profess to impart absolute knowledge which will enable others to direct their conduct under all circumstances. These teachers are criticised, not only for accepting fees, but for their fundamental claim. In this latter criticism he has in view the followers of Socrates and Plato, if not the great masters themselves. The second class of teachers criticised are the professors of political discourse, and that, too, in spite of the fact that it is to this class that Isocrates himself belongs. Here, however, he criticises the claim commonly put forth of power to make any one a good forensic speaker irrespective of his natural ability. The third class criticised are those who profess to write on the art of rhetoric, yet confine the whole art to the realm of forensic or political discourse.

The second selection was written 354 B.C., at the close

of his career. Isocrates was then eighty-two years old and was the leading representative of his profession. In this oration, *On the Exchange of Estates*, he gives not only a defence of himself and of his own career, but of his profession in general. In the latter half of the selection is stated the general theory of the Sophists, or of rhetorical education.

The fourth source relating to this period is the selection from the *Republic*, wherein Plato points out the evil of ill-directed education, and shows the distinction between the true philosopher and the false. This discussion gives Plato's conception of the group of teachers represented by Isocrates, just as the paragraph in *Against the Sophists* gave the Sophists' views of the philosophic or dialectic teachers. As the philosophers were visionaries and theorists to Isocrates, so the Sophists were simply corrupted, ignoble, incompletely formed philosophers to Plato. The value of the *Republic* as a source is discussed later (p. 130).

**The Changes in the Education** of the period are manifold and not confined to any one aspect, though they are more pronounced in what would now be called secondary and higher education. Using the testimony of the *Clouds* with caution and supplementing it with corroborative evidence, circumstantial or direct, from a great variety of sources, the following general changes can be indicated. The very source of education, the home itself, was affected by these changes. There was a decline in the rigid discipline of the boy and of the immediate personal supervision of the boy by his father. His early training was now left more largely to the direction of nurses and pedagogues in whose selection less care was exercised. There was no need for the old-time severity. There was greater ease and luxury in the home life. Even the change in table manners and in foods is marked by Aristophanes as being significant. The up-to-date youth recognized no rules in the choice of foods but his own tastes, and if what he desired was not given him willingly, he procured it himself. He was rude in his behaviour, he giggled, he crossed his legs, he interrupted the conversation; and was indulged by his father with weak good humor.

The changes in the school were more significant. A similar freedom or license prevailed there. In the music schools the simple music of old did not suffice: quavers and trills of the voice were indulged in; the old melodies were replaced by those more complex and more sentimental, for the dominant moral purpose now became largely intellectual and æsthetic. The cithera as a simple accompaniment for the voice no longer sufficed, and the flute and other wind instruments were now also used, though hitherto their use had been considered positively immoral. In the literary work of the music schools a similar change occurred. The old national songs and the Homeric poems were partially replaced by the newer literature of a reflective and didactic character, that stimulated discussion and introspective analysis, but furnished little incentive to the active life in public service that had hitherto been the purpose. A yet greater change occurred in the palæstra in that the severity of the physical training was much relaxed. The motive of the gymnastic period was no longer simply the production of strong, manly, healthy bodies, as an equipment for the enjoyment of life and the performance of civic and military duties, but rather the acquirement of physical beauty and sensuous enjoyment. We cannot believe that this criticism indicates a condition universally true, but it does indicate a tendency. Under these conditions the moral results of the old palæstra training could no longer be expected.

But the greatest change occurred in the character of the education from fifteen to twenty. Hitherto boys had spent the first three years of this period in the gymnasium, and in the political training in the agora, and the courts, and the last two years in the ephebic military service. During the time of conflict between the old ideas and the new, the education of the gymnastic period became predominantly intellectual. The substitution of discussion and rhetorical education for the old physical and civic training is quite clearly pictured in some of the dialogues of Plato in which youths participate. Whatever else may be said for the Platonic discussions, it must be admitted that they could never be brought to a close, and that they were without any immediate practical result. It can, therefore, be readily understood how these educational innovations appeared to the conservatives but a training in idleness. The new movement was at first but a vague general tendency, but by the opening of the fourth century it came to have a definite organization in the philosophical and rhetorical schools, while in its earlier stage it found its best representation in the Sophists.

**The Sophists** have been judged largely by what their opponents have said of them. The typical Sophists of the earlier period have left no writings; at least none are extant. It has been popular to consider them not only as the typical representatives of these innovations in Greek society during this period, but as being responsible for the growth in immorality and civic indifference. The more just view now accepted is that the Sophists were neither better nor worse than their times, but that they were the teachers who were able to give what the new Greece of that time demanded. In supplying these new demands, they became an influential factor in the civic and moral disintegration and in the intellectual advance that form the great characteristics of the times.

The first of the Sophists was Protagoras, who began to teach in Athens about 445 B.C. The term "Sophist," however, had been used earlier than this to indicate any one who professed wisdom, such as the Seven Sages of the earlier times. After Protagoras came a number of other noted teachers, including Gorgias, Prodicus, and Hippias. These men were received at Athens with great enthusiasm, and had much influence on such men as Pericles, Euripides, Socrates, Thucydides, and Isocrates. This group of Sophists soon raised up a multitude of lesser ones, pupils or imitators of less ability, putting forth more extravagant claims, and exerting a more detrimental influence. The influence of these men brought the entire class and the general tendency of their teachings into disrepute with the more conservative element in Athenian society, and aroused the opposition of such teachers as Socrates and Plato, just as the minor teachers of the Socratic type called forth the denunciation of Isocrates. The masses did not discriminate between the teachings of Socrates and that of the others, for in essentials Socrates was a Sophist, and so considered himself. Many of his pupils were no more of a credit to him than were those of the Sophists. In fact, the Phidippides of the *Clouds* is generally supposed to be a more or less faithful picture of young Alcibiades, who was a pupil of Socrates.

The essential characteristics of the Sophists were these:

they professed to have the knowledge that was necessary for a successful career in the public life of the times, and to be able to impart this by instruction; they devoted themselves largely to the instruction of boys between the age of fifteen and the time of their admission into full citizenship. This period, formerly devoted to gymnastic exercise, routine military service, and training in political duties through association with elders in the agora and the courts, was now largely given over to discussion and theoretical instruction. To the old Greek this would only appear as a training in idleness. The common method of instruction was to teach by continuous discourse, but in this respect Socrates was a marked exception, for he taught through conversation. This use of the dialogue developed into the specific dialectic method, and even more than the Sophists' method was responsible for making the Greeks "a nation of talkers instead of a nation of doers." A further distinction, not noted in the *Clouds*, between Socrates and the other Sophists was that while the latter taught for fees, the former did not. Even this distinction was not observed by the successors of Socrates, unless it was Plato. In their fundamental belief, that virtue, or wisdom, or practical guidance in life, could be gained by instruction instead of by the previous methods of a long training in the formation of social habits, Socrates and the Sophists were essentially at one. As an aid to popularizing their ideas and perhaps as a means to success, the Sophists travelled from city to city, though Athens naturally became the centre on account of the great freedom of thought allowed there, and on account of the intellectual superiority of its citizens. These Sophists were received everywhere with great enthusiasm by the younger generation. On account of this popularity and the rather spectacular character of their work, they were held responsible for the changes that Grecian society was undergoing at that time. They held no common doctrines and had no common organization as a school. They agreed, however, in their negative attitude toward old Greek speculation in its search for an explanation of the physical universe, and toward the old religion as a basis for moral action and social conduct. It is because of this critical attitude that they are condemned by Aristophanes. But the criticism of Plato is of a diametrically opposite sort. It is because they do not go far enough in rejecting the old and do not attempt to set up a radically new society instead of preparing for a successful career in the present, that he condemns them as corrupt or incompletely formed philosophers.

Not only was there no common ground in their beliefs, but in their purposes also they were wholly individualistic. The success which they professed to prepare for was success as an individual. It had little or no reference to the needs of the state, and was attained at the expense of the necessary military preparation demanded and most needed by the state at that time. Success in defending one's own interest, in rising to political and legal distinction, in acquiring wealth, in achieving renown through oratory or debate, was their aim. Virtue or wisdom becomes success or happiness, a wholly individualistic conception. In their ideas and in their influence they were wholly in accord with the individualistic tendencies of the time, and were responsible for accelerating this development. Their nearest approach to a common doctrine was this expression of individualism, "Man is the measure of all things."

The means to success emphasized by the Sophists constituted a training in formal oratory and in popular discussion. These were the most assured means to success in that period. This training led to a much greater attention than had ever been paid before to the form and structure of language, both in its oral and written forms, and, in consequence, higher education became almost exclusively literary.

**Literary Education.** — Ability to speak in public, in defence of one's own rights and in advocacy of personal views on public questions, was expected of all Athenian citizens. The Sophists deliberately proposed to create this ability through instruction. While they devoted most of their time to personal instruction, many of them wrote grammatical and rhetorical treatises, and from them date both these sciences. The efforts of the minor Sophists were largely directed toward clarifying the meaning of words and making more definite the structure of the language. In general their work had the same purpose as the teaching of rhetoric and composition at the present time. For this they were criticised, as were Socrates, Isocrates, Aristotle, Quintilian, and others whose reputations have survived the criticism. Sophistic instruction meant, however, an emphasis on the form of expression rather than on the thought. This distinction coincided with a further general one that arose under the influence of Socrates. The rhetorical education was largely a preparation for practical life, and was dominated chiefly by the hope of success or gain on the part of the individual. As opposed to this there was the tendency to investigate for the sake of truth itself, and in so doing to pursue a life that had little direct connection with the activities of the public, and that offered little opportunity for achieving success with, or reward from, the public. The method best adapted to such pursuits was the dialectic or conversational method of Socrates. Hence the general tendency popularly represented by the Sophists, divided by the opening of the fourth century into two distinct branches. One was the rhetorical education, that aimed to prepare for practical life, that was chiefly grammatical and rhetorical in its subject-matter, and that depended upon formal instruction of the lecture type for its method; the other was the philosophical, that had little or no connection with practical life, that devoted itself to speculation, to a search for truth in the subjective or thought world, and that was dialectic in its method. Therein lay the first broad distinction between the practical and the liberal education. Both dialectician and rhetorician had been included at first under the term "Sophist." But through the influence of such criticisms as those of Plato, the term "Sophists" was limited for the most part to the rhetoricians, while the other group assumed the term "philosophers." To the former group the philosophers were visionaries, lacking in public spirit, patriotism, and wisdom in the practical affairs of life. To the latter the rhetoricians, or the Sophists as they prefer to call them, were selfish, incapable of seeing or appreciating the truth, and concerned in seeking their own advancement at the expense of the public welfare. Each appeared to the other as the corrupters of youth; to the conservative public both appeared in this light. The work of the two groups was largely responsible for that versatility of mind that gave to the Greek the intellectual and literary leadership of all times. To the influence of both was due as well the culmination of the political decline and the rejection of the old religious and social ideals. On the other hand, it cannot be doubted that the germs of moral decay were inherent in classical society, and that they are discoverable long before the time of the Sophists. Education in Greece now became almost wholly literary and soon took the form it retained through the Græco-Roman period.

## *Selections from The Clouds of Aristophanes*

(SCENE — the interior of a sleeping apartment; STREPSIADES, PHIDIPPIDES, and two servants are seen in their beds; a small house is seen at a distance. Time — midnight.)

Strepsiades, formerly a wealthy country gentleman, without culture, has married out of his station to a luxury-loving Athenian woman. Their son, Phidippides, has squandered much of his father's fortune in horse racing and other extravagances. Anxiety concerning some of these debts, now due, causes the father a sleepless night. The son dreams of his racing and in his sleep talks of his sporting friends. The comedy opens with the lamentations of the father and the broken mutterings of the son.

* * * * * * *

(75–152.)

The occasion for resort to Sophists' teachings.

STREP. I have discovered one path for my course extraordinarily excellent; to which if I persuade this youth, I shall be saved. But first I wish to awake him. How then can I awake him in the most agreeable manner? — How? Phidippides, my little Phidippides?

PHID. What, father?

STREP. Kiss me, and give me your right hand!

PHID. There. What's the matter?

STREP. Tell me, do you love me?

PHID. Yes, by this Equestrian Neptune.[1]

STREP. Nay, do not by any means mention *this Equestrian* to me, for this god is the author of my misfortunes. But, if you really love me from your heart, my son, obey me.

[1] Patron god of his favorite sport. Probably represented in the bedchamber by a statue.

PHID. In what, then, pray, shall I obey you?

STREP. Reform your habits as quickly as possible; and go and learn what I advise.

PHID. Tell me now, what do you prescribe?

STREP. And will you obey me at all?

PHID. By Bacchus, I will obey you.

STREP. Look this way, then! Do you see this little door and little house?

PHID. I see it. What then, pray, is this, father?

STREP. This is a thinking-shop [1] of wise spirits. There dwell men who in speaking of the heavens persuade people that it is an oven, and that it encompasses us, and that we are the embers. These men teach, if one give them money, to conquer in speaking, right or wrong.

PHID. Who are they?

STREP. I do not know the name accurately. They are minute-philosophers, noble and excellent.

PHID. Bah! they are rogues; I know them. You mean the quacks, the pale-faced wretches, the bare-footed fellows, of whose number are the miserable Socrates and Chærephon.[2]

STREP. Hold! hold! be silent! Do not say anything foolish. But, if you have any concern for your father's patrimony, become one of them, having given up your horsemanship.

PHID. I would not, by Bacchus, if even you were to give me the pheasants [3] which Leogoras rears!

STREP. Go, I entreat you, dearest of men, go and be taught.

PHID. Why, what shall I learn?

STREP. They say, that among them are both the two causes,—the better cause, whichever that is, and the worse: they say, that the one of these two causes, the worse, prevails, though it speaks on the unjust side. If therefore you learn for me this unjust cause, I would not pay to any

[1] Or subtlety-shop.

[2] "A hanger-on of the philosopher, and appears to have been laughed at even by his fellow-scholars for the mad extremes to which he carried his reverential attachment." — WALSH.

[3] Reference to another extravagant taste of wealthy Athenians. Leogoras was noted for the luxury and dissipation in which he wasted his property.

one, not even an obolous of these debts, which I owe at present on your account.

PHID. I cannot comply; for I should not dare to look upon the Knights, having lost all my colour.

STREP. Then, by Ceres, you shall not eat any of my goods! neither you, nor your draught-horse, nor your blood-horse; but I will drive you out of my house to the crows.

PHID. My uncle Megacles will not permit me to be without a horse. But I'll go in, and pay no heed to you.

[*Exit* PHIDIPPIDES.

The Sophists' school caricatured.

STREP. Though fallen, still I will not lie prostrate: but having prayed to the gods, I will go myself to the thinking-shop and get taught. How then, being an old man, and having a bad memory, and dull of comprehension, shall I learn the subtleties of refined disquisitions? — I must go. Why thus do I loiter and not knock at the door? [*Knocks at the door.*] Boy! little boy!

DIS. [*from within*]. Go to the devil! Who is it that knocked at the door?

STREP. Strepsiades, the son of Phidon, of Cicynna.[1]

DIS. You are a stupid fellow, by Jove! who have kicked against the door so very carelessly, and have caused the mis-carriage[2] of an idea which I had conceived.

STREP. Pardon me; for I dwell afar in the country. But tell me the thing which has been made to miscarry.

DIS. It is not lawful to mention it, except to disciples.

STREP. Tell it, then, to me without fear; for I here am come as a disciple to the thinking-shop.

DIS. I will tell you; but you must regard these as mysteries. Socrates lately asked Chærephon about a flea, how many of its own feet it jumped; for after having bit the eyebrow of Chærephon, it leapt away on to the head of Socrates.

STREP. How, then, did he measure this?

DIS. Most cleverly. He melted some wax, and then took the flea and dipped its feet in the wax; and then a

[1] Strepsiades gives name, paternity, and deme (native place), as was required in judicial proceedings, thus adding to the serio-comic aspect.

[2] Referring to Socrates' characterization of himself as an intellectual midwife.

pair of Persian slippers[1] stuck to it when cooled. Having gently loosened these, he measured back the distance.

STREP. O king Jupiter! what subtlety of thought![2] . . .

(180–269.)

Open, open quickly the thinking-shop, and show to me Socrates as quickly as possible. For I desire to be a disciple. Come, open the door. — [*The door of the Thinking-shop opens, and the pupils of* SOCRATES *are seen, all with their heads fixed on the ground, while* SOCRATES *himself is seen suspended in the air in a basket.*] O Hercules, from what country are these wild beasts?

DIS. What do you wonder at? To what do they seem to you to be like?

STREP. To the Spartans, who were taken at Pylos.[3] But why in the world do these look upon the ground?

Subjects investigated by the Sophists ridiculed.

DIS. They are in search of the things below the earth.

STREP. Then they are searching for roots. Do not, then, trouble yourselves about this; for I know where there are large and fine ones. Why, what are these doing, who are bent down so much?

DIS. These are groping about in darkness under Tartarus.[4] . . . [*Turning to the pupils.*] But go in, lest he meet with us.

STREP. Not yet, not yet: but let them remain, that I may communicate to them a little matter of my own.

DIS. It is not permitted to them to remain without in the open air for a very long time.[5] [*The pupils retire.*]

STREP. [*discovering a variety of mathematical instruments*]. Why, what is this, in the name of heaven? Tell me.

DIS. This is Astronomy.

STREP. But what is this?

DIS. Geometry.

[1] Close-fitting shoes.

[2] Here follow a number of such incidents, designed to ridicule the practice of the Sophists and the "new" educators.

[3] Refers to their lean and haggard appearance after their long imprisonment.

[4] Beneath Tartarus there was nothing.

[5] They would lose their scholarly pallor.

STREP. What then is the use of this?

DIS. To measure out the land.

STREP. What belongs to an allotment?

DIS. No, but the whole earth.

STREP. You tell me a clever notion; for the contrivance is democratic and useful.

DIS. [*pointing to a map*]. See, here's a map of the whole earth. Do you see? this is Athens.

STREP. What say you? I don't believe you; for I do not see the Dicasts[1] sitting.

DIS. *Be assured* that this is truly the Attic territory.

STREP. Why, where are my fellow-tribesmen of Cicynna?

DIS. Here they are. And Eubœa here, as you see, is stretched out a long way by the side of it to a great distance.

STREP. I know that; for it was stretched by us and Pericles.[2] But where is Lacedæmon?

DIS. Where is it? Here it is.

STREP. How near it is to us! Pay great attention to this, to remove it very far from us.

DIS. By Jupiter, it is not possible.

Socrates represented as the chief of the Sophists.

STREP. Then you will weep for it. [*Looking up and discovering* SOCRATES.] Come, who is this man who is in the basket?

DIS. Himself.[3]

STREP. Who's "Himself"?

DIS. Socrates.

STREP. O Socrates! Come, you sir, call upon him loudly for me.

DIS. Nay, rather, call him yourself; for I have no leisure. [*Exit* DISCIPLE.

STREP. Socrates! my little Socrates!

SOC. Why callest thou me, thou creature of a day?

STREP. First tell me, I beseech you, what you are doing.

SOC. I am walking in the air, and speculating about the sun.

[1] Popular quiries or courts. Every year six thousand citizens were jurymen.

[2] Subdued by the Athenians under Pericles, twenty years previous to the presentation of the play.

[3] The usual designation of a teacher by a pupil or of a master by a slave.

STREP. And so you look down upon the gods[1] from your basket, and not from the earth? if, indeed, it is so.

Soc. For I should never have rightly discovered things celestial, if I had not suspended the intellect, and mixed the thought in a subtle form with its kindred air. But if, being on the ground, I speculated from below on things above, I should never have discovered them. For the earth forcibly attracts to itself the meditative moisture. Water-cresses also suffer the very same thing.[2]

STREP. What do you say? Does meditation attract the moisture to the water-cresses? Come then, my little Socrates, descend to me, that you may teach me those things, for the sake of which I have come.

[SOCRATES *lowers himself and gets out of the basket.*]

Soc. And for what did you come?

STREP. Wishing to learn to speak; for, by reason of usury, and most ill-natured creditors, I am pillaged and plundered, and have my goods seized for debt.

**Aristophanes presents the old Greek attitude toward the Sophists.**

Soc. How did you get in debt without observing it?

STREP. A horse-disease[3] consumed me,—terrible at eating. But teach me the other one of your two causes, that which pays nothing; and I will swear by the gods, I will pay down to you whatever reward you exact of me.

Soc. By what gods will you swear? for, in the first place, gods are not a current coin with us.

STREP. By what do you swear? By iron money, as in Byzantium?[4]

Soc. Do you wish to know clearly celestial matters, what they rightly are?

STREP. Yes, by Jupiter, if it be possible!

Soc. And to hold converse with the Clouds, our divinities?

STREP. By all means.

Soc. [*with great solemnity*]. Seat yourself, then, upon the sacred couch.

STREP. Well, I am seated!

[1] Strepsiades understands Socrates to mean the sun-god.

[2] In ridicule of Socrates' habit of drawing his illustrations from the affairs of common life.

[3] A cancerous ulcer.

[4] A Dorian colony at that time.

Soc. Take, then, this chaplet.

STREP. For what purpose a chaplet?[1] — Ah me! Socrates, see that you do not sacrifice me like Athamas![2]

Soc. No; we do all these to those who get initiated.

STREP. Then, what shall I gain, pray?

Moral and religious effects of the new teachings represented as subversive.

Soc. You shall become in oratory a tricky knave, a thorough rattle, a subtle speaker. — But keep quiet.

STREP. By Jupiter, you will not deceive me; for if I am besprinkled,[3] I shall become fine flour.

Soc. It becomes the old man to speak words of good omen, and to hearken to my prayer. — O sovereign King, immeasurable Air, who keepest the earth suspended, and thou bright Æther, and ye august goddesses, the Clouds[4] sending thunder and lightning, arise, appear in the air, O mistresses, to your deep thinker.

STREP. Not yet, not yet, till I wrap this around me, lest I be wet through. To think of my having come from home without even a cap, unlucky man! . . .

[*The* CHORUS *representing the clouds appears.*]

(320–416.)

STREP. Tell me, O Socrates, I beseech you by Jupiter, who are these that have uttered this grand song? Are they some heroines?

Soc. By no means; but heavenly Clouds, great divinities to idle men;[5] who supply us with thought and argument, and intelligence, and humbug and circumlocution, and ability to hoax, and comprehension.

STREP. On this account therefore my soul, having heard their voice, flutters, and already seeks to discourse subtilely, and to quibble about smoke, and having pricked a maxim with a little notion, to refute the opposite argu-

[1] It was the custom to crown with a chaplet the head of the victim for sacrifice.

[2] Recently reproduced on the stage. Athamas had been crowned by sacrifice to Zeus, but was saved by Heracles.

[3] The head of the sacrificial victim was sprinkled with meal.

[4] The transition to monotheism, with the early Greek philosophers, was usually by a combination of the three related deities, Air, Æther, Clouds.

[5] Referring to the Sophists, who took no part in public affairs.

ment. So that now I eagerly desire, if by any means it be possible, to see them palpably.

Soc. Look, then, hither, towards Mount Parnes;[1] for now I behold them descending gently.

STREP. Pray, where? Show me.

Soc. See! there they come in very great numbers through the hollows and thickets; there, obliquely.[2]

STREP. What's the matter? for I can't *see them*.

Soc. By the entrance.

[*Enter* CHORUS.]

STREP. Now at length with difficulty I just see them.

Soc. Now at length you assuredly see them, unless you have your eyes running pumpkins.

STREP. Yes, by Jupiter! O highly honoured Clouds, for now they cover all things.

Soc. Did you not, however, know, nor yet consider, these to be goddesses?

STREP. No, by Jupiter! but I thought them to be mist, and dew, and smoke.

Soc. For you do not know, by Jupiter, that these feed very many sophists, Thurian[3] soothsayers, practisers of medicine, lazy-longhaired-onyx-ring-wearers,[4] and song-twisters for the cyclic dances, and meteorological quacks. They feed idle people who do nothing, because *such men* celebrate them in verse.

A conversation follows in which Socrates demonstrates to Strepsiades that clouds can take any form, and that these forms of the Chorus which resemble women in reality are clouds.

STREP. O earth, what a voice! how holy, and dignified, and wondrous!

[1] In the south of Attica: frequently crowned with clouds, especially in the morning, though it was not visible from the stage where the comedy was presented.

[2] The entrance of the orchestra is here indicated.

[3] Thurii was founded 444 B.C., chiefly through the influence of the soothsayer Lampon. A number of Sophists and orators also took part in the movement.

[4] Dilettante philosophers of Athens, who paid great attention to their dress and toilet.

New gods substituted for old.

Soc. For, in fact, these alone are goddesses; and all the rest is nonsense.

STREP. But come, by the Earth, is not Jupiter, the Olympian, a god?

Soc. What Jupiter? Do not trifle. There is no Jupiter.

STREP. What do you say? Who rains, then? For first of all explain this to me.

Soc. These, to be sure. I will teach you it by powerful evidence.[1] Come, where have you seen him raining at any-time without Clouds? And yet he ought to rain in fine weather, and these to be absent. . . .

(423-487.)

Will you not, pray, now believe in no god, except what we *believe in*—this Chaos, and the Clouds, and the Tongue—these three?

STREP. Absolutely I would not even converse with the others, not even if I met them; nor would I sacrifice to them, nor make libations, nor offer frankincense.

CHO. Tell us then boldly, what we must do for you? for you shall not fail in getting it, if you honour and admire us, and seek to become clever.

STREP. O mistresses, I request of you then this very small favor, that I be the best of the Greeks in speaking by a hundred stadia.

CHO. Well, you shall have this from us, so that henceforward from this time no one shall get more opinions passed in the public assemblies than you.

Ancient moral ideas replaced by selfish utilitarian ones.

STREP. Grant me not to deliver important opinions; for I do not desire these, but only to pervert the right for my own advantage, and to evade my creditors.

CHO. Then you shall obtain what you desire; for you do not covet great things. But commit yourself without fear to our ministers.

STREP. I will do so in reliance upon you, for necessity oppresses me, on account of the blood-horses, and the marriage which ruined me. Now, therefore, let them use me as they please. I give up this my body to them to be

[1] The theory that rain was the result of natural causes, and not sent by Zeus, was held by some earlier philosophers.

beaten, to be hungered, to be troubled with thirst, to be squalid, to shiver with cold, to flay into a leathern bottle, if I shall escape clear from my debts, and appear to men to be bold, glib of tongue, audacious, impudent, shameless, a fabricator of falsehoods, inventive of words, a practised knave in lawsuits, a law-tablet, a thorough rattle, a fox, a sharper, a slippery knave, a dissembler, a slippery fellow, an imposter, a gallows-bird, a blackguard, a twister, a troublesome fellow, a licker-up of hashes. If they call me this, when they meet me, let them do to me absolutely what they please. And if they like, by Ceres, let them serve up a sausage out of me to the deep thinkers.

CHO. This man has a spirit not void of courage, but prompt. Know, that if you learn these matters from me, you will possess amongst mortals a glory as high as heaven.

STREP. What shall I experience?

CHO. You shall pass with me the most enviable of mortal lives the whole time.

STREP. Shall I then ever see this?

CHO. Yea, so that many be always seated at your gates, wishing to communicate with you and come to a conference with you, to consult with you as to actions and affidavits of many talents, as is worthy of your abilities. [*To* SOCRATES.] But attempt to teach the old man by degrees whatever you purpose, and scrutinize his intellect, and make trial of his mind.

**The methods of sophistic teaching caricatured.**

SOC. Come now, tell me your own turn of mind; in order that, when I know of what sort it is, I may now, after this, apply to you new engines.

STREP. What? By the gods, do you purpose to besiege me?

SOC. No; I wish to briefly learn from you if you are possessed of a good memory.

STREP. In two ways, by Jove. If any thing be owing to me, I have a very good memory; but if I owe, unhappy man, I am very forgetful.

SOC. Is the power of speaking, pray, implanted in your nature?

STREP. Speaking is not in me, but cheating is.

* * * * * * *

(743–846.)

Soc. Keep quiet; and if you be puzzled in any one of your conceptions, leave it and go; and then set your mind in motion again, and lock it up.

STREP. [*in great glee*]. O dearest little Socrates!

Soc. What, old man?

STREP. I have got a device for cheating them of the interest.

Soc. Exhibit it.

STREP. Now tell me this, pray; if I were to purchase a Thessalian witch, and draw down the moon by night, and then shut it up, as if it were a mirror, in a round crest-case, and then carefully keep it —

Soc. What good, pray, would this do you?

STREP. What? If the moon were to rise no longer anywhere, I should not pay the interest.

Soc. Why so, pray?

STREP. Because the money is lent out by the month.

Soc. Capital! But I will again propose to you another clever question. If a suit of five talents should be entered against you, tell me how you would obliterate it.

STREP. How? how? I do not know; but I must seek.

Soc. Do not then always revolve your thoughts about yourself; but slack away your mind into the air, like a cock-chafer tied with a thread by the foot.

STREP. I have found a very clever method of getting rid of my suit, so that you yourself would acknowledge it.

Soc. Of what description?

STREP. Have you ever seen this stone in the chemists' shops, the beautiful and transparent one, from which they kindle fire?

Soc. Do you mean the burning-glass? [1]

STREP. I do. Come, what would you say, pray, if I were to take this, when the clerk was entering the suit,[2] and were to stand at a distance, in the direction of the sun, thus, and melt out the letters of my suit?

Soc. Cleverly done, by the Graces!

[1] At that time ranked with precious stones.

[2] This was done upon a waxen tablet, which was then hung up in the court for public inspection.

STREP. Oh! how I am delighted, that a suit of five talents has been cancelled!

Soc. Come now, quickly seize upon this.

STREP. What?

Soc. How, when engaged in a lawsuit, you could overturn the suit, when you were about to be cast, because you had no witnesses.

STREP. Most readily and easily.

Soc. Tell me, pray.

The Sophists' claim that they could teach anyone ridiculed.

STREP. Well now, I tell you. If, while one suit was still pending, before mine was called on, I were to run away and hang myself.

Soc. You talk nonsense.

STREP. By the gods would I! for no one will bring an action against me when I am dead.

Soc. You talk nonsense. Begone; I can't teach you any longer.

STREP. Why so? Yea, by the gods, O Socrates!

Soc. You straightway forget whatever you learn. For, what now was the first thing you were taught? Tell me.

STREP. Come, let me see: nay, what *was* the first? What was the first? Nay, what *was* the thing in which we knead our flour? Ah me! what was it?

Soc. Will you not pack off to the devil, you most forgetful and most stupid old man?

STREP. Ah me, what then, will become of me, wretched man? For I shall be utterly undone, if I do not learn to ply the tongue. Come, oh, ye Clouds, give me some good advice.

CHO. We, old man, advise you, if you have a son grown up, to send him to learn in your stead.

STREP. Well, I have a fine handsome son, but he is not willing to learn. What must I do?

CHO. But you permit him?

STREP. Yes, for he is robust in body, and in good health, and is come of the high-plumed dames of Cœsyra. I will go for him, and if he be not willing, I will certainly drive him from my house. [*To* SOCRATES.] Go in and wait for me for a short time. [*Exit.*

CHO. Do you perceive that you are soon about to obtain the greatest benefits through us alone of the gods? For this man is ready to do everything that you bid him. But you, while the man is astounded and evidently elated, having perceived it, will quickly fleece him to the best of your power. [*Exit* SOCRATES.] For matters of this sort are somehow accustomed to turn the other way.

[*Enter* STREPSIADES *and* PHIDIPPIDES.]

STREP. By Mist,[1] you certainly shall not stay here any longer! but go and gnaw the columns of Megacles.[2]

The new ideas and practices, being superficial, are quickly gained, and are easily spread.

PHID. My good sir, what is the matter with you, O father? You are not in your senses, by Olympian Jupiter!

STREP. See, see! "Olympian Jupiter!" What folly! To think of your believing in Jupiter, as old as you are!

PHID. Why, pray, did you laugh at this?

STREP. Reflecting that you are a child, and have antiquated notions. Yet, however, approach, that you may know more; and I will tell you a thing, by learning which you will be a man. But see that you do not teach this to any one.

PHID. Well, what is it?

STREP. You swore now by Jupiter.

PHID. I did.

STREP. Seest thou, then, how good a thing is learning? There is no Jupiter, O Phidippides!

PHID. Who then?

STREP. Vortex reigns, having expelled Jupiter.

PHID. Bah! Why do you talk foolishly?

STREP. Be assured that it is so.

PHID. Who says this?

STREP. Socrates the Melian,[3] and Chærephon, who knows the footmarks of fleas.

PHID. Have you arrived at such a pitch of frensy, that you believe madmen?

[1] The new oath indicates the effect of the sophistic teaching on religious beliefs.

[2] The context indicates that, just before arriving on the stage, the boy has once more refused to obey his father and has alluded to his Uncle Megacles. The father's suggestion is that there is nothing to eat there save the columns, which are all that is left of the former splendor.

[3] A common expression for *atheist*, referring to Diagoras of Melos.

STREP. Speak words of good omen, and say nothing bad of clever men and wise; of whom, through frugality, none ever shaved or anointed himself, or went to a bath to wash himself; while you squander my property in bathing, as if I were *already* dead. But go as quickly as possible, and learn instead of me.

PHID. What good *could* any one learn from them?

STREP. What, really! Whatever wisdom there is amongst men. And you will know yourself, how ignorant and stupid you are. But wait for me here a short time. [*Runs off.*

PHID. Ah me! what shall I do, my father being crazed? Shall I bring him into court and convict him of lunacy, or shall I give information of his madness to the coffin-makers?

* * * * * * *

(865–1062.)

STREP. Come hither, come hither, O Socrates! come forth, for I bring to you this son of mine, having persuaded him against his will.

[*Enter* SOCRATES.]

SOC. For he is still childish, and not used to the baskets here.

PHID. You would yourself be used to them if you were hanged.

STREP. A mischief take you! do you abuse your teacher?

SOC. "Were hanged" quoth 'a! how sillily he pronounced it, and with lips wide apart! How can this *youth* ever learn an acquittal from a trial or a legal summons, or persuasive refutation? And yet Hyperbolus learnt this at the cost of a talent.[1]

STREP. Never mind; teach him. He is clever by nature. Indeed, from his earliest years, when he was a little fellow only so big, he was wont to form houses and carve ships within-doors, and make little wagons of leather, and make frogs out of pomegranate-rinds, you can't think how cleverly. But see that he learns those two causes; the better, whatever it may be; and the worse, which, by maintaining

[1] Referring to the claims of some of the Sophists that any art could be taught to any one, if proper payment was made.

what is unjust, overturns the better. If not *both*, at any rate the unjust one by all means.

Soc. He shall learn it himself from the two causes in person. [*Exit* SOCRATES.

STREP. I will take my departure. Remember this now, that he is to be able to reply to all just arguments.

The two causes representing "the old" and "the new" education.

[*Exit* STREPSIADES, *and enter* JUST CAUSE *and* UNJUST CAUSE.]

JUST. Come hither! show yourself to the spectators, although being audacious.

UNJUST. Go whither you please; for I shall far rather do for you, if I speak before a crowd.

JUST. You destroy me? Who are you?

UNJ. A cause.

JUST. Aye, the worse.

UNJ. But I conquer you, who say that you are better than I.

JUST. By doing what clever trick?

UNJ. By discovering new contrivances.

JUST. For these *innovations* flourish by the favour of these silly persons.

UNJ. No; but wise persons.

JUST. I will destroy you miserably.

UNJ. Tell me, by doing what?

JUST. By speaking what is just.

UNJ. But I will overturn them by contradicting them; for I deny that justice even exists at all.

JUST. Do you deny that it exists?

UNJ. For come, where is it?

JUST. With the gods.

UNJ. Now then, if justice exists, has Jupiter not perished, who bound his own father?

JUST. Bah! this profanity now is spreading! Give me a basin.

Their characteristics and methods in caricature.

UNJ. You are a dotard and absurd.

JUST. You are debauched and shameless.

UNJ. You have spoken roses of me.

JUST. And a dirty lickspittle.

UNJ. You crown me with lilies.

JUST. And a parricide.

UNJ. You don't know that you are sprinkling me with gold.

JUST. Certainly not so formerly, but with lead.

UNJ. But now this is an ornament to me.

JUST. You are very impudent.

UNJ. And you are antiquated.

JUST. And through you, no one of our youths is willing to go to school; and you will be found out some time or other by the Athenians, what sort of doctrines you teach the simple-minded.

UNJ. You are shamefully squalid.

JUST. And you are prosperous. And yet formerly you were a beggar, saying that you were the Mysian Telephus,[1] and gnawing the maxims of Pandeletus[2] out of your little wallet.

UNJ. Oh, the wisdom —

JUST. Oh, the madness —

UNJ. Which you have mentioned.

JUST. And of your city, which supports you who ruin her youth.

UNJ. You shan't teach this *youth*, you old dotard.

JUST. Yes, if he is to be saved, and not merely to practise loquacity.

UNJ. [*to* PHIDIPPIDES]. Come hither, and leave him to rave.

JUST. You shall howl, if you lay your hand on him.

CHO. Cease from contention and railing. But show to us, you, what you used to teach the men of former times, and you, the new system of education; in order that, having heard you disputing, he may decide and go to the school *of one or the other.*

JUST. I am willing to do so.

UNJ. I also am willing.

[1] Telephus, king of Mysia, wounded by Achilles during the Trojan War, sought a cure, at the direction of the Delphic oracle, from the one who had wounded him. This he did, disguised as a beggar, and through the mediation of Agamemnon was successful. In the play of Euripides he is presented as an accomplished Sophist in the guise of a beggar. Hence the reference.

[2] Pandeletus was one of the minor Sophists.

CHO. Come now, which of the two shall speak first?

UNJ. I will give him the precedence; and then, from these things which he adduces, I will shoot him dead with new words and thoughts. And at last, if he mutter, he shall be destroyed, being stung in his whole face and his two eyes by my maxims, as if by bees.

CHO. Now the two, relying on very dexterous arguments and thoughts, and sententious maxims, will show which of them shall appear superior in argument. For now the whole crisis of wisdom is here laid before them; about which my friends have a very great contest. But do you, who adorned our elders with many virtuous manners, utter the voice in which you rejoice, and declare your nature.

The "old education described by its friend.

JUST. I will, therefore, describe the ancient system of education, how it was ordered, when I flourished in the advocacy of justice, and temperance was the fashion. In the first place it was incumbent that no one should hear the voice of a boy uttering a syllable; and next, that those from the same quarter of the town should march in good order through the streets to the school of the Harp-master, naked, and in a body, even if it were to snow as thick as meal. Then again, *their master* would teach them, not sitting cross-legged, to learn by rote a song, either "Pallas Terrible Destroyer of Cities"[1] or "Far Reaching Shriek,"[2] raising to a higher pitch the harmony which our fathers transmitted to us. But if any of them were to play the buffoon, or turn any quavers like these difficult turns the present artists make after the manner of Phrynis,[3] he used to be thrashed, being beaten with many blows, as banishing the Muses. And it behoved the boys, while sitting in the school of the Gymnastic-master, to cover the thigh, so that they might exhibit nothing indecent to those outside; then again, after rising *from the ground*, to sweep *the sand* together, and to take care not to leave an impression of the person for their lovers. And no boy used in those days to

[1] First line of a song composed by Lamprocles, son of Didon, an ancient Athenian poet.

[2] First line of a song composed by Cydides, a harper of Hermione.

[3] Phrynis of Mitylene introduced a new species of modulation in music, deviating from the simplicity of the ancients.

anoint himself below the navel; so that their bodies wore the appearance of blooming health. Nor used he to go to his lover, having made up his voice in an effeminate tone, prostituting himself with his eyes. Nor used it to be allowed when one was dining to take the head of a radish, or to snatch from their seniors dill or parsley, or to eat fish, or to giggle, or to keep the legs crossed.[1]

UNJ. Aye, antiquated and Dipolia-like,[2] and full of grasshoppers, and of Cecydes,[3] and of the Buphonian festival![4]

JUST. Yet certainly these are those principles by which my system of education nurtured the men who fought at Marathon. But you teach the men of the present day, from their earliest years, to be wrapped up in himatia; so that I am choked, when at the Panathenaia[5] a fellow, holding his shield before his person, neglects Tritogenia,[6] when they ought to dance. Wherefore, O youth, choose, with confidence, me, the better cause, and you will learn to hate the Agora, and to refrain from baths, and to be ashamed at what is disgraceful, and to be enraged if any one jeer you, and to rise up from seats before your seniors when they approach, and not to behave ill toward your parents, and to do nothing else that is base, because you are to form in your mind an image of Modesty: and not to dart into the house of a dancing woman, lest, while gaping after these things, being struck with an apple by a wanton, you should be damaged in your reputation: and not to contradict your father in any thing; nor by calling him Iapetus,[7] to reproach him with the ills of age, by which you were reared in your infancy.

[1] "Among the remains of ancient art there is, perhaps, not one representing a man, woman, god, or dæmon sitting cross-legged." — FELTON.

[2] One of the most ancient festivals in Attica, in honor of Jupiter, the protector of cities. These ceremonies had become antiquated and were ridiculed.

[3] An ancient poet.

[4] Same festival as the Dipolia, mentioned above.

[5] The most ancient and most important of Athenian festivals, held in honor of Athene, the patron deity of Athens. The lesser festival held every year, the greater every fifth year.

[6] A surname of Athene.

[7] Son of Uranus and Gæa; regarded by the Greeks as the father of the human race.

Unj. If you shall believe him in this, O youth, by Bacchus, you will be like the sons of Hippocrates,[1] and they will call you a booby.

How the "new" education appears to an advocate of the "old."

Just. Yet certainly shall you spend your time in the gymnastic schools, sleek and blooming; not chattering in the market-place rude jests, like the youths of the present day; nor dragged into court for a petty suit, greedy, pettyfogging, knavish; but you shall descend to the Academy[2] and run races beneath the sacred olives along with some modest compeer, crowned with white reeds, redolent of yew, and careless ease, and of leaf-shedding white poplar, rejoicing in the season of spring, when the plane-tree whispers to the elm. If you do these things which I say, and apply your mind to these, you will ever have a stout chest, a clear complexion, broad shoulders, a little tongue, large hips, little lewdness. But if you practise what the youths of the present day do, you will have, in the first place, a pallid complexion, small shoulders, a narrow chest, a large tongue, little hips, great lewdness, a long psephism; and *this deceiver* will persuade you to consider every thing that is base to be honourable, and what is honourable to be base; and, in addition to this, he will fill you with the lewdness of Antimachus.[3]

Cho. O thou that practisest most renowned high-towering wisdom! how sweetly does a modest grace attend your words! Happy, therefore, were they who lived in those days, in the times of former men! In reply, then, to these, O thou that hast a dainty-seeming muse, it behoveth thee to say something new; since the man has gained renown. And it appears you have need of powerful arguments against him, if you are to conquer the man, and not incur laughter.

Ideals of the "new" education as viewed by the "old."

Unj. And yet I was choking in my heart, and was longing to confound all these with contrary maxims. For I have been called among the deep thinkers the "worse cause," on this very account, that I first contrived how to

[1] A nephew of Pericles. His sons were often derided for their silliness.

[2] A public grove in the suburbs of Athens, where Plato and his followers taught.

[3] A composer of lewd songs.

speak against both law and justice: and this *art* is worth more than ten thousand staters, that one should choose the worse cause, and nevertheless be victorious. But mark how I will confute the system of education on which he relies, who says, in the first place, that he will not permit you to be washed with warm water. And yet, on what principle do you blame the warm baths?

JUST. Because it is most vile, and makes a man cowardly.

UNJ. Stop! For immediately I seize and hold you by the waist without escape. Come, tell me, which of the sons of Jupiter do you deem to have been the bravest in soul, and to have undergone most labours? Method of the "new" education caricatured.

JUST. I consider no man superior to Hercules.

UNJ. Where, pray, did you ever see cold Heraclean baths?[1] And yet, who was more valiant *than he?*

JUST. These are the very things which make the bath full of youths always chattering all day long, but the palæstras empty.

UNJ. You next find fault with their living in the market-place; but I commend it. For if it had been bad, Homer would never have been for representing Nestor as an orator; nor all the *other* wise men. I will return, then, from thence to the tongue, which this fellow says our youths ought not to exercise, while I maintain *they should.* And, again, he says they ought to be modest: two very great evils. For tell me to whom you have ever seen any good accrue through modesty; and confute me by your words. . . . (1071–1112.) For [*to* PHIDIPPIDES] consider, O youth, all that attaches to modesty, and of how many pleasures you are about to be deprived — of women, of games at cottabus,[2] of dainties, of drinking-bouts, of giggling. And yet, what is life worth to you, if you be deprived of these *enjoyments?* Well, I will pass from thence to the necessities of our nature. You have gone astray, you have fallen in love, you have been guilty of some adultery, and then have been

[1] Herculean baths were warm baths, for Athena had called the warm springs of Thermopylæ into existence in order that Heracles might refresh himself. This passage is a type of the "sophistic" reasoning.

[2] A Greek game, popular at drinking bouts.

caught. You are undone, for you are unable to speak. But if you associate with me, indulge your inclination, dance, laugh, and think nothing disgraceful. For if you should happen to be detected as an adulterer, you will make this reply to him, "that you have done him no injury": and then refer him to Jupiter, how even he is overcome by love. And yet, how could you, who are a mortal, have greater power than a god?

JUST. But what, if he should suffer the radish through obeying you, and be depillated with hot ashes? What argument will he be able to state, *to prove* that he is not a blackguard?

Popularity of the new educators and of their methods of gaining converts.

UNJ. And if he be a blackguard, what harm will he suffer?

JUST. Nay, what could he ever suffer still greater than this?

UNJ. What then will you say, if you be conquered by me in this?

JUST. I will be silent: what else *can I do*?

UNJ. Come now, tell me; from what class do the advocates come?

JUST. From the blackguards.

UNJ. I believe you. What then? from what class do the tragedians come?

JUST. From the blackguards.

UNJ. You say well. But from what class do the public orators come?

JUST. From the blackguards.

UNJ. Then have you perceived that you say nothing to the purpose? And look which class among the audience is the more numerous.

JUST. Well now, I'm looking.

UNJ. What, then, do you see?

JUST. By the gods, the blackguards *to be* far more numerous. This fellow, at any rate, I know; and him yonder; and this fellow with the long hair.

UNJ. What, then, will you say?

JUST. We are conquered. Ye blackguards, by the gods, receive my cloak,[1] for I desert to you.

[1] An allusion to Socrates' ceremony of stripping his disciples before they were initiated into his school.

[*Exeunt the two* CAUSES, *and reënter* SOCRATES *and* STREPSIADES.]

SOC. What then? Whether do you wish to take and lead away this your son, or shall I teach him to speak?

STREP. Teach him, and chastise him; and remember that you train him properly; on the one side able for petty suits; but train his other jaw able for the more important causes.

SOC. Make yourself easy; you shall receive him back a clever sophist. . . .

**Phidippides receives instruction from the Sophists. Meanwhile the creditors with summons-witnesses call upon Strepsiades. These he first confounds with "Sophists'" arguments and then drives away with a whip.**

(1265–1346.)

AMYNIAS. Do not jeer me, my friend; but order your son to pay me the money which he received; especially as I have been unfortunate.

**The newly acquired learning put to a test.**

STREP. What money is this?

AMYN. That which he borrowed.

STREP. Then you were really unlucky, as I think.

AMYN. By the gods, I fell while driving my horses.

STREP. Why, pray, do you talk nonsense, as if you had fallen from an ass?

AMYN. Do I talk nonsense, if I wish to recover my money?

STREP. You can't be in your senses yourself.

AMYN. Why, pray?

STREP. You appear to me to have had your brains shaken as it were.

AMYN. And you *appear* to me, by Hermes, to be going to be summoned, if you will not pay me the money.

STREP. Tell me now, whether do you think that Jupiter always rains fresh rain on each occasion, or that the sun draws from below the same water back again?[1]

AMYN. I know not which; nor do I care.

STREP. How then is it just that you should recover your money, if you know nothing of meteorological matters?

[1] A common subject of discussion.

AMYN. Well, if you are in want, pay me the interest of my money.

STREP. What sort of an animal is this interest?

AMYN. Most assuredly the money is always becoming more and more every month and every day as the time slips away.

STREP. You say well. What then? Is it possible that you consider the sea to be greater now than formerly?

PAS. No, by Jupiter, but equal: for it is not fitting that it should be greater.

STREP. And how then, you wretch, does this become no way greater, though the rivers flow into it, while you seek to increase your money? Will you not take yourself off from my house? Bring me the goad. [*Enter servant with a goad.*]

AMYN. I call you to witness these things.

STREP. [*beating him*]. Go! why do you delay? Won't you march, Mr. Blood-horse?

AMYN. Is not this an insult, pray?

STREP. Will you move quickly? [*Pricks him behind with the goad.*] I'll lay on you, goading you behind, you out-rigger. Do you fly? [AMYNIAS *runs off.*] I thought I should stir you, together with your wheels and your two-horse chariots. [*Exit* STREPSIADES.

CHO. What a thing it is to love evil courses! For this old man, having loved them, wishes to withhold the money which he borrowed. And he will certainly meet with something to-day, which will perhaps cause this Sophist to suddenly receive some misfortune, in return for the knaveries he has begun. For I think that he will presently find what has been long boiling up, that his son is skilful to speak opinions opposed to justice, so as to overcome all with whomsoever he holds converse, even if he advance most villanous doctrines; and perhaps, perhaps *his father* will wish that he were even speechless.

The immoral character of the new learning furnishes the plot to the comedy.

STREP. [*running out of the house pursued by his son*]. Hollo! Hollo! O neighbors and kinsfolk and fellow-tribesmen, defend me, by all means, who am being beaten! Ah me, unhappy man, for my head and jaw! Wretch! do you beat your father?

PHID. Yes, father.

STREP. You see him owning that he beats me.

PHID. Certainly.

STREP. O wretch, and parricide, and house-breaker!

PHID. Say the same things of me again, and more. Do you know that I take pleasure in being much abused?

STREP. You blackguard!

PHID. Sprinkle me with roses in abundance.

STREP. Do you beat your father?

PHID. And will prove, too, by Jupiter, that I beat you with justice.

STREP. O thou most rascally! Why, how can it be just to beat a father?

PHID. I will demonstrate it, and will overcome you in argument.

STREP. Will you overcome me in this?

PHID. Yea, by much and easily. But choose which of the two Causes you wish to speak.[1]

STREP. Of what two Causes?

PHID. The better, or the worse?

STREP. Marry, I did get you taught to speak against justice, by Jupiter, my friend, if you are going to persuade me of this, that it is just and honourable for a father to be beat by his sons!

PHID. I think I shall certainly persuade you: so that, when you have heard, not even you yourself will say any thing against it.

STREP. Well, now, I am willing to hear what you have to say.

* * * * * * *

(1408-1450.)

PHID. I will pass over to that part of my discourse where you interrupted me; and first I will ask you this: Did you beat me when I was a boy?

STREP. I did, through good will and concern for you.

**The new learning is destructive to old Greek morality,**

PHID. Pray tell me, is it not just that I also should be well inclined towards you in the same way, and beat you, since this is to be well inclined — to give a beating? For why ought your body to be exempt from blows, and mine

[1] It was characteristic of the Sophists to be indifferent as to which side of a question they should support.

not? And yet I too was born free. The boys weep, and do you not think it right that a father should weep? You will say that it is ordained by law that this should be the lot of boys. But I would reply, that old men are boys twice over, and that it is the more reasonable that the old should weep than the young, inasmuch as it is less just that they should err.

STREP. It is no where ordained by law that a father should suffer this.

PHID. Was it not then a man like you and me, who first proposed this law, and by speaking persuaded the ancients? Why then is it less lawful for me also in turn to propose henceforth a new law for the sons, that they should beat their fathers in turn? But as many blows as we received before the law was made, we remit; and we concede to them our having been well thrashed without return. Observe the cocks and these other animals, how they punish their fathers; and yet, in what do they differ from us, except that they do not write decrees?

STREP. Why then, since you imitate the cocks in all things, do you not sleep on a perch?

PHID. It is not the same thing, my friend; nor would it appear so to Socrates.

STREP. Therefore do not beat me; otherwise you will one day blame yourself.

PHID. Why, how?

STREP. Since I am justly entitled to chastise you; and you *to chastise* your son, if you should have one.

PHID. But if I should not have one, I shall have wept for nothing, and you will die laughing at me.

STREP. To me indeed, O comrades, he seems to speak justly; and I think we ought to concede to them what is fitting. For it is proper that we should weep, if we do not act justly.

PHID. Consider still another maxim.

STREP. *No;* for I shall perish *if I do.*

PHID. And yet perhaps you will not be vexed at suffering what you now suffer.

STREP. How, pray? for inform me what good you will do me by this?

PHID. I will beat my mother, just as I have you.

STREP. What do you say? what do you say? This other again, is a greater wickedness.

PHID. But what if, having the worst Cause, I shall conquer you in arguing, *proving* that it is right to beat one's mother?

STREP. Most assuredly, if you do this, nothing will hinder you from casting yourself and your Worse Cause into the pit[1] along with Socrates. — These evils have I suffered through you, O Clouds, having intrusted all my affairs to you. . . .

**and to old Greek religion.**

## *Against the Sophists: An Oration by Isocrates*

**Many ignorant or unscrupulous teachers have brought the entire profession of "Sophists" into disrepute.**

If all those who undertake instruction, would speak the truth, nor make greater promises than they can perform, they would not be accused by the illiterate. Now, those who inconsiderately have dared to boast, have been the cause that those men seem to have reasoned better, who indulge their indolence, than such as study philosophy: for, first, who would not detest and despise those who pass their time in sophistic chicanery? who pretend indeed, that they seek truth, but, from the beginning of their promises, labour to speak falsities; for I think it manifest to all, that the faculty of foreknowing future things is above our nature: nay, we are so far from such prudence, that Homer, who, for his wisdom, has acquired the highest fame, has sometimes introduced gods in his poem, consulting about futurity; not that he knew the nature of their minds, but that he would show to us, that this was one of those things which are impossible for man. These men are arrived at that pitch of insolence, that they endeavor to persuade the younger, that, if they will be their disciples, they shall know what is best to be done, and thereby be made happy; and, after they have erected themselves into teachers of such sublime things, they are not ashamed to ask of them four or five minæ; though, did they sell any other possession for much less than its value, they would not hesitate to grant themselves mad. But now exposing to sale

[1] At the base of the Hill of the Nymphs, into which criminals or their bodies were cast.

all virtue and happiness (if we will believe them), they dare argue, that, as being wise men, they ought to be the preceptors of others; yet they say indeed, that they are not indigent of money, while, to diminish its idea, they call it pitiful gold and silver; though they require a trifling gain, and only promise to make those next to immortal, who will commence their disciples. But what is the absurdest of all, is, that they are diffident of those very persons from whom they are to receive their reward, though they themselves are to teach them justice; for they make an agreement, that the money shall be deposited with those whom they never taught. Doing right in regard of their own security, but acting contrary to their own promises: for it becomes those who teach any other thing, by a cautious bargain to avoid controversy (for nothing impedes, but that those who are ingenious in other respects, may not be honest in regard of contracts); yet how can it be but absurd, that they, who pretend to teach virtue and temperance as an art, should not chiefly trust to their own disciples; for they who are just towards other men, will certainly not trespass against those, by whom they were made both good and equitable.

**Material gain placed above moral influence.**

When therefore some of the unlearned, considering all these things, see those who profess teaching wisdom and happiness, indigent themselves of many things, requiring a small sum of their scholars, and observing contradictions in silly sentences, though they see them not in actions; professing likewise, that they know futurity, yet not capable of speaking or deliberating properly of things present; and that those are more consistent with themselves, and do more things right who follow common opinions, than those who say they are possessed of wisdom: when they see this, I say, they think such disputations mere trifles, a loss of time in idle things, and not a real improvement of the human mind.

**Their false claims bring all instruction into disrepute.**

Nor is it just to blame these men only, but those likewise who profess to teach civil science to the citizens; for they also disregard truth; and think it artful, if they draw as many as possible, by the smallness of the recompence, and the greatness of their promises, and so receive something of them: and they are so stupid, and imagine

**They profess to teach civic wisdom and to give oratorical power.**

others so, that though they write orations more inaccurate than some who are unlearned speak extempore, yet they promise they will make their disciples such orators, that they shall omit nothing in the nature of things; nay, that they will teach them eloquence, like grammar; not considering the nature of each, but thinking, that on account of the excellence of their promises, they will be admired, and the study of eloquence seem of higher value; not knowing, that arts render not those famous who insolently boast of them, but those who can find out and express whatever is in them. But I would purchase willingly, at a great price, that philosophy could effect this; perhaps, then, I should not be left the farthest behind, nor have the least share of its benefits: but as the nature of the thing is not so, I would have these triflers to be silent; for I see reflections not only cast upon the faculty, but that all are accused who are conversant in the same studies. I wonder when I see those thought worthy of having scholars, who perceive not they produce a fixed art, and bound down by rules, for example of that which depends chiefly on genius. Is there any one, excepting them, who is ignorant, that, as for letters and grammar, they are unchangeable, and the same, and that we always use the same words about those things; but that the nature of eloquence is quite the contrary: for what has been said by another is not equally useful to him who speaks after; but he is the most excellent in this art, who speaks worthily indeed of his subject, but also those things which never were invented by others. The greatest difference betwixt these arts is this: it is impossible orations should be good, unless there be in them an observation of time and decorum; but there is no need of this in letters. Wherefore those who use such foreign examples, ought rather to pay than receive money, because, wanting much instruction themselves, they pretend to teach others. But if I ought not only to accuse others, but explain my own sentiments, all wise men, I believe, will agree with me, that many, studious of philosophy, have led a private life; but that some others, though they never were the scholars of sophists, were skilled both in eloquence and governing the state; for the faculty of eloquence, and all other in-

**Rhetoric and grammar can be taught; not so, eloquence.**

**Eloquence depends upon natural ability, improved by instruction.**

genuity, is innate in men, and is the portion of such as are exercised by use and experience; though instruction renders such more knowing in art, and better qualified for life: for learning has taught them to draw, as it were, from a store, what else perhaps they would but casually light on. But as for those who are of a weaker genius, it will never render them adroit pleaders, or good orators; but it will make them excel themselves, and become more prudent in many things. Since I am advanced so far, I will speak more clearly of this topic; I say then, it is no difficult matter to learn those forms or orders of things, by which we know how to compose orations, if any one puts himself under the care not of such as easily vaunt themselves, but such as have the real science; but, in regard of what relates to particular things, which we must first see, and mix together, and dispose in order, and, besides, not lose opportunities, but vary the whole discourse with arguments, and conclude it in a harmonious and musical manner: these things, I say, require great care, and are the province of a manly and wise mind; and the scholar must, besides his having necessary ingenuity, perfectly instruct himself in the different kinds of orations, and be exercised in the practice: but it becomes the master to explain all these as accurately as possible, so as to omit nothing which may be taught. As for the rest, show himself such an example, that they who can imitate and express it, may be able to speak in a more beautiful and elegant manner than others. In whatever regard any thing of what I have mentioned is wanting, it must follow, that his disciples will be less perfect.

Kind of instruction necessary.

These Sophists are wrong, not only in their method of education, but also in their purpose.

And for those sophists who have lately sprung up, and fallen into this arrogance, though numerous now, they will be forced at last to conform to my rules. Now, there remain those who were born before us, and have dared to write of arts, not to be dismissed without just reprehension; who have professed, that they would teach how we should plead under an accusation, choosing out the most odious expression of all, which their enviers ought to have done, and not they who preside over this institution; since this, as far as it can be taught, can conduce no more to the composing of law-orations than all others: yet the sophists

Virtue and temperance cannot be so taught.

are worse than those who grovel amidst contentions, because, while they recite such miserable orations, as did any one imitate, he must become unfit for all things, yet affirm, that virtue and temperance are taught in them; but the latter, exhorting to popular orations, and neglecting the other advantages they were possessed of, have suffered themselves to be esteemed teachers of bustling in business, and of gratifying avarice; yet they will sooner assist those who will obey the precepts of this learning, in the habit of equity than eloquence. But let no one think, that I imagine justice can be taught; for I do not think there is any such art which can teach those who are not disposed by nature, either temperance or justice; though I think the study of popular eloquence helps both to acquire and practice it. But that I may not seem to accuse other men's promises, and magnify things more than I ought, I judge I shall easily manifest to any one by the same arguments with which I have persuaded myself that these things are so.

### *On the Exchange of Estates; an Oration by Isocrates*

'If this speech were an ordinary specimen of the Forensic [1] or Epideictic [2] class, it would need no preface. As it is of a new kind, its origin must be explained. I had long known that some of the sophists slandered my pursuits, and represented me as a writer of speeches for the law-courts. They might as well have called Phidias [3] a doll-maker, Zeuxis [4] or Parrhasios [5] a sign-painter. Believing that I had made it clear that my subjects are not private disputes but the greatest and highest questions,

The occasion of this speech, in which Isocrates defends himself and his profession.

[1] While the speech is in the general form of addresses in the law courts, yet its style is not. It is a defence before the public.

[2] Demonstrative as opposed to deliberative oratory; oratory of purely rhetorical character. This oration of Isocrates falls between the two.

[3] The greatest of Grecian sculptors. Lived during the fifth century B.C.

[4] A celebrated painter of the Ionic school. Lived during the fifth century B.C.

[5] After Zeuxis, the chief representative of the Ionic school of painting. A contemporary of Zeuxis. These artists were in the celebrated contest in which Zeuxis deceived the birds, while Parrhasius deceived even Zeuxis himself.

I supposed such idle calumnies to be powerless. Now, however, at the age of 82, I have discovered that they influence the general public. A person who had been called upon to serve as trierarch[1] challenged me to exchange properties with him, or else to take the duty.[2] A lawsuit followed.[3] The plaintiff dwelt upon the evil tendency of my writings, upon my wealth and the number of my pupils; and the court imposed the trierarchy upon me. The expense I bore with equanimity; but I wish to correct the prejudices which led to such a verdict. This discourse is meant as an image of my mind and life. It is cast into the form of a defence in an imaginary trial. It contains some things that might be said in a law-court; some, unsuited to such a place, but illustrative of my philosophy; some, which may profit young men anxious to learn; some, taken from my former writings and intro-

[1] Trierarch was one called upon to equip a ship of war. It was the most expensive of the liturgies, or services performed for the public, required of Athenian citizens. This service was required of the wealthiest citizens only, and was imposed on them in regular rotation, the nominations being made each year by the strategi. The state furnished the vessel, — that is, the hull and mast, — the trierarch all the necessary equipment and complement of oarsmen, keeping it in readiness for a year.

[2] When such a service was imposed upon a citizen, he might take advantage of a law, called the antidosis or "an exchange," popularly ascribed to Solon, though probably originating in more democratic times. The antidosis provided that a person nominated to perform a liturgy might call upon any qualified person not so charged to take the office in his stead, or to submit to a complete exchange of property. In case the exchange was made, the first party bore the expense of the liturgia. Courts were opened for these proceedings at stated times of the year. In the case of the trierarchy the magistrates were the strategi, the ten popular magistrates elected from the several tribes and having charge of all military affairs.

[3] The trierarchy had recently been imposed upon Isocrates after such a trial, in which he had been challenged to an exchange of estates. He discharged the duties. This apology resulted, not as the actual defence made in court, but as a discourse, issued later, to combat the general prejudice against his profession. In the actual trial, Isocrates had not been able to appear on account of illness, his place being taken and his defence made by his adopted son. Isocrates and his son had borne the trierarchy as well as other liturgies. They were enrolled among the twelve hundred richest citizens.

duced here in harmony with a special purpose. The resulting whole must not be judged as representing any one class of speech, but as made up of several distinct elements brought in with several distinct aims. It ought to be read, not continuously, but part by part.

'The worst knave is he who brings against another charges to which he himself is liable. Lysimachos,[1] delivering a composed speech, has dwelt most of all upon the insidious skill of my compositions. Do not be swayed by calumny; remember the oath taken yearly by judges that they will hear impartially accuser and accused. Ere now Athens has regretted a hasty verdict; and it would be shameful that Athenians, reputed in all else the most merciful of the Greeks, should be rashly cruel in their own law-courts. No one of you, the judges, can tell that he will not be the next victim of Lysimachos. A good life is no protection from such men; they show their power upon the innocent in order to be bribed by the guilty. Never till this day have I been brought before judge or arbitrator; now, if you will hear me, I hope to prove my real character.— Read the indictment. . . .

**"Informers" responsible for this charge and for the disrepute of the Sophists.**

'Here, in the indictment, he charges me with corrupting the youth[2] by teaching them to be tricky litigants. In his speech, on the other hand, he represents me as the most wonderful of men; — as one among whose pupils have been public speakers, generals, kings, despots. He thinks that I shall be envied on the latter account, and detested on the former. Dismiss prejudice, and decide upon the merits of the case. That my literary skill has not been used for bad purposes, appears from the fact that I have no enemies. If I had, they would have profited by this trial to appear against me. This skill itself, if it has been well used, is a claim to esteem. The difference between me and a writer of law-speeches will appear if you compare our modes of life. Men frequent the places

**Charges made against Isocrates; incidentally against all Sophists.**

**His defence.**

[1] A fictitious person, who stands for the challenger in the real trial and for demagogues in general; for the decision against Isocrates was the result of the appeals to popular prejudices made by the challenger.

[2] The common charge against the Sophists and the new educators in general.

His interest has been, not in forensic rhetoric,

from which they draw their subsistence. Those who subsist by your litigations almost live in the law-courts. No one has ever seen me in a council-chamber, at the archon's office, before judges, before arbitrators. Pettifoggers thrive at home; my prosperity has always been found abroad. Is it probable that Nikokles[1] of Cyprus, sovereign judge among his people, should have rewarded me for aiding him to become a pleader? No mere writer of law-speeches has ever had pupils; I have had many. But it is not enough to show that my line of work has not been this. I will show you what it has been.

but in Panhellenic politics.

'First, it must be remembered that there are as many branches of prose as of poetry. Some prose-writers have spent their lives in tracing the genealogies of the Heroes. Others have been critics of the poets. Others have compiled histories of wars. Others have woven discussions into dialogues. My work has lain in yet another field,— in the composition of discourses bearing upon the politics of all Hellas, and fitted for recitation at Panhellenic gatherings. Such discourses evidently stand nearer to poetry than to forensic rhetoric. Their language is more imaginative and more ornate; there is greater amplitude, more scope for originality, in the thoughts which they strive to express. They are as popular as poems; and the art of writing them is much studied. Unlike forensic speeches, they deal with matters of universal interest; they have a lasting value, independent of any special occasion. Besides, he who is a master of these could succeed also in a law-court; but not *vice versa*. At these I have worked; and have got by them a reputation better than law-courts could give.

His influence not harmful, but beneficial to the public.

'I am ready to impose the severest terms upon myself. Punish me, not merely if my writings are proved harmful but if they are not shown to be matchless. It is not necessary here to argue on probabilities. My writings are themselves the facts in question. Samples of them shall be shown to you, and you shall judge for yourselves. The

[1] King of Salamis, in Cyprus. When he succeeded his father in 374 B.C. he celebrated the latter's obsequies with great splendor. Isocrates was engaged to deliver the eulogy.

discourse from which the first sample shall be taken was written when Sparta was at the head of Greece and Athens in a low estate. It seeks to rouse Hellas against Persia; and disputes the claim of Sparta to sole leadership.[1] . . .

'Is the writer of this a "corrupter of young men," or their inciter to noble daring? Does he deserve punishment; or is he to be thanked for having so praised Athens and your ancestors that former writers on the same theme feel remorse, and intending ones, despair?

'Some who, themselves unable to create, can only criticise, will say that this is 'graceful' (they could not bring themselves to say 'good'); but that praise of the past is less valuable than censure of present mistakes. You shall hear, then, part of another speech in which I assume this office of censor. Its immediate subject is the peace with Chios, Rhodes and Byzantium; it goes on to show the drawbacks to a maritime supremacy; and ends by addressing to Athens exhortation, censure and advice.[2] . . .

**Evidence from various speeches.**

'You have now heard parts of two discourses; a short passage from a third shall be read, in order that you may see how the same tendency goes through all that I have written. Here, addressing Nikokles of Cyprus, I did not aim at regular composition, but merely strung together a number of detached precepts upon government. It is not for their literary merit, but simply as showing the spirit of my dealing with princes as well as with private men, that they are quoted here. One who so boldly advised a king to care for his people, would surely be no less frank in the popular cause under a democracy.—I begin by blaming the usual neglect of special preparation by a monarch; and then urge Nikokles to regard his office as a task calling for serious labor.[3] . . .

'This shall be the last of these long extracts; but I reserve the right of referring in detail to my own writings whenever it can be useful. I offered just now to bear any

[1] Here is read an extract from the *Panegyrikos*, secs. 51–99.

[2] Here is read an extract from the speech *On the Peace*, secs. 25–56; secs. 132 to end.

[3] Here is read an extract from the discourse *To Nikokles*, secs. 14–39.

penalty, not merely if it could be shown that my writings were harmful, but unless it could be shown that they were incomparable. That boast has been justified. What attempt could be holier or more righteous than the attempt to praise our ancestors worthily of their exploits; what theme nobler than his who urges Hellenes to unite against barbarians? Good laws are allowed to be the greatest blessings to human life. Yet these benefit only the individual city; my discourses profit all Hellas. It is easier to be a legislator than to be a competent adviser of Athens and Hellas. The legislator, in an advanced stage of civilisation, is often little more than a compiler; the thoughts of an effective speaker must be his own. Teachers of moral philosophy differ from each other and from the world as to what is virtue; the virtue which I inculcate is recognised by all. Those theorists seek only to draw disciples to themselves; my object is to impress a public duty upon Athens. The alleged vices of my teaching are disproved by the affection of my pupils; who, at the end of three or four years, have left me with regret. Lysimachos has accused me, without a shadow of proof, of corrupting them; but I will refute him formally.

Character of his teaching proven by the character of his pupils,

and of his friends,

'You know my writings; you shall now hear who have been my associates from childhood, and the evidence of my contemporaries shall prove the statement. Among my friends in youth were Eunomos, Lysitheides, Kallippos; afterwards Onetor, Antikles, Philonides, Philomelos, Charmantides.[1] All these were crowned with golden crowns for their services to Athens. Whether you suppose me to have been their adviser and teacher, or merely their companion, my character is vindicated. If it is not, what would it have been if among my intimates had been such a man as Lysimachos? Some will perhaps say that I am citing good men whom I barely knew, but keeping out of sight the rascals who were my pupils. I am ready to waive all credit for honourable friendships, and to bear the full discredit of any which can be shown to have been disreputable.

and by his influence on public officers.

'The general charge against me in the indictment—that

[1] Some of these are now unknown; some are identified with prominent or wealthy citizens of Athens.

of corrupting my associates—has been sufficiently answered. But special stress has been laid upon my friendship with Timotheos;[1] and, since the interests which he long controlled were so great, especial pains have been taken to slander him. I, therefore, who am supposed to have been his adviser and teacher, cannot be silent. If he is shown to have been a bad man, let me share the blame. If he is proved to have been incomparable as a general and as a citizen, let the honour be his alone. Now, in the first place, no general ever took so many and such important cities. Corcyra, important in regard to the Peloponnesos, —Samos, for Ionia,—Sestos and Krithôte, for the Hellespont,—Potidæa, for Thrace,—were taken by him with slender resources. He forced Lacedæmon into the present peace,[2] the most advantageous ever concluded by Athens. In a word, he took twenty-four towns at a smaller outlay than the single siege of Melos cost our fathers. These exploits were achieved at a time when we were weak and our enemies strong. By what qualities did Timotheos achieve them? He was not of the ordinary type of your generals,—neither of a robust frame, nor trained in the camps of mercenaries. But he knew against whom, and with whose aid, to make war; how to form, and to use, a force suitable for each attempt; how to bear privations, and to remedy them; how to win for Athens the trust and the love of Greece. A general who, like Lysander, has one brilliant success is less great than one who for years deals wisely with ever-varying difficulties. Yet Timotheos was brought to trial for treason; and, although Iphikrates[3] took the responsibility for what had been done, Menestheus[3] for what had been spent, they were acquitted, while Timotheos was fined in an unheard-of sum. Ignorance, envy,

[1] A famous Athenian general, first appointed to command in 378 B.C. In 356 he was associated in command of the Athenian fleet. In consequence of his failure to relieve Samos, he was fined one hundred talents—more than $100,000. He was unable to pay the fine and died shortly after. Nine-tenths of the fine was subsequently remitted; the remaining tenth his son Colon expended in repair of the walls.

[2] Peace of Kallias, 371 B.C.

[3] Associates of Timotheos in the command of the fleet.

excitement, go far to explain this result; but it must be owned that the character of Timotheos contributed to it. He was no anti-democrat, no misanthrope, not arrogant; but his unbending loftiness of mind made him liable to seem all this. Against my advice, he refused to conciliate the speakers who sway the ekklesia[1] and those who direct the opinion of private circles. These men made it their business to frame falsehoods about him — falsehoods which, had I space, I could bring you to see and hate. But I must go back to my own case.

Difficulty of defence before Athenian democracy. A corrupt society.

'I hardly know how to arrange the topics on which it remains for me to speak; perhaps it will be best to take each as it occurs. But here I am checked by the warning of a friend, — which you shall hear. "If you describe your blameless life," he said, "you will only provoke jealousy. That you should have so written as to deserve public gratitude, and that your intimates should have been men whom Athens delighted to honor; that, till now, you should have been a stranger to lawsuits; that, while seeking no public emoluments, you should have enrolled yourself and your son among the twelve hundred who pay the war-tax and bear the public services; that you and he should thrice have discharged the trierarchy, and performed the other services at a greater cost than the laws enjoin; that you should receive presents from abroad, and avoid all display at home — these things will but irritate your judges." When my friend said this, it seemed to me that it would be strange if any reasonable men could object to my bearing the city's burdens and yet declining its rewards. I decline its rewards not from arrogance, but from preference for a quiet life. It is not because I am very rich that I take so large a share of its burdens. No sophist has ever made a great fortune. Gorgias[2] of Leontini,[3] who passed

Rewards of Sophists exaggerated.

[1] The public assembly, which had the final decision in public affairs. At Athens every citizen in full possession of his civic rights was entitled to take part in it after his twentieth year.

[2] A Sophist and rhetorician who came to Athens late in life. He practically introduced rhetoric into Athens. He was a contemporary of Socrates. His philosophy, as opposed to the Platonic idealism, was nihilistic.

[3] In Sicily.

much time in Thessaly when it was the richest part of Greece — whose life was spent in seeking wealth from city to city, and who had no family burdens — left only 1000 staters. The income of a sophist must not be judged by that of a popular actor. Compare me, if you will, with the most successful men in my own profession; and you will find that I have been at once a thrifty householder and a liberal citizen. Things have changed at Athens since I was a boy. Then wealth was not only dignified but safe, and every one affected to be richer than he was. Now it is more dangerous to be suspected of wealth than of the worst crime. When my fortune was wrecked in the Peloponnesian war, and I resolved to repair it by teaching, I hoped that success in my new profession would bring credit and respect. It has brought, however, only envy and slander. Lysimachos, who lives by the informer's trade, is accuser — I, who have not preyed on you, but have prospered through the gratitude of men whom I had saved, stand in danger. Our ancestors made Pindar[1] their public friend,[2] and voted him 10,000 drachmas[3] because he bore witness that Athens is the stay of Hellas It would be hard if I, who have given her praise ampler and nobler than that, should not be allowed even to end my days in peace.

Democratic jealousy of wealth and influence.

'The indictment has now been answered. But from the first I have foreseen that I should have to combat, not merely the charges against myself, but the prejudice against these studies generally. Reflection, however, assured me that among you I should find fairness, and that the cause of Philosophy could be satisfactorily defended. In the fact of the prejudice against it there is nothing strange. Athens is large and populous. Public opinion

Not Isocrates alone, but education is attacked.

[1] The greatest of Greek lyric poets, born in Thebes, 522 B.C. His support of Athens was due to her part in the Persian Wars. For this praise the Thebans fined him and the Athenians reimbursed him twofold, adding statues and other honors.

[2] The proxenos might be either an honorary appointment, or it might be similar to modern consular appointments made from citizens of the country in which they reside, by a foreign country which they are to represent.

[3] About $1800 in our money.

here is irregular and vehement as a winter-torrent. It sweeps down all men and all things that it chances to seize. This has befallen my studies. But you must decide calmly. Remember that it is not my case alone which is at issue, but the education of our youth — upon which the future of Athens must depend. If Philosophy is a bad thing, it should be absolutely banished; if it is a good thing, it should be encouraged, and its detractors should be silenced. I wish that this accusation had been brought against me (if it was to be brought) at a time when I could have pleaded the cause of philosophy with the vigour of a younger man. However, I will try to set before you, as well as I can, its nature — its power — its relation to other sciences — the benefits which it is able to confer — and the degree in which I profess to impart them. If the style of the defence is singular, pardon it to the difficulty of the subject.

Defence of the higher education. Analogy with gymnastic.

'What Gymnastic is for the body, Philosophy is for the mind. In the one as in the other, the pupil learns first the technical rudiments, and then how to combine them. The physical and the mental training will alike improve natural powers. But the master of the palæstra cannot make a great athlete, nor the teacher of Philosophy a great speaker. To make the latter, three things are needed — capacity, training, and practice. Capacity — which includes intellect, voice, and nerve — is the chief requisite. Practice, however, can by itself make a good speaker. Training is by far the least important of the three. It may be complete, and yet may be rendered useless by the absence of a single quality — nerve.

Proof that Isocrates had discountenanced false claims, proven by his essay, *Against the Sophists.*

'Do not suppose that my claims are modest only when I address you, but larger when I speak to my pupils. In an essay published when I first began to teach, the excessive pretensions of some teachers are expressly blamed. — This passage will explain my view.[1] . . . You see, then, that at the outset as at the close of my career, in safety as in danger, I have held this language.

'This, I well know, will not satisfy those against whose prejudices I am contending. Much more must be said before they can be converted or refuted. Their prejudice

[1] Here is read an extract from the essay, *Against the Sophists.*

utters itself in one of two assertions:—that the system of the sophists is futile; or that it is effectual, but immoral.

'Those who say that it is futile try it by a standard which they apply to none of those arts in which they believe. They demand that all its disciples shall become finished speakers in a year. The success of the sophists is, in fact, equal to that of any other class of teachers. Some of their pupils become powerful debaters; others become competent teachers; all become more accomplished members of society, better critics, more prudent advisers. And what proves the training to be scientific, is that all bear the stamp of a common method. These who despise such culture assume that practice, which develops every other faculty, is useless to the intellect; that the human mind can educate the instincts of horses and dogs, but cannot train itself; that tame lions and learned bears are possible, but not instructed men.

The sophistic education is effectual,

'Others maintain that Philosophy has an immoral tendency, and hold it responsible for the faults of a few who pervert it. I am not going to defend all who *say* that they are sophists, but only those who say so truly. And first—What are the objects which tempt men to be dishonest? I answer that the object is always one of three things—pleasure, profit, or honour. Could it be pleasant, profitable, or honourable for a sophist that his pupils should be known as rascals? It may perhaps be replied that men do not always calculate; that a margin must be left for intemperate impulse. But, even if a sophist indulged such impulses in himself, it could be no more for his pleasure than for his interest to encourage them in his pupil. Are the strangers who come from Sicily, from the Euxine and other quarters to the rhetorical schools of Athens brought hither by the desire to become knaves? Or, if that were their wish, could they not find teachers at home? But the whole tenor of their life among us proves them honest men. Again, if power in discourse is in itself a corrupting thing, all those who have possessed it, and not some only, ought to have been tainted by it. Yet the best statesmen of our generation and of the last were those who had most studied oratory. To go back to old times, Solon, Kleisthenes, Themistocles, Perikles, were all distinguished orators:

and not immoral.

The best statesmen have had some kind of training.

Solon was even called one of the Seven Sophists. Perikles studied under Anaxagoras[1] of Klazomenæ, and under Damon,[2] who was the ablest Athenian of his time.

The real corrupters are the sycophants.

'But I can point out the places in which may be found those who are really liable to the charges falsely brought against the sophists. Read the tablets, giving notice of lawsuits, which are published by the Thesmothetæ,[3] by the Eleven, and by the Forty.[4] Among the names of wrongdoers and of false accusers which figure there will be found those of Lysimachos and his friends,—not mine, nor that of any member of our profession. Were we really corrupters of youth, our accusers would have been the fathers and relatives of those whom we corrupted,—not such men as Lysimachos, whose interest it is that Athens should be demoralised. Just now I spoke of the hostility which some educated men feel towards our art. That hostility, I venture to hope, will have been disarmed by these plain statements. But there is, I think, a jealousy which is even more widely spread. It is because all ambitious men wish to be able speakers, but are too indolent to work for that end, that they dislike those who are ready to go through the necessary toil. It is strange that, while Athenians reproach the Thebans and others with neglecting culture, they should revile their fellow-citizens for seeking it; that the goddess of Persuasion should be honoured with yearly sacrifice, while those who wish to share her power should be regarded as desiring something evil; that bodily training should be esteemed, while mental training—to which Athens owes her place in Hellas—is slighted.

Prejudice against the Sophists is due to jealousy.

Speech is man's noblest gift.

'If a man used his inherited wealth, his skill as a hoplite[5] or as an athlete, in doing harm to his fellow-citizens, he

[1] A Greek philosopher of Klazomenæ in Asia Minor. He first introduced philosophy into Athens in the fifth century B.C.

[2] A celebrated musician and music teacher. Plato commends him as a desirable companion for young men.

[3] The six junior archons at Athens, who administered justice in all cases not specifically under the jurisdiction of the three senior archons, or some other authority.

[4] Judges who went on circuit through the Attic demes trying minor cases.

[5] A heavy-armed soldier.

would be punished, though the founders of his fortune, the teachers of his skill, might be praised. The gods have given us speech—the power which has civilised human life; and shall we not strive to make the best use of it?

**Opposition between the rhetorical and the philosophical education.**

'Lysimachos and such as he are not the only enemies of Rhetoric. It is attacked also by the professors of Eristic.[1] Instead of retorting their reproaches, I wish simply to aid you in estimating their studies relatively to ours. Eristic discussion, like Astrology or Geometry, seems to me not to deserve the name of Philosophy, since it has no practical bearing; but, rather, to be a good preparation for Philosophy. Schoolboys are trained to work and to think accurately by grammar and literary study; Philosophy forms a more manly discipline of the same sort for young men. But no one should allow his mind to be dried up by barren subtleties, or to drift into such speculations as those with which the Ionic physicists juggled.

**The true nature of philosophical education.**

'Having said what Philosophy is not, I must try to explain what (as I think) it is. My view is very simple. A wise man is one who can make a good guess (knowledge being impossible) as to what he ought to say and do. A philosopher, a lover of wisdom, is one who spends his time in the pursuits by which he may best gain such perception. And what are these pursuits? My answer will probably shock you; but I should be ashamed to betray the truth for the sake of peace in the fraction of life remaining to me. Well, then, I hold that there is no communicable science of Virtue or Justice; but that a man ambitious of speaking well, of persuading others, and (in the true sense) of *gain*, will incidentally become more virtuous and more just. Desirous of speaking with applause, he will occupy himself with the noblest themes, and dwell upon the worthiest topics of these. Desirous of persuading, he will strive to be just, since nothing is so persuasive as a character which is felt to be upright. Desirous of real gain, he will seek the approval of the gods and the esteem of his fellow-citizens. It is only by a perversion of language that the "desire of gain" has been associated with knavery; as "wittiness" with buffoonery, and "philosophy" with the mystifications

**Virtue cannot be taught; but the philosopher will be virtuous.**

[1] Controversial philosophical discussion of the character of the Socratic and Platonic schools.

of the elder sophists. This conception of philosophy as something unpractical — this tendency to discourage all systematic training for affairs — has its result in the lives of our youth. Their occupations are to cool wine in the Enneakrunos, — to drink in taverns, — to gamble, — to haunt the music-schools. The informers do not molest those who foster *these* pursuits. They attack us, who discourage them; and say that youths who spend on their education a tithe of what others spend on vice, are being corrupted.

The sophistic or rhetorical education is the glory of Athens.

'Power of speaking, when simply natural, is admired; it is strange, then, that blame should be cast upon the attempt to cultivate it. When acquired by labour, the faculty is more likely to be used discreetly than when it is an accident of genius. Athenians, of all men, ought not to despise culture. It is cultivated intelligence which distinguishes men from beasts, Hellenes from barbarians, Athenians from Hellenes. Athens is regarded as the teacher of all who can speak or teach others to speak; the greatest prizes, the best schools, the most constant practice are supplied by her. For her to disown the study of eloquence would be as if Sparta laid disabilities on military education or the Thessalians on skill in horsemanship. In athletic prowess, Athens has many rivals; in culture, none. Her intellectual culture is what most commands the admiration of foreigners; as the prevalence of informers is the one blot to which they can point. You ought to punish those who bring disgrace upon you, and honour those who do you credit. Miltiades, Themistokles, Perikles, became great by the pursuits which these informers vilify. Remembering this, strive to keep the law-courts pure for the citizens generally; and honour the ablest and most cultivated among them as the truest guardians of the democracy.

Contrast between ancient respect for education and the modern.

'The length of my defence has already passed due limits; but there are still a few words that I would say to you. It is bitter to me to see the informer's trade prospering better than the cause of education. Would our ancestors have looked for this? Solon, eldest of the Sophists, was put by them at the head of the State; against informers they appointed not one mode of procedure only but many,

—indictment before the Thesmothetæ, impeachment before the Senate, plaint to the Assembly. And informers are worse now than they were then. Their audacity has grown with the licence of those demagogues to whom our fathers entrusted the protection of the Athenian empire; who, by reproaching our most distinguished citizens as oligarchs and partisans of Sparta, made them such,—who harassed, and so estranged, our allies,—who brought Athens to the verge of slavery. Time is failing me; I must cease. Others conclude by committing their cause to the mercy of their judges, and the entreaties of their friends; *I* appeal to my past life. The gods, who have protected it hitherto, will protect it now. Your verdict, whatever it may be, will be for my good. Let each of you give what sentence he will.'

**Power of the demagogue.**

## *Selections from the Republic of Plato relating to the Sophists*

### BOOK VI

(491–497.)

**Education wrongly directed, a greater evil than ignorance.**

And may we not say, Adeimantus, that the most gifted minds, when they are ill-educated, become the worst? Do not great crimes and the spirit of pure evil spring out of a fulness of nature ruined by education rather than from any inferiority, whereas weak natures are scarcely capable of any very great good or very great evil?

There I think that you are right.

And our philosopher follows the same analogy—he is like a plant which, having proper nurture, grows and matures into all virtue, but, if sown and planted in an alien soil, becomes the most noxious of all weeds, unless saved by some divine help. Do you really think, as people are fond of saying, that our youth are corrupted by Sophists, or that private teachers of the art corrupt them in any degree worth speaking of? Are not the public who say these things the greatest of all Sophists? And do they not educate to perfection alike young and old, men and women, and fashion them after their own hearts?

When is this accomplished? he said.

When they meet together, and the world sits down at an

assembly, or in a court of law, or a theatre, or a camp, or at some other place of resort, and there is a great uproar, and they praise some things which are being said or done, and blame other things, equally exaggerating in both, shouting and clapping their hands, and the echo of the rocks and the place in which they are assembled redoubles the sound of the praise or blame — at such a time will not a young man's heart leap within him? Will the influences of education stem the tide of praise or blame, and not rather be carried away in the stream? And will he not have the notions of good and evil which the public in general have — he will do as they do, and as they are, such will he be?

Yes, Socrates; necessity will compel him.

And yet, I said, there is a still greater necessity, which has not been mentioned.

What is that?

The gentle force of attainder or confiscation or death, which, as you are aware, these new Sophists and educators, who are the public, apply when their words are powerless.

Indeed they do: of that there can be no doubt.

Now what opinion of any other Sophist, or of any private man, can be expected to overcome in such an unequal contest?

None, he replied.

No, indeed, I said, even to make the attempt is a piece of folly; for there neither is, has been, nor ever can be, as I think, a better type of character, trained to virtue in despite of them — I speak, my friend, of man only; what is more than man, as the proverb says, is not included: for I would not have you ignorant that, in the present evil state of governments, whatever is saved and comes to good is saved by the power of God, as you may truly say.

I quite assent, he replied.

Then let me crave your assent also to a further observation.

The Sophists are but exponents of the popular corruption.

What are you going to say?

Why, that all those mercenary individuals, whom the world calls Sophists and esteems rivals, do but teach the collective opinion of the many, which are the opinions of their assemblies; and this is their wisdom. I might compare them to a man who should study the tempers and desires of a mighty strong beast who is fed by him — he would learn how to approach and handle him, also at what times and from what causes he is dangerous or the reverse, and what is the meaning of his several cries, and by what sounds, when another utters them, he is soothed or infuriated; and you may suppose further, that when, by constantly living with him, he has become perfect in all this he calls his knowledge wisdom, and makes a system or art, which he proceeds to teach, not that he has any real notion of what he is teaching, but he names this honourable and that dishonourable, or good or evil, or just or unjust, all in accordance with the tastes and tempers of the great brute, when he has learnt the meaning of his inarticulate grunts. Good he pronounces to be what pleases him and evil what he dislikes; and he can give no other account of them except that the just and noble are the necessary, having never himself seen, and having no power of explaining to others the nature of either, or the immense difference between them. Would not he be a rare educator?

Indeed he would.

And in what respects does he who thinks that wisdom is the discernment of the tastes and pleasures of the assembled multitude, whether in painting or music, or, finally, in politics, differ from such an one? For I suppose you will agree that he who associates with the many, and exhibits to them his poem or other work of art or the service which he has done the State, making them his judges, except under protest, will also experience the fatal necessity of producing whatever they praise. And yet the reasons are utterly ludicrous which they give in confirmation of their notions about the honourable and good. Did you ever hear any of them which were not?

No, nor am I likely to hear.

**Popular opinion opposed to philosophical knowledge.**

You recognise the truth of what has been said? Then let me ask you to consider further whether the world will ever be induced to believe in the existence of absolute beauty rather than of the many beautiful, or of the absolute in each kind rather than of the many in each kind?

Certainly not.

Then the world cannot possibly be a philosopher?

Impossible.

And therefore philosophers must inevitably fall under the censure of the world?

They must.

And of individuals who consort with the mob and seek to please them?

That is evident.

Then, do you see any way in which the philosopher can be preserved in his calling to the end? and remember what we were saying of him, that he was to have knowledge and memory and courage and magnanimity — these were admitted by us to be the true philosopher's gifts.

Yes.

Now, will not such an one be, from the first, in all things first among all, especially if his bodily endowments are like his mental ones?

Certainly, he said.

And his friends and fellow-citizens will want to use him as he gets older for their own purposes?

No question.

Falling at his feet, they will make requests to him and do him honour and flatter him, because they want to get into their hands now, the power which he will one day possess.

That often happens, he said.

And what will he do under such circumstances, especially if he be a citizen of a great city, rich and noble, and a tall proper youth? Will he not be full of boundless aspirations, and fancy himself able to manage the affairs of Hellenes and of barbarians, and therefore will he not dilate and elevate himself in the fulness of vain pomp and senseless pride?

To be sure he will.

Why philosophy is unpopular.

Now, when he is in this state of mind, if some one gently comes to him and tells him that he is without sense, which he must have, but can only get it by slaving for it, do you think that, under such adverse circumstances, he will be easily induced to listen?

He would be very unlikely to listen.

But suppose further that there is one person who has feeling, and who, either from some excellence of disposition or natural affinity, is inclined or drawn towards philosophy, and his friends think that they are likely to lose the advantages which they were going to reap from his friendship, what will be the effect upon them? Will they not do and say anything to prevent his learning and to make his teacher powerless, using to this end private intrigues as well as public prosecutions?

There can be no doubt of it.

And how can one who is thus circumstanced ever become a philosopher?

Impossible.

Then were we not right in saying that even the very qualities which make a man a philosopher may, if he be ill-educated, serve to divert him from philosophy, no less than riches and their accompaniments and the other so-called goods of life?

We were quite right.

Thus, my excellent friend, is brought about the ruin and failure of the natures best adapted to the best of all pursuits, who, as we assert, are rare at any time; and this is the class out of whom come those who are the authors of the greatest evil to States and individuals; and also of the greatest good when the tide carries them in the direction of good; but a small man never was the doer of any great thing either to individuals or States.

The Sophist is the corrupted philosopher.

That is most true, he said.

They fall away, and philosophy is left desolate, with her marriage rite incomplete: for her own have forsaken her, and while they are leading a false and unbecoming life, other unworthy persons, seeing that she has no protector, enter in and dishonour her; and fasten upon her the reproaches which her reprovers utter, who say of her votaries that some of them are good for nothing, and the greater number deserving of everything that is bad.

That is certainly said.

Yes; and what else would you expect, I said, when you think of the puny creatures who, seeing this land open to them—a land well stocked with fair names and showy titles—like prisoners who run away out of prison into a sanctuary, take a leap out of the arts into philosophy; those who do so being probably the cleverest hands at their own miserable crafts? For, although philosophy be in this evil case, still there remains a dignity about her which is not found in the other arts. And many are thus attracted by her whose natures are imperfect and whose souls are marred and disfigured by their meannesses, as their bodies are by their arts and crafts. Is not that true?

Yes.

**The ranks of the Sophists are recruited from those unworthy of an education.**

Are they not exactly like a bald little tinker who has just got out of durance and come into a fortune; he washes the dirt off him and has a new coat, and is decked out as a bridegroom going to marry his master's daughter, who is left poor and desolate?

The figure is exact.

And what will be the issue of such marriages? Will they not be vile and bastard?

There can be no question of it.

And when persons who are unworthy of education approach philosophy and make an alliance with her who is in a rank above them, what sort of ideas and opinions are likely to be generated? Will they not be sophisms captivating to the ear, yet having nothing in them genuine, or worthy of or akin to true wisdom?

No doubt, he said.

**The character of the true philosopher.**

Then there is a very small remnant, Adeimantus, I said, of worthy disciples of philosophy: perchance some noble nature, brought up under good influences, and detained by exile in her service, who in the absence of temptation remains devoted to her; or some lofty soul born in a mean city, the politics of which he contemns or neglects; and perhaps there may be a few who, having a gift for philosophy, leave other arts, which they justly despise, and come to her; — and peradventure there are some who are restrained by our friend Theages' bridle (for Theages, you know, has had everything to draw him away; but his ill-health keeps him from politics). My own case of the internal sign is indeed hardly worth mentioning, as very rarely, if ever, has such a monitor been vouchsafed to any one else. Those who belong to this small class have tasted how sweet and blessed a possession philosophy is, and have also seen and been satisfied of the madness of the multitude, and known that there is no one who ever acts honestly in the administration of States, nor any helper who defends the cause of the just, by whose aid he may be saved. Such a defender may be compared to a man who has fallen among wild beasts — he would not join in the wickedness of his fellows, but neither would he be able alone to resist all their fierce natures, and therefore he would be of no use to the State or to his friends, and would have to throw away his life before he had done any good to himself or others. When he reflects upon all this, he holds his peace, and does his own business. He is like one who retires under the shelter of a wall in the storm of dust and sleet which the driving wind hurries along; and when he sees the rest of mankind full of wickedness, he is content if only he can live his own life and be pure from evil or unrighteousness, and depart in peace and good-will, with bright hopes.

Yes, he said, and he will have done a great work before he departs.

A great work — yes; but not the greatest, unless he find a State suitable to him; for in a State which is suitable to him, he will have a larger growth and be the saviour of his country, as well as of himself.

Enough, then, of the causes why philosophy is in such an evil name; how unjustly, has been explained; and now is there anything more which you wish to say?

## IV. GREEK EDUCATIONAL THEORISTS: THE HISTORICAL VIEW

**The Period and the Sources in General.** — This phase of Greek education does not constitute a distinct period in time, but falls in that of the New Greek Education. In fact, these writings form but one portion of the literature of the Attic period, which is one of the essential features or results of the new education. At the same time the writings of the theorists present an aspect of Greek education wholly different from those treated as the old and the new education. The literature on this topic is more voluminous than that on any of the others so far treated, and includes the writings of Plato and Aristotle as well as the selection from Xenophon first given. Incidentally these selections, especially those from Aristotle, give much information concerning the actual practices of Greek schools.

**The Problem of the Theorists.** — The writers of this group, while for the most part contemporary with the Sophists, differ from them in two important respects. The Sophists were practical teachers and were interested in the educational movement of the times chiefly in a personal way. They claimed to be able to prepare for a successful career, and were primarily concerned in achieving such a success for themselves. They taught for money and for reputation, as do most teachers at the present. Some of them, as Socrates, had a profound public interest as well, but the earlier Sophists were not native Athenians, and had little patriotic or national interest. On the other hand, the theorists were profoundly interested in education on account of its national importance, and so far as practical teachers, they were wholly disinterested and refused to accept any remuneration for their efforts. The second distinction is a more important one. The teachings of the Sophists were wholly critical and destructive in character. Their influence accorded with the current tendency to reject the old interpretations of legend and religious myth, and to produce a religious scepticism. At the same time, the claims of the state upon the individual were being questioned, and an indifference or a self-centred individualism replaced the old patriotic ardor. In fact, the old religious and political morality was being replaced by an individualism that made the individual man "the measure of all things." On the other hand, while the theorists recognized the validity of the criticisms upon the old order, they were unwilling to accept the wholly negative and disintegrating view. Their attempt was to supply new moral, religious, and political motives and ideals that would replace the old, now no longer effective. The Sophists believed that the interest of the individual was a sufficient motive and an adequate ideal. The theorists sought to find this in higher forms of life than had hitherto been realized, and strove to develop a higher morality and a broader patriotism than had hitherto existed, for the most part, by some reform in education. Some of these new educational schemes suggested, such as the *Republic*, are wholly idealistic; others, such as the *Cyropædia* and the *Laws*, are but modifications or purifications of the old régime.

**Socrates** was the source of, and furnished the inspiration for, this entire movement in educational thought. Though he has left no writings, the character and the substance of his teachings can be quite accurately reproduced from the writings of his pupils, Xenophon and Plato. Socrates lived from 469 to 399 B.C. The earlier portion of his life was spent as a sculptor, but the middle and later portion, though from what exact date is not known, as a teacher. Yet he never opened a school or delivered public lectures, in these respects differing from the Sophists and from the philosophers who continued his line of thought and work. His method was to engage in conversation any interested person, either old or young, in the market-place, the shop, or the gymnasium. In the latter places he found abundant opportunity, and there his teachings were especially influential upon those just entering that period of their education, hitherto devoted wholly to physical training and the service of the state. With these, his influence was wholly at variance with the old training, and was at one with that of the Sophists in inclining the youth to neglect the old training and to devote their time to intellectual development. His custom of teaching wholly through conversation was of importance educationally in that it introduced an entirely new method of study and teaching. As opposed to the old methods of the early philosophers and of the popular Sophists, this method was essentially inductive; though with Socrates it was applied to a limited field only, that of the phenomena of human conduct, as opposed to the old interest in physical investigation or speculation. It is through this new method that Socrates came to be the founder of ethics and of philosophy as it relates to the theory of knowledge. At the same time the new method was responsible for the sharp distinction between the practical life which was essentially unworthy and to be escaped from, and the ideal life devoted to subjective good, to be attained by withdrawing from, or rising above, the ordinary cares and interests in life. Hence, so far as the effects upon the political and religious obligation of Greek society as then organized were concerned, the influence of Socrates was identical with the individualistic teachings of the Sophists. Yet the whole purpose and spirit of the teaching of Socrates was to oppose this individualism.

He agreed with them in rejecting the external authority of the state or of the old religion in shaping the purpose of education or of life itself; on the other hand, he rejected their conclusion that the individual man furnished the sole standard. To Socrates this standard was furnished by the universal in man, — by that which he possessed in common with all others. This common possession was "knowledge," as opposed to the opinion of the individual, which the Sophists had exalted as the sole criterion of conduct. Socrates sought to develop this knowledge by his method of conversation. The subject-matter of his conversation and of his teaching, then, was knowledge, but knowledge in the limited sense already indicated. The ancients expressed this influence of Socrates in the saying that he brought down philosophy from heaven to earth. Hitherto the advanced intellectual life of the Greeks was concerned with astronomy and physics; hereafter it was concerned with man's moral and intellectual nature. Concerning such investigation, Socrates asks: "Do these inquirers think that they already know human affairs well enough, that they thus begin to meddle with the divine? Do they think that they shall be able to excite or calm the winds and the rain at pleasure, or have they no other view than to gratify an idle curiosity? Surely, they must see that such matters are beyond human investigation. Only let them recollect how much the greatest men, who attempted the investigation, differ in their pretended results, holding opinions extreme and opposite to each other, like those of madmen."[1] On the other hand, "Socrates," says Xenophon, "continued discussing human affairs; investigating, What is piety? What is impiety? What is the honorable and the base? What is the just and the unjust? What is temperance or the unsound mind? What is courage or cowardice? What is a city? What is the character fit for a citizen? What is authority over men? What is the character befitting the exercise of such authority? and other similar questions. Men who knew these matters he accounted good and honorable; men who were ignorant of them he assimilated to slaves." While Socrates gave a new purpose to education, that of discovering what knowledge was, thus furnishing a new ideal to life and a new basis for society; while he suggested a new content to education, the study of man's moral and intellectual natures; while he gave a new method, the dialectic or conversational inductive, — he did not suggest any means for making his teachings effective either through establishing a school for disseminating his ideas, or by outlining a scheme of education. His followers did both of these things.

**Xenophon** was a pupil of Socrates and gave the practical aspect of his master's character and teachings, just as Plato gave the more intellectual aspect of his character and the speculative tendency of his teaching. Selections

[1] Xenophon, *Memorabilia*, I. i. 12, etc. *Grote's* translation.

from the Socratic writings of Xenophon have already been given. Xenophon's solution of the educational problem set by the changes occurring in Grecian society in the fifth and fourth centuries, is the simplest of all solutions offered. It is found in the opening chapters of the *Cyropædia*, one of his latest works. In fact, it was not written till near the middle of the fourth century. The *Cyropædia* is a political romance, and is even less reliable, in its historical data, than Xenophon's other historical works. It purports to be a biography of the Persian monarch, Cyrus, and a description of the great Oriental monarch. It is, in reality, an exposition of Xenophon's ideal of government drawn from his own theories, and his intimate knowledge of Spartan institutions, with Oriental coloring supplied from his earlier experience. It has little value as a source of information concerning Persian education, notwithstanding its use for this purpose. Nor is it of more worth as a source concerning the actual practices of Grecian education, though many of its features are wholly Spartan. Xenophon was an Athenian by birth but a Spartan in sympathies, and was wholly opposed to the democratic tendency in the Athenian government and society. His military career was either in the service of the Spartan state or with Grecian mercenaries, chiefly Spartan. His children were educated at Sparta, and his fondness for Spartan customs is evident in his writings. Even his long exile from Athens was spent, though not at Sparta, at least in neighboring Dorian territory.

Xenophon's solution of the educational problem was a return to the old education, in which the means and the system should be largely Spartan, with the ideals those of the old Athenian period. In his scheme education is largely social, that is, military and moral in its purposes. The intellectual element is wholly eliminated, as at Sparta. In respect to its application to various classes in society and to women, it resembles Athenian rather than Spartan custom. The classification into periods is Spartan, as are also the means used, such as military drill, hunting, conversation with elders, the passing of judgment upon the conduct of companions, and the severe physical and dietetic discipline. In depending upon the general organization of society as an educational institution rather than upon the special institution of schools of a private character, the scheme is Spartan. The selective character of each stage in the educational system resembles Athenian customs in that it restricted the higher stages of training, and hence the most important political positions to the youths that came from the wealthiest families. In this respect it also resembles the ideal state of Plato, though, with the communism of the *Republic*, merit rather than wealth and birth formed the essential element in worth. In general Xenophon's plan was simply a restatement of the old conservative position, formulated in Persian rather than Spartan terms, probably in deference to the intense dislike at Athens for things Spartan as a result of the Peloponnesian conflict. The solutions offered by Plato and Aristotle are much more elaborate and original, and of much greater influence upon thought.

## *Selections from the Cyropædia of Xenophon*

### CHAPTER II

1. Cyrus is said to have had for his father Cambyses, king of the Persians. Cambyses was of the race of Perseidæ, who were so called from Perseus. It is agreed that

he was born of a mother named Mandane; and Mandane was the daughter of Astyages, king of the Medes. Cyrus is described, and is still celebrated by the Barbarians, as having been most handsome in person, most humane in disposition, most eager for knowledge, and most ambitious of honour; so that he would undergo any labour and face any danger for the sake of obtaining praise. 2. Such is the constitution of mind and body that he is recorded to have had; and he was educated in conformity with the laws of the Persians.

**Comparison of character of Persian laws with the laws of other countries.**

These laws seem to begin with a provident care for the common good; not where they begin in most other governments; for most governments, leaving each individual to educate his children as he pleases, and the advanced in age to live as they please, enjoin their people not to steal, not to plunder, not to enter a house by violence, not to strike any one whom it is wrong to strike, not to be adulterous, not to disobey the magistrates, and other such things in like manner; and, if people transgress any of these precepts, they impose punishments upon them. 3. But the Persian laws, by anticipation, are careful to provide from the beginning, that their citizens shall not be such as to be inclined to any action that is bad and mean. This care they take in the following manner.

**Their educational institution.**

They have an Agora,[1] called the Free, where the king's palace and other houses for magistrates are built; all things for sale, and the dealers in them, their cries and coarsenesses, are banished from hence to some other place; that the disorder of these may not interfere with the regularity of those who are under instruction. 4. This Agora, round the public courts, is divided into four parts; of these, one is for the boys, one for the youth, one for the full-grown men, and one for those who are beyond the years for military service.

**Training of the boys.**

Each of these divisions, according to the law, attend in their several quarters; the boys and full-grown men as soon as it is day; the elders when they think convenient, except upon appointed days, when they are obliged to be present. The youth pass the night round the courts, in their light arms, except such as are married; for these are not required to do so, unless orders

[1] An open square, free from buying and selling.

have been previously given them; nor is it becoming in them to be often absent. 5. Over each of the classes there are twelve presidents, for there are twelve distinct tribes of the Persians. Those over the boys are chosen from amongst the elders, and are such as are thought likely to make them the best boys; those over the youth are chosen from amongst the full-grown men, and are such as are thought likely to make them the best youth; and over the full-grown men, such as are thought likely to render them the most expert in performing their appointed duties, and in executing the orders given by the chief magistrate. There are likewise chosen presidents over the elders, who take care that these also perform their duties. What it is prescribed to each age to do, we shall relate, that it may be the better understood how the Persians take precautions that excellent citizens may be produced.

Justice, the aim and the substance of Persian education.

6. The boys attending the public schools, pass their time in learning justice; and say that they go for this purpose, as those with us say who go to learn to read. Their presidents spend the most part of the day in dispensing justice amongst them; for there are among the boys, as among the men, accusations for theft, robbery, violence, deceit, calumny, and other such things as naturally occur; and such as they convict of doing wrong, in any of these respects, they punish; 7. they punish likewise such as they find guilty of false accusation; they appeal to justice also in the case of a crime for which men hate one another excessively, but for which they never go to law, that is, ingratitude; and whomsoever they find able to return a benefit, and not returning it, they punish severely. For they think that the ungrateful are careless with regard to the gods, their parents, their country, and their friends; and upon ingratitude seems closely to follow shamelessness, which appears to be the principal conductor of mankind into all that is dishonourable.

Training in self-control, obedience, and temperance.

8. They also teach the boys self-control; and it contributes much towards their learning to control themselves, that they see every day their elders behaving themselves with discretion. They teach them also to obey their officers; and it contributes much to this end, that they

see their elders constantly obedient to their officers. They teach them temperance with respect to eating and drinking; and it contributes much to this object, that they see that their elders do not quit their stations to satisfy their appetites, until their officers dismiss them, and that the boys themselves do not eat with their mothers, but with their teachers, and when the officers give the signal. They bring from home with them bread, and a sort of cresses to eat with it; and a cup to drink from, that, if any are thirsty, they may take water from the river. They learn, besides, to shoot with the bow, and to throw the javelin. These exercises the boys practise until they are sixteen or seventeen years of age, when they enter the class of young men.

**Education of the young men.**

**Military.**

9. The young men pass their time thus: For ten years after they go from the class of boys, they pass the night round the courts, as I have said before, both for the security and guard of the city, and for the sake of practising self-restraint; for this age seems most to need superintendence. During the day they keep themselves at the command of their officers, in case they want them for any public service; and when it is necessary they all wait at the courts. But whenever the king goes out to hunt, he takes half the guard out with him, and leaves half of it behind; and this he does several times every month. Those that go out must have their bow, with a quiver, a bill or small sword in a sheath, a light shield, and two javelins, one to throw, and the other, if necessary, to use at hand. 10. They attend to hunting as a matter of public interest, and the king, as in war, is their leader, hunting himself, and seeing that others do so; because it seems to them to be the most efficient exercise for all such things as relate to war. It accustoms them to rise early in the morning, and to bear heat and cold; it exercises them in long marches, and in running; it necessitates them to use their bow against the beast that they hunt, and to throw their javelin, wherever he falls in their way, their courage must, of necessity, be often sharpened in the hunt, when any of the strong and vigorous beasts present themselves; for they must come to blows with the animal if he comes up to them, and must be upon their

**In hunting.**

guard as he approaches; so that it is not easy to find what single thing, of all that is practised in war, is not to be found in hunting. 11. They go out to hunt provided with a dinner, larger, indeed, as is but right, than that of the boys, but in other respects the same; and during the hunt perhaps they may not eat it; but if it be necessary to remain on the ground to watch for the beast, or if for any other reason they wish to spend more time in the hunt, they sup upon this dinner, and hunt again the next day till supper time, and reckon these two days as but one, because they eat the food of but one day. This abstinence they practise to accustom themselves to it, so that, should it be necessary in war, they may be able to observe it. Those of this age have what they catch for meat with their bread; or, if they catch nothing, their cresses. And, if any one think that they eat without pleasure when they have cresses only with their bread, and that they drink without pleasure when they drink only water, let him recollect how pleasant barley cake or bread is to eat to one who is hungry, and how pleasant water is to drink to one who is thirsty.

Practice reënforces early training.

12. The parties that remain at home pass their time in practising what they learned while they were boys, as well as other things, such as using the bow and throwing the javelin; and they pursue these exercises with mutual emulation, as there are public contests in their several accomplishments, and prizes offered; and in whichsoever of the tribes there are found the most who excel in skill, in courage, and in obedience, the citizens applaud and honour, not only the present commander of them, but also the person who had the instruction of them when they were boys. The magistrates likewise make use of the youth that remain at home, if they want them, to keep guard upon any occasion, to search for malefactors, to pursue robbers, or for any other business that requires strength and agility. In these occupations the youth are exercised.

Manhood in the service of the state.

But when they have completed their ten years, they enter into the class of full-grown men; 13. who, from the time they leave the class of youth, pass five and twenty years in the following manner. First, like the youth, they keep themselves at the command of the magistrates, that they may use their services, if it should be necessary, for the public good, in whatever employments require the exertions of such as have discretion, and are yet in vigour. If it be necessary to undertake any military expedition, they who are in this state of discipline do not march out with bows and javelins, but with what are called arms for close fight, a corslet over the breast, a shield in the left hand, such as that with which the Persians are painted, and, in the right, a large sword or bill. All the magistrates are chosen from this class, except the teachers of the boys; and, when they have completed five and twenty years in this class, they will then be something more than fifty years of age, and pass into the class of such as are elders, and are so called. 14. These elders no longer go on any military service abroad, but, remaining at home, have the dispensation of public and private justice; they take cognizance of matters of life and death, and have the choice of all magistrates; and, if any of the youth or full-grown men fail in anything enjoined by the laws, the several magistrates of the tribes, or any one that chooses, gives information of it, when the elders hear the cause, and pass sentence upon it; and the person that is condemned remains infamous for the rest of his life.

**in war, in rendering justice, and in training the boys.**

15. But that the whole Persian form of government may be shown more clearly, I shall go back a little; for, from what has been already said, it may now be set forth in a very few words. The Persians are said to be in number about a hundred and twenty thousand; of these no individual is excluded by law from honours and magistracies, but all are at liberty to send their boys to the public schools of justice. Those who are able to maintain their children without putting them to work, send them to these schools; they who are unable, do not send them. Those who are thus educated under the public teachers, are at liberty to pass their youth in the class of young men; they who are not so educated, have not that liberty. They who pass their term among the young men, discharging all things enjoined by the law, are allowed to be incorporated amongst the full-grown men, and to partake of all honours and magistracies; but they who do not complete

**Character of Persian institutions.**

**A class education.**

their course in the class of youth, do not pass into that of full-grown men. Those who make their progress through the order of full-grown men unexceptionably, are then enrolled among the elders; so that the order of elders stands composed of men who have pursued their course through all things good and excellent. Such is the form of government among the Persians, and such the care bestowed upon it, by the observance of which they think that they become the best citizens. 16. . . .

These particulars I had to state concerning the Persians in general. I will now relate the actions of Cyrus, upon whose account this narrative was undertaken, beginning from his boyhood.

## V. GREEK EDUCATIONAL THEORISTS: THE PHILOSOPHICAL VIEW

**The Period and the Authority.** — As has been already indicated, the period is that of the conflict between the old and the new educational ideas. Plato is the most important representative of the educational theorists, whether judged from the extent, the immediate influence, or the permanent suggestiveness, of his writings. Plato was born in 428 or 427 B.C., probably in Athens. Until the age of twenty his interest was centred in poetry and music. He then fell under the influence of Socrates. From that time until the death of Socrates, eight years later, Plato was one of his most devoted pupils. The thirteen years following the death of his master, Plato devoted to travel and to the study of philosophy, mathematics, and kindred subjects, chiefly in Italy, Sicily, and Egypt. In 386 Plato returned permanently to Athens and began his continuous formal teaching. Here, in a private home and garden adjoining the sacred garden and gymnasium of Academus, Plato established his school, the first of the permanent philosophical schools. For thirty-six years Plato taught a distinguished group of pupils, drawn not only from Athens, but also from many distant places as well. During this long period most of the dialogues were produced, though not one of them contains any definite internal evidence of its date. For thirty-three years after the death of Plato the school was under the direction of teachers that had been in close personal contact with the founder. During this period the Platonic writings were carefully preserved and copies made, so that it is believed that the complete works are extant. In the latest group of the dialogues fall the two that contain the educational discussions, — the *Republic* and the *Laws*.

**The *Republic*** is the great constructive work of Plato. Its professed subject is, What is Justice? But this subject is expanded to include a theory of psychology, a theory of knowledge, a theory of the soul, a theory of the state or of politics, a theory of human society, or of ethics, and a theory of education, with the last of which alone these selections have to do. Plato's solution of the problem raised by the conflict between the new education and the old, is the formation of a new state based upon the principle of justice, that principle in the state coinciding with happiness, or rather virtue, in the individual. To determine the nature of justice and the means of establishing it, is the chief purpose of the dialogue. The Platonic scheme of education is the result. Since justice is to be developed from the "knowledge" or "intelligence" of Socrates, the nature of justice and of the state can be most readily discovered by an analysis of the individual. The faculties of the individual are three: the intelligence, seated in the head; courage or spirit, a function of the heart; the appetites, lodged in the abdomen. Each has its proper function, which constitutes its worth. When properly performed, the functioning of the intelligence constitutes prudence; that of courage, fortitude; that of the appetites, temperance. The combination of these three produces individual well-being, or virtue.

By a similar analysis, the faculties of society are found

in the three great classes, the philosophic, the military, and the industrial. The virtues of these classes correspond to the virtues of the faculties of the individual. The proper function of the first class is to rule; of the second, is to protect; of the third, to support. The combination of these virtues in society produces justice.

Plato defines the principles that are yet recognized as the basis of society, the reciprocity of needs and services, and the education of each individual for the performance of some function in this interchange of services. If the Platonic restriction of these needs and services to special classes is a marked limitation, it is to be recalled that this discussion forms one of the earliest analyses in the history of ethics.

It will be recalled that the Socratic solution of the educational problem was that the new state of society was to be based on knowledge, that the germs of knowledge were inherent in every human being, by virtue of his own experience, and that these germs could be developed by the dialectic process. Plato departs from this solution in two important respects. He elaborates a definite theory of knowledge, more restricted than that of Socrates. As with Socrates, knowledge in the Platonic sense consists of whole thoughts; but whole thoughts are ideas, are universals as opposed to individuals. Such knowledge can be attained only by a few; while the germs of knowledge are present in the experience of every one, and can be developed by reflection and the dialectic process, knowledge itself can be attained only by those who have a higher, a sixth sense, the sense for ideas. Those who have this sense form the philosophic class, and they alone are free, — they alone should rule society. This is the second important divergence from the Socratic teaching. Knowledge is not an actual possession, or even a possible possession, of every human being. Hence every one cannot be free, cannot control his own conduct by the knowledge which he may attain. It is only a certain limited class, the philosophers, that can do so. The appropriate function of these philosophers, then, since they alone can see the truth, is not only to direct their own conduct, but that of all members of the other classes. The philosophers are to be the rulers of the new society, when "philosophers are kings, or the kings and the princes of this world have the spirit and power of philosophy." The production of this class of guardians, and the perpetuation of this ideal state, forms the aim of the scheme of education elaborated in the *Republic.*

The educational system of the *Republic* is designed especially for the guardian class; though all classes are to profit by the earlier stages of instruction, since one chief purpose of the system is to select the guardians. The *Republic* itself falls into two general divisions, each containing a discussion of a state and of a type of education. Both the state and the education of the first division, Books I. to V., inclusive, are very closely modelled after the actual Athenian conditions; in the second division, Books V. to X., the state becomes the ideal kingdom of the philosophers and the education there given is that suited to develop a philosophic class. The two schemes are really in opposition, though, as Plato suggests, the earlier sketch may be taken as an introduction to the later scheme. The education of the first four books is based upon the accepted Hellenic ideas of religion and morality, but in some respects is supplemented and purified. Plato holds that the

Greeks in their education had really "builded better than they knew." In this portion of the *Republic* he aims to base their practices on theory instead of upon experience, and to make explicit that which has hitherto been but non-rational custom. Education is comprehended in its two aspects, music and gymnastic; but the literary element of music is purified by the exclusion of the early poetry dealing with mythical subjects and is supplemented by a mathematical discipline, while gymnastic is now organized as a moral as well as physical discipline, and becomes largely military in character. The chief purpose of the discussion presented in the first selections is to clarify the principles underlying the old Greek educational practices, which had been developed empirically and not as a result of reflection. This scheme of education is designed for the first seventeen or eighteen years of life, and is for all youths, preparatory to the more rigid discipline for those who can profit by the highest theoretical education.

The education of the select guardian class is described in detail in Book VII. For those who have demonstrated themselves worthy of this higher discipline, the period from twenty to thirty is devoted to scientific study, chiefly of a mathematical character. This division between the elementary and the higher education forms the basis for the subsequent division of the curriculum into the trivium and the quadrivium of the "seven liberal arts." The purpose of this prolonged discipline is to perfect the future philosophers in the grasp of fundamental laws and principles underlying all life and thought. This study is not to be separated from practical duties of military and civic character. The effect of this combined training of practical and theoretical character is to eliminate a large number of those who have passed through the elementary training, and to indicate a yet more select class that can profit by the highest discipline of all, the philosophical. For the elect, the period from thirty to thirty-five is to be devoted wholly to philosophical pursuits and dialectic training. Only the ablest minds and the most stable characters can profit by this highest of intellectual efforts. From thirty-five to fifty these philosophers are to be the guardians of society, and are to devote themselves to the practical duties of public life. After the fiftieth year the practical life, now much less onerous in its character, is again merged in philosophical pursuits; that is, the philosopher who has meanwhile tested principle by experience is prepared to deepen his insight into fundamental truth, not only for his own sake, but for the benefit of society as well.

While Plato's ideal state was never realized, the idea education, separated from practical civic life, was approximated in the formation of the philosophical schools and the mystical religious societies and, in a later religious form, in the Christian church. Yet there remains the educational truth, essential for all times, that education is a life process, and that it should not be divorced at any time from actual life. In this latter respect the influence of Plato was quite at variance with his doctrine.

**The *Laws*** form a marked contrast with the *Republic* both in the theory of the state there advanced and in the scheme of education there advocated. So sharp is this contrast in some points that the authenticity of the *Laws* has been questioned. This scepticism is based upon inferiority of style as well as of ideas, but it finds no general support. This work is probably the last of Plato's compositions, being written during the last seven years of his life, when he was over seventy years of age. In many minor characteristics the *Laws* are in contrast with the other Platonic dialogues, these formal differences indicating a real change in the author's convictions. This dialogue is one of the few in which Socrates does not appear, and is the only one the scene of which is not located at Athens. This accords with the fact that the speculative element is almost wholly wanting, and that throughout it is dogmatic in a way wholly at variance with that of Socrates. The attitude of Socrates in the dialogues is that of an inquirer for knowledge, not that of a possessor: the Athenian in the *Laws*, who represents Plato's views, speaks with the utmost assurance on all topics, with the assumption that truth needs no longer to be sought for, but has been discovered. There is, indeed, a manifest intolerance, especially in religious matters, which is in such marked contrast with the usual Platonic attitude that it has formed an important feature in the argument against the Platonic authorship. In a similar way there is a marked contrast in the manner of treatment. The style is no longer conversational, but is more in the form of continuous discourse. In the latter half of the work the dialogue practically disappears. The selections from the *Republic* illustrate the dialectic method popularized, if not introduced, by Socrates; the *Laws* in its continuous, dogmatic, formal discourse exemplifies the method of the rhetorical schools.

The relation of the *Laws* to the *Republic* is indicated in paragraph 739 of the former. "The first and highest form of the state, and of the government and of the law is that in which there prevails most widely the ancient saying, that 'Friends have all things in common.' . . . Such a state, whether inhabited by Gods or by sons of

Gods, will make them blessed who dwell therein: and therefore to this we are to look for the pattern of the state, and to cling to this, and, so far as possible, to seek for one which is like this. The state which we now have in hand when created will be nearest to immortality and unity in the next degree." The *Republic* is an ideal impossible of attainment: the *Laws* forms the nearest possible approximation to the ideal. The events at Athens, and the failure of the attempt at Syracuse to realize the government by philosophers, led Plato to the radical modification of the scheme outlined in the *Republic*. Elsewhere Plato indicates the relation of the two types of government and of education. The most perfect state is that in which there are no rigid laws, but which is under the direction of the intelligent despot that possesses all wisdom, or of a class of such philosophers. In case such an ideal is unrealizable, the next best government is one in which a rigid scheme of laws framed by philosophers is enforced by officials who have no power to modify the laws. Such a government Plato formulates in the *Laws*. The first four books are merely introductory; the fifth gives the outline of the constitution; the last six are devoted to the laws in detail. The class of guardians now gives place to an hereditary prince, a commissioner of education, an elective senate, and a body of officials chosen by lot.

As it calls for no guardian class, for which the whole scheme of education must be shaped, the *Laws* offers a scheme of education radically different from that presented in the *Republic*. Not only are poets banished, as in the *Republic*, but there is now no place for philosophers, who, if not banished, are at least ignored. Hence, the phase of education in the earlier work devoted to philosophy is entirely eliminated. Education culminates in science and mathematics, but after the manner of the Pythagoreans, it is a mathematics closely allied to religion. Arithmetic and geometry, developing the idea of harmony, culminate in astronomy, which is closely allied with astrology. This astrological religion forms the basis of society. Plato praises the religious and ethical conditions in primitive society, quite after the manner of Aristophanes; but finding it impossible to advise a return to the gross polytheism of the early Greeks, he substitutes for it a mixture of Pythagorean philosophy and Oriental or Egyptian astrology. This education, no longer having any connection with his doctrine of ideas, is the same for all. The outline of education, with the omission of the higher stage, is quite similar to that of the *Republic*, though animated throughout by a different spirit. The literary element now becomes small. It is most strictly guarded by the state, on the assumption that social decay in Athenian society has been due to a corruption in music and in literature. In detail the entire scheme more nearly approximates the accepted Greek education. It is, however, a combination of selected Athenian and Spartan elements rather than a close imitation of either. The common meals, the education of both sexes, the public character of the education, its uniformity, the close superintendence of private life, are Spartan; the literary elements, the philosophy of the curriculum, the Bacchic choruses, its festive character, are Athenian. The strong emphasis on mathematics represents the Pythagorean influence that became so strong in Plato's later life. While in immediate importance and in permanent value the education of the *Laws* cannot compare with that of the *Republic*, its historic elements are of somewhat greater value.

## *Selections from the Republic of Plato*

PERSONS OF THE DIALOGUE

| | |
|---|---|
| SOCRATES, who is the narrator. | CEPHALUS. |
| GLAUCON. | THRASYMACHUS. |
| ADEIMANTUS. | CLEITOPHON. |
| POLEMARCHUS. | |

And others who are mute auditors.

The scene is laid in the house of CEPHALUS at the Piræus; and the whole discourse is narrated the day after it actually took place, to TIMÆUS, HERMOCRATES, CRITIAS, and a nameless person.

### BOOK II

* * * * * * *

Then he who is to be a really good and noble guardian of the State will require to unite in himself philosophy and spirit and swiftness and strength?

Undoubtedly.

Justice or the end of the state dependent upon education.

Then we have found the desired natures; and now that we have found them, how are they to be reared and educated? Is this an enquiry which may be fairly expected to throw light on the greater enquiry which is our final end — How do justice and injustice grow up in States? for we do not want to be tedious and irrelevant, or to leave out anything which is really to the point.

Adeimantus thought that the enquiry would be of great use to us.

Then, I said, my dear friend, the task must not be given up, even if somewhat long.

Certainly not.

Come then, and let us pass a leisure hour in story telling, and our story shall be the education of our heroes.

By all means.

Divisions of education.

And what shall be their education? Can we find a better than the old-fashioned sort? — and this has two divisions, gymnastic for the body, and music for the soul.

True.

Shall we begin education with music, and go on to gymnastic afterwards?

By all means.

And when you speak of music, do you rank literature under music or not?

**What use shall be made of literature?**

I do.

And literature may be either true or false?

Yes.

And the young are trained in both kinds, and in the false before the true?

I do not understand your meaning, he said.

You know, I said, that we begin by telling children stories which, though not wholly destitute of truth, are in the main fictitious; and these stories are told them when they are not of an age to learn gymnastics.

Very true.

That was my meaning in saying that we must teach music before gymnastics.

Quite right, he said.

You know also that the beginning is the chiefest part of any work, especially in a young and tender thing; for that is the time at which the character is being formed and most readily receives the desired impression.

Quite true.

And shall we just carelessly allow children to hear any casual tales which may be framed by casual persons, and to receive into their minds notions which are the very opposite of those which are to be held by them when they are grown up?

We cannot.

Then the first thing will be to have a censorship of the writers of fiction, and let the censors receive any tale of fiction which is good, and reject the bad; and we will desire mothers and nurses to tell their children the authorised ones only. Let them fashion the mind with these tales, even more fondly than they form the body with their hands; and most of those which are now in use must be discarded.

Of what tales are you speaking? he said.

You may find a model of the lesser in the greater, I said; for they are necessarily cast in the same mould, and there is the same spirit in both of them.

That may be very true, he replied; but I do not as yet know what you would term the greater.

Objections to the use of the Homeric poems and the early literature of the Greeks.

Those, I said, which are narrated by Homer and Hesiod, and the rest of the poets, who have ever been the great story-tellers of mankind.

But which stories do you mean, he said; and what fault do you find with them?

A fault which is most serious, I said; the fault of telling a lie, and, what is more, a bad lie.

But when is this fault committed?

Whenever an erroneous representation is made of the nature of gods and heroes,—like the drawing of a limner which has not the shadow of a likeness to the truth.

Yes, he said, that sort of thing is certainly very blameable; but what are the stories which you mean?

First of all, I said, there was that greatest of all lies in high places, which the poet told about Uranus, and which was a bad lie too,—I mean what Hesiod says that Uranus did, and what Cronus did to him. The doings of Cronus, and the sufferings which in turn his son inflicted upon him, even if they were true, ought certainly not to be lightly told to young and simple persons; if possible, they had better be buried in silence. But if there is an absolute necessity for their mention, a chosen few might hear them in a mystery, and in order to reduce the number of hearers they should sacrifice not a common (Eleusinian) pig, but some huge and unprocurable victim.

Why, yes, said he, those stories are certainly objectionable.

Their moral influence bad.

Yes, Adeimantus, they are stories not to be narrated in our State; the young man should not be told that in committing the worst of crimes he is far from doing anything outrageous; and that if he chastises his father when he does wrong, in any manner that he likes, he will only be following the example of the first and greatest among the gods.

I quite agree with you, he said; in my opinion those stories are not fit to be repeated.

Neither, if we mean our future guardians to regard the habit of quarrelling as dishonourable, should anything be said of the wars in heaven, and of the plots and fightings of the gods against one another, which are quite untrue. Far be it from us to tell them of the battles of the giants, and embroider them on garments; or of all the innumerable other quarrels of gods and heroes with their friends and relations. If they would only believe us we would tell them that quarrelling is unholy, and that never up to this time has there been any quarrel between citizens; this is what old men and old women should begin by telling children, and the same when they grow up. And the poets should be required to compose accordingly. But the narrative of Hephæstus binding Here his mother, or how on another occasion Zeus sent him flying for taking her part when she was being beaten,—such tales must not be admitted into our State, whether they are supposed to have an allegorical meaning or not. For the young man cannot judge what is allegorical and what is literal; anything that he receives into his mind at that age is apt to become indelible and unalterable; and therefore the tales which they first hear should be models of virtuous thoughts.

There you are right, he replied; that is quite essential: but, then, where are such models to be found? and what are the tales in which they are contained? when that question is asked, what will be our answer?

Criticism of the character of religious ideas imparted.

I said to him, You and I, Adeimantus, are not poets in what we are about just now, but founders of a State: now the founders of a State ought to know the general forms in which poets should cast their tales, and the limits which should be observed by them, but actually to make the tales is not their business.

Very true, he said; but what are these forms of theology which you mean?

Something of this kind, I replied:—God is always to be represented as he truly is; that is one form which is equally to be observed in every kind of verse, whether epic, lyric, or tragic.

Right.

And is he not truly good? and must he not be represented as such?

Certainly.

And no good thing is hurtful?

No, indeed.

And that which is not hurtful hurts not?

Certainly not.

And that which hurts not does no evil?

No.

And that which does no evil is the cause of no evil?

Impossible.

And the good is the advantageous?

Yes.

And the good is the cause of well-being?

Yes.

The good is not the cause of all things, but of the good only, and not the cause of evil?

Assuredly.

Then God, if he be good, is not the author of all things, as the many assert, but he is the cause of a few things only, and not of most things that occur to men. For few are the goods of human life, and many are the evils, and the good is to be attributed to God alone; of the evils the cause is to be sought elsewhere, and not in him.

That appears to me to be most true, he said.

Then we must not listen to Homer or to any other poet who is guilty of the folly of saying that two casks

> 'Lie at the threshold of Zeus, full of lots, one of good, the other of evil lots,'

and that he to whom Zeus gives a mixture of the two

> 'Sometimes meets with evil fortune, at other times with good;'

but that he to whom is given the cup of unmingled ill

> 'Him wild hunger drives over the divine earth.'

And again:—

> 'Zeus, who is the dispenser of good and evil to us.'

And if any one asserts that the violation of oaths and treaties of which Pandarus was the real author, was brought about by Athene and Zeus, or that the strife and conflict of the gods was instigated by Themis and Zeus, he shall not have our approval; neither will we allow our young men to hear the words of Æschylus, that

> 'God plants guilt among men when he desires utterly to destroy a house.'

And if a poet writes of the sufferings of Niobe, which is the subject of the tragedy in which these iambic verses occur, or of the house of Pelops, or of the Trojan war, or any similar theme, either we must not permit him to say that these are the works of God, or if they are of God, he must devise some explanation of them such as we are seeking: he must say that God did what was just and right, and they were the better for being punished; but that those who are punished are miserable, and that God is the author of their misery — the poet is not to be permitted to say; though he may say that the wicked are miserable because they require to be punished, and are benefited by receiving punishment from God; but that God being good is the author of evil to any one, is to be strenuously denied, and not allowed to be sung or said in any well-ordered commonwealth by old or young. Such a fiction is suicidal, ruinous, impious.

I agree with you, he replied, and am ready to give my assent to the law.

Let this then be one of the rules of recitation and invention, — that God is not the author of evil, but of good only.

That will do, he said.

And what do you think of another principle? Shall I ask you whether God is a magician, and of a nature to appear insidiously now in one shape, and now in another — sometimes himself changing and becoming different in form, sometimes deceiving us with the semblance of such transformations; or is he one and the same immutably fixed in his own proper image?

I cannot answer you without more thought.

Well, I said; but if we suppose a change in anything, that change must be effected either by the thing itself, or by some other thing?

That is most certain.

And things which are at their best are also least liable to be altered or discomposed; for example, when healthiest and strongest the human frame is least liable to be affected by meats, and drinks and labours, and the plant which is in the fullest vigour also suffers least from heat and wind, or other similar accidents.

Of course.

And this is true of the soul as well as of the body; the bravest and wisest soul will be least confused or deranged by any external influence.

True.

And further, as I should suppose, the same principle applies to all works of art — vessels, houses, garments; and that when well made and in good condition, they are least altered by time and circumstances.

Very true.

Then everything which is good, whether made by art or nature, or both, is liable to receive the least change at the hands of others?

True.

But surely God and the things of God are absolutely perfect?

Of course they are.

He is therefore least likely to take many forms.

He is.

But suppose again that he changes and transforms himself?

Clearly, he said, that must be the case if he is changed at all.

And will he then change himself for the better, or for the worse?

If he change at all he must change for the worse, for we cannot suppose that he is deficient in virtue or beauty.

Very true, Adeimantus; but then, would any one, whether God or man, desire to change for the worse?

Impossible.

Then God too cannot be willing to change; being, as is supposed, the fairest and best that is conceivable, every God remains absolutely and for ever in his own form.

That necessarily follows, he said, in my judgment.

Then, I said, my dear friend, let none of the poets tell us that

> 'The gods, taking the disguise of strangers, haunt cities in all sorts of forms;'

and let no one slander Proteus and Thetis, neither let any one, either in tragedy or any other kind of poetry, introduce Here disguised in the likeness of a priestess asking an alms

'For the life-giving daughters of the river Inachus;

let us have no more lies of that sort. Neither must we have mothers under the influence of the poets scaring their children with abominable tales of certain gods who, as they say:—

Condemnation of use of religious and legendary tales to frighten children.

'Go about by night in the likeness of strangers from every land;'

let them beware lest they blaspheme against the gods, and at the same time make cowards of their children.

Heaven forbid, he said.

But although the gods are themselves unchangeable, still by witchcraft and deception they may make us think that they appear in various forms?

Suppose that, he replied.

Well, but can you imagine that God will be willing to lie, or make a false representation of himself, whether in word or deed?

I cannot say, he replied.

Do you not know, I said, that the true lie, if I may use such an expression, is hated of gods and men?

What do you mean? he said.

I mean this, I said,—that no one will admit falsehood into that which is the truest and highest part of himself, or about the truest and highest matters; there he is most afraid of a lie having possession of him.

Still, he said, I do not comprehend you.

The reason is, I replied, that you attribute some grand meaning to me; but I am only saying that deception, or being deceived or uninformed about realities in the highest faculty, which is the soul, and in that part of them to have and to hold the lie, is what mankind least like;—that, I say, is what they utterly detest.

There is nothing more hateful to them.

And, as I was just now remarking, this ignorance in the soul of him who is deceived may be called the true lie; for the lie in words is only a kind of imitation and shadowy image of a previous affection of the soul, not pure unadulterated falsehood. Am I not right?

Perfectly right.

The true lie is hated not only by the gods, but also by men?

Yes.

Whereas the lie in words is in certain cases useful and not hateful; in dealing with enemies — that would be an instance; or again, as a cure or preventive of the madness of those who are called your friends; also in the tales of mythology, of which we were just now speaking — because we do not know the truth about ancient traditions, we make falsehood as much like truth as may be, and so of use.

Misrepresentations of the idea of God by the poets.

Very true, he said.

But can any of these reasons apply to God? Can we suppose that he is ignorant of antiquity, and therefore has recourse to invention?

That would be ridiculous, he said.

Then the lying poet has no place in our idea of God?

I should say not.

Peradventure again he may tell a lie because he is afraid of enemies?

That is inconceivable.

But he may have friends who are senseless or mad?

But no mad or senseless person can be a friend of God.

Then no motive can be imagined why God should lie?

None.

Then the superhuman and divine is absolutely incapable of falsehood?

Yes.

Then is God perfectly simple and true both in deed and word; he changes not; he deceives not, either by dream or waking vision, by sign or word.

Your words, he answered, are the very expression of my own feelings.

You agree with me, I said, that this is the second type or mould in which we are to cast our ideas about divine things. The Gods are not magicians who transform themselves, neither do they deceive mankind in word or deed.

I grant that.

Then, although we are lovers of Homer, we do not love the lying dream which Zeus sends to Agamemnon; neither will we praise the verses of Æschylus in which Thetis says that Apollo at her nuptials

> 'Was celebrating in song her fair progeny whose days were to be long, and to know no sickness. And in conclusion he raised a note of triumph over the blessedness of my lot, and cheered my soul. And I thought that the word of Phœbus, being divine and full of prophecy, would not fail. And now he himself who uttered the strain, he who was present at the banquet, and who said this — he is the very god who has slain my son.'

These are the kind of sentiments about the gods which will arouse our anger; and he who utters them shall be refused a chorus; neither shall we allow them to enter into education, meaning, as we do, that our guardians, as far as men can be, should be true worshippers of the gods and like them.

I entirely agree, he said, in the propriety of these principles, and promise to make them my laws.

## BOOK III

Such then, I said, are our principles of theology — some tales are to be told, and others are not to be told to our disciples from their youth upwards, if we mean them to honour the gods and their parents, and to value friendship with one another.

**Courage or cowardice are promoted through the tales of the poets.**

Yes; and I think that our principles are right, he said.

But if they are to be courageous, must they not learn, besides these, other lessons also, such as will have the effect of taking away the fear of death? Can any man be courageous who has the fear of death in him?

Certainly not, he said.

And can he be fearless of death, or will he choose death in battle rather than defeat and slavery, who believes in the reality and the terror of the world below?

Impossible.

Then we must assume a control over this class of tales as well as over the others, and beg the relaters of them not simply to revile, but rather to commend the world below, intimating to them that their descriptions are untrue, and will do no good to our future warriors.

That will be our duty, he said.

Then, I said, we shall have to obliterate obnoxious passages, beginning with the verse, —

> 'I would rather be a serf on the land of a poor portionless man who is not well to do, than rule over all the dead who have come to nought.'

We must also expunge the verse, which tells us how Pluto feared,

> 'Lest the mansions grim and squalid which the gods abhor should be seen both of mortals and immortals.'

And again : —

> 'O heavens ! verily in the house of Hades there is soul and ghostly form but no mind !'

Again of Tiresias : —

> 'To him alone did Persephone give mind, that he should be wise even after death ; but the other souls are flitting shades.'

Again : —

> 'The soul flying from the limbs had gone to Hades, lamenting her fate, leaving strength and youth.'

Again : —

> 'And the soul, with shrilling cry, passed like smoke beneath the earth.'

And : —

> 'As bats in hollow of mystic cavern, whenever any of them dropped out of the string falls from the rock, fly shrilling and hold to one another, so did they with shrilling cry hold together as they moved.'

And we must beg Homer and the other poets not to be angry if we strike out these and similar passages, not because they are unpoetical, or unattractive to the popular ear, but because the greater the charm of them as poetry, the less are they meet for the ears of boys and men who are to be sons of freedom, and are to fear slavery more than death.

Undoubtedly.

Also we shall have to reject all the terrible and appalling names which describe the world below — Cocytus and Styx, ghosts under the earth, and sapless shades, and any similar words of which the very mention causes a shudder to pass through the inmost soul of him who hears them. I do not say that these horrible stories may not have a use of some kind; but there is a danger that the nerves of our guardians may become affected by them.

We have reason to fear that, he said.

Then there must be no more of them.

True.

Another and a nobler strain will be ours.

Clearly.

**Objection to the examples of cowardice of famous men,**

And shall we proceed to get rid of the weepings and wailings of famous men?

They will go with the others.

But shall we be right in getting rid of them? Reflect: our principle is that the good man will not consider death terrible to a good man.

Yes; that is our principle.

And therefore he will not sorrow for his departed friend as though he had suffered anything terrible?

He will not.

Such an one, as we further maintain, is enough for himself and his own happiness, and therefore is least in need of other men.

True, he said.

And for this reason the loss of a son or brother, or the deprivation of fortune, is to him of all men least terrible.

Assuredly.

And therefore he will be least likely to lament, and will bear with the greatest equanimity any misfortune of this sort which may befall him.

Yes, he will feel such a misfortune far less than another.

Then we shall be right in getting rid of the lamentations of famous men, and making them over to women (and not even to women who are good for anything), or to men of a baser sort, that those who are being educated by us to be the defenders of their country may scorn to do the like.

That will be very right.

Then we will once more entreat Homer and the other poets not to depict Achilles, who is the son of a goddess, first lying on his side, then on his back, and then on his face; then starting up and sailing in a frenzy along the shores of the barren sea; now taking the dusky ashes in both his hands and pouring them over his head, or bewailing and sorrowing in the various modes which Homer has delineated. Nor should he describe Priam the kinsman of the gods as praying and beseeching:—

> 'Rolling in the dirt, calling each man loudly by his name.'

and of the gods.

Still more earnestly will we beg of him not to introduce the gods lamenting and saying:—

> 'Alas! my misery! Alas! that I bore the bravest to my sorrow.'

But if he must introduce the gods, at any rate let him not dare so completely to misrepresent the greatest of the gods, as to make him say—

> 'O heavens! with my eyes I behold a dear friend of mine driven round and round the city, and my heart is sorrowful.'

Or again:—

> 'Woe is me that I am fated to have Sarpedon, dearest of men to me, subdued at the hands of Patroclus the son of Menœtius.'

For if, my sweet Adeimantus, our youth seriously believe in such unworthy representations of the gods, instead of laughing at them as they ought, hardly will any of them deem that he himself, being but a man, can be dishonored by similar actions; neither will he rebuke any inclination which may arise in his mind to say and do the like. And instead of having any shame or self-control, he will be always whining and lamenting on slight occasions.

Yes, he said, that is very certain.

Yes, I replied; but that is just what ought not to be, as the argument proved to us; and we must abide by our conviction until we find a better.

True.

Poets often represent the gods as examples of levity and intemperance.

Neither ought our guardians to be given to laughter. For a fit of laughter which has been indulged to excess almost always produces a violent reaction.

So I believe.

Then persons of worth, even if only mortal, must not be

represented as overcome by laughter, and still less must such a representation of the gods be allowed.

Still less of the gods, as you say, he replied.

Then we shall not suffer such an expression to be used about the gods as that in which Homer describes how

> 'Inextinguishable laughter arose among the blessed gods, when they saw Hephæstus bustling about the mansion.'

On your views, we must not admit them.

On my views, if you like to father them on me; that we must not admit them is certain.

Again, truth should be highly valued; if, as we were saying, a lie is useless to the gods, and useful only as a medicine to men, then the use of such medicines should be restricted to physicians; private individuals have no business with them.

Clearly not, he said.

Then if any persons are to have the privilege of lying, either at home or abroad, they will be the rulers of the State; and they may be allowed to lie for the public good. But nobody else is to meddle with anything of the kind; and for a private man to lie in return to the rulers is to be deemed a more heinous fault than for the patient or the pupil of a gymnasium not to speak the truth about his own bodily illnesses to the physician or trainer, or for a sailor not to tell the captain truly how matters are going on in the ship.

Most true, he said.

If, then, the ruler catches anybody beside himself lying in the State,

> 'Any of the craftsmen, whether he be priest or physician or carpenter,'

he will punish him for introducing a practice which is equally subversive of ship or State.

Yes, he said, if our theory is carried into execution.

Next, will not our youth require temperance?

Certainly.

Under temperance, speaking generally, are included obedience to commanders and command of self in sensual pleasures.

True.

Then would you praise or blame the injunction of Diomede in Homer,

> 'Friend, sit still and obey my word,'

and the verses which follow,

> 'The Greeks marched breathing prowess,
> . . . in silent awe of their leaders,'

and other sentiments of the same kind?

They are good.

What again of this line,

> 'O heavy with wine, who hast the eyes of a dog and the heart of a stag,'

and of the verses which follow? Would say that in these, or any other impertinent words which private men are supposed to address to their rulers, whether in verse or prose, are well or ill spoken?

They are ill spoken.

They may very possibly afford some amusement, but they do not conduce to temperance. And therefore they are likely to do harm to our young men — you would agree with me in that?

Yes.

And then, again, to make the wisest of men say that nothing in his opinion is more glorious than

> 'When the tables are full of bread and meat, and the cup-bearer carries round wine which he draws from the bowl and pours into the cups;'

is this fit or improving for a young man to hear? Or that other verse which affirms that

> 'The saddest of fates is to die and meet destiny from hunger?'

What would you say again to the tale of Zeus, who, while other gods and men were asleep and he the only person awake, lay devising plans, but forgot them all in a moment through his lust, and was so completely overcome at the sight of Here that he would not even go into the hut, but wanted to lie with her on the ground, declaring that he had never been in such a state of rapture before, even when they first met one another without the knowledge of their parents; or that other tale of how Hephæstus, in consequence of a similar piece of work, bound Ares and Aphrodite?

Indeed, he said, I am strongly of opinion that they ought not to hear that sort of thing.

But any deeds of endurance which are done or told by famous men, these they ought to see and hear; as, for example, what is said in the verses,

> 'He beat his breast, and thus reproached his heart,
> Endure, my heart; far worse hast thou endured!'

Certainly, he said.

In the next place, we must not let them be receivers of gifts or lovers of money.

Certainly not.

Neither must we sing to them of

> 'Gifts persuading gods, and persuading reverend kings.'

Objection to the examples of impiety and insolence given by the poets.

Neither is Phœnix, the tutor of Achilles, to be approved or regarded as having given his pupil good counsel when he told him that he should take the gifts of the Greeks and assist them; but that without a gift he should not be reconciled to them. Neither will we believe or allow Achilles himself to have been such a lover of money that he took Agamemnon's gifts, or required a price as the ransom of the dead.

Undoubtedly, he said, these are not sentiments which ought to be approved.

Loving Homer as I do, I hardly like to say what I must say nevertheless, that in speaking thus of Achilles, or in believing these words when spoken of him by others, there is downright impiety. As little can I credit the narrative of his insolence to Apollo, where he says:—

> 'Thou hast wronged me, O far-darter, most abominable of deities.
> Verily I would be even with thee, if I had only the power;'

or his insubordination to the river-god, on whose divinity he is ready to lay hands; or the dedication to the dead Patroclus of his own hair, which had been previously dedicated to the other river-god Spercheius; or his dragging Hector round the tomb of Patroclus, and his slaughter of the captives at the pyre; of all this I cannot believe that he was guilty, any more than I can allow our citizens to believe that he, Cheiron's pupil, the son of a goddess and of Peleus who was the gentlest of men and third in descent from Zeus, was in such rare perturbation of mind as to be at one time the slave of two seemingly inconsistent passions, meanness, not untainted by avarice, combined with overwhelming contempt of gods and men.

You are quite right, he replied.

And let us equally refuse to believe, or allow to be repeated, the tale of Theseus son of Poseidon, or of Perithous son of Zeus, going forth to perpetrate such a horrid rape; or of any other hero or son of a god daring to do such impious and horrible things as they falsely ascribe to them in our day: and let us compel the poets to declare either that these acts were not done by them, or that they were not the sons of gods; — both in the same breath they shall not be permitted to affirm. We will not have them teaching our youth that the gods are the authors of evil, and that heroes are no better than men; undoubtedly these sentiments, as we were saying, are neither pious or true, for they are at variance with our demonstration that evil cannot come from God.

Undoubtedly.

And further they are likely to have a bad effect on those who hear them; for everybody will begin to excuse his own vices when he is convinced that similar wickednesses are always being perpetrated by the kindred of the gods,

> 'The relatives of Zeus, whose paternal altar is in the heavens and on the mount of Ida,'

and who have

> 'The blood of deities yet flowing in their veins.'

And therefore let us put an end to such tales, lest they engender laxity of morals among the young.

By all means, he replied.

* * * * * * *

I will beg you also to recall what I began by saying, that we had done with the subject and might proceed to the style.

Objection to the form of the art of the poets,

Yes, I remember.

In saying this, I meant to imply that we must come to an understanding about the mimetic art,—whether the poets, in narrating their stories, are to be allowed to imitate, and if so, whether in whole or in part, and if the latter, in what parts; or should all imitation be prohibited?

You mean, I suspect, to ask whether tragedy and comedy shall be admitted into our State?

Yes, I said; but there may be more than this in question: I really do not know as yet, but whither the argument may blow, thither we go.

And go we will, he said.

Then, Adeimantus, let me ask you whether our guardians ought to be imitators, or whether in fact this question has not been already answered by our previous recognition of the principle that one man can only do one thing well, and not many; and that if he attempt many, he will altogether fail of gaining much reputation in any?

Certainly.

And this is equally true of imitation; no one man can imitate many things as well as he would imitate a single one?

He cannot.

Then the same person will hardly be able to play the serious part of life, and at the same time be an imitator and imitate many other parts as well; for even when two species of imitation are nearly allied, the same persons cannot succeed in both, as is plain in the case of tragedy and comedy—did you not say that they are imitations?

on the ground that it is imitation.

Yes, I did; and you are right in thinking that the same persons cannot succeed in both.

Any more than they can be rhapsodists and actors at once.

True.

Neither are actors the same as comic and tragic poets; yet all these are imitations.

Yes, they are imitations.

And human nature, Adeimantus, appears to have been

coined into yet smaller pieces, and to be as incapable of imitating many things well, as of performing well the actions of which the imitations are copies.

Quite true, he replied.

Youths should be trained to imitate the true character, not every phase of character as does the poet.

If then we would retain the notion with which we began, that our guardians are to be released from every other art, and to be the special artificers of freedom, and to minister to this and have no other end, they ought not to practise or imitate anything else; and, if they imitate at all, they should imitate from youth upward the characters which are suitable to their profession — the temperate, holy, free, courageous, and the like; but they should not depict or be skilful at imitating any kind of illiberality or other baseness, lest from imitation they should come to be what they imitate. Did you never observe how imitations, beginning in early youth, at last sink into the constitution and become a second nature of body, voice, and mind?

Yes, certainly, he said.

Then, I said, we will not allow those for whom we profess a care and desire that they should be good men, to imitate a woman, whether young or old, quarrelling with her husband, or striving and vaunting against the gods in conceit of her happiness, or when she is in affliction, or sorrow, or weeping; and certainly not one who is in sickness, love, or labour.

Very right, he said.

Neither must they represent slaves, male or female, doing the offices of slaves?

They must not.

And surely not rogues or cowards, or any who do the reverse of what we have prescribed — jesting, scolding, reviling, in drink or out of drink; or otherwise sinning against themselves or others in word or deed, as the manner of such is. Neither should they be trained to imitate the action or speech of madmen; for madness, like vice, is to be known only to be avoided.

Very true, he replied.

Any more than they may imitate smiths or other artificers, or oarsmen, or boatswains, or the like?

Impossible, he said; how can they imitate that with which they will have no concern at all?

And would you have them imitate the neighing of horses, the bellowing of bulls, the murmur of rivers and roll of the ocean, thunder, and all that sort of thing?

Nay, he said, if madness is forbidden, then neither may they copy the behaviour of madmen.

You mean, I said, if I understand you rightly, that there is one sort of narration which may be used or spoken by a truly good man, and that there is another sort which will be exclusively adapted to a man of another character and education.

And which are these two sorts? he asked.

Suppose, I answered, that a just and good man in the course of narration comes on some saying or action of another good man, — I should imagine that he will like to personate him, and will not be ashamed of this sort of imitation: he will be most ready to play the part of the good man when he is acting firmly and wisely; in a less degree when his steps falter owing to sickness or love, or from intoxication or any other mishap. But when he comes to a character which is unworthy of him, he will not make a study of that; he will disdain his inferiors, and will wear their likeness, if at all, for a moment only when they are doing some good; at other times he will be ashamed to play a part which he has never practised, nor will he like to fashion and frame himself after the baser models; he feels that the serious use of such an art would be beneath him, and his mind revolts at it.

That is what I should expect, he replied.

Then he will adopt a mode of narration such as we have illustrated out of Homer, that is to say, his style will be both imitative and narrative; but there will be very little of the former, and a great deal of the latter. Do you agree?

Certainly, he said; that is the model which such a speaker must necessarily take.

But another sort of character will narrate anything, and, the worse he is, the more unscrupulous he will be; nothing will be beneath him: moreover he will be ready to imitate anything, not as a joke, but in right good earnest, and before a large audience. As I was just now saying, he will attempt to represent the roll of thunder, the noise of wind and hail, or the creaking of wheels, and pulleys, and the various sounds of flutes, pipes, trumpets, and all sorts of instruments: also he will bark like a dog, bleat like a sheep, and crow like a cock; his entire art will consist in imitation of voice and gesture, and there will be very little narration.

That, he said, will be his mode of speaking.

These, then, are the two kinds of style?

Yes.

And you would agree with me in saying that one of them is simple and has but slight changes; and if the harmony and rhythm are also chosen for their simplicity, the result is that the speaker, if he speaks correctly, is always pretty much the same in style, and keeps within the limits of a single harmony (for the changes are not great), and also keeps pretty nearly the same rhythm?

That is quite true, he said.

Whereas the other style requires all sorts of harmonies and all sorts of rhythms, if the music is to be expressive of the variety and complexity of the words?

That is also perfectly true, he replied.

And do not the two styles, or the mixture of the two, comprehend all poetry, and every form of expression in words? No one can say anything except in one or other of them or in both together.

They include all, he said.

And shall we receive one or both of the two pure styles? or would you include the mixed?

I should prefer only to admit the pure imitator of virtue.

**Poets to be excluded from the ideal state.**

Yes, I said, Adeimantus; but the mixed style is also very charming and indeed the pantomimic, which is the opposite of the one chosen by you, is the most popular style with children and their instructors, and with the world in general.

I do not deny it.

But I suppose you mean to say that such a style is unsuitable to our State, in which human nature is not twofold or manifold, for one man plays one part only?

Yes; quite unsuitable.

And this is the reason why in our State, and in our State only, we shall find a shoemaker to be a shoemaker and not a pilot also, and a husbandman to be a husbandman and not a dicast also, and a soldier a soldier and not a trader also, and the same of all the other citizens?

True, he said.

And therefore when any one of these clever multiform gentlemen, who can imitate anything, comes to us, and makes a proposal to exhibit himself and his poetry, we will fall down and worship him as a sweet and holy and wonderful being; but we must also inform him that there is no place for such as he is in our State,—the law will not allow them. And so when we have anointed him with myrrh, and set a garland of wool upon his head, we shall send him away to another city. For we mean to employ for our souls' health the rougher and severer poet or storyteller, who will imitate the style of the virtuous only, and will follow those models which we prescribed at first when we began the education of our soldiers.

That, he said, we certainly will, if we have the power.

Then now, my friend, I said, that part of music or literary education which relates to the story or myth may be considered to be finished; for the matter and manner have both been discussed.

I think so too, he said.

Next in order will follow melody and song.

Melody and song from the remainder of music.

That is plain.

Every one can see what we ought to say about them, if we are to be consistent with ourselves.

I fear, said Glaucon, laughing, that the word 'every one' hardly includes me, for I cannot at the moment say, though I may guess.

At any rate you can tell that a song or ode has three parts—the words, the melody, and the rhythm;—that degree of knowledge I may presuppose?

Yes, he said; so much as that you may.

And as for the words, there will be no difference between words which are and which are not set to music; both will conform to the same laws, and these have been already determined by us?

Yes.

Also the melody and rhythm will go with the subject?

Certainly.

And we were saying, as you may remember, in speaking the words, that we had no need of lamentation and strains of of sorrow?

True.

And which are the harmonies expressive of sorrow? As you are a musician, I wish that you would tell me.

These to conform to the same rules as literature.

The harmonies which you mean are the mixed or tenor Lydian, and the full-toned or bass Lydian, and others which are like them.

These then, I said, must be banished; even to women of virtue and character they are of no use, and much less to men.

Certainly.

In the next place, drunkenness and softness and indolence are utterly at variance with the character of our guardians.

Of course.

Then I must ask you again, which are the soft or drinking harmonies?

The Ionian, he replied, and the Lydian; they are termed 'solute.'

Well, and are these of any military use?

Quite the reverse, he replied; but then the Dorian and the Phrygian appear to be the only ones which remain.

I answered: Of the harmonies I know nothing, but I want to have one warlike, which will sound the word or note which a brave man utters in the hour of danger and stern resolve, or when his cause is failing, and he is going to wounds or death or is overtaken by some other evil, and at every such crisis meets fortune with calmness and endurance; and another to be used by him in times of peace and freedom of action, when there is no pressure of necessity, and he is seeking to persuade God by prayer, or man by instruction and advice; or on the other hand, which expresses his willingness to listen to persuasion or entreaty or advice, and which represents him when he has accomplished his aim, not carried away by success, but acting moderately and wisely, and acquiescing in the event. These two harmonies I ask you to leave; the strain of necessity and the strain of freedom, the strain of the unfortunate and the strain of the fortunate, the strain of courage, and the strain of temperance; these, I say, leave.

And these, he replied, are the very ones of which I was speaking. **Types of music**

Then, I said, if only the Dorian and Phrygian harmonies are used in our songs and melodies, we shall not want multiplicity of notes or a panharmonic scale?

I suppose not.

Then we shall not maintain the artificers of lyres with three corners and complex scales, or of any other many-stringed, curiously-harmonised instruments? **and of instruments approved.**

Certainly not.

But what do you say to flute-makers and flute-players? Would you admit them when you reflect that in this composite use of harmony the flute is worse than all the stringed instruments put together, for even the panharmonic music is only an imitation of the flute?

Clearly not.

There remain then only the lyre and the harp for use in the city, and you may have a pipe in the country.

Yes, certainly; thus far the argument is clear.

* * * * * * *

But shall our superintendence go no further, and are the poets only to be required by us to express the image of the good in their works as the condition of producing in our State? Or is the same control to be exercised over other artists, and are they also to be prohibited from exhibiting the opposite forms of vice and intemperance and meanness and indecency in sculpture and building and the other creative arts; and is he who does not conform to this rule of ours to be prevented from practising his art in our State, lest the taste of our citizens be corrupted by him? We would not have our guardians grow up amid images of moral deformity, as in some noxious pasture, and there browse and feed upon many a baneful herb and flower day by day, little by little, until they silently gather a festering mass of corruption in their own soul. Let our artists rather be those who are gifted to discern the true nature of beauty and grace; then will our youth dwell in the land of health, amid fair sights and sounds; and beauty, the effluence of fair works, will visit the eye and ear, like a healthful breeze from a purer region, and insen- **Similar control over other artists by the state.**

sibly draw the soul even in childhood into harmony with the beauty of reason.

There can be no nobler training than that, he replied.

And therefore, I said, Glaucon, musical training is a more potent instrument than any other, because rhythm and harmony find their way into the secret places of the soul, on which they mightily fasten, imparting grace, and making the soul graceful of him who is rightly educated, or ungraceful of him who is ill-educated; and also because he who has received this true education of the inner being will most shrewdly perceive omissions or faults in art and nature, and with a true taste, while he praises and rejoices over and receives into his soul the good, and becomes noble and good, he will justly blame and hate the bad, now in the days of his youth, even before he is able to know the reason why; and when reason comes he will recognise and salute her as a friend with whom his education has made him long familiar.

Yes, he said, I quite agree with you in thinking that on these grounds education should be in music.

Just as in learning to read, I said, we want to know the various letters in all their recurring sizes and combinations; not slighting them as unimportant whether they be large or small, but everywhere eager to make them out; and not thinking ourselves perfect in the art until we recognise them wherever they are found:

True —

Or, as we recognise the reflection of letters in the water, or in a mirror, only when we know the letters themselves; the same art giving us the knowledge of both:

Exactly —

Even so, as I maintain, neither we nor our guardians, whom we have to educate, can ever become musical until we and they know the essential forms of temperance, courage, liberality, magnificence, and their kindred, as well as the contrary forms, in all their combinations, and can recognise them and their images wherever they are found, not slighting them either in small things or great, but believing them all to be within the sphere of one art and study.

Most assuredly.

* * * * * * *

After music comes gymnastic, in which our youth are next to be trained.

Gymnastic, the second part of education.

Certainly.

And gymnastic as well as music should receive careful attention in childhood, and continue through life. Now my belief is, — and this is a matter upon which I should like to have your opinion, but my own belief is, — not that the good body improves the soul, but that the good soul improves the body. What do you say?

Yes, I agree.

Then, if we have educated the mind, the minuter care of the body may properly be committed to the mind, and we need only describe the outlines of the subject for brevity's sake.

The mind educated by music may direct gymnastic, the education of the body.

Very good.

That they must abstain from intoxication has been already remarked by us; for of all persons a guardian should be the last to get drunk and not know where in the world he is.

Yes, he said; that a guardian should require another to guard him is ridiculous indeed.

But next, what shall we say of their food; for the men are athletes in the great contest of all — are they not?

Yes, he said.

And will the usual gymnastic exercises be suited to them?

I cannot say.

I am afraid, I said, that such exercise is but a sleepy sort of thing, and rather perilous to health. Do you not observe that athletes sleep away their lives, and are liable to most dangerous illnesses if they depart, in ever so slight a degree, from their customary regimen?

Yes, I do.

Then, I said, a finer sort of training will be required for our warrior athletes, who are to be like wakeful dogs, and to see and hear with the utmost keenness; in the many changes of water and also of food, of summer heat and winter cold, which they will have to endure, they must not be liable to break down in health.

That is quite my view, he said.

Gymnastic should be of a military type.

The really excellent gymnastic is twin sister of that simple music which we were just now describing.

How so?

Why, I conceive that there is a gymnastic also which is simple and good; and that such ought to be the military gymnastic.

* * * * * * *

Examination of the theory that the youth should experience evil in order to judge of it.

All that, Socrates, is excellent; but I should like to put a question to you. Ought there not to be good physicians in a State, and are not the best those who have treated the greatest number of constitutions good and bad, just as good judges are those who are acquainted with all sorts of moral natures?

Yes, I said, I quite agree about the necessity of having good judges and good physicians. But do you know whom I think good?

Will you inform me?

Yes, if I can. Let me however note that in the same question you join two things which are not the same.

How so? he asked.

Why, I said, you join physicians and judges. Now skilful physicians are those who, from their youth upwards, have combined with the knowledge of their art the greatest experience of disease; they had better not be robust in health, and should have had all manner of diseases in their own persons. For the body, as I conceive, is not the instrument with which they cure the body; in that case we would not allow them ever to be sickly; but they cure the body with the mind, and the mind which is or has become sick can cure nothing.

That is very true, he said.

But with the judge the case is different; he governs mind by mind, and he ought not therefore to have been reared among vicious minds, and to have associated with them from youth upwards, in order that, having gone through the whole calendar of crime, he may quickly infer the crimes of others like their diseases from the knowledge of himself; but the honourable mind which is to form a healthy judgment ought rather to have had no experience or contamination of evil habits when young. And this is the reason why in youth good men often appear to be simple, and are easily practised upon by the evil, because they have no examples of what evil is in their own souls.

Yes, he said, that very often happens with them.

Therefore, I said, the judge should not be young; he should have learned to know evil, not from his own soul, but from late and long observation of the nature of evil in others: knowledge, and not his own experience, should be his guide.

Such knowledge should be gained by observing the nature and results of evil in others.

Yes, he said, that is the ideal of a judge.

Yes, I replied, and he will be a good man (which is my answer to your question); for he is good whose soul is good. Whereas your cunning and suspicious character, who has committed many crimes, and fancies himself to be a master in wickedness, when he is among men who are like himself, is wonderful in his precautions against others, because he judges of them by himself: but when he gets into the company of men of virtue, who have the experience of age, he appears to be a fool again, owing to his unseasonable suspicion; he cannot recognise an honest man, because he has nothing in himself which will tell him what an honest man is like; at the same time, as the bad are more numerous than the good, and he meets with them oftener, he thinks himself, and others think him, rather wise than foolish.

Most true, he said.

Then the good and wise judge whom we are seeking is not this man; the other is better suited to us; for vice cannot know virtue, but a virtuous nature, educated by time, will acquire a knowledge both of virtue and vice: the virtuous, and not the vicious man has wisdom—in my opinion.

Only the virtuous man can have wisdom.

And in mine also.

This is the sort of medicine, and this is the sort of law, which you will sanction in your state. They will minister to better natures, giving health both of soul and of body; but the bad nature they will in the case of the body leave to die, and the diseased and incurable soul they will put to death themselves.

That is clearly best both for them and for the State.

Both music and gymnastic have this wisdom for their end.

And thus our youth, having been educated only in that simple music which infuses temperance, will be reluctant to go to law.

Clearly.

And in the same way simple gymnastic will incline him to have as little as possible to do with medicine.

That I quite believe.

The very exercises and toils which he undergoes are intended to stimulate the spirited elements of his nature, and not to increase his strength; he will not, like common athletes, use exercise and regimen to develope his muscles.

Very right, he said.

Neither are the two arts of music and gymnastic really designed, the one for the training of the soul, the other for the training of the body.

But what is the real object?

I believe, I said, that the teachers of both have in view chiefly the improvement of the soul.

How can that be? he asked.

Did you never observe, I said, the effect on the mind of exclusive devotion to gymnastic, or the opposite effect of an exclusive devotion to music?

In what way shown? he said.

In producing a temper of hardness and ferocity, or again of softness and effeminacy, I replied.

Yes, he said, I am quite aware that your mere athlete becomes too much of a savage, and that the mere musician is melted and softened beyond what is good for him.

Yet surely, I said, the fierce quality gives spirit, and, if educated rightly, will be valiant, but, if exaggerated, is likely to become hard and brutal.

That I quite think.

The philosopher will have the quality of gentleness. And this, when too much indulged, will turn to softness, but, if educated rightly, will be gentle and modest.

True.

Whereas in our judgment the guardians ought to have both these qualities?

Certainly they ought.

The qualities should be harmonized?

Beyond question.

And the harmonious soul is both temperate and valiant?

Yes.

And the inharmonious is cowardly and boorish?

Very true.

And, when a man allows music to play and pour over his soul through the funnel of his ears those sweet and soft and melancholy airs of which we were just now speaking, and his whole life is passed in warbling and the delights of song; in the first stage of the process the passion or spirit which is in him is tempered like iron, and made useful, instead of brittle and useless. But, if he carries on the softening process, in the next stage he begins to melt and waste, until he has wasted away his spirit and cut out the sinews of his soul; and he makes a feeble warrior.

Very true.

**Only such music and exercise as have a temperate effect to be used.**

If the element of spirit is naturally weak in him this is soon accomplished, but if he have a good deal, then the power of music weakening the spirit renders him excitable; — he soon flames up, and is speedily extinguished; instead of having spirit he becomes irritable and violent and very discontented.

Exactly.

And so in gymnastics, if a man takes violent exercise and is a great feeder, and the reverse of a great student of music and philosophy, at first the high condition of his body fills him with pride and spirit, and he becomes twice the man that he was.

Certainly.

But if he do nothing else, and never cultivates the Muses, even that intelligence which there may be in him, having no taste of any sort of learning or enquiry or thought or music, grows feeble and dull and blind, because never roused or sustained, and because the senses are not purged of their mists.

True, he said.

And he ends by becoming a hater of philosophy, uncivilized, never using weapon of persuasion, — he is like a wild beast, all violence and fierceness, and knows no other way of dealing; and he lives in all ignorance and evil conditions, and has no sense of propriety and grace.

That is quite true, he said.

And as there are two principles of human nature, one the spirited and the other the philosophical, some God, as I should say, has given mankind two arts answering to them (and only indirectly to the soul and body), in order that these two principles may be duly attuned and harmonised with one another.

That I am disposed to believe.

And he who mingles music with gymnastic in the fairest proportions, and best attempers them to the soul, may be called the true musician and harmonist in a far higher sense than the tuner of the strings.

I dare say, Socrates.

And such a presiding genius will be always required in our State if the government is to last.

Yes, he will be absolutely necessary.

**Further details of education follow the same principles.**

Such, then, are our principles of nurture and education. There would be no use in going into further details about their dances, their hunting or chasing with dogs, their gymnastic and equestrian contests; for these all follow the general principle, and having found that, we shall have no difficulty in discovering them.

* * * * * * *

BOOK IV

* * * * * * *

These things, my good Adeimantus, are not, as might be supposed, a number of great principles, but trifles all, if care be taken, as the saying is, of the one great thing,— a thing, however, which I would rather call not great, but enough for our purpose.

What may that be? he asked.

**Supreme importance of education.**

Education, I said, and nurture. For if our citizens are well educated, and grow into sensible men, they will easily see their way through all these, as well as other matters which I do not mention; such, for example, as marriage, the possession of women and the procreation of children, which will all follow the general principle that friends have all things in common, as the proverb says.

That will be the best way of settling them.

Also, I said, the State, if once started well, goes on with accumulating force like a wheel. For good nurture and education implant good constitutions, and these good constitutions having their roots in a good education improve more and more, and this improvement affects the breed in man as in other animals.

True, he said.

Then to sum up: This is the point to which, above all, the attention of our rulers should be directed, — that music and gymnastic be preserved in their original form, and no innovation made. They must do their utmost to maintain this. And when any one says that mankind most regard

**No innovations permitted.**

> 'The song which is the newest that the singers have,'

they will be afraid that he may be praising, not new songs, but a new kind of song; and this ought not to be praised, nor is this to be regarded as the meaning of the poet; for any musical innovation is full of danger to the State, and ought to be prevented. So Damon tells me, and I can quite believe him; — he says that when modes of music change, the fundamental laws of the State always change with them.

Yes, said Adeimantus; and you may add my suffrage to Damon's and your own.

Then, I said, our guardians must lay the foundations of their fortress in music?

Yes, he said; and the licence of which you speak very easily creeps in.

Yes, I replied, in the form of amusement; and at first sight appears harmless.

Why, yes, he said, and there is no harm; were it not that little by little the spirit of licence, finding a home, penetrates into manners and customs; whence, issuing with greater force, it invades agreements between man and man, and from agreements goes on to laws and constitutions, in utter recklessness, and ends, Socrates, by an overthrow of all things, private as well as public.

Is that true? I said.

That is my belief, he replied.

Then, as I was saying, our youth should be educated in a stricter rule from the first, for if education becomes lawless, and the youths themselves become lawless, they can never grow up into well-conducted and meritorious citizens.

**Importance of the earlier stages of education.**

Very true, he said.

And the education must begin with their plays. The

spirit of law must be imparted to them in music, and the spirit of order, attending them in all their actions, will make them grow; and if there be any part of the State which has fallen down, will raise it up again.

Very true, he said.

Thus educated, they will have no difficulty in rediscovering any lesser matters which have been neglected by their predecessors.

What do you mean?

Rigid laws concerning education obviate the necessity for detailed regulations in other respects.

I mean such things as these: — when the young are to be silent before their elders; how they are to show respect to them by sitting down and rising up; what honour is due to parents; what garments or shoes are to be worn; the mode of dressing the hair; deportment and manners in general. You would agree with me?

Yes.

You would think, as I do, that there is small wisdom in legislating about such matters, — I doubt if it is ever done; nor are any precise verbal enactments about them likely to be lasting.

Impossible.

We may assume, Adeimantus, that the direction in which education starts a man will determine his future life. Does not like always attract like?

To be sure.

Until he reaches some one rare and grand result, which may be good, and may be the reverse of good.

That is not to be denied.

And for this reason, I said, I shall not attempt to legislate further about them.

Naturally enough, he replied.

Well, and about the business of the agora, and the ordinary dealings between man and man, or again about agreements with artisans; about insult and injury, or the order in which causes are to be tried, and the appointment of juries, what would you say? there may be also questions about any impositions and exactions of market and harbour dues which may be required, and in general about the regulations of markets, police, harbours, and the like. But, oh heavens! shall we condescend to legislate on any of these particulars?

I think, he said, that there is no need to impose laws about them on good men; what regulations are necessary they will find out soon enough for themselves.

Yes, I said, my friend, if God will only guard the laws which we have given them.

And without divine help, said Adeimantus, they will go on forever making and mending their laws and their lives in the hope of attaining perfection.

You would compare them, I said, to those invalids who, having no self-restraint, will not leave off their habits of intemperance?

Exactly.

Yes, I said; and what a delightful life they lead! they are always doctoring and increasing and complicating their disorders, and always fancying that they will be cured by some nostrum which somebody advises them to try.

That is often the case, he said, with invalids such as you describe.

Yes, I replied; and the charming thing is that they deem him their worst enemy who tells them the truth, which is simply that, unless they give up eating and drinking and lusting and sleeping, neither drug nor cautery nor spell nor amulet nor any other remedy will avail.

Charming! he replied. I see nothing charming in going into a passion with a man who tells you what is good.

These gentlemen, I said, do not seem to be in your good graces.

Assuredly not.

Nor would a State which acts like them stand high in your estimation. And do not States act like them, which are ill governed? For they begin by proclaiming to their citizens that no one, under penalty of death, shall alter the constitution of the State; and at the same time, he who conforms to their politics and most sweetly serves them, who indulges them and fawns upon them and has a presentiment of their wishes, and is skilful in gratifying them, he is deemed to be their good man, and the wise and mighty one who is to be held in honour by them?

Yes, he said; the States are as bad as the men; and I am far from approving of them.

But do you not admire, I said, the coolness and dexterity of these ready ministers of political corruption?

Yes, he said, I do; but not of all of them, for there are some whom the applause of the multitude has deluded into the belief that they are really statesmen, and they are not much to be admired.

What do you mean? I said; you should have more feeling for them. When a man cannot measure, and a great many others who cannot measure declare that he is four cubits high, can he help believing what they say?

He cannot.

Well, then, do not be angry with them; for are they not as good as a play, trying their hand at legislation, and always fancying that by reforming they will make an end of frauds between man and man, and the other rascalities which I was mentioning, not knowing that they are in reality cutting away the heads of a hydra?

Yes, he said; that is just what they are doing.

I conceive, I said, that the true legislator will not trouble himself with enactments of this sort in an ill-ordered any more than in a well-ordered State; for in the former they are useless, and in the latter there will be no difficulty in inventing them, and many of them will naturally flow out of our previous regulations.

What, then, he said, is still remaining to us of the work of legislation?

**Religious sanction essential.**

Nothing to us, I replied; but to Apollo, the god of Delphi, there remains the ordering of the greatest and noblest and chiefest of all.

What is that? he said.

The institution of temples and sacrifices, and in general the service of gods, demigods, and heroes; also the ordering of the repositories of the dead, and the rites which have to be observed in order to propitiate the inhabitants of the world below. For these are matters of which we are ignorant, and as founders of a city we should be unwise in trusting them to any interpreter but our ancestral deity. He is the god who sits in the centre, on the navel of the earth, and he is the interpreter of religion to all mankind.

You are right, and we will do as you propose.

* * * * * * *

BOOK V

• • • • • • •

Let us proceed now to give the women a similar training and education, and see how far that accords with our design.

**The education of women**

What do you mean?

What I mean may be put into the form of a question, I said: Do we divide dogs into hes and shes, and take the masculine gender out to hunt, or have them to keep watch and ward over the flock, while we leave the females at home, under the idea that the bearing and suckling their puppies hinder them from sharing in the labours of the males?

No, he said, they share alike; the difference between them is in degrees of strength.

But can you use different animals for the same purpose, unless they are bred and fed in the same way?

You cannot.

Then, if women are to have the same duties as men, they must have the same education?

Yes.

The education which was assigned to the men was music and gymnastic.

**to be similar to that of men.**

Yes.

Then women must be taught music and gymnastic and also the art of war, which they must practise like the men?

That is the inference, I suppose.

I should rather expect, I said, that several of our proposals, if they are carried out, being unusual, may appear ridiculous.

No doubt of it.

Yes, and the most ridiculous thing of all will be the sight of women naked in the palæstra, exercising with the men, especially when they get old; they certainly will not be a vision of beauty, any more than the wrinkled old men who have anything but an agreeable appearance when they take to gymnastics—this, however, does not deter them.

Yes, indeed; he said: according to present notions the proposal would appear ridiculous.

But then, I said, as we have determined to speak our

Explanation of the difficulties to be encountered.

minds, we must not fear the jests of the wits which will be directed against this sort of innovation; how they will talk of women's attainments in music as well as in gymnastic, and above all about their wearing armour and riding upon horseback!

Very true, he replied.

Yet having begun we must go on and attack the difficulty; at the same time begging of these gentlemen for once in their life to be serious. Not long ago, as we shall remind them, the Greeks were of the opinion, which is still generally received among the barbarians, that the sight of a naked man was ridiculous and improper; and when first the Cretans and then the Lacedæmonians introduced naked exercises, the wits of that day might have ridiculed them equally.

No doubt.

But when experience showed that to let all things be uncovered was far better than to cover them up, and the ludicrous effect to the outward eye vanished before the approval of reason, then the man was seen to be a fool who laughs or directs the shafts of his ridicule at any other sight but that of folly and vice, or seriously inclines to measure the beautiful by any other standard but that of the good.

Very true, he replied.

Argument of the question whether woman has the same nature as man,

First, then, whether the question is to be put in jest or in earnest, let us ask about the nature of woman: Is she capable of sharing either wholly or partially in the actions of men, or not at all? And is the art of war one of those arts in which she can or cannot share? That will be the best way of commencing the enquiry, and will probably lead to the fairest conclusion.

That will be best.

Suppose that we take the other side and begin by arguing against ourselves, and so the adversary's position will be fairly defended.

Why not? he said.

Then let us put a speech into the mouths of our opponents. They will say: 'Socrates and Glaucon, no adversary need convict you, for you yourselves, at the first foundation of the State, admitted the principle that every one was to do his own work according to his nature.' And certainly, if I am not mistaken there was such an admission made by us. Then he will proceed to say: 'Is there not the greatest difference between the natures of men and women?' And we shall reply: Of course, there is. And he will ask 'whether men and women ought not to have different tasks imposed upon them, such as are agreeable to their different natures?' Certainly they ought. 'Have you not then fallen into a great inconsistency in saying that men and women, who are entirely different, ought to perform the same actions?'—What defence will you make for us, my good Sir, against any one who offers these objections?

That is not an easy question to answer when asked suddenly; and I shall and I do beg of you to draw out the case on our side.

There, Glaucon, is the difficulty which made me unwilling to take in hand any law about women and children; and this is not the only difficulty.

Why yes, he said, there is something of a difficulty.

Yes, I said, but the fact is that when a man is out of his depth, whether he has fallen into a swimming bath or into the ocean, he has to swim all the same.

Very true.

And must not we swim and make for some haven, in the hope that Arion's dolphin or some other miraculous help may save us?

I suppose so, he said.

Well then, let us see if we can discover any way of escape. Our principle was that different natures ought to have different pursuits, and that men's and women's natures are different. And now what are we saying?—that different natures ought to have the same pursuits,—this is the inconsistency which is charged upon us.

Precisely.

Verily, Glaucon, I said, glorious is the power of the art of contradiction.

Why do you say so?

Because I think that many a man falls into the practice against his will. When he thinks that he is reasoning he is really disputing, just because he cannot define and divide, and so know that of which he is speaking; and he will pursue a merely verbal opposition in the spirit of contention and not of fair discussion.

Yes, he replied, such is very often the case; but what has that to do with us and our argument?

A great deal; for there is certainly a danger of our getting unintentionally into a verbal opposition.

In what way?

Why we valiantly and pugnaciously insist upon the verbal truth, that different natures ought to have different pursuits, but we never considered at all what was the meaning of sameness or difference of nature, or why we distinguished them when we assigned different pursuits to different natures.

Why, no, he said, that was never considered by us.

I said: Suppose that by way of illustration we were to ask the question whether there is not an opposition in nature between bald men and hairy men; and if there is, then, if bald men are cobblers, forbid the hairy men, or if the hairy men are cobblers, then forbid the bald men to be cobblers.

That would be a jest, he said.

Yes, I said, a jest; and why? because we never meant when we constructed the State, that the opposition of natures should extend to every difference, but only to those differences which affected the pursuit in which the individual is engaged; we should have said, for example, that a man and a woman when they both have the soul of a physician may be said to have the same nature.

True.

Whereas the physician and the carpenter are different?

Certainly.

And if, I said, the male and female sex appear to differ in their fitness for any art or pursuit, we should say that such pursuit or art ought to be assigned to one or the other of them; but if the difference consists only in women bearing and men begetting children, this does not amount to a proof that a woman differs from a man in that respect of which we are speaking; and we shall therefore continue to maintain that our guardians and their wives ought to have the same pursuits.

settled in the affirmative.

Very true, he said.

The next step will be to desire our opponent to show how, in reference to any of the pursuits or arts of citizens, the nature of a woman differs from that of a man?

That will be fair.

And perhaps he, like yourself, will reply that to give an answer on the instant is not easy; a little reflection is needed.

Yes, perhaps.

Suppose then that we invite him to come along with us in the argument, and then we may hope to show him that there is no special function which a woman has in the administration of the State.

By all means.

Let us say to him: Come now, and we will ask you a question:—when you said that one man has natural gifts and another not, was this your meaning?—that the former will acquire a thing easily which the latter will have a difficulty in acquiring; a little learning will lead the one to discover a great deal; whereas the other, after a great deal of learning and application, will only forget what he has learned; or again, you may mean, that the one has a body which is a good servant to his mind, while the body of the other is at war with his mind;—would these be the sort of differences which distinguish the man of capacity from the man who is wanting in capacity?

The existence of such differences, he said, will be universally allowed.

Women possess the same characteristics, only in an inferior degree.

Can you mention any pursuit of man in which the male sex has not all these qualities in a far higher degree than the female? Need I waste time in speaking of the art of weaving, and the management of pancakes and preserves, in which womankind does really appear to be great, and in which for her to be beaten is the most absurd of all things?

You are quite right, he replied, in maintaining the general inferiority of the female sex; at the same time many women are in many things superior to many men, though, speaking generally, what you say is true.

And so, I said, my friend, in the administration of a State neither a woman as a woman, nor a man as a man has any special function, but the gifts of nature are equally diffused in both sexes; all the pursuits of men are the pursuits of women also, and in all of them a woman is only a weaker man.

Very true.

Then are we to impose all our enactments on men and none of them on women?

That will never do.

One woman has a gift of healing, another not; one is a musician, and another is not a musician?

Very true.

And one woman has a turn for gymnastic and military exercises, and another is unwarlike and hates gymnastics?

Beyond question.

And one woman is a philosopher, and another is an enemy of philosophy; one has spirit, and another is without spirit?

That is also true.

Then one woman will have the temper of a guardian, and another not; for was not the selection of the male guardians determined by these sort of differences?

Very true.

Then the woman has equally with the man the qualities which make a guardian; she differs only in degrees of strength?

Obviously.

**Education of women to be settled on the same general principles as that of men,**

And those women who have such qualities are to be selected as the companions and colleagues of our guardians, since they resemble them in ability and character?

Very true.

And being of the same nature with them, ought they not to have the same pursuits?

They ought.

Then, as we were saying before, there is nothing unnatural in assigning music and gymnastic to the wives of the guardians: to that point we come round again.

Very good.

The law which thus enacted, instead of being an impossibility or mere aspiration, was agreeable to nature, and the contrary practice, which prevails at present, is in reality a violation of nature.

That appears to be true.

There was, first, the possibility, and secondly, the advantage of our proposed arrangement, which had to be considered?

Yes.

And the possibility has been allowed?

Yes.

The very great advantage has next to be acknowledged?

Clearly.

You will admit that the same education which makes a man a good guardian will make a woman a good guardian; for their original nature is the same?

Yes.

I should like to ask you a question: Would you say that all men are equal in excellence, or is one man better than another?

The latter.

And in our imaginary commonwealth which do you reckon the better, the guardians who have been brought up on our model system or the cobblers whose education has been cobbling?

What a ridiculous question!

You have answered me, I replied. Well, and may we not further say that our guardians are the best of our citizens?

Far the best.

And will not their wives be the best women?

Yes, again I say the very best.

**and to include the same subjects.**

And can there be anything better for the interests of the State than that the men and women of a State should be as good as possible?

There can be nothing better.

And our course of music and gymnastic will accomplish this?

Certainly.

Then we have made an enactment not only possible but in the highest degree advantageous to the State?

True.

* * * * * * *

Then you must not insist on my proving that the actual State will in every respect coincide with the ideal: if we are only able to discover how a city may be governed nearly as we proposed, you will admit that we have discovered the possibility which you demand; and will be contented. I am sure that I should be contented — will not you?

Yes, I will.

Then let me next endeavour to show what is that fault in States which is the cause of their present maladministration, and what is the least change which will enable a State to pass into the truer form; and let the change, if possible, be of one thing only, or, if not, of two; at any rate, let the changes be as few and slight as possible.

Certainly, he replied.

I think then, I said, that there might be a revolution if there were just one change, which is not a slight or easy though still a possible one.

What is it? he said.

Now then, I said, I go to meet that which I liken to the greatest of waves, yet shall the word be spoken, even though the overflowing of the laughing wave shall drown me in laughter and dishonour; and do you attend to me.

Proceed.

The ideal state is to be produced by education, such as outlined for the guardian class.

I said: Until, then, philosophers are kings, or the kings and princes of this world have the spirit and power of philosophy, and political greatness and wisdom meet in one, and those commoner natures who follow either to the exclusion of the other are compelled to stand aside, cities will never cease from ill — no, nor the human race, as I believe — and then only will our State have a possibility of life and behold the light of day. This was the thought, my dear Glaucon, which I was wanting to utter if it had not seemed too extravagant; for to be convinced that in no other state can there be private or public happiness is indeed a hard thing.

Socrates, what do you mean? I would have you consider that the word which you have spoken, is one at which numerous persons, and very respectable persons too, pulling off their coat in a moment, and seizing any weapon that comes to hand, will run at you might and main, intending to do heaven knows what; and if you don't prepare an answer, and put yourself in motion, you will be 'pared by their fine wits,' and no mistake.

You got me into the scrape, I said.

And I was quite right; however, I will do all I can to get you out; but I can only give you wishes and exhortations, and also, perhaps, I may be able to fit answers to your questions better than another — that is all. And now, having such an auxiliary, you must do your best to show the unbelievers that you are right.

Character of the philosopher, the ideal of this education.

I ought to try, I said, since you offer me such valuable assistance. And I think that, if there is to be a chance of our escaping, we must define who these philosophers are who, as we say, are to rule in the State; then we shall be able to defend ourselves: There will be discovered to be some natures who ought to rule and to study philosophy; and others who are not born to be philosophers, and are meant to be followers rather than leaders.

Then now for a definition, he said.

Follow me, I said, and I hope that I may somehow or other be able to give you a satisfactory explanation.

Proceed.

I dare say that you remember, and therefore I need not remind you, that a lover, if he is worthy of the name, ought to show his love, not to some one part of that which he loves, but to the whole.

I believe that I must ask you to explain, for I really do not understand.

Another, I replied, might fairly answer thus; but a man of pleasure like you ought to know that all who are in the flower of their youth do somehow or other raisc a pang or emotion in a lover's breast, and are thought by him to be worthy of his affectionate regards. Is not this a way which you have with the fair: one has a snub nose, and you praise his pleasant face; another's beak, as you say, has a royal look; while he who is neither snub nor hooked has the grace of regularity: the dark visage is manly, and the fair are angels; and as to the sweet 'honey-pale,' as they are called, what is the very name but the invention of a lover who uses these pet names, and is not averse to paleness on the cheek of youth? In a word, there is no excuse which you will not make, and nothing which you will not say, in order to preserve for your use every flower that has the bloom of youth.

If you will make me an authority in matters of love, for the sake of the argument, I assent.

And what do you say of lovers of wine? Do you not see them doing the same? They are glad of any pretext of drinking any wine.

Very good.

And the same is true of ambitious men; if they cannot be generals, they are willing to be captains; and if they cannot be honoured by really great and important persons, they are glad to be honoured by inferior people, — but honour of some kind they must have.

Exactly.

Once more let me ask: Does he who desires any class of goods, desire the whole class or a part only?

The whole.

And may we not say of the philosopher that he is a lover, not of a part of wisdom only, but of the whole?

True.

They are lovers of knowledge,

Then he who dislikes knowledge, especially in youth, when he has no power of judging what is good and what is not, such an one we maintain not to be a philosopher or a lover of knowledge, just as he who refuses his food is not hungry, and may be said to have a bad appetite and not a good one?

There we are right, he said.

Whereas he who has a taste for every sort of knowledge and who is curious to learn and is never satisfied, may be justly termed a philosopher? Am I not right?

Glaucon said: If curiosity makes a philosopher, you will find many a strange being claiming the name. For all the lovers of sights have a delight in learning, and will therefore have to be included. Musical amateurs, too, are a folk wonderfully out of place among philosophers, for they are the last persons in the world who would come to anything like a philosophical discussion, if they could help, while they run about at the Dionysiac festivals as if they had let out their ears to hear every chorus; whether the performance is in town or country — that makes no difference — they are there. Now are we to maintain that all these and any who have similar tastes, as well as the professors of minor arts, are philosophers?

Certainly not, I replied, they are only an imitation.

He said: But who are the true philosophers?

Those, I said, who are lovers of the vision of truth. **and of truth.**

That is also good, he said; but I should like to know what you mean?

To another, I replied, I might have a difficulty in explaining; but I am sure that you will admit a proposition which I am about to make.

What proposition?

That since beauty is the opposite of ugliness, they are two?

Certainly.

And inasmuch as they are two, each of them is one?

True again.

And of just and unjust, good and evil, and of every other class, the same remark holds: taken singly, each of them is one; but from the various combinations of them with things and persons and with one another, they are seen in various lights and appear many?

Very true.

And this is the distinction which I draw between the sight-loving, art-loving, busy class and those of whom I am speaking, and who are alone worthy of the name of philosophers.

How do you distinguish them? he said.

The lovers of sounds and sights, I replied, are, as I conceive, fond of fine tones and colours and forms and all the artificial products that are made out of them, but their mind is incapable of seeing or loving absolute beauty.

True, he replied.

Few are they who are able to attain the sight of this.

Very true.

And he who, having a sense of beautiful things has no sense of absolute beauty, or who, if another lead him to a knowledge of that beauty is unable to follow—of such an one I ask, Is he awake or in a dream only? Reflect: is not the dreamer, sleeping or waking, one who puts the resemblance in the place of the real object?

I should certainly say that such an one was dreaming.

But take the case of the other, who recognises the existence of absolute beauty and is able to distinguish the idea

**He is the one who can distinguish the object and the idea,**

from the objects which participate in the idea, neither putting the objects in the place of the idea nor the idea in the place of the objects — is he a dreamer, or is he awake?

He is wide awake.

And may we not say that the mind of the one has knowledge and that the mind of the other has opinion only?

Certainly.

But suppose that the latter quarrels with us and disputes our statement, can we administer any soothing cordial or advice to him, without revealing to him that there is sad disorder in his wits?

Good advice is what he certainly wants, he replied.

Come, then, and let us think of something to tell him. Suppose we begin by assuring him that he is welcome to any knowledge he may have, and that we are rejoiced at his having any. But we should like to ask him a question: Does he who has knowledge know something or nothing? (You must answer for him.)

I answer that he knows something.

Something that is or is not?

Something that is; for how can that which is not ever be known?

And are we assured, after looking at the matter in every point of view, that absolute being is or may be absolutely known, but that not-being is utterly unknown and unknowable?

Nothing can be more certain.

Good. But if there be anything which is of such a nature as to be and not to be, that will have a place intermediate between pure being and the absolute negation of being?

Yes, between them.

**who possesses knowledge as opposed to opinion.**

And, as knowledge corresponded to being and ignorance to not-being, for that intermediate between being and not-being there has to be discovered a corresponding intermediate between ignorance and knowledge, if there be such?

Certainly.

Do we admit the existence of opinion?

Undoubtedly.

As being the same with knowledge, or another faculty?

Another faculty.

**Discussion concerning the relation of knowledge and opinion.**

Then opinion and knowledge have to do with different kinds of matter corresponding to this difference of faculties?

Yes.

And knowledge is relative to being and knows being. But before I proceed I will make a division.

What division?

I will begin by placing faculties in a class by themselves: they are powers in us, and in all other things, by which we do as we do. Sight and hearing, for example, I should call faculties. Have I clearly explained the class which I mean?

Yes, I quite understand.

Then let me tell you my view about them. I do not see them, and therefore the distinctions of figure, color, and the like, which enable me to discern the differences of some things, do not apply to them. In speaking of a faculty I think only of the end and the operation; and that which has the same end and the same operation I call the same faculty, but that which has another end and another operation I call different. Would that be your way of speaking?

Yes.

To return. Would you place knowledge among faculties, or in some other class?

Certainly knowledge is a faculty, and the most powerful of all faculties.

And is opinion also a faculty?

Certainly, he said; for opinion is that with which we are able to form an opinion.

And yet you were surely admitting a little while ago that knowledge is not the same as opinion?

Why, yes, said he; for how can any reasonable being ever identify that which is infallible with that which errs?

That is very good, I said, and clearly shows that we are conscious of a distinction between them?

Yes.

Then knowledge and opinion having distinct powers have also distinct ends or subject-matters?

That is certain.

Being is the end or subject-matter of knowledge, and knowledge is the knowledge of being?

Yes.

And opinion is to have an opinion?

Yes.

And is the subject-matter of opinion the same as the subject-matter of knowledge?

Nay, he replied, that is already disproven; if difference in faculty implies difference in the end or subject-matter, and opinion and knowledge are distinct faculties, the subject-matter of knowledge cannot be the same as the subject-matter of opinion.

Then if being is the subject-matter of knowledge, something else must be the subject-matter of opinion?

Yes, something else.

Well then, is not-being the subject-matter of opinion? or, rather, how can there be an opinion at all about not-being? Reflect: when a man has an opinion, has he not an opinion about something? Can he have an opinion which is an opinion about nothing?

Impossible.

He who has an opinion has an opinion about some one thing?

Yes.

And not-being is not one thing but, properly speaking, nothing?

True.

Of not-being, ignorance was assumed to be the necessary correlative; of being, knowledge?

True, he said.

Then opinion is not concerned either with being or with not-being?

Not with either.

And can therefore neither be ignorance nor knowledge?

That seems to be true.

Then is opinion to be sought without and beyond either of them, in a greater clearness than knowledge, or in a greater darkness than ignorance?

Neither.

Then I suppose that opinion appears to you darker than knowledge, but lighter than ignorance?

Both; and in no small degree.

And also to be within and between them?

Yes.

Then you would infer that opinion is intermediate?

No question.

But were we not saying before, that if anything appeared to be of a sort which is and is not at the same time, that sort of thing would appear also to lie in the interval between pure being and absolute not-being; and that the corresponding faculty is neither knowledge nor ignorance, but will be found in the interval between them?

True.

And in that interval there has now been discovered a thing which we call opinion?

There has.

Then what remains to be discovered is the object which partakes equally of the nature of being and not-being, and cannot rightly be termed either, pure and simple; this unknown term, when discovered, we may truly call the subject of opinion, and assign to each their due — to the extremes the faculty of the extreme and to the mean the faculty of the mean.

True.

This being premised, I would ask the gentleman who is of opinion that there is no absolute or unchangeable idea of beauty — in whose opinion the beautiful is the diverse — he, I say, your lover of beautiful sights, who cannot bear to be told that the just is one, and the beautiful is one, or that anything is one — to him I would appeal, saying, Best of men, of all these beautiful things is there one which will not be found ugly; or of the just, which will not be found unjust; or of the holy, which will not also be unholy?

No, he replied; the beautiful will in some point of view be found ugly; and the same is true of the rest.

And may not the many which are doubles be also halves? — doubles, that is, of one thing, and halves of another?

Yes.

And things great and small, heavy and light, will not be denoted by these any more than by the opposite names?

True; both those and the opposite names will always attach to all of them.

And can any one of those many things which are called

by particular names be said to be this rather than not to be this?

He replied: They are like the punning riddles which are asked at feasts or the children's puzzle about the eunuch aiming at the bat, with what he hit him, as they say in the puzzle, and what the bat was sitting upon; for these immediate objects of which I am speaking are a riddle also, and have a double sense: nor can you fix them in your mind, either as being or not-being, or both or neither.

Then what do you do with them? I said. Can they have a better place than between being and not-being? For they are clearly not in greater darkness or negation than not-being, or more full of light and existence than being.

That is quite true, he said.

Thus then we seem to have discovered that the many things which are esteemed beautiful or good by the multitude, are tossing about in some region which is half-way between pure being and pure not-being?

We have.

**Knowledge relates to ideas to the absolute, while opinion relates to phenomenal existence.**

Yes; and we had before agreed that anything of this kind which we might find was to be described as matter of opinion, and not as matter of knowledge; being the intermediate flux which is caught and detained by the intermediate faculty.

Granted.

Then those who see the many beautiful, and who yet neither see, nor can be taught to see, absolute beauty; who see the many just, and not absolute justice, and the like, — such persons may be said to have opinion but not knowledge?

That is certain.

But those who see the absolute and eternal and immutable may be said to know, and not to have opinion only?

Neither can that be denied.

The one love and embrace the subjects of knowledge, the other those of opinion? The latter are the same, as I dare say you will remember, who listened to sweet sounds and gazed upon fair colours, but would not tolerate the existence of absolute beauty.

Yes, I remember.

Shall we then be guilty of any impropriety in calling them lovers of opinion rather than lovers of wisdom, and will they be very angry with us for thus describing them?

I shall tell them that they ought not to be angry at a description of themselves which is true.

But those who love the truth of each thing are to be called lovers of wisdom and not lovers of opinion.

Assuredly.

## BOOK VI

And thus, Glaucon, after the argument has gone a weary way, the true and the false philosophers have at length appeared in view.

I do not think, he said, that the way could have been shortened.

I suppose not, I said; and yet I believe that we might have a nearer view of both of them if there were not many other questions awaiting us, which he who desires to see in what the life of the just differs from that of the unjust must consider.

And what question is next in order? he asked.

Surely, I said, there can be no doubt about that. Inasmuch as philosophers only are able to grasp the eternal and unchangeable, and those who wander in the region of the many and variable are not philosophers, I must ask you which of the two kinds should be the rulers of our State?

And how can we truly answer that question?

Philosophers are the true rulers of the state.

Ask yourself, I replied, which of the two are better able to guard the laws and institutions of our State; and let them be our guardians.

Very good.

Neither, I said, can there be any question that the guardian who is to keep anything should have eyes rather than no eyes?

There can be no question of that.

And are not those who are truly and indeed without the knowledge of the true being of each thing, and have in their souls no clear pattern, and are unable as with a painter's eye to look at the very truth and to that original to repair, and having perfect vision of the other world to order the laws about beauty, goodness, justice in this, if not already ordered, and to guard and preserve the order of them — are they not, I say, simply blind?

Assuredly, he replied, that is very much their condition.

And shall they be our guardians when there are others who, besides being their equals in experience and not inferior to them in any particular of virtue, have also the knowledge of the truth?

There can be no reason, he said, for rejecting those who have this great and pre-eminent quality, if they do not fail in any other respect.

Suppose then, I said, that we determine how far they can unite this and the other excellences.

By all means.

Their qualifications.

In the first place, as we began by observing, the nature of the philosopher was to be ascertained; about which, if we are agreed, then, if I am not mistaken, we shall also be agreed that such an union of qualities is possible, and that those in whom they are united, and those only, should be rulers in the State. Let us assume that philosophical minds always love knowledge of a sort which shows them the eternal nature not varying from generation and corruption.

Agreed.

For they possess knowledge;

And further, I said, let us admit that they are lovers of all true being; there is no part whether greater or less, or more or less honourable, which they are willing to renounce; as we said before of the lover and the man of ambition.

True.

they are truthful;

There is another quality which they will also need if they are to be what we were saying.

What quality?

Truthfulness: they will never intentionally receive falsehood, which is their detestation, and they will love the truth.

Yes, that may be affirmed of them.

'May be,' my friend, I replied, is not the word; say rather, 'must be affirmed': for he whose nature is amorous of anything cannot help loving all that belongs or is akin to the object of his affections.

Right, he said.

And is there anything more akin to wisdom than truth?

How can there be?

Or can the same nature be a lover of wisdom and a lover of falsehood?

Never.

The true lover of learning then must from his earliest youth, as far as in him lies, desire all truth?

Assuredly.

But then again, he whose desires are strong in one direction will have them weaker in others; they will be like a stream which has been drawn off into another channel.

True.

He whose desires are drawn towards knowledge in every form will be absorbed in the pleasures of the soul, and will hardly feel bodily pleasure — I mean, if he be a true philosopher and not a sham one.

That is most certain.

Such an one is sure to be temperate and the reverse of covetous; for the motives which make another man desirous to have and to spend, are no part of his character. **they are temperate;**

Very true.

Another criterion of the philosophical nature has also to be considered.

What is that?

There should be no secret corner of meanness; for littleness is the very opposite of a soul which is ever longing after the whole of things both divine and human.

Most true, he replied.

Then how can he who has magnificence of mind and is the spectator of all time and all existence, think much of human life?

He cannot.

Or can such an one account death fearful? **they are brave and magnanimous;**

No indeed.

Then the cowardly and mean nature has no part in true philosophy?

Certainly not.

Or again: can he who is harmoniously constituted, who is not covetous or mean, or a boaster, or a coward — can he, I say, ever be unjust or hard in his dealings?

Impossible.

*they are just and gentle;* Then you will note whether a man is just and gentle, or rude and unsociable; these are the signs which distinguish even in youth the philosophical nature from the unphilosophical.

True.

And there is another point which should be remarked.

What point?

Whether he has or has not a pleasure in learning; for no one will love that which gives him pain, and in which after much toil he makes little progress.

Certainly not.

*they are not forgetful.* And again, if he is forgetful and retains nothing of what he learns, will he not be an empty vessel?

That is certain.

Labouring in vain, he must end in hating himself and his fruitless occupation?

Yes.

Then the forgetful soul cannot be ranked among philosophers; a philosopher ought to have a good memory?

Certainly.

Yet again, the inharmonious and unseemly nature can only tend to disproportion?

Undoubtedly.

And do you consider truth to be akin to proportion or to disproportion?

To proportion.

Then, besides other qualities, let us seek for a well-proportioned and gracious mind, whose own nature will move spontaneously towards the true being of everything.

Certainly.

Well, and do not all these qualities go together, and are they not necessary to a soul, which is to have a full and perfect participation of being?

They are absolutely necessary, he replied.

And must not that be a blameless study which he only can pursue who has a good memory, and is quick to learn, noble, gracious, the friend of truth, justice, courage, temperance, who are his brethren?

The god of jealousy himself, he said, could find no fault with such a study.

And to these, I said, when perfected by years and education, and to these only you will entrust the State.

Here Adeimantus interposed and said: To this, Socrates, no one can offer a reply; but there is a feeling which those who hear you talk as you are now doing often experience, and which I may describe in this way: they fancy that they are led astray a little at each step in the argument, owing to their own want of skill in asking and answering questions; these littles accumulate, and at the end of the discussion they are found to have sustained a mighty overthrow and reversal of their first notions. And as unskilful players of draughts are at last shut up by their skilled adversaries and have no piece to move, so they find themselves at last shut up and have no word to say in this new game of which words are the counters; and yet all the time they are in the right. The observation is suggested to me by what is now occurring. For any one of us might say, that although in words he is not able to meet you at each step in the argument, as a fact he sees that the votaries of philosophy who carry on the study, not only in youth with a view to education, but as the pursuit of their maturer years, for the most part grow into very strange beings, not to say utter rogues, and that those who may be considered the best of them, are made useless to the world by the very study which you extol.

Well, I said; and do you think that they are wrong?

I cannot tell, he replied; but I should like to know what is your opinion.

**This opinion concerning philosophers as the proper rulers, the reverse of popular belief.**

Hear my answer; I am of opinion that they are quite right.

Then how can you be justified in saying that cities will not cease from evil until philosophers rule in them, when philosophers are acknowledged by us to be of no use to them?

You ask a question, I said, to which I can only reply in a parable.

Yes, Socrates; and that is a way of speaking to which you are not at all accustomed, I suppose.

I perceive, I said, that you are vastly amused at having plunged me into such a hopeless discussion; and now you shall hear the parable in order that you may judge better of the meagreness of my imagination: for the treatment which the best men experience from their States is so grievous that no single thing on earth can be compared with them; and therefore if I would defend them I must have recourse to fiction, and make a compound of many things, like the fabulous unions of goats and stags which are found in pictures. Imagine then a fleet or a ship in which there is a captain who is taller and stronger than any of the crew, but he is a little deaf and has a similar infirmity in sight, and his knowledge of navigation is not much better. Now the sailors are quarrelling with one another about the steering; every one is of opinion that he ought to steer, though he has never learned and cannot tell who taught him or when he learned, and will even assert that the art of navigation cannot be taught, and is ready to cut in pieces him who says the contrary. They throng about the captain, and do all that they can to make him commit the helm to them; and if he refuses them and others prevail, they kill the others or throw them overboard, and having first chained up the noble captain's senses with drink or some narcotic drug, they mutiny and take possession of the ship and make themselves at home with the stores; and thus, eating and drinking, they continue their voyage with such success as might be expected of them. Him who is their partisan and zealous in the design of getting the ship out of the captain's hands into their own, whether by force or persuasion, they compliment with the name of sailor, pilot, able seaman, and abuse the other sort of man and call him a good-for-nothing; but they have not even a notion that the true pilot must pay attention to the year and seasons and sky and stars and winds, and whatever else belongs to his art, if he intends to be really qualified for the command of a ship; while at the same time he must and will be the steerer, whether other people like or not; and they think that to combine the exercise of command with the steerer's art is impossible. Now in vessels which are thus circumstanced and among sailors of this class, how will the true pilot be regarded? Will he not be called by the mutineers a prater, a star-gazer, a good-for-nothing?

The objection answered by a parable.

Of course, said Adeimantus.

I do not suppose, I said, that you would care to hear the

interpretation of the figure, which is an allegory of the true philosopher in his relation to the State; for you understand already.

Certainly.

Then suppose you now take the parable to the gentleman who is surprised at finding that philosophers have no honour in their cities, and explain to him and try to convince him that their having honour would be far more extraordinary.

I will.

Say to him, that, in deeming the best of the votaries of philosophy to be useless to the rest of the world, he is right; but he ought to attribute their uselessness to the fault of those who will not use them, and not to themselves. The pilot should not humbly beg the sailors to be commanded by him — that is not the order of nature; neither are the wise to go to the doors of the rich (the ingenious author of this saying told a lie), for the truth is, that, when a man is ill, whether he be rich or poor, he must go to the physician's door — the physician will not come to him — and he who is asking to be governed, to the door of him who is able to govern. The ruler who is good for anything ought not to ask his subjects to obey him; he is not like the present governors of mankind, who may be compared to the mutinous sailors, and the true helmsman to those whom they call good-for-nothings and stargazers.

Precisely, he said.

For these reasons, and among men like these, philosophy, the noblest pursuit of all, is not likely to be much esteemed by her adversaries; not that the greatest and most lasting injury is done to her by them, but by her own professing followers, the same of whom you suppose the accuser to say, that the greater number of them are arrant rogues, and the best are useless; in which opinion I agreed.

Yes.

And the reason why the good are useless has been now explained?

True.

Then shall we now endeavour to show that the corruption of the greater number is also unavoidable, and that this is

**Philosophy is not responsible for the ignorance and corruption of the masses.**

not to be laid to the charge of philosophy any more than the other?

By all means.

And let us ask and answer in turn, first going back to the description of the gentle and noble nature. Truth, as you will remember, was his captain, whom he followed always and in all things; failing in this, he was an impostor, and had no part or lot in true philosophy.

Yes, that was said.

Well, and is not this quality alone greatly at variance with our present notions of him?

Certainly, he said.

And have we not a right to say in his defence, that the true lover of knowledge is always striving after being — that is his nature; he will not rest in the multiplicity of individuals which is an appearance only, but will go on — the keen edge will not be blunted, neither the force of his desire abate until he have attained the knowledge of the true nature of every essence by a kindred power in the soul, and by that power drawing near and mingling and becoming incorporate with very being, having begotten mind and truth, he will know and live and grow truly, and then, and not till then, will he cease from his travail.

Nothing, he said, can be more just than such a description of him.

And will the love of a lie be any part of a philosopher's nature? Will he not utterly hate a lie?

He will.

And when truth is the captain, we cannot suspect any evil of the band which he leads?

Impossible.

Justice and health will be of the company, and temperance will follow after?

True, he replied.

Neither is there any reason why I should again set in array the philosopher's virtues, as you will doubtless remember that courage, magnanimity, apprehension, memory, were his natural gifts. And you objected that, although no one could deny what I then said, still, if you leave words and look at facts, the persons who are thus described are some of them manifestly useless, and the greater number wholly depraved; we were then led to inquire into the grounds of these accusations, and we had arrived at the point of asking why are the many bad, which question of necessity brought us back to the examination and definition of the true philosopher.

Exactly.

And now we have to consider the corruptions of the philosophical nature, why so many are spoiled and so few escape spoiling — I am speaking of those whom you call useless but not wicked — and after that we will consider the imitators of philosophy, what manner of natures are they who aspire after a profession which is above them and of which they are unworthy, and then, by their manifold inconsistencies, bring upon philosophy, and upon all philosophers, that universal reprobation of which we speak.

The corrupt types of philosophical nature.

What are these corruptions, he said?

I will see if I can explain them to you. Every one will admit that a nature having in perfection all the qualities which make a philosopher, is a plant that rarely grows among men — there are not many of them.

They are very rare.

And what numberless causes may tend utterly to destroy these rare natures!

What causes?

In the first place there are their own virtues, their courage, temperance, and the rest of them, every one of which praiseworthy qualities (and this is a most singular circumstance) destroys and distracts from philosophy the soul which is the possessor of them.

That is very singular, he replied.

Then there are all the ordinary goods of life — beauty, wealth, strength, rank, and great connections in the State — which I have described generally, and therefore need not enlarge upon them; — these also have a corrupting and distracting effect.

I know the goods which you mean, and I should like to know more precisely what you mean about them.

Grasp the truth as a whole, I said, and in the right way; you will then have no difficulty in understanding the preceding remarks, and they will no longer appear strange to you.

And how am I to do so? he asked.

Why, I said, we know that when any germ or seed, whether vegetable or animal, fails to meet with proper nutriment or climate or soil, the greater the vigour, the more will it lack its proper qualities, for evil is a greater enemy to good than to the not-good.

Very true.

There is reason in supposing that the finest natures, when under alien conditions, receive more injury than the inferior, because the contrast is greater.

Very true.[1]

* * * * * * *

## BOOK VII

* * * * * * *

Yes, my friend, I said; and there lies the point. You must contrive for your future rulers another and a better life than that of a ruler, and then you may have a well-ordered State; for only in the State which offers this, will they rule who are truly rich, not in silver and gold, but in virtue and wisdom, which are the true blessings of life. Whereas if they go to the administration of public affairs, poor and hungering after their own private advantage, thinking that hence they are to snatch the good of life, order there can never be; for they will be fighting about office, and the civil and domestic broils which thus arise will be the ruin of the rulers themselves and of the whole State.

Most true, he replied.

And the only life which looks down upon the life of political ambition is that of true philosophy? Do you know of any other?

No, indeed, he said.

And those who govern ought not to be lovers of the task? For if they are, there will be rival lovers, and they will fight.

No question.

Whom then would you choose rather than those who are

[1] The extract relating to the Sophists is given in Chapter III.

wisest about affairs of State, and who at the same time have other honours and another and a better life?

**How the guardian class is to be created.**

They are the men, and I will choose them, he replied.

Would you like us then to consider in what way such guardians may be called into existence, and how they are to be brought from darkness to light,—as some are said to have ascended from the world below to the gods?

Certainly I should, he replied.

The process, I said, is not the turning over of an oyster-shell, but the turning round of a soul from darkness visible to the upward path of truth and being.

Very true.

And should we not enquire what sort of knowledge has the power of effecting such a change?

Certainly.

What sort of knowledge is there which would draw the soul from becoming to being? And another consideration has just occurred to me: You will remember that our young men are to be warrior athletes?

Yes, that was said.

Then this new kind of knowledge must have another quality?

What quality?

Usefulness in war.

Yes, if possible.

There were two parts in our former scheme of education, were there not?

**What subjects of study in addition to those previously discussed?**

True.

There was gymnastic which presided over the growth and decay of the body, and may therefore be regarded as having to do with generation and corruption?

True.

Then that is not the knowledge which we are seeking to discover?

No.

But what do you say of music, for that also entered to a certain extent into our scheme?

That, he said, as you will remember, was the counterpart of gymnastic, and trained the guardians by the influences of habit, by harmony making them harmonious, and by rhythm rhythmical, although not giving them science;

and the words, whether fabulous or partly true, had kindred elements of rhythm and harmony in them. But musical knowledge was not of a kind which tended to that good which you are now seeking.

You are most accurate, I said, in your recollection; for in music there certainly was nothing of the kind. But what branch of knowledge is there, my dear friend, which is of the desired nature; since all the useful arts were reckoned mean by us?

Undoubtedly; and yet if music and gymnastic are excluded, and the arts are also excluded, what remains?

Well, I said, there may be nothing left; and then we shall have to take something which is of universal application.

What may that be?

A something which all arts and sciences and intelligences use in common, and which every one ought to learn among the elements of education.

What is that?

**Arithmetic.** The little matter of distinguishing one, two, and three —in a word, number and calculation:—do not all arts and sciences necessarily partake of them?

Yes.

Then the art of war partakes of them?

To be sure.

Then Palamedes, when he appears in the play, proves Agamemnon ridiculously unfit to be a general. Did you never remark how he declares that he had invented number, and had numbered and set in array the ranks of the army at Troy; which implies that they had never been numbered before, and Agamemnon must be supposed literally to have been incapable of counting his own feet—how could he if he was ignorant of number? And if that is true, what sort of general must he have been?

I should say a very strange one, certainly.

Must not a warrior, then, I said, in addition to his military skill, have a knowledge of arithmetic?

**Its value.** Certainly he must, if he is to have the least understanding of military tactics, or indeed, I should rather say, if he is to be a man at all.

I should like to know whether you have the same notion which I have of this study?

What is your notion?

It appears to me to be a study which leads naturally to reflection, and is of the kind which we are seeking, but has never been rightfully used; for it is really of use in drawing us towards being.

Will you explain your meaning? he said.

I will try, I said; and I wish you would consider and help me, and say 'yes' or 'no' when I attempt to distinguish in my own mind what branches of knowledge have this attracting power, in order that we may have clearer proof that arithmetic is one of them.

Explain, he said.

I mean to say that objects of sense are of two kinds; some of them do not invite thought because the sense is an adequate judge of them; while in the case of other objects there is a mistrust of the senses which imperatively demands enquiry.

You must be referring, he said, to the manner in which the senses are imposed upon by distance, and by painting in light and shade.

No, I said, that is not my meaning.

Then what is your meaning?

When speaking of uninviting objects, I mean those which do not pass from one sensation to another; inviting objects are those which give opposite sensations; in this latter case the sense coming upon the object, whether at a distance or near, gives no more vivid idea of anything in particular than of its opposite. An illustration will make my meaning clearer:— here are three fingers — a little finger, a second finger, and a middle finger.

Very good.

You may suppose that they are seen quite close And here comes the point.

What is that?

Each of them equally appears a finger, whether seen in the middle or at the extremity, whether white or black, or thick or thin — it makes no difference; a finger is a finger all the same. And in all these cases the ordinary soul is not compelled to ask of thought the question what is a finger? for the sight never intimates to her that a finger is other than a finger.

True.

And therefore, I said, there is nothing here which invites or excites intelligence.

There is not, he said.

But is this equally true of the greatness and smallness of the fingers? Can sight adequately perceive them? and is no difference made by the circumstance that one of the fingers is in the middle and another at the extremity? And in like manner does the touch adequately perceive the qualities of thickness or thinness, or softness or hardness? And so of the other senses; do they give perfect intimations of such matters? Is not their mode of operation rather on this wise — the sense which is concerned with the quality of hardness is necessarily concerned also with the quality of softness, and only intimates to the soul that the same thing is felt to be hard and soft?

Very true, he said.

And must not the soul be perplexed at this intimation of a hard which is also soft? What, again, is the meaning of light and heavy, if that which is light is also heavy, and that which is heavy, light?

Yes, he said, these intimations are very curious and have to be explained.

Yes, I said, and in these perplexities the soul naturally summons to her aid calculation and intelligence, that she may see whether the several objects announced are one or two.

True.

And if they turn out to be two, is not each of them one and different?

Certainly.

And if each is one, and both are two, she will conceive the two as in a state of division, for if they were undivided they could only be conceived of as one?

True.

The eye certainly did behold both small and great, not divided but confused.

Yes.

Whereas the thinking mind, intending to light up the chaos, was compelled to reverse the process, and look at small and great as separate and not confused.

Very true.

And was not this the beginning of the inquiry "What is great?" and "What is small?"

Exactly so.

Here began the distinction of the visible and the intelligible.

Most true.

And that is an illustration of my meaning in describing impressions as inviting to the intellect, or the reverse—the inviting impressions are simultaneous with opposite impressions.

I understand, he said, and agree with you.

And to which class do unity and number belong?

I do not know, he replied.

**Arithmetic a means for developing the sense for ideas.**

Think a little and you will see that what has preceded will supply the answer; for if simple unity, and that only, can be adequately perceived by the sight or by any other sense, then, as we were saying in the case of the fingers, there will be nothing to attract towards being; but when there is some contradiction always present, and one is the reverse of one and involves the conception of plurality, then thought begins to be aroused within, and the soul perplexed and wanting to arrive at a decision asks "What is absolute unity?" And this is the way in which the study of the one has a power of drawing and converting the mind to the contemplation of true being.

And surely, he said, this occurs notably when we look at one, for the same thing is seen by us as one and as infinite in multitude?

Yes, I said; and this being true of one must be equally true of all number?

Certainly.

And all arithmetic and calculation have to do with number?

Yes.

And they are conductors to truth?

Yes, in an eminent degree.

Then this is the sort of knowledge of which we are in search, having a double use, military and philosophical; for the man of war must learn the art of number that he may know how to array his troops, and the philosopher also, because he has to rise out of the sea of change and lay hold of true being, if he would be an arithmetician.

That is true.

And our guardian is both warrior and philosopher?

Certainly.

Then this is a kind of knowledge which legislation may fitly prescribe; and we must endeavour to persuade the principal men of our State to go and learn arithmetic, not as amateurs, but they must carry on the study until they see the nature of numbers in the mind only; nor again, in the spirit of merchants or traders, with a view to buying or selling, but for the sake of their military use, and of the soul herself; and because this will be the easiest way for her to pass from becoming to truth and being.

That is excellent, he said.

Yes, I said; and now having spoken of it, I must add how charming the science is! and in how many ways it conduces to our desired end, if pursued in the spirit of a philosopher, and not of a shopkeeper!

How do you mean?

I mean, as I was saying, that arithmetic has a very great and elevating effect, compelling the soul to reason about abstract number, and rebelling against the introduction of visible or tangible objects into the argument. You know how steadily the masters of the art repel and ridicule any one who attempts to divide absolute unity when he is calculating, and if you divide, they multiply, taking care that one shall continue one and not become lost in fractions.

That is very true.

Now, suppose a person were to say to them: O my friends, what are these wonderful numbers about which you are reasoning, in which, as you say, there is a unity such as you require, and each unit is equal, invariable, indivisible, — what would they answer?

They would answer, as I suppose, that they were speaking of those numbers which are only realized in thought.

Then you see that this knowledge may be truly called necessary, necessitating as it does the use of the pure intelligence in the attainment of pure truth?

Yes; that is a marked characteristic of it.

And have you further remarked, that those who have a

natural talent for calculation are generally quick at every other kind of knowledge; and even the dull, if they have had an arithmetical training, gain in quickness, if not in any other way?

Very true, he said.

And indeed, you will not easily find a more difficult study, and not many as difficult.

You will not.

And, for these reasons, arithmetic is a kind of knowledge in which the best natures should be trained, and which must not be given up.

I agree.

Let this then be made one of our subjects of education. And next, shall we enquire whether the kindred science also concerns us?

You mean geometry?

Geometry: — its practical and its theoretical value.

Yes.

Certainly, he said; that part of geometry which relates to war is clearly our concern; for in pitching a camp, or taking up a position, or closing or extending the lines of an army, or any other military manœuvre, whether in actual battle or on a march, there will be a great difference in a general, according as he is or is not a geometrician.

Yes, I said, but for that purpose a very little of either geometry or calculation will be enough; the question is rather of the higher and greater part of geometry, whether that tends towards the great end—I mean towards the vision of the idea of good; and thither, as I was saying, all things tend which compel the soul to turn her gaze towards that place, where is the full perfection of being, of which she ought, by all means, to attain the vision.

True, he said.

Then if geometry compels us to view being, it concerns us; if becoming only, it does not concern us?

Yes, that is what we assert.

Nevertheless, such a conception of the science is in flat contradiction to the ordinary language of geometricians, as will hardly be denied by those who have any acquaintance with their study: for they speak of squaring and applying and adding, having in view use only, and absurdly confuse the necessities of geometry with those of daily life; whereas knowledge is the real object of the whole science.

Certainly, he said.

Then must not a further admission be made?

What admission?

The admission that this knowledge at which geometry aims is of the eternal, and not of the perishing and transient.

That, he replied, may be readily allowed, and is true.

Then, my noble friend, geometry will draw the soul towards truth, and create the spirit of philosophy, and raise up that which is now unhappily allowed to fall down.

Nothing will be more effectual.

Then nothing should be more effectually enacted than that the inhabitants of your fair city should learn geometry. Moreover the science has indirect effects, which are not small.

Of what kind are they? he said.

**Its indirect advantages.** There are the military advantages of which you spoke, I said; and in all departments of study, as experience proves, any one who has studied geometry is infinitely quicker of apprehension than one who has not studied it.

Yes, he said, the difference between a geometrician and one who is not a geometrician is very great indeed.

Then shall we propose this as a second branch of knowledge which our youth will study?

Let us make the proposal, he replied.

**Astronomy: — its practical value.** And suppose we make astronomy the third — what do you say?

I am strongly inclined to it, he said; the observation of the seasons and of months and years is quite essential to husbandry and navigation, and not less essential to military tactics.

I am amused, I said, at your fear of the world, which makes you guard against the appearance of insisting upon useless studies; and I quite admit the difficulty of believing that in every man there is an eye of the soul which, when by other pursuits lost and dimmed, is by these purified and re-illumined; and is more precious far than ten thousand bodily eyes, for by this alone is truth seen. Now there are two classes of persons: one class who will agree with you and will take your words as a revelation; another class who have no understanding of them, and to whom they will naturally seem to be idle tales. And you had better decide at once with which of the two you are arguing; or, perhaps, you will say with neither, and that your chief aim in carrying on the argument is your own improvement; at the same time not grudging to others any benefit which they may derive.

I think that I should prefer to carry on the argument on my own behalf.

Then take a step backward, for we have gone wrong in the order of the sciences.

What was the mistake? he said.

After plane geometry, I said, we took solids in revolution, instead of taking solids in themselves; whereas after the second dimension the third, which is concerned with cubes and dimensions of depth, ought to have followed.

That is true, Socrates; but these subjects seem to be as yet hardly explored.

Why, yes, I said, and for two reasons:—in the first place, no government patronises them, which leads to a want of energy in the study of them, and they are difficult; in the second place, students cannot learn them unless they have a teacher. But then a teacher can hardly be found, and even if he could, as matters now stand, the students, who are very conceited, would not mind him. That, however, would be otherwise if the whole State patronised and honoured these studies; then they would find disciples, and there would be continuous and earnest search, and discoveries would be made; since even now, disregarded as they are by the world, and maimed of their fair proportions, and although none of their votaries can tell the use of them, still these studies force their way by their natural charm, and very likely they may emerge into light.

Yes, he said, there is a remarkable charm in them. But I do not clearly understand the change in the order. First you began with a geometry of plane surfaces?

Yes, I said.

And you placed astronomy next, and then you made a step backward?

Yes, and I have delayed you by my haste; the ludicrous state of solid geometry made me pass over this branch and go on to astronomy, or motion of solids.

True, he said.

Then assuming that the science now omitted would come into existence if encouraged by the State, let us go on to astronomy, which will be fourth.

The right order, he replied. And now, Socrates, as you rebuked the vulgar manner in which I praised astronomy before, my praise shall be more worthy of your own spirit. For every one, as I think, must feel that astronomy compels the soul to look upwards, and leads us from this world to another.

I am an exception then, for I should rather say that those who elevate astronomy into philosophy make us look downwards and not upwards.

What do you mean? he asked.

The theoretic value of astronomy.

You, I replied, have in your mind a sublime conception of how we know the things above. And I dare say that if a person were to throw his head back and study the fretted ceiling, you would still think that his mind was the percipient, and not his eyes. And you are very likely right, and I may be a simpleton: but, in my opinion, that knowledge only which is of being and of the unseen can make the soul look upwards, and whether a man gapes at the heavens or blinks on the ground, seeking to learn some particular of sense, I would deny that he can learn, for nothing of that sort is matter of science; his soul is looking, not upwards, but downwards, whether his way to knowledge is by water or by land, in whichever element he may lie on his back and float.

I acknowledge, he said, the justice of your rebuke. Still, I should like to ascertain how astronomy can be learned in any manner more conducive to that knowledge of which we speak?

I answered: The starry heaven which we behold is wrought upon a visible ground, and therefore, although the fairest and most perfect of visible things, must necessarily be deemed inferior far to the true motions of absolute swiftness and absolute slowness, which are relative to each other, and carry with them that which is contained in them, in the true number and in every true figure. Now, these are to be apprehended by reason and intelligence, but not by sight.

True, he replied.

The spangled heavens should be used as a pattern and with a view to that higher knowledge; their beauty is like the beauty of figures or pictures wrought by the hand of Dædalus, or some other great artist, which we may chance to behold; any geometrician who saw them would appreciate the exquisiteness of their workmanship, but he would never dream of thinking that in them he could find the true equal or the true double, or the truth of any other proportion.

No, he said, to think so would be ridiculous.

And will not a true astronomer have the same feeling when he looks at the movements of the stars? Will he not think that heaven and the things in heaven are framed by the Creator in the most perfect manner? But when he reflects that the proportions of night and day, or of both to the month, or of the month to the year, or of the other stars to these and to one another, are of the visible and material, he will never fall into the error of supposing that they are eternal and liable to no deviation — that would be monstrous; he will rather seek in every possible way to discover the truth of them.

I quite agree now that you tell me so.

Then, I said, in astronomy, as in geometry, we should use problems, and let the heavens alone if we desire to have a real knowledge of the science, and to train the reasoning faculty by the aid of it.

That, he said, is a work infinitely beyond our present astronomers.

Yes, I said; and there are many other things which must also have a similar extension given to them, if our legislation is to be of any use.

Can you tell me of any other suitable study?

No, he said, not without thinking.

Motion, I said, has many forms, and not one only; two of them are obvious enough; and there are others, as I imagine, which may be left to wiser heads than ours.

But where are the two?

There is a second, I said, which is the counterpart of the one already named.

And what may that be?

The science of music or of harmony.

The second, I said, would seem relatively to the ears to be what the first is to the eyes; for I conceive that as the eyes are designed to look up at the stars, so are the ears to hear harmonious motions, and these are sister sciences — as the Pythagoreans say, and we, Glaucon, agree with them?

Yes, he replied.

But this, I said, is a laborious study, and therefore we had better go and learn of them; and they will tell us whether there are any other applications of these sciences. At the same time, we must not lose sight of our own higher object.

What is that?

There is a perfection which all knowledge ought to reach, and which our pupils ought also to attain, and not to fall short of, as I was saying that they did in astronomy. For in the science of harmony, as you probably know, they are equally empirical. The sounds and consonances which they compare are those which are heard only, and their labour, like that of the astronomers, is in vain.

Yes, by heaven! he said; and 'tis as good as a play to hear them talking about their condensed notes, as they call them; they put their ears alongside of their neighbours as if to get a sound out of them — one set of them declaring that they catch an intermediate note and have found the least interval which should be the unit of measurement; the others maintaining the opposite theory that the two sounds have passed into the same — either party setting their ears before their understanding.

You mean, I said, those gentlemen who tease and torture the strings and rack them on the pegs of the instrument: I might carry on the metaphor and speak after their manner of the blows which the plectrum gives, and make accusations against the strings, both of backwardness and forwardness to sound; but this would be tedious, and therefore I will only say that these are not the men, but that I am speaking of the Pythagoreans, of whom I was just now proposing to enquire about harmony. For they too are in error, like the astronomers; they investigate the numbers of the harmonies which are heard, but they never attain to problems—that is to say, they never reach the natural harmonies of number, or reflect why some numbers are harmonious and others not.

That, he said, is a thing of more than mortal knowledge.

A thing, I replied, which I would rather call useful; that is, if pursued with a view to the beautiful and good; but if pursued in any other spirit, useless.

Very true, he said.

Now, when all these studies reach the point of intercommunion and connection with one another, and come to be considered in their mutual affinities, then, I think, but not till then, will the pursuit of them have a value for our objects; otherwise they are useless.

I suspect so; but you are speaking, Socrates, of a vast work.

These four studies form a prelude to the study of dialectic.

What do you mean? I said; the prelude or what? Do you not know that all this is but the prelude to the actual strain which we have to learn? For you surely would not regard the skilled mathematician as a dialectician?

Assuredly not, he said; I have hardly ever known a mathematician who was capable of reasoning.

But do you imagine that men who are unable to give and take a reason will have the knowledge which we require of them?

Neither can this be said any more than the other.

And so, Glaucon, we have at last arrived at dialectic. This is that strain which is of the intellect only, but which the faculty of sight will nevertheless be found to imitate; for sight, as you may remember, was finally imagined by us to behold real animals and the stars, and last of all the sun himself. And so with dialectic; when a person starts on the discovery of the absolute by the light of reason only, and without any assistance of sense, if he perseveres by pure intelligence, he attains at last to the idea of good, and finds himself at the end of the intellectual world, as in the other case at the end of the visible.

Exactly, he said.

Then this is the progress which you call dialectic?

True.

But the release of the prisoners from chains, and their translation from the shadows to the images and to the light, and the ascent from the underground den to the sun, while their eyes are weak and in his presence are vainly trying to look on animals and plants and the light of the sun, but are able to look upon the divine images in the water, which are the shadows of true existence (not shadows of images cast by a light of fire, which compared with the sun is only an image) — this power of elevating the highest principle in the soul to the contemplation of that which is best in existence, with which we may compare the raising of the most luminous of the senses to the sight of that which is brightest in the visible world — this power is given, as I was saying, by all that study and pursuit of the arts which has been described.

**The nature and the divisions of dialectic.**

I agree in what you are saying, he replied, which may be hard to believe, yet, from another point of view, is harder still to deny. But whether denied or not, let us assume all this, which may be the theme of many another discussion; and now proceed at once from the prelude or preamble to the chief strain, and describe that in like manner. Say, then, what is the nature and what are the divisions of dialectic, and what are the paths which lead thither; for these paths will also lead to our final rest.

Dear Glaucon, I said, you will not be able to follow me here, though I would do my best, and you should behold not an image only but the absolute truth, according to my notion. Although I am not confident that I could tell you the exact truth, I am certain that you would behold something like the truth.

Doubtless, he replied.

But I must add, that the power of dialectic alone can reveal this, and only to one who is a disciple of the previous sciences.

Of that assertion you may be as certain as of the last.

**The previous arts and sciences are partially concerned with opinion;**

And certainly no one will argue that there is any other method or way of comprehending all true existence; for the arts in general are concerned with the wants or opinions of men, or are cultivated for the sake of production and construction, or for the care of such productions and constructions; and as to the mathematical arts which, as we were saying, have some apprehension of true being — geometry and the like — they only dream about being, but never can they behold the waking reality so long as they leave the hypotheses which they use unexamined, and are unable to give an account of them. For when a man knows not his own first principle, and when the conclusion and intermediate steps are also constructed out of he knows not what, how can he imagine that such a conventional statement will ever become science?

Impossible, he said.

Then dialectic, and dialectic alone, goes directly to the first principle and is the only science which does away with hypotheses in order to make certain of them; the eye of the soul, which is literally buried in an outlandish slough, is by her taught to look upwards; and she uses as handmaids, in the work of conversion, the sciences which we have been discussing. Custom terms them sciences, but they ought to have some other name, implying greater clearness than opinion and less clearness than science: and this, in our previous sketch, was called understanding. But there is no use in our disputing about names when we have realities of such importance to consider.

**dialectic, alone, deals with ideas, with truth.**

No, he said; any name will do which expresses the thought clearly.

At any rate, we are satisfied, as before, to have four divisions; two for intellect and two for opinion, and to call the first division science, the second understanding, the third belief, and the fourth knowledge of shadows, opinion being concerned with becoming, and intellect with being; and so to make a proportion —

As being : becoming :: pure intellect : opinion.
As science : belief :: understanding : knowledge of shadows.

But let us leave the further distribution and division of the objects of opinion and of intellect, which will be a long enquiry, many times longer than this has been.

As far as I understand, he said, I agree.

And do you also agree, I said, in describing the dialectician as one who has a conception of the essence of each thing? And may he who is unable to acquire and impart this conception, in whatever degree he fails, in that degree also be said to fail in intelligence? Will you admit that?

Yes, he said; how can I deny it?

And you would say the same of the conception of the good? Until a person is able to abstract and define the idea of good, and unless he can run the gauntlet of all objections, and is ready to disprove them, not by appeals to opinion, but to true existence, never faltering at any step of the argument — unless he can do all this, you would say that he knows neither absolute good nor any other good; he apprehends only a shadow, which is given by opinion and not by knowledge; — dreaming and slumbering in this life, before he is well awake here, he arrives at the world below, and has his final quietus.

In all that I should most certainly agree with you.

Dialectic forms the culmination of the education of the guardian class — of philosophers.

And surely you would not have the children of your ideal State, whom you are nurturing and educating — if the ideal ever becomes a reality — you would not allow the future rulers to be like posts, having no reason in them, and yet to be set in authority over the highest matters?

Certainly not.

Then you will enact that they shall have such an education as will enable them to attain the greatest skill in asking and answering questions?

Yes, he said, I will, with your help.

Dialectic, then, as you will agree, is the coping-stone of the sciences, and is placed over them; no other science can be placed higher — the nature of knowledge can no further go?

I agree, he said.

But to whom we are to assign these studies, and in what way they are to be assigned, is a question which remains to be considered.

Yes, plainly.

You remember, I said, how the rulers were chosen before?

Certainly, he said.

The same natures must still be chosen, and the preference again given to the surest and the bravest, and, if possible, to the fairest; and, having noble and manly tempers, they should also have the natural gifts which will facilitate their education.

And what are they?

Such gifts as keenness and ready powers of acquisition; for the mind more often faints from the severity of study than from the severity of gymnastics: the toil is more entirely the mind's own, and is not shared with the body.

Very true, he replied.

Further, he of whom we are in search should have a good memory, and be an unwearied solid man who is a lover of labour in any line, or he will never be able to undergo the double toil and trouble of body and mind.

Certainly, he said; he must have natural gifts.

The mistake at present is, that those who study philosophy have no vocation, and this, as I was before saying, is the reason why she has fallen into disrepute: her true sons should study her and not bastards.

How do you mean?

In the first place, her votary should not have a lame or one-legged industry — I mean, that he should not be half industrious and half idle: as, for example, when a man is a lover of gymnastic and hunting, and all other bodily exercises, but a hater rather than a lover of the labour of learning or hearing or enquiring. Or he may have the other sort of lameness, and the love of labour may take an opposite form, and the man may be lame in another way.

Certainly, he said.

And as to truth, I said, is not a soul equally to be deemed halt and lame which hates voluntary falsehood and is extremely indignant at himself and others when they tell lies, but is patient of involuntary falsehood, and does not mind wallowing like a swinish beast in the mire of ignorance, and has no shame at being detected?

To be sure.

And, again, as to temperance and courage and magnanimity, and every other virtue, should they not discern between the ways of the true son and of the bastard? for wherever States and individuals fail in discrimination, they unconsciously make a friend or perhaps a ruler of one who is in a figure a lame man or a bastard, from a defect in some one of these qualities.

That is very true, he said.

All these things, then, will have to be carefully considered, and those whom we introduce to this vast system of education and training must be sound in limb and mind, and then justice herself will have nothing to say against us, and we shall be the saviours of the State; but, if our pupils are men of another stamp, the reverse will happen, and we shall pour a still greater flood of ridicule on philosophy.

That would be discreditable.

Yes, certainly, I said; and yet, perhaps, in thus turning jest into earnest I am equally ridiculous.

In what respect?

I had forgotten, I said, that we were not in earnest, and spoke with too much excitement. For when I saw philosophy trampled under foot of men I could not help feeling a sort of indignation at the authors of her disgrace: and my anger made me vehement.

Indeed! I did not observe that you were more vehement than was right.

The proper period for the respective stages of education.

But I felt that I was. And now let me remind you that, although in our former selection we chose old men, we must not do so in this. Solon was under a delusion when he said that a man as he is growing older may learn many things — for he can no more learn than he can run; youth is the time of toil.

Very true.

Education of children;

And, therefore, calculation and geometry and all the other elements of instruction, which are a preparation for dialectic, should be presented to the mind in childhood; not, however, under any notion of forcing them.

Why not?

Because a freeman ought to be a freeman in the acquisition of knowledge. Bodily exercise, when compulsory, does no harm; but knowledge which is acquired under compulsion has no hold on the mind.

Very true.

Then, my good friend, I said, do not use compulsion, but let early education be a sort of amusement; you will then be better able to find out the natural bent.

You are right there.

Do you remember our saying that the children, too,

must be taken to see the battle on horseback; and that if there were no danger they might be led close up and, like young hounds, have a taste of blood given them?

Yes, I remember.

The same practice may be followed, I said, in other things — labours, lessons, dangers — and he who is most at home in all of them ought to be enrolled in a select number.

At what age?

At the age when the necessary gymnastics are over: the period whether of two or three years which passes in this sort of training is useless for any other purpose; for sleep and exercise are unpropitious to learning; and the trial of who is first in gymnastic exercises is one of the most important tests to which they are subjected.

Certainly, he replied.

After that time those who are selected from the class of twenty years old will be promoted to higher honour, and the sciences which they learned without any order in their early education will now be brought together, and they will be able to see the natural relationship of them to one another and to true being.

**after twenty years of age, devoted to study of the sciences.**

Yes, he said, that is the only kind of knowledge which is everlasting.

Yes, I said; and the capacity for such knowledge is the great criterion of dialectical talent: the comprehensive mind is always the dialectical.

I agree with you, he said.

These, I said, are the points which you must consider; and those who have most of this comprehension, and who are most steadfast in their learning, and in their military and other public duties, when they arrive at the age of thirty will have to be chosen by you out of the select class, and elevated to higher honour; and you will have to prove them by the help of dialectic, in order to learn which of them is able to give up the use of sight and other senses, and in company with truth to attain absolute being. And here, my friend, great caution is required.

**Dialectic studied from thirty to thirty-five.**

Why great caution?

Do you not remark, I said, how great the evil is which dialectic has introduced?

What evil? he said.

The lawlessness of which the professors of the art are full.

Very true, he said.

Do you think that there is anything unnatural in their case? or may I ask you to make some allowance for them?

What sort of allowance?

I want you, I said, by way of parallel, to imagine a supposititious son who is brought up in great wealth; he is one of a large and numerous family, and has many flatterers. When grown up he learns that his alleged are not his real parents; but who the real are he is unable to discover. Can you guess how he will be likely to behave towards his flatterers and his supposed parents, first of all during the period when he is ignorant of the false relation, and then again when he knows? Or shall I guess for you?

If you please.

Then I guess, that while he is ignorant of the truth he will be likely to honour his father and his mother and his supposed relations more than the flatterers; he will be less willing to see them in want, or to do any violence to them, or say anything evil of them, and he will be less willing to disobey them in important matters.

He will.

But when he has made the discovery, I should imagine that he would diminish his honour and regard for them, and would become more devoted to the flatterers; their influence over him would greatly increase; he would now live after their ways, and openly associate with them, and, unless he were of an unusually good disposition, he would think no more of his parents or other supposed friends.

Well, all that is extremely probable. But how is the image applicable to the disciples of philosophy?

In this way: you know that there are certain principles about justice and honour, which were taught us in childhood, and under their parental authority we have been brought up, obeying and valuing them.

That is true.

There are also opposite maxims and habits of pleasure which flatter and attract our soul, but do not influence those who have any sense of right, and they continue to obey and value the maxims of their fathers.

True.

Now, when a man is in this state, and the questioning spirit asks what is fair or honourable, and he answers as the legislator has taught him, and then arguments come again and again and refute his words, and he is driven into believing that nothing is fair any more than foul, or just and good any more than the opposite, and the same of all his time-honoured notions, do you think that he will still obey and value them?

Impossible.

And when he ceases to think them honourable and natural as heretofore, and he fails to discover the true, can he be expected to pursue any life other than that which flatters his desires?

He cannot.

And from being a keeper of the law he is converted into a breaker of it?

Unquestionably.

Now all this is very natural in students of philosophy such as I have described, and also, as I was just now saying, most excusable.

Yes, he said; and, I may add, pitiable.

Therefore, that your feelings may not be moved to pity about our citizens who are thirty years of age, every care must be taken in introducing them to dialectic.

Certainly.

**Danger in too early study of dialectic.**

There is a danger lest they should taste the dear delight too early; for young men, as you may have observed, when they first get the taste in their mouths, argue for amusement, and are always contradicting and refuting others in imitation of those who refute them; like puppy-dogs, they delight to tear and pull at all who come near them.

Yes, he said, there is nothing of which they are fonder.

And when they have made many conquests and received defeats at the hands of many, they violently and speedily get into a way of not believing anything that they believed before, and hence, not only they, but philosophy generally, has a bad name with the rest of the world.

Too true, he said.

But when a man begins to get older, he will no longer be guilty of such insanity; he will imitate the dialectician who is seeking for truth, and not the eristic, who is contradicting for the sake of amusement; and the greater moderation of his character will increase instead of diminishing the honour of the pursuit.

Very true, he said.

And did we not make special provision for this, when we said that the disciples of philosophy were to be orderly and steadfast, not, as now, any chance aspirant or intruder?

Very true.

Suppose, I said, that the study of philosophy be continued diligently and earnestly and exclusively for twice the number of years which were passed in bodily exercise — will that be enough?

Would you say six or four years? he asked.

A period of active political service should follow the training in dialectic.

Say five years, I replied; at the end of that time they must be sent down into the den and compelled to hold any military or other office which young men are qualified to hold: in this way they will get their experience of life, and there will be an opportunity of trying whether, when they are drawn all manner of ways by temptation, they will stand firm or flinch.

And how long is this stage of their lives to last?

This to last until the fiftieth year of age.

Fifteen years, I answered; and when they have reached fifty years of age, then let those who still survive and have distinguished themselves in every deed and in all knowledge come at last to their consummation: the time has now arrived at which they must raise the eye of the soul to the universal light which lightens all things, and behold the absolute good; for that is the pattern according to which they are to order the State and the lives of individuals, and the remainder of their own lives also, making philosophy their chief pursuit; but, when their turn comes, toiling also at politics and ruling for the public good, not as if they were doing some great thing, but of necessity; and when they have brought up others like themselves and left them in their place to be governors of the State, then they will depart to the Islands of the Blest and dwell there; and the city will give them public memorials and sacrifices and honour them, if the Pythian oracle consent, as demigods, and at any rate as blessed and divine.

You are a sculptor, Socrates, and have made statues of our governors quite faultless.

Yes, I said, Glaucon, and of our governesses too; for you must not suppose that what I have been saying applies to men only and not to women as far as their natures can go.

There you are right, he said, if, as we described, they are to have all things in common with the men.

Well, I said, and you would agree (would you not?) that what has been said about the State and the government is not a mere dream, and although difficult not impossible, but only possible in the way which has been supposed; that is to say, when the true philosopher kings, one or more of them, are born in a State, despising the honours of this present world which they deem mean and worthless, above all esteeming right and the honour that springs from right, and regarding justice as the greatest and most necessary of all things, whose ministers they are, and whose principles will be exalted by them when they set in order their own city?

How will they proceed?

**The ideal state to be realized through education.**

They will begin by sending out into the country all the inhabitants of the city who are more than ten years old, and will take possession of their children, who will be unaffected by the habits of their parents; they will then train them in their own habits and laws, that is to say, in those which we have given them: and in this way the State and constitution of which we were speaking will soonest and most easily succeed, and the nation which has such a constitution will be most benefited.

Yes, that will be the best way. And I think, Socrates, that you have very well described how, if ever, such a constitution might come into being.

And have we not said enough of the State, and of the man who corresponds to the State, for there is no difficulty in seeing how we shall describe him?

There is no difficulty, he replied, and I say with you, enough.

## *Selections from the Laws of Plato*

PERSONS OF THE DIALOGUE

AN ATHENIAN STRANGER. CLEINIAS, a Cretan.
MEGILLUS, a Lacedæmonian.

### BOOK II

* * * * * * *

(653–660.)

ATH. Let me once more recall our doctrine of right education; which, if I am not mistaken, depends on the due regulations of convivial intercourse.

CLE. You talk rather grandly.

ATH. Pleasure and pain I maintain to be the first perceptions of children, and I say that they are the forms under which virtue and vice are originally present to them. As to wisdom and true and fixed opinions, happy is the man who acquires them, even when declining in years; and he who possesses them, and the blessings which are contained in them, is a perfect man. Now, I mean by education that training which is given by suitable habits to the first instincts of virtue in children; — when pleasure, and friendship, and pain, and hatred, are rightly implanted in souls not yet capable of understanding the nature of them, and who find them, after they have attained reason, to be in harmony with her. This harmony of the soul, when perfected, is virtue; but the particular training in respect to pleasure and pain, which leads you always to hate what you ought to hate, and love what you ought to love, from the beginning to the end, may be separated off; and, in my view, will be rightly called education.

Nature of education.

CLE. I think, Stranger, that you are quite right in all that you have said and are saying about education.

ATH. I am glad to hear that you agree with me; for, indeed, the true discipline of pleasure and pain which, when rightly ordered, is a principle of education, has been often relaxed and corrupted in human life. And the Gods, pitying the toils which our race is born to undergo, have appointed holy festivals, in which men alternate rest with labour; and have given them the Muses and Apollo the leader of the Muses, and Dionysus, to be partners in their revels, that they may improve what education they have, at the festivals of the Gods and by their aid. I should like to know whether a common saying is true to nature or not. For what men say is that the young of all creatures cannot be quiet in their bodies or in their voices; they are always wanting to move, and cry out; at one time leaping and skipping, and overflowing with sportiveness and delight at something, and then again uttering all sorts of cries. But, whereas other animals have no perception of order or disorder in their movements, that is, of rhythm or harmony, as they are called, to us, the Gods, who, as we say, have been appointed to be our partners in the dance, have given the pleasurable sense of harmony and rhythm; and so they stir us into life, and we follow them and join hands with one another in dances and songs; and these they call choruses, which is a term naturally expressive of cheerfulness. Shall we begin, then, with the acknowledgment that education is first given through Apollo and the Muses? What do you say?

**Beginnings of education found in the sense for harmony.**

CLE. I assent.

ATH. And the uneducated is he who has not been trained in the chorus, and the educated is he who has been well trained?

CLE. Certainly.

ATH. And the chorus is made up of two parts, dance and song?

CLE. True.

ATH. Then he who is well educated will be able to sing and dance well?

**Music and gymnastic as the subject-matter of education.**

CLE. I suppose that he will.

ATH. Let us see; what are we saying?

CLE. What?

ATH. He sings well and dances well; now must we add that he sings what is good and dances what is good?

CLE. Let us make the addition.

ATH. We will suppose that he knows the good to be good, and the bad to be bad, and makes use of them accordingly: which now is the better trained in dancing and music; — he who is able to move his body and to use his voice in what is understood to be the right manner, but has no delight in good or hatred of evil; or he who is incorrect in gesture and voice, but is right in his sense of pleasure and pain, and welcomes what is good, and is offended at what is evil?

CLE. There is a great difference, Stranger, in the two kinds of education.

ATH. If we know what is good in song and dance, then we know also who is rightly educated and who is uneducated; but if not, then we certainly shall not know wherein lies the safeguard of education, and whether there is any or not.

CLE. True.

Character of the music and gymnastic determine the character of the education.

ATH. Let us follow the scent like hounds, and go in pursuit of beauty of figure, and melody, and song, and dance; if these escape us, there will be no use in talking about true education, whether Hellenic or barbarian.

CLE. Yes.

ATH. And what is beauty of figure, or beautiful melody? When a manly soul is in trouble, and when a cowardly soul is in a similar case, are they likely to use the same figures and gestures, or to give utterance to the same sounds?

CLE. How can they, when the very colours of their faces differ?

ATH. Good, my friend; I may observe, however, in passing, that in music there certainly are figures and there are melodies: and music is concerned with harmony and rhythm, so that you may speak of a melody or figure having rhythm or harmony; the term is correct enough, but you cannot speak correctly, as the masters of choruses have a way of talking metaphorically of the 'colour' of a melody or figure, although you can speak of the melodies or figures of the brave and the coward, praising the one and censuring the other. And not to be tedious, the figures and melodies which are expressive of virtue of soul or body, or of images of virtue, are without exception good, and those which are expressive of vice are the reverse of good.

CLE. You are right in calling upon us to make that division.

ATH. But are all of us equally delighted with every sort of dance?

CLE. Far otherwise.

ATH. And what, then, is the cause of error or division among us? Are beautiful things not the same to us all, or are they the same in themselves, but not in our opinion of them? For no one will admit that forms of vice in the dance are more beautiful than forms of virtue, or that he himself delights in the forms of vice, and others in a muse of another character. And yet most persons say, that the excellence of music is to give pleasure to our souls. But this is intolerable and blasphemous; there is, however, a more plausible account of the delusion.

CLE. What is that?

ATH. There is a way of making our likes and dislikes the criterion of excellence. Choric movements are imitations of manners occurring in various actions, chances, characters,—each particular is imitated, and those to whom the words, or songs, or dances are suited, either by nature or habit or both, cannot help feeling pleasure in them and applauding them, and calling them beautiful. But those whose natures, or ways, or habits are unsuited to them, cannot delight in them or applaud them, and they call them base. There are others, again, whose natures are right and their habits wrong, or whose habits are right and their natures wrong, and they praise one thing, but are pleased at another. For they say that certain things are pleasant, but not good. And in the presence of those whom they think wise, they are ashamed of dancing and singing in the baser manner, or of deliberately lending their countenance to such proceedings; and yet, they have a secret pleasure in them.

CLE. Very true.

ATH. And is any harm done to the lover of vicious dances or songs, or any good done to the approver of the opposite sort of pleasure?

CLE. I think that there is.

**They are to be determined by public ends, not by personal choice.**

ATH. 'I think' is not the word, but I would say, rather, 'I am certain.' For must they not have the same effect as when a man is in evil company, whom he likes and approves rather than dislikes, and only censures them playfully as if he has a suspicion of his own badness? In that case, he who takes pleasure in them will surely become like those in whom he takes pleasure, even though he be ashamed to praise them. And what greater good or evil can any destiny ever make us undergo?

CLE. I know of none.

ATH. Then in a city which has or in future ages is to have good laws, and where there is a due regard to the instruction and amusement which the Muses give, can we suppose that the poets are to be allowed to teach in the dance anything which the poet himself likes, in the way of rhythm, or melody, or words, to the children and youth of well-conditioned parents? Is he to train his choruses as he pleases, without reference to virtue or vice?

CLE. That is surely quite unreasonable, and is not to be thought of.

ATH. And yet he may do this in almost any state with the exception of Egypt.

CLE. And what are the laws about music and dancing in Egypt?

Static ideals of Egyptian education praised as a model.

ATH. You will wonder when I tell you: Long ago they appear to have recognised the very principle of which we are now speaking — that their young citizens must be habituated to forms and strains of virtue. These they fixed, and exhibited the patterns of them in their temples; and no painter or artist is allowed to innovate upon them, or to leave the traditional forms and invent new ones. To this day, no alteration is allowed either in these arts, or in music at all. And you will find that their works of art are painted or moulded in the same forms which they had ten thousand years ago; — this is literally true and no exaggeration, — their ancient paintings and sculptures are not a whit better or worse than the work of to-day, but are made with just the same skill.

CLE. How extraordinary!

ATH. I should rather say, how wise and worthy of a great legislator! I know that other things in Egypt are not so good. But what I am telling you about music is true and deserving of consideration, because showing that a lawgiver may institute melodies which have a natural truth and correctness without any fear of failure. To do this, however, must be the work of God, or of a divine person; in Egypt they have a tradition that their ancient chants are the composition of the Goddess Isis. And therefore, as I was saying, if a person can only find in any way the natural melodies, he may confidently embody them in a fixed and legal form. For the love of novelty which arises out of pleasure in the new and weariness of the old, has not strength enough to vitiate the consecrated song and dance, under the plea that they have become antiquated. At any rate, they are far from being antiquated in Egypt.

CLE. Your arguments seem to prove your point.

ATH. May not the true use of music and choral festivities be described as follows: we rejoice when we think that we prosper, and again we think that we prosper when we rejoice? **Use of music and the dance.**

CLE. Exactly.

ATH. And when rejoicing is our good fortune, we are unable to be still?

CLE. True.

ATH. Our young men break forth into dancing and singing, and we who are their elders deem that we are fulfilling our part in life when we look on at them. Having lost the agility of youth, we delight in their sports and merry-making; because we love to think of our former selves, and gladly institute contests for those who are able to awaken in us the memory of what we once were.

CLE. Very true.

ATH. People say that we ought to regard him as the wisest of men, and the winner of the palm, who gives us the greatest amount of pleasure and mirth. For when mirth is to be the order of the day, he ought to be honoured most, and, as I was saying, bear the palm, who gives most mirth to the greatest number. Now I want to know whether this is a true way of speaking or of acting?

CLE. Possibly.

ATH. But, my dear friend, let us distinguish between different cases, and not be hasty in forming a judgment: One way of considering the question will be to imagine a festival at which there are entertainments of all sorts, including gymnastic, musical, or equestrian contests: the citizens are assembled, and proclamation is made that any **How the criterion of excellencies are to be determined.**

one who likes may enter the lists, and that he is to bear the palm who gives the most pleasure to the spectators — there is to be no regulation about the manner how; but he who is most successful in giving pleasure is to be crowned victor, and is deemed to be the pleasantest of the candidates: What is likely to be the result of such a proclamation?

CLE. In what respect?

ATH. There would be various exhibitions: the Homeric bard would exhibit a rhapsody, another a performance on the lute; one would have a tragedy, and another a comedy. Nor would there be anything astonishing in some one imagining that he could gain the prize by exhibiting a puppet-show. Suppose these competitors to meet, and not these only, but innumerable others as well, can you tell me who ought to be the victor?

CLE. I do not see how I can answer you, unless I myself hear the several competitors; the question is absurd.

ATH. Well, then, if neither of you can answer, shall I answer this question which you deem absurd?

CLE. By all means.

ATH. If very small children are to determine the question, they will decide for the puppet-show?

CLE. Of course.

ATH. The older children will be advocates of comedy; educated women, and young men, and people in general, will favour tragedy.

CLE. Very likely.

ATH. And I believe that we old men would have the greatest pleasure in hearing a rhapsodist recite well the Iliad and Odyssey, or one of the Hesiodic poems, and would award the victory to him? But, who would really be the victor? that is the question.

CLE. Yes.

Censors of music should lead, not follow, public opinion.

ATH. Clearly you and I will be compelled to reply that the old men are right; their way of thinking is far better than any other which now prevails in the world.

CLE. Certainly.

ATH. Thus far I too should agree with the many, that the excellence of music is to be measured by pleasure. But the pleasure must not be that of chance persons; the fairest music is that which delights the best and best educated, and especially that which delights the one man who is pre-eminent in virtue and education. And therefore the judges will require virtue — they must possess wisdom and also courage; for the true judge ought not to learn from the theatre, nor ought he to be panic-stricken at the clamour of the many and his own incapacity; nor again, knowing the truth, ought he through cowardice and unmanliness carelessly to deliver a lying judgment, out of the very same lips which have just appealed to the Gods before he judged. He is sitting not as the disciple of the theatre, but, in his proper place, as their instructor, and he ought to be the enemy of all pandering to the pleasure of the spectators. The ancient and common custom of Hellas, which still prevails in Italy and Sicily, did certainly leave the judgment to the body of spectators, who determined the victor by the show of hands; yet this custom has been the destruction of the poets; — for they are now in the habit of composing with a view to please the bad taste of their judges, and the result is that the spectators instruct themselves, which has been the ruin of the theatre; — when they ought to be having characters put before them better than their own, and so receiving a higher pleasure, they themselves make them inferior. Now what is the inference to be deduced from all this? Shall I tell you?

CLE. What?

**Aims of education determined by the experience of the race.**

ATH. The inference at which we arrive for the third or fourth time is, that education is the constraining and directing of youth towards that right reason, which the law affirms, and which the experience of the best of our elders has agreed to be truly right. In order, then, that the soul of the child may not be habituated to feel joy and sorrow in a manner at variance with the law, and those who obey the law, but may rather follow the law and rejoice and sorrow at the same things as the aged — in order, I say, to produce this effect, songs appear to have been invented, which are really charms, and are designed to implant that harmony of which we speak. And, because the mind of the child is incapable of enduring serious training, they are called plays or songs, and are performed in play; just as when men are sick and ailing in their bodies, their attendants give them wholesome diet in pleasant meats and drinks, but unwholesome diet in disagreeable things, in order that they may learn, as they ought, to like the one, and to dislike the other. And similarly the true legislator will persuade, and, if he cannot persuade, will compel the poet to express, as he ought, by fair and noble words, in his rhythms, the figures, and in his melodies, the music of temperate and brave and in every way good men. . . . (672–673.) The whole choral art is also in our view the whole of education; and of this art, rhythms and harmonies, having to do with the voice, form a part.

**Education identical with music, the dance, and gymnastic.**

CLE. Yes.

ATH. And the movement of the body and the movement of the voice have a common form which is rhythm, but they differ, in that the one is gesture, and the other song.

CLE. Most true.

ATH. And the sound of the voice which reaches and educates the soul, we have ventured to term music.

CLE. True.

ATH. And the movement of the body, which, when regarded as an amusement, we termed dancing; when pursued with a view to the improvement of the body, according to rules of art, may be called gymnastic.

CLE. Quite true.

ATH. Music, which was one half of the choral art, may be said to have been completely discussed. Shall we proceed to the other half or not? What would you like?

CLE. My good friend, when you are talking with a Cretan and Lacedæmonian, and we have discussed music and not gymnastic, what answer are either of us likely to make to you?

ATH. That question is pretty much of an answer; and I understand and accept what you say both as an answer, and also as a command to proceed with gymnastic.

CLE. You quite understand me; do as you say.

ATH. I will; and there will be small difficulty in speaking intelligibly to you about a subject with which both of you are far more familiar than with music.

CLE. That is very true.

ATH. Is not the origin of gymnastics, too, to be sought in the tendency to rapid motion which exists in all animals; man, as we were saying, having attained the sense of rhythm, created and invented dancing; and melody arousing and awakening rhythm, both united formed the choral art?

**Origin of gymnastic.**

CLE. Very true.

* * * * * * *

### BOOK VII

* * * * * * *

(793-823.)

ATH. Up to the age of three years, whether of boy or girl, if a person strictly carries out our previous regulations and makes them a principal aim, he will do much for the advantage of the young creatures. But at three, four, five, and six years the childish nature will require sports; now is the time to get rid of self-will in him, punishing him, not so as to disgrace him. As we were saying about slaves, that we ought neither to punish them in hot blood or so as to anger them, nor yet to leave them unpunished lest they become self-willed, a like rule is to be observed in the case of the free-born. Children at that age have certain natural modes of amusement which they find out for themselves when they meet. And all the children who are between the ages of three and six ought to meet at the temples of the villages, several families of a village uniting on one spot, and the nurses seeing that the children behave properly and orderly, — they themselves and their whole company being under the care of one of the twelve women aforesaid annually appointed out of their number by the guardians of the law to inspect and order each company. Let the twelve be appointed by the women who have authority over marriage, one out of each tribe and all of the same age; and when appointed, let them hold office and go to the temples every day, punishing all offenders, male or female, who are slaves or strangers, by the help of some of the public servants; but if any citizen disputes the punishment, let

**Training of children from three to six.**

her bring him before the wardens of the city; or, if there be no dispute, let her punish him herself. After the age of six years the time has arrived for the separation of the sexes, — let boys live with boys, and girls in like manner with girls. Now they must begin to learn — the boys going to teachers of horsemanship and the use of the bow, the javelin, and sling; and if they do not object, let women also go to learn if not to practise; above all, they ought to know the use of arms; for I may note, that the practice which now almost universally prevails is due to ignorance.

**Instruction to begin at the sixth year.**

CLE. In what respect?

ATH. In this respect, that the right and left hand are supposed to differ by nature when we use them; whereas no difference is found in the use of the feet and the lower limbs; but in the use of the hands we are in a manner lame, by reason of the folly of nurses and mothers; for although our several limbs are by nature balanced, we create a difference in them by bad habit. In some cases this is of no consequence, as, for example, when we hold the lyre in the left hand, and the plectrum in the right, but it is downright folly to make the same distinction in other cases. The custom of the Scythians proves our error; for they not only hold the bow from them with the left hand and draw the arrow to them with their right, but use either hand for both purposes. And there are many similar examples in charioteering and other things, from which we may learn that those who make the left side weaker than the right act contrary to nature. In the case of the plectrum, which is of horn only, and similar instruments, as I was saying, it is of no consequence, but makes a great difference, and may be of very great importance to the warrior who has to use iron weapons, bows and javelins, and the like; above all, when in heavy armour, he has to fight against heavy armour. And there is a very great difference between one who has learnt and one who has not, and between one who has been trained in gymnastic exercises and one who has not been. For as he who is perfectly skilled in the Pancratium or boxing or wrestling, is not unable to fight from his left side, and does not limp and draggle in confusion when his opponent makes him

**Training of the hands. Ambi-dexterity.**

change his position, so in heavy-armed fighting, and in all other things, if I am not mistaken, the like holds — he who has these double powers of attack and defence ought not in any case to leave them either unused or untrained; and if a person had the nature of Geryon[1] or Briareus he ought to be able with his hundred hands to throw a hundred darts. Now, the rulers, male and female, should see to all these things; the women superintending the nursing and amusements of the children, and the men superintending their education, that all of them, boys and girls alike, may be sound in hand and foot, and may not, if they can help, spoil the gifts of nature by bad habits.

The two branches of education,— music and gymnastic.

Education has two branches, — one of gymnastic, which is concerned with the body, and the other of music, which is designed for the improvement of the soul. And gymnastic has also two parts — dancing and wrestling; and one sort of dancing imitates musical recitation, and aims at preserving dignity and freedom; the other aims at producing health, agility, and beauty of the limbs and parts of the body, giving the proper flexion and extension to each of them, diffusing and accompanying the harmonious motion of the dance everywhere. As regards wrestling, the tricks which Antæus and Cercyon devised in their systems out of a vain spirit of competition, or the tricks of boxing which Epeius or Amycus invented, are useless for war, and do not deserve to have much said about them; but the art of wrestling erect and keeping free the neck and hands and sides, working with energy and constancy, with a composed strength, and for the sake of health — these are always useful, and are not to be neglected, but to be enjoined alike on masters and scholars, when we reach that part of legislation; and we will desire the one to give their instructions freely, and the others to receive them thankfully. Nor, again, must we omit suitable imitations of war in our dances; in Crete there are the armed sports of the Curetes, and in Lacedæmon of the Dioscori. And our virgin lady, delighting in the sports of the dance,

Proper character of gymnastic.

[1] A giant with three bodies and powerful wings, that dwelt in the island of Erythia, guarding a herd of cattle. It was one of the labors of Heracles to carry off these cattle and slay Geryon.

thought it not fit to dance with empty hands; she must be clothed in a complete suit of armour, and in this attire go through the dance; and youths and maidens should in every respect imitate her example, honouring the Goddess both with a view to the actual necessities of war, and to festive amusements: it will be right also for the boys until such time as they go out to war to make processions and supplications to the Gods in goodly array, armed and on horseback, in dances and marches, fast or slow, offering up prayers to the Gods and to the sons of Gods; and also engaging in contests and preludes of contests, if at all, with these objects. For these sort of exercises, and no others, are useful both in peace and war, and are beneficial both to states and to private houses. But other labours and sports and excessive training of the body are unworthy of freemen, O Megillus and Cleinias.

I have now completely described the kind of gymnastic which I said at first ought to be described; if you know of any better, will you communicate your thoughts?

CLE. It is not easy, Stranger, to put these principles of gymnastic aside and to enunciate better ones.

ATH. Next in order follow the gifts of the Muses and of Apollo: before, we fancied that we had said all, and that gymnastic alone remained to be discussed; but now we see clearly what points have been omitted, and should be first proclaimed; of these, then, let us proceed to speak.

CLE. By all means.

ATH. Hear me once more, although you have heard me say the same before — that caution must be always exercised, both by the speaker and by the hearer, about anything that is singular and unusual. For my tale is one which many a man would be afraid to tell, and yet I have a confidence which makes me go on.

CLE. What have you to say, Stranger?

Importance of play in education.

ATH. I say that in states generally no one has observed that the plays of childhood have a great deal to do with the permanence or want of permanence in legislation. For when plays are ordered with a view to children having the same plays and amusing themselves after the same manner, and finding delight in the same playthings, the more solemn institutions of the state are allowed to remain undisturbed. Whereas if sports are disturbed and innovations are made in them, and they constantly change, and the young never speak of their having the same likings, or the same established notions of good and bad taste, either in the bearing of their bodies or in their dress, but he who devises something new and out of the way in figures and colours and the like is held in special honour, we may truly say that no greater evil can happen in a state; for he who changes the sports is secretly changing the manners of the young, and making the old to be dishonoured among them and the new to be honoured. And I affirm that there is nothing which is a greater injury to all states than saying or thinking thus. Will you hear me tell how great I deem it to be?

**Innovations to be avoided.**

CLE. You mean the evil of blaming antiquity in states?

ATH. Exactly.

CLE. If you are speaking of that, you will find in us hearers who are disposed to receive what you say not unfavourably but most favourably.

ATH. I should expect so.

CLE. Proceed.

**Importance of reverence for antiquity.**

ATH. Well, then, let us give all the greater heed to one another's words. The argument says that to change from anything except the bad is the most dangerous of all things; this is true in the case of the seasons and of the winds, in the management of our bodies and the habits of our minds—true of all things except, as I said before, of the bad. He who looks at the constitution of individuals accustomed to eat any sort of meat or drink any drink or do any work which they could get, may see that they are at first disordered but afterwards, as time goes on, their bodies grow adapted to them, and they learn to know and like variety, and have good health and enjoyment of life; and if ever afterwards they are confined again to a superior diet, at first they are troubled with disorders, and with difficulty become habituated to their new food. A similar principle we may imagine to hold good about the minds of men and the nature of their souls. For when they have been brought up in certain laws, which by some Divine Providence have remained unchanged during long ages, so that no one has any memory or tradition of their ever having been otherwise than they are, then every one is afraid and ashamed to change that which is established. The legislator must somehow find a way of implanting this reverence for antiquity, and I would propose the following way: — People are apt to fancy, as I was saying before, that when the plays of children are altered they are merely plays, not seeing that the most serious and detrimental consequences arise out of the change; and they readily comply with the child's wishes instead of deterring him, not considering that these children who make innovations in their games, when they grow up to be men will be different from the last generation of children, and, being different, will desire a different sort of life, and under the influence of this desire will want other institutions and laws; and no one ever apprehends that there will follow what I just now called the greatest of evils to states. Changes in bodily fashions are no such serious evils, but frequent changes in the praise and censure of manners are the greatest of evils, and require the utmost prevision.

CLE. To be sure.

ATH. And now do we still hold to our former assertion, that rhythms and music in general are imitations of good and evil characters in men? What say you?

CLE. That is the only doctrine which I can admit.

ATH. Must we not, then, try in every possible way to prevent our youth desiring imitations and novelties either in dance or song? nor must any one be allowed to offer them varieties of pleasures.

CLE. Most true.

ATH. Can any better mode of effecting this object be imagined by any of us than that of the Egyptians?

CLE. What is their method?

How secured by the Egyptians.

ATH. They consecrate every sort of dance or melody, first ordaining festivals, — calculating for the year what they ought to be, and at what time, and in honour of what Gods, sons of Gods, and heroes they ought to be celebrated; and, in the next place, what hymns ought to be sung at the several sacrifices, and with what dances the particular festival is to be honoured. This is to be arranged at first by certain persons, and, when arranged, the whole assembly of the citizens are to offer sacrifices and libations to the Fates and all the other Gods, and to consecrate the several odes to Gods and heroes: and if any one offers any other hymns or dances to any one of the Gods, the priests and priestesses, with the consent of the guardians of the law, shall religiously and lawfully exclude him, and he who is excluded, if he do not submit, shall be liable all his life long to have a suit of impiety brought against him by any one who likes.

CLE. Very good.

ATH. In the consideration of this subject, let us remember what is due to ourselves.

CLE. To what are you referring?

ATH. I mean that any young man, and much more any old one, when he sees or hears anything strange or unaccustomed, does not at once run to embrace the paradox, but he stands considering, like a person who is at a place where three ways meet, and does not very well know his way — he may be alone or he may be walking with others, and he will say to himself and them, 'Which is the way?' and will not move forward until he is satisfied that he is going right. And this is our case, for a strange discussion on the subject of law has arisen, which requires the utmost consideration, and we should not at our age be too ready to speak about such great matters, or be confident that we can say anything certain all in a moment.

CLE. Most true.

ATH. Then we will allow time for reflection, and decide when we have given the subject sufficient consideration. But that we may not be hindered from completing the natural arrangement of our laws, let us proceed to the conclusion of them in due order; for very possibly, if God will, the exposition of them, when completed, may throw light on our present perplexity.

CLE. Excellent, Stranger; let us do as you propose.

**Music serves as a restraining force, as do laws.**

ATH. Let us then affirm the paradox that strains of music are our laws (*νόμος*), and this latter being the name which the ancients gave to lyric songs, they probably would not have very much objected to our proposed application of the word. Some one, either asleep or awake, must have had a dreamy suspicion of their nature. And let our decree be as follows: — No one in singing or dancing shall offend against public and consecrated models, and the general fashion among the youth, any more than he would offend against any other law. And he who observes this law shall be blameless; but he who is disobedient, as I was saying, shall be punished by the guardians of the laws, and by priests and priestesses: suppose that we imagine this to be our law.

CLE. Very good.

ATH. Can any one who makes such laws escape ridicule? Let us see. I think that our only safety will be in first framing certain models for them. One of these models shall be as follows: — If when a sacrifice is going on, and the victims are being burnt according to law, — if, I say, any one who may be a son or brother, standing by another at the altar and over the victims, horribly blasphemes, will he not inspire despondency and evil omens and forebodings in the mind of his father and of his other kinsmen?

CLE. Of course.

Influence of music on the people.

ATH. And this is just what takes place in almost all our cities. A magistrate offers a public sacrifice, and there come in not one but many choruses, who stand by themselves a little way from the altar, and from time to time pour forth all sorts of horrible blasphemies on the sacred rites, exciting the souls of the audience with words and rhythms, and melodies most sorrowful to hear; and he who can at the instant the city is sacrificing make the citizens weep most, carries away the palm of victory. Now, ought we not to forbid such strains as these? And if ever our citizens must hear such lamentations, then on some unblest and inauspicious day let there be choruses of foreign and hired minstrels, like those who accompany the departed at funerals with barbarous Carian chants. That is the sort of thing which will be appropriate if we have such strains at all; and let the apparel of the singers be not circlets and ornaments of gold, but the reverse. Enough of the description. And now I will ask once more whether we shall lay down as one of our principles of song —

CLE. What?

ATH. That we should avoid every evil word. I need

hardly ask again, but shall assume that you agree with me.

**Music and poetry shall conform to these laws.**

CLE. By all means; that law is approved by the suffrage of all of us.

ATH. But what shall be our next musical law or type? Ought not prayers to be offered up to the Gods when we sacrifice?

CLE. Certainly.

ATH. And our third law, if I am not mistaken, will be to the effect, that our poets understanding prayers to be requests which we make to the Gods, will take especial heed that they do not by mistake ask for evil instead of good. To make such a prayer would surely be too ridiculous.

CLE. Very true.

ATH. Were we not a little while ago quite determined that no silver or golden Plutus should dwell in our state?

CLE. To be sure.

ATH. And what did this illustration mean? Did we not imply that the poets are not always quite capable of knowing what is good or evil? And if one of them utters a mistaken prayer in song or words, he will make our citizens pray for the opposite of what is good in matters of the highest import; than which, as I was saying, there can be few greater mistakes. Shall we then propose as one of our laws and models relating to the Muses —

CLE. What? — will you explain the law more precisely?

ATH. Shall we make a law that the poet shall compose nothing contrary to the ideas of the lawful, or just, or beautiful, or good, which are allowed in the state? nor shall he be permitted to communicate his compositions to any private individuals, until he shall have shown them to the appointed judges, and the guardians of the law, and they are satisfied with them. As to the persons whom we appoint to be our legislators about music and directors of education, they have been already indicated. Once more then, as I have asked more than once, shall this be our third law, and type, and model — What do you say?

CLE. Yes, by all means.

ATH. Next it will be proper to have hymns and praises of the Gods, intermingled with prayers; and after the

Gods prayers and praises should be offered in like manner to demigods and heroes, suitable to their several characters.

CLE. Certainly.

ATH. In the third place there will be no objection to a law, that citizens who are departed and have done good and energetic deeds, either with their souls or with their bodies, and have been obedient to the laws, should receive eulogies; this will be very fitting.

CLE. Quite true.

Selection of proper music by public judges.

ATH. But to honour with hymns and panegyrics those who are still alive is not safe; a man should run his course, and make a fair ending, and then we will praise him; and let praise be given equally to women as well as men who have been distinguished in virtue. The order of songs and dances shall be as follows: — There are many ancient musical compositions and dances which are excellent, and from these the government may freely select what is proper and suitable; and they shall choose judges of not less than fifty years of age, who shall make the selection, and any of the old poems which they deem sufficient they shall include; any that is deficient or altogether unsuitable, they shall either utterly throw aside, or examine and amend, taking into their counsel poets and musicians, and making use of their poetical genius; but explaining to them the wishes of the legislator in order that they may regulate dancing, music, and all choral strains, according to his mind; and not allowing them to indulge, except in some minor matters, their individual pleasures and fancies. Now, the irregular strain of music is always made ten thousand times better by attaining to law and order, and rejecting the honied Muse — not however that we mean wholly to exclude pleasure, which is the characteristic of all music. And if a man be brought up from childhood to the age of discretion and maturity in the use of the orderly and severe music, when he hears the opposite he detests it, and calls it illiberal; but if trained in the sweet and vulgar music, he deems the opposite cold and displeasing. So that, as I was saying before, while he who hears them gains no more pleasure from the one than from the other, the one has the advantage of making those who are trained in it better men, whereas the other makes them worse.

CLE. Very true.

ATH. Again, we must distinguish and determine on some general principle what songs are suitable to women, and what to men, and must assign to them their proper melodies and rhythms. It is shocking for a whole harmony to be inharmonical, or for a rhythm to be unrhythmical, and this will happen when the melody is inappropriate to them. And, therefore, the legislator must assign to them also their forms. Now, both sexes have melodies and rhythms which of necessity belong to them; and those of women are clearly enough indicated by their natural difference. The grand, and that which tends to courage, may be fairly called manly; but that which inclines to moderation and temperance, may be declared both in law and in ordinary speech to be the more womanly quality: this, then, will be the general order of them. **Different selections for men and for women.**

Let us now speak of the manner of teaching and imparting them, and the persons to whom, and the time when, they are severally to be imparted. As the shipwright first lays down the lines of the keel, and draws the design in outline, so do I seek to distinguish the patterns of life, and lay down their keels according to the nature of different men's souls; seeking truly to consider by what means, and in what ways, we may go through the voyage of life best. Now, human affairs are hardly worth considering in earnest, and yet we must be in earnest about them,—a sad necessity constrains us. And having got thus far, there will be a fitness in our completing the matter, if we can only find some suitable means of doing so. But what am I saying? and yet very probably there may be a meaning latent in these very words. **How taught.**

CLE. To be sure.

ATH. I say, that about serious matters a man should be serious, and about a matter which is not serious he should not be serious; and that God is the natural and worthy object of a man's most serious and blessed endeavours; who, as I said before, is made to be the plaything of God, and that this, truly considered, is the best of him; wherefore every man and woman should walk seriously, and pass life in the noblest of pastimes, and be of another mind from what they now are. **For serious purposes.**

CLE. In what respect?

Proper aims in life

ATH. Now they think that their serious pursuits should be for the sake of their sports, for they deem war a serious pursuit, which must be managed well for the sake of peace; but the truth is, that there neither is, nor has been, nor ever will be, either amusement or instruction in any degree worth speaking of in war, which is nevertheless deemed by us to be the most serious of our pursuits. And therefore, as we say, every one of us should live the life of peace as long and as well as he can. And what is the right way of living? Are we to live in sports always? If so, in what kind of sports? We ought to live sacrificing, and singing, and dancing, and then a man will be able to propitiate the Gods, and to defend himself against his enemies and conquer them in battle. The type of song or dance by which he will propitiate them has been described, and the paths along which he is to proceed have been cut for him. He will go forward in the spirit of the poet: —

> 'Telemachus, some things thou wilt thyself find in thy heart, but other things God will suggest; for I deem that thou wast not born or brought up without the will of the Gods.'

determined by tradition and by nature.

And this ought to be the view of our alumni; they ought to think that what has been said is enough for them, and that any other things some God or a demigod will suggest to them — he will tell them to whom, and when, and to what Gods severally they are to sacrifice and perform dances, and how they may propitiate the deities, and live according to the appointment of nature; being for the most part puppets, but having some little share of reality.

MEG. You have a low opinion of mankind, Stranger.

ATH. Nay, Megillus, I was only comparing them with the Gods; and under that feeling I spoke. Let us grant, if you wish, that the human race is not to be despised, but is worthy of some consideration.

Schools of various types.

Next follow the buildings for gymnasia and schools open to all; these are to be in three places in the midst of the city; and outside the city and in the surrounding country there shall be schools for horse exercise, and open spaces also in three places, arranged with a view to archery and the throwing of missiles, at which young men may learn and practise. Of these mention has already been made; and if the mention be not sufficiently explicit, let us speak further of them and embody them in laws. In these several schools let there be dwellings for teachers, who shall be brought from foreign parts by pay, and let them teach the frequenters of the school the art of war and the art of music, and the children shall come, not only if their parents please, but if they do not please; and if their education is neglected, there shall be compulsory education, as the saying is, of all and sundry, as far as this is possible; and the pupils shall be regarded as belonging to the state rather than to their parents. My law would apply to females as well as males; they shall both go through the same exercises. I assert without fear of contradiction that gymnastic and horsemanship are as suitable to women as to men. Of the truth of this I am persuaded from ancient tradition, and at the present day there are said to be myriads of women in the neighbourhood of the Black Sea, called Sauromatides,[1] who not only ride on horseback like men, but have enjoined upon them the use of bows and other weapons equally with the men. And I further affirm, that if these things are possible, nothing can be more absurd than the practice which prevails in our own country of men and women not following the same pursuits with all their strength and with one mind, for thus the state, instead of being a whole, is reduced to a half, and yet has the same imposts to pay and the same toils to undergo; and what can be a greater mistake for any legislator to make?

**Education should be compulsory and the same for both sexes.**

CLE. Very true; and much of what has been asserted by us, Stranger, is contrary to the custom of states; still, in saying that the discourse should be allowed to proceed, and that when the discussion is completed, we should choose what seems best, you have spoken very properly, and have made me feel compunction for what I said. Tell me, then, what you would next wish to say.

ATH. I should wish to say, Cleinias, as I said before, that if the possibility of these things were not sufficiently proven in fact, then there might be an objection to the argument, but the fact being as I have said, he who rejects

[1] Scythians, of what is now Southern Russia.

the law must find some other ground of objection; and, failing this, our exhortation will still hold good, nor will any one deny that women ought to share as far as possible in education and in other ways with men, for consider; — if women do not share in their whole life with men, then they must have some other order of life.

CLE. Certainly.

Other ideas concerning the education of women.

ATH. And what arrangement of life to be found anywhere is preferable to this community which we are now assigning to them? Shall we prefer that which is adopted by the Thracians and many other races who use their women to till the ground and to be shepherds of their herds and flocks, and to minister to them like slaves? Or shall we do as we and people in our part of the world do? getting together, as the phrase is, all our goods and chattels into one dwelling — these we entrust to our women, who are the stewards of them; and who also preside over the shuttles and the whole art of spinning. Or shall we take a middle course, as in Lacedæmon, Megillus, letting the girls share in gymnastic and music, while the grown-up women, no longer employed in spinning wool, are actively engaged in weaving the web of life, which will be no cheap or mean employment, and in the duty of serving and taking care of the household and bringing up children in which they will observe a sort of mean, not participating in the toils of war; and if there were any necessity that they should fight for their city and families, unlike the Amazons, they would be unable to take part in archery or any other skilled use of missiles, nor could they, after the example of the Goddess, carry shield or spear, or stand up nobly for their country when it was being destroyed, and strike terror into their enemies, if only because they were seen in regular order? Living as they do, they would never dare at all to imitate the Sauromatides, whose women, when compared with ordinary women, would appear to be like men. Let him who will, praise your legislators, but I must say what I think. The legislator ought to be whole and perfect, and not half a man only; he ought not to let the female sex live softly and waste money and have no order of life, while he takes the utmost care of the male sex, and leaves half of life only blest with happiness, when he might have made the whole state happy.

MEG. What shall we do, Cleinias? Shall we allow a stranger to run down Sparta in this fashion?

CLE. Yes; for as we have given him liberty of speech we must let him go on until we have perfected the work of legislation.

MEG. Very true.

ATH. Then now I may proceed?

CLE. By all means.

ATH. What will be the manner of life among men who may be supposed to have their food and clothing provided for them in moderation, and who have entrusted the practice of the arts to others, and whose husbandry, committed to slaves paying a part of the produce, brings them a return sufficient for men living temperately; who, moreover, have common tables in which the men are placed apart, and near them are the common tables of their families, of their daughters and mothers, which day by day, the rulers, male and female, are to inspect and look to their mode of life and so dismiss them; after which the magistrate and his attendants shall honour with libations those Gods to whom that day and night are dedicated, and then go home? To men whose lives are thus ordered, is there no work to be done which is necessary and fitting, but shall each one of them live fattening like a beast? Such a life is neither just nor honourable, nor can he who lives it fail of meeting his due; and the due reward of the idle fatted beast is that he should be torn in pieces by some other valiant beast whose fatness is worn down by labours and toils. These regulations, if we duly consider them, will never perfectly take effect under present circumstances, nor as long as women and children and houses and all other things are the private property of individuals; but if we can attain the second-best form of polity, with that we may be satisfied. And to men living under this second polity there remains a work to be accomplished which is far from being small or insignificant, but is the greatest of all works, and ordained by the appointment of righteous law. For a life which is wholly concerned with the virtue of body and soul may truly be said to be twice,

**Life of leisure desirable,**

**in order to provide exercise for the body and education for the soul.**

or more than twice, as full of toil and trouble as the pursuit after Pythian[1] and Olympic victories, which debars a man from every employment of life. For there ought to be no bye-work interfering with the greater work of providing the necessary exercise and nourishment for the body, and instruction and education for the soul. Night and day are not long enough for the accomplishment of their perfection and consummation; and therefore to this end all freemen ought to arrange the time of their employments during the whole course of the twenty-four hours, from morning to evening and from evening to the morning of the next sunrise. There may seem to be some impropriety in the legislator determining minutely the little details of the management of the house, including such particulars as the duty of wakefulness in those who are to be perpetual watchmen of the whole city; for that any citizen should continue during the whole night in sleep, instead of being seen by all his servants, always the first to awake and the first to rise — this, whether the regulation is to be called a law or only a practice, should be deemed base and unworthy of a freeman; also that the mistress of the house should be awakened by her handmaidens instead of herself first awakening them, is what her slaves, male and female, and her children, and, if that were possible, everything in the house should regard as base. If they rise early, they may all of them do much of their public and of their household business, as magistrates in the city, and masters and mistresses in their private houses, before the sun is up. Much sleep is not required by nature, either for our souls or bodies, or for the actions in which they are concerned. For no one who is asleep is good for anything, any more than if he were dead; but he of us who has the most regard for life and reason keeps awake as long as he can, reserving only so much time for sleep as is expedient for health; and much sleep is not required, if the habit of not sleeping be once formed. Magistrates in states who keep awake at night

[1] After the Olympic games, the most important of Greek national festivals. Held every fourth year at Delphi in honor of Apollo. They consisted of musical and gymnastic contests.

are terrible to the bad, whether enemies or citizens, and are honoured and reverenced by the just and temperate, and are useful to themselves and to the whole state.

**Difficulties of educating children.**

A night which is short and devoted to work, in addition to all the above-mentioned advantages, infuses a sort of courage into the minds of the citizens. When the day breaks, the time has arrived for youth to go to their schoolmasters. Now, neither sheep nor any other animals can live without a shepherd, nor can children be left without tutors, or slaves without masters. And of all animals the boy is the most unmanageable, inasmuch as he has the fountain of reason in him not yet regulated; he is the most insidious, sharp-witted, and insubordinate of animals. Wherefore he must be bound with many bridles; in the first place, when he gets away from mothers and nurses, he must be under the control of tutors on account of his childishness and foolishness; then, again, being a freeman, he must have teachers and be educated by them in anything which they teach, and must learn what he has to learn; but he is also a slave, and in that regard any freeman who comes in his way may punish him and his tutor and his instructor, if any of them does anything wrong; and he who comes across him and does not inflict upon him the punishment which he deserves, shall incur the greatest disgrace; and let the guardian of the law, who is the director of education, see to him who coming in the way of the offences which we have mentioned, does not chastise them when he ought, or chastises them in a way which he ought not; let him keep a sharp look-out, and take especial care of the training of our children, directing their natures, and always turning them to good according to the law.

**Training and work of the teacher.**

And how can our law sufficiently train the director of education himself; for as yet all has been imperfect, and nothing has been said either clear or satisfactory? Now, as far as possible, the law ought to leave nothing to him, but to explain everything, that he may be the interpreter and tutor of others. About dances and music and choral strains, I have already spoken both as to the character of the selection of them, and the manner in which they are to be improved and consecrated. But we have not yet spoken, O illustrious guardian of education, of the manner in which your pupils are to use those strains which are written in prose, although you have been informed what martial strains they are to learn and practise; what relates in the first place to the learning of letters, and secondly, to the lyre, and also to calculation, which, as we were saying, is needful for them all to learn, and any other things which are required with a view to war and the management of house and city, and, looking to the same object, what is useful in the revolutions of the heavenly bodies — the stars and sun and moon, and the various regulations about these matters which are necessary for the whole state — I am speaking of the arrangements of days in periods of months, and of months in years, which are to be observed, in order that times and sacrifices and festivals may proceed in regular and natural order, and keep the city alive and awake, the Gods receiving the honours due to them, and men having a better understanding about them; all these things, O my friend, have not yet been sufficiently declared by the legislator. Attend, then, to what I am now going to say: We were telling you, in the first place, that you were not sufficiently informed about letters, and the objection made was to this effect, — 'That you were never told whether he who was meant to be a respectable citizen should apply himself in detail to that sort of learning, or not apply himself at all'; and the same remark was made about the lyre. But now we say that he ought to attend to them. A fair time for a boy of ten years old to spend in letters is three years; at thirteen years he should begin to handle the lyre, and he may continue at this for another three years, neither more nor less, and whether his father or himself like or dislike the study, he is not to be allowed to spend more or less time in learning music than the law allows. And let him who disobeys the law be deprived of those youthful honours of which we shall hereafter speak. Hear, however, first of all, what the young ought to learn in the early years of life, and what their instructors ought to teach them. They ought to be occupied with their letters until they are able to read and write; but the acquisition of perfect beauty or quickness in writing, if nature has not stimulated them

Period of literary education; of musical education.

to acquire these accomplishments in the given number of years, they should let alone. And as to the learning of compositions committed to writing which are unaccompanied by song, whether metrical or without rhythmical divisions, compositions in prose, as they are termed, having no rhythm or harmony — seeing how dangerous are the writings handed down to us by many writers of this class — what will you do with them, O most excellent guardians of the law? or how can the lawgiver rightly direct you about them? I believe that he will be in great difficulty.

**Difficulties in the literary education.**

CLE. What troubles you, Stranger? and why are you so perplexed in your mind?

ATH. You naturally ask, Cleinias, and to you, who are my partners in the work of education, I must state the difficulties of the case.

CLE. To what do you refer in this instance?

ATH. I will tell you. There is a difficulty in opposing many myriads of mouths.

CLE. Well, and have we not already opposed the popular voice in many important enactments?

ATH. That is quite true; and you mean to imply that the road which we are taking may be disagreeable to some but is agreeable to as many others, or if not to as many, at any rate to persons not inferior to the others, and in company with them you bid me, at whatever risk, proceed along the path of legislation which has opened out of our present discourse, and to be of good cheer, and not to faint.

CLE. Certainly.

**Objections to the poets.**

ATH. And I do not faint; I say, indeed, that we have a great many poets writing in hexameter, trimeter, and all sorts of measures — some who are serious, others who aim only at raising a laugh — and all mankind declare that the youth who are rightly educated should be brought up and saturated with them; they should be constantly hearing them read at recitations, and some would have them learn by heart entire poets; while others select choice passages and long speeches, and make compendiums of them, saying that these shall be committed to memory, and that in this way only can a man be made good and wise by experience and learning. And you want me to say plainly in what they are right and in what they are wrong.

CLE. Yes, I do.

ATH. But how can I in one word rightly comprehend all of them? I am of opinion, and, if I am not mistaken, there is a general agreement, that every one of these poets has said many things well and many things the reverse of well; and if this be true, then I do affirm that much learning brings danger to youth.

CLE. Then how would you advise the guardian of the law to act?

ATH. In what respect?

CLE. I mean to what pattern should he look as his guide in permitting the young to learn some things and forbidding them to learn others? Do not shrink from answering.

ATH. My good Cleinias, I rather think that I am fortunate.

CLE. In what?

Socratic dialogues the best literary subject-matter.

ATH. I think that I am not wholly in want of a pattern, for when I consider the words which we have spoken from early dawn until now, and which, as I believe, have been inspired by Heaven, they appear to me to be quite like a poem. When I reflected upon all these words of ours, I naturally felt pleasure, for of all the discourses which I have ever learnt or heard, either in poetry or prose, this seemed to me to be the justest, and most suitable for young men to hear; I cannot imagine any better pattern than this which the guardian of the law and the educator can have. They cannot do better than advise the teachers to teach the young these and the like words, and if they should happen to find writings, either in poetry or prose, or even unwritten discourses like these of ours, and of the same family, they should certainly preserve them, and commit them to writing. And, first of all, they shall constrain the teachers themselves to learn and approve them, and any of them who will not, shall not be employed by them, but those whom they find agreeing in their judgment, they shall make use of and shall commit to them the instruction and education of youth. And here and on this wise let my fanciful tale about letters and teachers of letters come to an end.

CLE. I do not think, Stranger, that we have wandered

out of the proposed limits of the argument; but whether we are right or not in the whole design I cannot be very certain.

ATH. The truth, Cleinias, may be expected to become clearer when, as we have often said, we arrive at the end of the whole discussion about laws.

CLE. Yes.

ATH. And now that we have done with the teacher of letters, the teacher of the lyre has to receive orders from us.

Principles controlling the teacher of the lyre.

CLE. Certainly.

ATH. I think that we have only to recollect our previous discussions, and we shall be able to give suitable regulations touching all this part of instruction and education to the teachers of the lyre.

CLE. To what do you refer?

ATH. We were saying, if I remember rightly, that the sixty years' old choristers of Dionysus were to be specially quick in their perceptions of rhythm and musical composition, that they might be able to distinguish good and bad imitation, or in other words, the imitation of the good or bad soul when under the influence of passion, rejecting the one and displaying the other in hymns and songs, charming the souls of youth, and inviting them to follow and attain virtue by the way of imitation.

CLE. Very true.

ATH. And with this view the teacher and the learner ought to use the sounds of the lyre because its notes are pure, the player who teaches and his pupil giving note for note in unison; but complexity, and variation of notes, when the strings give one sound and the poet or composer of the melody gives another; also when they make concords and harmonies in which lesser and greater intervals, slow and quick, or high and low notes, are combined; or, again, when they make complex variations of rhythms, which they adapt to the notes of the lyre, — all that sort of thing is not suited to those who have to acquire a speedy and useful knowledge of music in three years; for opposite principles are confusing, and create a difficulty in learning, and our young men should learn quickly, and their mere necessary acquirements are not few or trifling, as will be shown in due course. Let our educator attend to the principles concerning music which we are laying down. As to the songs and words themselves which the masters of choruses are to teach and the character of them, they have been already described by us, and are the same which we said were to be consecrated as may suit the several feasts, and so furnish an innocent and useful amusement to cities.

CLE. That, again, is true.

ATH. Then let the musical president who has been elected receive these rules from us as the very truth; and may he prosper in his office! Let us now proceed to lay down other rules about dancing and gymnastic exercise in general. Having said what remained to be said about the teaching of music, let us speak in like manner about gymnastic. For boys and girls ought to learn to dance and practise gymnastic exercises — ought they not?

Rules concerning dancing and gymnastic.

CLE. Yes.

ATH. Then the boys ought to have dancing masters, and the girls dancing mistresses to exercise them.

CLE. Very good.

ATH. Then once more let us call him who will have the chief trouble, the superintendent of youth; he will have plenty to do, if he is to have the charge of music and gymnastic.

CLE. But how will an old man be able to attend to such great charges?

ATH. O, my friend, there will be no difficulty, for the law has already given and will give him permission to select as his assistants in this charge any citizens, male or female, whom he desires; and he will know whom he ought to choose, and will be anxious not to make a mistake, from a sense of responsibility, and from a consciousness of the importance of his office, and also because he will consider that if young men have been and are well brought up, then all things go swimmingly, but if not, it is not meet to say, nor do we say, what will follow, lest the regarders of omens should take alarm about our infant state. Many things have been said by us about dancing and about gymnastic movements in general; for we include under gymnastics all military exercises, such as archery, and all hurling of

Branches of gymnastic.

weapons, and the use of the light shield, and all fighting with heavy arms, and military evolutions, and movements of armies, and encampments, and all that relates to horsemanship. Of all these things there ought to be public teachers, receiving pay from the state, and their pupils should be the men and boys in the state, and also the girls and women, who are to know all these things. While they are yet girls they should have practised dancing in arms and the whole art of fighting — when they are grown-up women, applying themselves to evolutions and tactics, and the mode of grounding and taking up arms; if for no other reason, yet in case the whole people should have to leave the city and carry on operations of war outside, that the young who are left to guard and the rest of the city may be equal to the task; and, on the other hand (what is far from being an impossibility), when enemies, whether barbarian or Hellenic, come from without with mighty force and make a violent assault upon them, and thus compel them to fight for the possession of the city, great would be the disgrace to the state, if the women had been so miserably trained that they could not fight for their young, as birds will, against any creature however strong, and die or undergo any danger, but must instantly rush to the temples and crowd at the altars and shrines, and bring upon human nature the reproach, that of all animals man is the most cowardly.

CLE. Such a want of education, Stranger, is certainly an unseemly thing to happen in a state, and also a great misfortune.

ATH. Suppose that we carry our law to the extent of saying that women ought not to neglect military matters, but that all citizens, male and female alike, shall attend to them?

CLE. I quite agree.

ATH. Of wrestling we have spoken in part, but of what I should call the most important part we have not spoken, and cannot easily speak without showing at the same time by gesture as well as in word what we mean; when word and action combine, and not till then, we shall explain clearly what has been said, pointing out that of all movements wrestling is most akin to the military art, and is to be pursued for the sake of this, and not this for the sake of wrestling.

CLE. Excellent.

Dancing.

ATH. Thus far we have spoken of the palæstra, and we will now proceed to speak of other movements of the body. Such motion may be in general called dancing, and is of two kinds: one of nobler figures, imitating the honourable, the other of the more ignoble figures, imitating the mean; and of both these there are two further sub-divisions. Of the serious, one kind is of those engaged in war and vehement action, and is the exercise of a noble person and a manly heart; the other exhibits a temperate soul in the enjoyment of prosperity and modest pleasures, and may be truly called and is the dance of peace. The warrior dance is different from the peaceful one, and may be rightly termed Pyrrhic; this imitates the modes of avoiding blows and darts, by dropping or giving way, or springing aside, or rising up or falling down; also the opposite of postures which are those of action, as, for example, the imitation of archery and the hurling of javelins, and of all sorts of blows. And when the imitation is of brave bodies and souls, and the action is direct and muscular, giving for the most part a straight movement to the limbs of the body — that, I say, is the true sort; but the opposite is not right. In the dance of peace the consideration is whether a man bears himself naturally and gracefully, and after the manner of well-conditioned men. But before proceeding I must distinguish the dancing about which there is any doubt, from that about which there is no doubt. How shall we distinguish them? There are dances of the Bacchic sort, in which they imitate, as they say, the Nymphs, and Pan, and drunken Silenuses, and Satyrs, after whom they name them, making purifications and celebrating mysteries, — all this sort of dancing cannot be distinguished as having either a peaceful or a warlike character, or indeed as having any meaning whatever, and may, I think, be most truly described as distinct from the warlike dance, and distinct from the peaceful, and not suited for a city at all. Having left this behind us, we will now proceed to the dances of war and peace, about which there can be no doubt in our state. Now the unwarlike muse, which honours in dance the Gods and the sons of

Warrior dances.

Dance of peace.

Types to be approved; their uses.

the Gods, is associated with the consciousness of prosperity; and this may be sub-divided into classes, of which one is expressive of an escape from some labour or danger into good, and has greater pleasures; the other expressive of preservation and increase of former good, in which the pleasure is less exciting;—in all these cases, every man when the pleasure is greater, moves his body more, and less when the pleasure is less; and, again, if he be more orderly and disciplined he moves less; but if he be a coward, and has no training or self-control, he makes greater and more violent movements, and in general when he is speaking or singing he is not altogether able to control his body; and so out of the imitation of words in gestures the art of dancing has originated. And in these various kinds of imitation one man moves in an orderly, another in a disorderly manner; and as the ancients may be observed to have given many names which are according to nature and deserving of praise, so there is an excellent one which they have given to those dances of men in their times of prosperity, who are moderate in their pleasures—whoever he was gave them a very true, and poetical, and rational name, when he called them Emmeleiai, or dances of order; thus establishing two kinds of dances of the nobler sort, the dance of war which he called the Pyrrhic, and the dance of peace which he called Emmeleia, or the dance of order; giving to each their appropriate and becoming name. These things the legislator should indicate in general outline, and the guardian of the law should enquire into them and search them out, combining dancing with music, and assigning to the several sacrificial feasts that which is suitable to them; and when he has consecrated them all in due order, he shall for the future change nothing, whether of dance or song. Thenceforward the city and the citizens shall continue to have the same pleasures, themselves being as far as possible alike, and shall live well and happily.

**Comic dances have their use; not to be indulged in by freemen.**

I have described the dances which are appropriate to noble bodies and generous souls. But it is necessary also to consider and know uncomely persons and thoughts, and those which are intended to produce laughter in comedy, and have a comic character both in respect to style, and song, and dance, whether real or imitated. For serious things cannot be understood without laughable things, nor opposites at all without opposites, if a man is really to have intelligence of either; but he cannot carry out both in action, if he is to have any degree of virtue. And for this very reason he should learn them both, in order that he may not in ignorance do or say anything which is ridiculous and out of place — he should command slaves and hired strangers to imitate such things, but he should never take any serious interest in them himself, nor should any freeman or freewoman be discovered learning them; and there should always be some element of novelty in the imitation. Let these then be laid down, both in law and in our narrative, as the regulations of laughable amusements which are generally called comedy. And, if any of the serious or tragic poets, as they are termed, come to us and say — 'O strangers, may we go to your city and country or may we not, and shall we bring with us our poetry — what is your will about these matters?' How shall we answer the divine men? I think that our answer should be as follows: — Best of strangers, we will say to them, we also according to our ability are tragic poets, and our tragedy the best and noblest; for our whole state is an imitation of the best and noblest life, which we affirm to be indeed the very truth of tragedy. You are poets and we are poets, your rivals and antagonists in the noblest of dramas, which true law will carry out in act, as our hope is. Do not then suppose that we shall all in a moment allow you to erect your stage in the agora, or introduce the fair voice of your actors, speaking above our own, and permit you to harangue our women and children, and the mass of mankind, about our institutions, in language other than our own, and very often the opposite of our own. For a state would be mad which gave you this licence, until the magistrates had determined whether your poetry might be recited, and was fit for publication or not. Wherefore, O ye sons and scions of the softer Muses, first of all show your songs to the magistrates, and let them compare them with our own, and if they are the same or better we will give you a chorus; but if not, then, my friends, we cannot. Let these, then, be the customs

Tragedies also to be excluded, unless permitted after examination by the magistrates.

ordained by law about all dances and the teaching of them, and let matters relating to slaves be separated from those relating to masters, if you do not object.

CLE. We can have no hesitation in assenting when you put the matter thus.

Mathematical studies for the few.

ATH. There still remains three studies suitable for freemen. Arithmetic is one of them; the measurement of length, surface, and depth is the second; and the third has to do with the revolutions of the stars in relation to one another. Not every one has need to toil through all these things in a strictly scientific manner, but only a few, and who they are to be, we will hereafter indicate in the proper place; not to know what is necessary for mankind in general, and what is the truth, is disgraceful to every one: and yet to enter into these matters minutely is neither easy, nor at all possible for every one; but there is something in them which is necessary and cannot be set aside, and probably he who made the proverb about God originally had this in view when he said, 'that not even God himself can fight against necessity';—he meant, if I am not mistaken, divine necessity; for as to the human necessities of which men often speak when they talk in this manner, nothing can be more ridiculous than such an application of the words.

CLE. And what necessities of knowledge are there, Stranger, which are divine and not human?

Mathematics the basis of the highest kinds of knowledge.

ATH. I conceive them to be those of which he who has no use nor any knowledge at all cannot be a God, or demi-god, or hero to mankind, or able to take any serious thought or charge of them. And very unlike a divine man would he be, who is unable to count one, two, three, or to distinguish odd and even numbers; or is unable to count at all, or reckon night and day, and who is totally unacquainted with the revolution of the sun and moon, and the other stars. There would be great folly in supposing that all these are not necessary parts of knowledge to him who intends to know anything about the highest kinds of knowledge; but which these are, and how many there are of them, and when they are to be learned, and what is to be learned together and what apart, and the whole correlation of them, must be rightly apprehended first; and these leading the way we may proceed to the other parts of knowledge. For so necessity grounded in nature constrains us, against which we say that no God contends, or ever will contend.

CLE. I think, Stranger, that what you have now said is very true and agreeable to nature.

ATH. Yes, Cleinias, I quite agree with you. But it is difficult for the legislator to begin with these studies; at a more convenient time we will make regulations for them.

CLE. You seem, Stranger, to be afraid of our habitual ignorance of the subject: there is no reason why that should prevent you from speaking out.

ATH. I certainly am afraid of the difficulties to which you allude, but I am still more afraid of those who apply themselves to this sort of knowledge, and apply themselves badly. For entire ignorance is not so terrible or extreme an evil, and is far from being the greatest of all; too much cleverness and too much learning, accompanied with ill bringing up, are far more fatal.

CLE. True.

**Extent of and method of teaching arithmetic.**

ATH. All freemen, I conceive, should learn as much of these branches of knowledge as every child in Egypt is taught when he learns his alphabet. In that country arithmetical games have been actually invented for the use of children, which they learn as a pleasure and amusement. They have to distribute apples and garlands, using the same number sometimes for a larger and sometimes for a lesser number of persons; and they arrange pugilists and wrestlers as they pair together by lot or remain over, and show the order in which they follow. Another mode of amusing them is by distributing vessels, some in which gold, brass, silver, and the like are mixed, others in which they are unmixed; as I was saying, they adapt to their amusement the numbers in common use, and in this way make more intelligible to their pupils the arrangements and movements of armies and expeditions, and in the management of a household they make people more useful to themselves, and more wide awake; and again in measurements of things which have length, and breadth, and depth, they free us from that natural ignorance of all these things which is so ludicrous and disgraceful.

CLE. What kind of ignorance do you mean?

ATH. O my dear Cleinias, I, like yourself, have late in life heard with amazement of our ignorance in these matters; to me we appear to be more like pigs than men, and I am quite ashamed, not only of myself, but of all Hellenes.

**Need of mathematical training for the Greeks.**

CLE. About what? Say, Stranger, what you mean?

ATH. I will; or rather I will show you my meaning by a question, and do you please to answer me: You know, I suppose, what length is?

CLE. Certainly.

ATH. And what breadth is?

CLE. To be sure.

ATH. And you know that these are two distinct things, and that there is a third thing called depth?

CLE. Of course.

ATH. And do not all these seem to you to be commensurable with one another?

CLE. Yes.

ATH. That is to say, length is naturally commensurable with length, and breadth with breadth, and depth in like manner with depth?

CLE. Undoubtedly.

ATH. But if some things are commensurable and others wholly incommensurable, and you think that all things are commensurable, what is your position in regard to them?

CLE. Clearly, far from good.

ATH. Concerning length and breadth when compared with depth, or breadth and length when compared with one another, are not all the Hellenes agreed that these are commensurable with one another in some way?

CLE. Quite true.

ATH. But if they are absolutely incommensurable, and yet all of us regard them as commensurable, have we not reason to be ashamed of our compatriots; and might we not say to them:—O ye best of Hellenes, is not this one of the things of which we were saying that not to know them is disgraceful, and of which to know only what is necessary is no great distinction?

CLE. Certainly.

ATH. And there are other things akin to these, in which there springs up other errors of the same family.

CLE. What are they?

ATH. The natures of commensurable and incommensurable quantities in their relation to one another. A man who is good for anything ought to be able, when he thinks, to distinguish them; and different persons should compete with one another in asking questions, which will be a far better and more graceful way of passing their time than the old man's game of draughts.

CLE. I dare say; and these pastimes are not so very unlike a game of draughts.

ATH. And these, as I maintain, Cleinias, are the studies which our youth ought to learn, for they are innocent and not difficult; the learning of them will be an amusement, and they will benefit the state. If any one is of another mind, let him say what he has to say.

CLE. Of course you are right.

ATH. Then if these studies are such as we say, we will include them; if not, they shall be excluded.

CLE. Assuredly: but may we not now, Stranger, prescribe these studies as necessary, and so fill up the lacunæ of our laws?

ATH. They shall be regarded as pledges which may be refused hereafter by the state, if they do not please either us who impose them, or you upon whom they are imposed.

CLE. A fair condition.

ATH. Next let us see whether we are willing that the study of astronomy shall or shall not be proposed for our youth.

Astronomy.

CLE. Proceed.

ATH. Here occurs a strange phenomenon, which certainly cannot in any point of view be tolerated.

CLE. To what are you referring?

ATH. Men say that we ought not to enquire into the supreme God and the nature of the universe, nor busy ourselves in searching out the causes of things, and that such enquiries are impious; whereas the very opposite is the truth.

CLE. What do you mean?

ATH. Perhaps what I am saying may seem paradoxical, and at variance with the usual language of age. But when any one has any good and true notion which is for the advantage of the state and in every way acceptable to God, he cannot abstain from expressing it.

CLE. Your words are reasonable enough; but shall we find any good or true notion about the stars?

ATH. My good friends, at this day all of us Hellenes speak falsely, if I may use such an expression, of those great Gods, the Sun and the Moon.

CLE. What is the falsehood?

ATH. We say that they and divers other stars do not keep the same path, and we call them planets or wanderers.

CLE. Very true, Stranger; and in the course of my life I have often myself seen the morning star and the evening star and divers others not proceeding in their own path, but wandering out of their path in all manner of ways, and I have seen the sun and moon doing what we all know that they do.

**Religious purpose in its study.**

ATH. Just so, Megillus and Cleinias, and I maintain that our citizens and our youth ought to learn about the nature of the Gods in heaven, so far as to be able to offer sacrifices and pray to them in pious language, and not to blaspheme about them.

CLE. There you are right, if such a knowledge be only attainable; and if we are wrong in our mode of speaking now, and can be better instructed and learn to use better language, then I quite agree with you that such a degree of knowledge as will enable us to speak rightly should, if attainable, be acquired by us. And now do you try to explain to us your whole meaning, and we, on our part, will endeavor to understand you.

ATH. There is some difficulty in understanding my meaning, but not a very great one, nor will any great length of time be required; and of this I am myself a proof; for I did not know these things long ago, nor in the days of my youth; and yet I can explain them to you in a brief space of time, whereas if they had been difficult I could certainly never have explained them all, old as I am, to old men like yourselves.

CLE. True; but what is this study which you describe as wonderful and fitting for youth to learn, but of which we are ignorant? Try and explain the nature of it to us as clearly as you can.

ATH. I will. For, O my good friends, that other doctrine about the wandering of the sun and the moon and the other stars is not the truth, but the very reverse of the truth. Each of them moves in the same path — not in many paths, but in one only, which is circular, and the varieties are only apparent. Nor are we right in supposing that the swiftest of them is the slowest, nor conversely, that the slowest is the quickest. And if what I say is true, only just imagine that we had a similar notion about horses running at Olympia, or about men who ran in the long course, and that we addressed the swiftest as the slowest and the slowest as the swiftest, and sang the praises of the vanquished as though he were the victor, — in that case our praises would not be true, nor very agreeable to the runners, though they be but men; and now, to commit the same error about the Gods which would have been ludicrous and erroneous in the case of men, — is not that ludicrous and erroneous?

Education of "The Laws" to terminate in religion.

CLE. Worse than ludicrous, I should say.

ATH. At all events, the Gods cannot like us to be spreading a false report of them.

CLE. Most true, if such is the fact.

ATH. And if we can show that such is really the fact, then all these matters ought to be learned so far as is necessary for the avoidance of impiety; but if we cannot, they may be let alone, and let this be our decision.

CLE. Very good.

ATH. Enough of laws relating to education and learning. But hunting and similar pursuits in like manner claim our attention. For the legislator appears to have a duty imposed upon him which goes beyond mere legislation. There is something over and above law which lies in a region between admonition and law, and has several times occurred to us in the course of discussion; for example, in the education of very young children there were things, as we maintain, which are not to be defined, and to regard them as matters of positive law is a great absurdity. Now, our laws and the whole constitution of our state having been thus delineated, the praise of the virtuous citizen is not complete when he is described as the person who serves the laws best and obeys them most, but the highest form of praise is that which describes him as the good citizen who goes through life undefiled and is obedient to the words of the legislator, both when he is giving laws and when he assigns praise and blame. This is the truest word that can be spoken in praise of a citizen; and the true legislator ought not only to write his laws, but also to interweave with them all such things as seem to him honourable and dishonourable. And the perfect citizen ought to seek to strengthen these no less than the principles of law which are sanctioned by punishments. I will adduce an example which will clear up my meaning. Hunting is of wide extent, and has a name under which many things are included, for there is a hunting of creatures in the water, and of creatures in the air; and there is a great deal of hunting of land animals of all sorts, and not of wild beasts only; the hunting after man is also worthy of consideration; there is the hunting after him in war, and there is often a hunting after him in the way of friendship, which is praised and also blamed; and there is thieving, and the hunting which is practised by robbers, and that of armies against armies. Now the legislator, in laying down laws about hunting, can neither abstain from noting these things, nor can he make threatening ordinances which will assign rules and penalties about all of them. What is he to do? He will have to praise and blame hunting with a view to the discipline and exercise of youth. And, on the other hand, the young man must listen obediently; neither pleasure nor pain should hinder him, and he should regard as his standard of action the praises and injunctions of the legislator rather than the punishments which he imposes by law. This being premised, there will follow next in order moderate praise and censure of hunting; the praise being assigned to that which will make the souls of young men better, and the censure to that which has the opposite effect. And now let us address young men in the form of a pious wish for their welfare: O, my friends, we will say to them, may no desire or love of hunting in the sea, or of angling or of catching the creatures in the sea, ever take possession of you, either when you are awake or when you are asleep, by hook or with weels, which latter is a very lazy contri-

**Hunting as an educational means.**

**Kinds of hunting forbidden.**

vance; and let not any desire of catching men and of piracy by sea enter into your souls and make you cruel and lawless hunters. And as to the desire of thieving in town or country, may it never enter into your most passing thoughts; nor let the insidious fancy of catching birds, which is hardly worthy of freemen, come into the head of any youth. There remains therefore for our athletes only the hunting and catching of land animals, of which the one sort is called hunting by night, in which the hunters sleep in turn and are lazy; this is not to be commended any more than that which has intervals of rest, in which the wild strength of beasts is subdued by nets and snares, and not by the victory of a laborious spirit. Thus, only the best kind of hunting is allowed at all — that of quadrupeds, which is carried on with horses and dogs and men's own persons, and they get the victory over the animals by running them down and striking them and hurling at them, those who have a care of godlike manhood taking them with their own hands. The praise and blame which is assigned to all these things has now been declared; and let the law be as follows: Let no one hinder our sacred hunters from following the chase wherever and whithersoever they will; but the nightly hunter, who trusts to his nets and springs, shall not be allowed to hunt anywhere. The fowler in the mountains and waste places shall be permitted, but on cultivated ground and on consecrated wilds he shall not be permitted; and any one who meets him may stop him. As to the hunter in waters, he may hunt anywhere except in harbours or sacred streams or marshes or pools, provided only that he do not trouble the water with poisonous mixtures. And now we may say that all our enactments about education are complete.

**The law concerning hunting.**

CLE. Very good.

## VI. THE SCIENTIFIC VIEW OF EDUCATION

**The Period and the Authority.** — Aristotle was the last of the great contributors to Greek educational theory, and his life (384–322 B.C.) forms a connecting link between the earlier theorists and the later cosmopolitan period which begins with the Macedonian supremacy. In philosophy Aristotle represents the culmination of the movement which passed through successive stages with the Sophists, Socrates and Plato. In his specific treatment of the subject of education he makes no great advance beyond Plato, though in later ages educational method and subject-matter are profoundly influenced through the *Organon* and *Metaphysics*. It is only with this specific treatment of education, in which he presents his own views, that the present discussion deals.

The adult life of Aristotle falls into three periods. The first is that from the seventeenth to the thirty-seventh years of his life, during which time he was under the instruction of Plato, or closely connected with the work of the Academy. Then it was that he showed opposition to the teachings of the master. Some of Aristotle's writings not now extant raise for debate the chief doctrine of the Platonic school, though the form of these writings is supposed to have been wholly in imitation of that of the master of the dialogue. This lack of orthodoxy and perhaps of intellectual sympathy led Aristotle to leave Athens at the death of Plato in 347 B.C., and for twelve years thereafter, in Asia Minor and Macedonia, he devoted himself to study and investigation. Some portion of the latter years of this period was devoted to the education of the young Alexander. While there are absolutely no details left to modern times concerning the nature of these duties and the manner in which they were performed, it has been suggested that Aristotle's chief influence on Greek education was through instilling into the mind of the future conqueror the ideas that led to the Hellenization of the East. Certain it is that the scheme of education outlined in the *Politics* is for the narrow limit of the city state, and that it was a scheme which had little or no immediate practical influence on Greek life. In 335 Aristotle returned to Athens to establish in the Lyceum his own school of philosophy, since the contrast between his own thought and that of the Academicians had now become more marked, both because his own ideas and method had developed, and because the work of the Academy had now degenerated into mere exposition and comment. Here he continued to teach for eighteen years. The aim of Aristotle was broader than that of the Platonic or of the other schools; it was nothing less than to produce an encyclopædia of all the sciences, — an organization of all human knowledge. During this period was produced the substance of the Aristotelian writings as we know them now. The character, order, and origin of these writings are all matters of debate. Leaving out of the question the pseudo-Aristotelian productions, it is generally admitted that not one of the works as we now have them is complete; that some of them are rather compilations or combinations of monographs than continuous treatises; that some contain parts or whole chapters that are mere summaries by pupils; that some are probably nothing more than very full notes taken by students at Aristotle's lectures. Even concerning the work of immediate interest to us, Jowett suggests that "we cannot be sure that any single sentence of the *Politics* proceeded from the pen of Aristotle." The whole question of authorship is complicated by the fact that the list of the 146 Aristotelian writings, made by the librarian of the great library at Alexander about 220 B.C., does not contain the name of a single one of his works, at least under the title by which we now know them. On the other hand, concerning the accepted works, it is quite as generally admitted that the substance, the spirit and the general form, if not the exact wording, are wholly Aristotelian. Where the efforts of the school supplemented those of the master, they were wholly under the dominance and direction of the latter, so that the same may be said of resulting collaborations. The fragmentary condition of some of the work, such as the treatment of education, is undoubtedly due to the fact that Aristotle purposely left the theme incomplete in presentation, with the expectation, and in some places with the explicit promise, of a return to the subject. This incompleteness, as well as the form in which some of the works have come down to us, is due to the manner of publication. This consisted merely in presentation through lectures in the schools, with the multiplication of texts through notes or more exact copies. It was therefore a process continuing over a considerable space of time, rather than an event of a given date. That during the period of publication the author's ideas would develop is evidenced by the *Republic* and the *Laws*, as well as by the *Politics*. At Aristotle's death it appears that the work of the Peripatetic school consisted largely in collecting and editing the master's works, and in some respects in completing them by a combination of fragments. The interest of the school was largely in those works of the philosopher produced during his headship of the Lyceum. There does not seem to have been any such multiplication of copies of the works as was the case with the other philosophical schools. Some thirty-five years after the death of Aristotle, the head of the school, who fell heir to the works, removed them to Asia Minor. Shortly after this, to save them from destruction, they were hidden in a vault, and there remained lost to the world until recovered a century and a half later. They were then restored to Greece and later transferred to Rome. This indicates in part the reason why these educational writings had no immediate influence upon Greek education.

The *Politics* contains Aristotle's specific treatment of education in the main; though the discussions of the general purpose of education could be supplemented with selections from the *Ethics*, and the discussion of the place of literature in education with selections from the *Poetics*. It is indicative of the importance of the subject of education in Grecian thought that it should form an integral part of the science of politics, — a fact to be gathered from the *Republic* and the *Laws*, as well as from the *Politics*. The *Politics* differs from the *Republic* and the *Laws* in being primarily a scientific investigation in comparative politics. In addition to being an inductive study based on his previous collection of constitutions, now lost, it contains many views that are simply a part of the ordinary aristocratic view of the Grecians, especially of those not in sympathy with the Athenians, and other views, largely metaphysical, that are made to appear scientific by referring them to "nature." The discussion of education, however, is for the most part a scientific exposition of the actual practices of Greek states, especially the Athenian, tested by Aristotle's standard of the natural. This standard, while in form often metaphysical, is nevertheless derived from a wide comparative study of existing practices.

Aristotle holds that there are three normal forms of government, — monarchy, aristocracy, and the constitutional or republican; and that there are perversions of each. Of the three he holds that the monarchical is best if not perverted, but that it is the most liable to abuse; that the republican is least liable to perversion, and hence the one to be recommended. It is for this best practicable form of government that he elaborates his approved scheme of education. One must bear in mind the fact that the state is still the very restricted city state of the Greeks. Aristotle sees the possibility of the larger nation and of the confederacy; but both of these have for their aims mere expediency, while the city state alone can aim at virtue. As a further essential to this ideal state the industrial and commercial classes, as well as the slave population, are excluded from citizenship. Only those who are relieved from the necessity of all economic activities can become good citizens. Those engaged in the practical or industrial life are to be educated by participation in the occupations which they are to follow, — in other words, by apprenticeship. All such persons need a practical education only, and a practical education calls for a training, but for no instruction.

The only education discussed in the *Politics* is the liberal education necessary as a preparation for citizenship in this state wherein all citizens are successively ruled and rulers. It is from this thought of the interchange of rulers and ruled that the consideration of education departs. The remainder of the seventh and all of the eighth book are devoted to this discussion, which, however, is only fragmentary. Education in infancy and childhood are treated of, but the passage closes without any mention of the most important phase of education, that of the immediate preparation of youth for citizenship. This is the stage of education concerning which there was then the greatest interest, and in which there had occurred the most radical changes. Either the latter portion of the treatise has been lost to modern times, or the author left it incomplete, with the expectation of returning to the subject.

On the training of infancy, the views of Aristotle do not depart materially from the approved custom at Athens or from the views of Plato, though he rejects the communistic scheme and insists upon the importance of the family. Of the physical well-being of the child, great care is to be taken, this care extending even to prenatal regulations. The child's morals are to be well guarded in various ways, amongst others by exclusion from contact with public life, and by the care of pedagogues and of guardians of public education — an institution borrowed from the Spartans. Concerning the education of childhood and youth, the periods from seven to fourteen and from fourteen to twenty, Aristotle again is substantially in accord with accepted Grecian practices. The greater part of the eighth book is devoted to a discussion of gymnastic and music as the component parts of the curriculum. The views here expressed are essentially those of the thoughtful Greek.

Neither gymnastic nor music should aim to produce the expert, but should be wholly liberalizing in their purpose. This exposition is the clearest statement to be found of the use of music in Greek education. The approved uses are for instruction, for purgation, and for leisure and recreation. To music and gymnastic are added drawing and letters as component parts of the curriculum, though little consideration is accorded either. In regard to letters Aristotle rejects the conclusions of Plato concerning Homer and the drama, but he fails to give any presentation of his own ideas concerning the proper scope of literary instruction. This omission is one of the best evidences of the fragmentary nature of the *Politics*. In all probability he would have made letters include the remainder of the liberal arts, thus completing the liberal education so far as it related to institutionalized instruction.

No correct concept of Aristotle's views of education can be gained, unless it be recognized that, as with Plato and Greek thinkers in general, the state itself is by him identified with education. The state is not only the end of education but, in every detail, a means to education. While Aristotle has no place for the guardians of the Platonic state, and consequently no elaborate philosophical education looking to the production of such a class, yet civic and military activities are to be organized for educational ends, and the education of the citizen does not cease until he has fully participated therein. These social activities are of two general classes: the one practical and executive, the other deliberative and advisory. After the age of twenty-one the young men are to engage in active civic and military duties. With their growing experience these are gradually to be exchanged for those that are advisory and judicial. Much of this time is to be spent in cultured leisure, and finally all of it is to be devoted to the life of contemplation. In this way the end of the state, as found in the happiness of the individuals composing it, is to be attained. This happiness of the individual is largely intellectual. Thus the problem of Greek politics and education is solved by the gradual development into the contemplative or intellectual life; neither is to be separated from the activities essential to the welfare of the state.

## *Selections from the Politics of Aristotle*

### BOOK V

**Education as the basis of stable government.**

9. But of all the things which I have mentioned that which most contributes to the permanence of constitutions is the adaptation of education to the form of government, and yet in our own day this principle is universally neglected. The best laws, though sanctioned by every citizen of the state, will be of no avail unless the young are trained by habit and education in the spirit of the constitution, if the laws are democratical, democratically, or oligarchically, if the laws are oligarchical. For there may be a want of self-discipline in states as well as in individuals. Now, to have been educated in the spirit of the constitution is not to perform the actions in which oligarchs or democrats delight, but those by which the existence of an oligarchy or of a democracy is made possible. Whereas among ourselves the sons of the ruling class in an oligarchy live in luxury, but the sons of the poor are hardened by exercise and toil, and hence they are both more inclined and better able to make a revolution. And in democracies of the more extreme type there has arisen a false idea of freedom which is contradictory to the true interests of the state. For two principles are characteristic of democracy, the government of the majority and freedom. Men think that what is just is equal; and that equality is the supremacy of the popular will; and that freedom and equality

mean the doing what a man likes. In such democracies every one lives as he pleases, or in the words of Euripides, 'according to his fancy.' But this is all wrong; men should not think it slavery to live according to the rule of the constitution; for it is their salvation.

* * * * * * *

BOOK VII

**Virtue and goodness of a state depend upon virtue and goodness of individual citizens.**

13. It follows then from what has been said that some things the legislator must find ready to his hand in a state, others he must provide. And therefore we can only say: May our state be constituted in such a manner as to be blessed with the goods of which fortune disposes (for we acknowledge her power): whereas virtue and goodness in the state are not a matter of chance but the result of knowledge and purpose. A city can be virtuous only when the citizens who have a share in the government are virtuous, and in our state all the citizens share in the government; let us then enquire how a man becomes virtuous. For even if we could suppose all the citizens to be virtuous, and not each of them, yet the latter would be better, for in the virtue of each the virtue of all is involved.

**Three elements of virtue: (1) nature, (2) habit, (3) reason.**

There are three things which make men good and virtuous: these are nature, habit, reason. In the first place, every one must be born a man and not some other animal; in the second place, he must have a certain character, both of body and soul. But some qualities there is no use in having at birth, for they are altered by habit, and there are some gifts of nature which may be turned by habit to good or bad. Most animals lead a life of nature, although in lesser particulars some are influenced by habit as well. Man has reason, in addition, and man only. Wherefore nature, habit, reason must be in harmony with one another (for they do not always agree); men do many things against habit and nature, if reason persuades them that they ought. We have already determined what natures are likely to be most easily moulded by the hands of the legislator. All else is the work of education; we learn some things by habit and some by instruction.

14. Since every political society is composed of rulers

Rulers and ruled are to interchange.

and subjects, let us consider whether the relations of one to the other should interchange or be permanent. For the education of the citizens will necessarily vary with the answer given to this question. Now, if some men excelled others in the same degree in which gods and heroes are supposed to excel mankind in general, having in the first place a great advantage even in their bodies, and secondly in their minds, so that the superiority of the governors over their subjects was patent and undisputed, it would clearly be better that once for all the one class should rule and the others serve. But since this is unattainable, and kings have no marked superiority over their subjects, such as Scylax[1] affirms to be found among the Indians, it is obviously necessary on many grounds that all the citizens alike should take their turn in governing and being governed. Equality consists in the same treatment of similar persons, and no government can stand which is not founded upon justice. For (if the government be unjust) every one in the country[2] unites with the governed in the desire to have a revolution, and it is an impossibility that the members of the government can be so numerous as to be stronger than all their enemies put together. Yet that governors should excel their subjects is undeniable. How all this is to be effected, and in what way they will respectively share in the government, the legislator has to consider. The subject has been already mentioned. Nature herself has given the principle of choice when she made a difference between old and young (though they are really the same in kind), of whom she fitted the one to govern and the others to be governed. No one takes offence at being governed when he is young, nor does he think himself better than his governors, especially if he will enjoy the same privilege when he reaches the required age.

Relation to education. All must know both how to command and how to obey.

We conclude that from one point of view governors and governed are identical, and from another different. And therefore their education must be the same and also different. For he who would learn to command well must, as men say, first of all learn to obey. As I observed in the

[1] An ancient geographer; cf. Herodotus, IV. 44.

[2] *I.e.* the perioeci.

first part of this treatise, there is one rule which is for the sake of the rulers and another rule which is for the sake of the ruled; the former is a despotic, the latter a free government. Some commands differ not in the thing commanded, but in the intention with which they are imposed. Wherefore, many apparently menial offices are an honour to the free youth by whom they are performed; for actions do not differ as honourable or dishonourable in themselves so much as in the end and intention of them. But since we say that the virtue of the citizen and ruler is the same as that of the good man, and that the same person must first be a subject and then a ruler, the legislator has to see that they become good men, and by what means this may be accomplished, and what is the end of the perfect life.

**Two parts of the soul; the end to be sought in reason.**

Now the soul of man is divided into two parts, one of which has reason in itself, and the other, not having reason in itself, is able to obey reason. And we call a man good because he has the virtues of these two parts. In which of them the end is more likely to be found is no matter of doubt to those who adopt our division; for in the world both of nature and of art the inferior always exists for the sake of the better or superior, and the better or superior is that which has reason. The reason too, in our ordinary way of speaking, is divided into two parts for there is a practical and a speculative reason, and there must be a corresponding division of actions; the actions of the naturally better principle are to be preferred by those who have it in their power to attain to both or to all, for that is always to every one the most eligible which is the highest attainable by him. The whole of life is further divided into two parts, business and leisure, war and peace, and all actions into those which are necessary and useful, and those which are honourable. And the preference given to one or the other class of actions must necessarily be like the preference given to one or other part of the soul and its actions over the other; there must be war for the sake of peace, business for the sake of leisure, things useful and necessary for the sake of things honourable. All these points the statesman should keep in view when he frames his laws; he should consider the parts of the soul

**Two classes of actions and two corresponding kinds of education: a higher and a lower.**

and their functions, and above all the better and the end; he should also remember the diversities of human lives and actions. For men must engage in business and go to war, but leisure and peace are better; they must do what is necessary and useful, but what is honourable is better. In such principles children and persons of every age which requires education should be trained. Whereas even the Hellenes of the present day, who are reputed to be best governed, and the legislators who gave them their constitutions, do not appear to have framed their governments with a regard to the best end, or to have given them laws and education with a view to all the virtues, but in a vulgar spirit have fallen back on those which promised to be more useful and profitable. Many modern writers have taken a similar view: they commend the Lacedæmonian constitution, and praise the legislator for making conquest and war his sole aim, a doctrine which may be refuted by argument and has long ago been refuted by facts. For most men desire empire in the hope of accumulating the goods of fortune; and on this ground Thibron and all those who have written about the Lacedæmonian constitution have praised their legislator, because the Lacedæmonians, by a training in hardships, gained great power. But surely they are not a happy people now that their empire has passed away, nor was their legislator right. How ridiculous is the result, if, while they are continuing in the observance of his laws and no one interferes with them, they have lost the better part of life. These writers further err about the sort of government which the legislator should approve, for the government of freemen is noble, and implies more virtue than despotic government. Neither is a city to be deemed happy or a legislator to be praised because he trains his citizens to conquer and obtain dominion over their neighbours, for there is great evil in this. On a similar principle any citizen who could, would obviously try to obtain the power in his own state, — the crime which the Lacedæmonians accuse king Pausanias of attempting, although he had so great honour already. No such principle and no law having this object is either statesmanlike or useful or right. For the same things are best both for individuals and for states, and

**Inadequacy of the Spartan education, which trained for the lower.**

**The military ideal is inadequate and is useless in peace.**

these are the things which the legislator ought to implant in the minds of his citizens. Neither should men study war with a view to the enslavement of those who do not deserve to be enslaved; but first of all they should provide against their own enslavement, and in the second place obtain empire for the good of the governed, and not for the sake of exercising a general despotism, and in the third place they should seek to be masters only over those who deserve to be slaves. Facts, as well as arguments, prove that the legislator should direct all his military and other measures to the provision of leisure and the establishment of peace. For most of these military states are safe only while they are at war, but fall when they have acquired their empire; like unused iron they rust in time of peace. And for this the legislator is to blame, he never having taught them how to lead the life of peace.

**War is for the sake of peace; business for the sake of leisure.**

15. Since the end of individuals and of states is the same, the end of the best man and of the best state must also be the same; it is therefore evident that there ought to exist in both of them the virtues of leisure; for peace, as has often been repeated, is the end of war, and leisure of toil. But leisure and cultivation may be promoted, not only by those virtues which are practised in leisure, but also by some of those which are useful to business. For many necessaries of life have to be supplied before we can have leisure. Therefore a city must be temperate and brave, and able to endure; for truly, as the proverb says, 'There is no leisure for slaves,' and those who cannot face danger like men are the slaves of any invader. Courage and endurance are required for business and philosophy for leisure, temperance and justice for both, more especially in times of peace and leisure, for war compels men to be just and temperate, whereas the enjoyment of good fortune and the leisure which comes with peace tends to make them insolent. Those then, who seem to be the best-off and to be in the possession of every good, have special need of justice and temperance,—for example, those (if such there be, as the poets say) who dwell in the Islands of the Blest; they above all will need philosophy and temperance and justice, and all the more the more leisure they have, living in the midst of abundance. There is no difficulty in seeing

why the state that would be happy and good ought to have these virtues. If it be disgraceful in men not to be able to use the goods of life, it is peculiarly disgraceful not to be able to use them in time of peace, — to show excellent qualities in action and war, and when they have peace and leisure to be no better than slaves. Wherefore we should not practise virtue after the manner of the Lacedæmonians. For they, while agreeing with other men in their conception of the highest goods, differ from the rest of mankind in thinking that they are to be obtained by the practice of a single virtue. And since these goods and the enjoyment of them are clearly greater than the enjoyment derived from the virtues of which they are the end, we must now consider how and by what means they are to be attained.

The highest goods not the result of a single virtue,— courage.

We have already determined that nature and habit and reason are required, and what should be the character of the citizens has also been defined by us. But we have still to consider whether the training of early life is to be that of reason or habit, for these two must accord, and when in accord they will then form the best of harmonies. Reason may make mistakes and fail in attaining the highest ideal of life, and there may be a like evil influence of habit. Thus much is clear in the first place, that, as in all other things, birth implies some antecedent principle, and that the end of anything has a beginning in some former end. Now, in men reason and mind are the end towards which nature strives, so that the birth and moral discipline of the citizens ought to be ordered with a view to them. In the second place, as the soul and body are two, we see also that there are two parts of the soul, the rational and the irrational, and two corresponding states — reason and appetite. And as the body is prior in order of generation to the soul, so the irrational is prior to the rational. The proof is that anger and will and desire are implanted in children from their very birth, but reason and understanding are developed as they grow older. Wherefore, the care of the body ought to precede that of the soul, and the training of the appetitive part should follow: none the less our care of it must be for the sake of the reason, and our care of the body for the sake of the soul.

The education of the body precedes that of the mind; and the formation of habit precedes instruction.

* * * * * * *

17. After the children have been born, the manner of rearing them may be supposed to have a great effect on their bodily strength. It would appear from the example of animals, and of those nations who desire to create the military habit, that the food which has most milk in it is best suited to human beings; but the less wine the better, if they would escape diseases. Also all the motions to which children can be subjected at their early age are very useful. But in order to preserve their tender limbs from distortion, some nations have had recourse to mechanical appliances which straighten their bodies. To accustom children to the cold from their earliest years is also an excellent practice, which greatly conduces to health, and hardens them for military service. Hence many barbarians have a custom of plunging their children at birth into a cold stream; others, like the Celts, clothe them in a light wrapper only. For human nature should be early habituated to endure all which by habit it can be made to endure; but the process must be gradual. And children, from their natural warmth, may be easily trained to bear cold. Such care should attend them in the first stage of life.

**Young children.** **Their food,** **exercise,** **clothing,**

The next period lasts to the age of five; during this no demand should be made upon the child for study or labour, lest its growth be impeded; and there should be sufficient motion to prevent the limbs from being inactive. This can be secured, among other ways, by amusement, but the amusement should not be vulgar or tiring or riotous. The Directors of Education, as they are termed, should be careful what tales or stories the children hear,[1] for the sports of children are designed to prepare the way for the business of later life, and should be for the most part imitations of the occupations which they will hereafter pursue in earnest. Those are wrong who (like Plato) in the Laws[2] attempt to check the loud crying and screaming of children, for these contribute towards their growth, and, in a manner, exercise their bodies. Straining the voice has an effect similar to that produced by the retention of the breath in violent exertions. Besides other duties, the

**amusements,** **tales and stories.**

[1] Cf. Plato, *Republic*, II. 377; p. 140 of this volume.

[2] Cf. Plato, *Laws*, I. 643; VII. 799.

Directors of Education should have an eye to their bringing up, and should take care that they are left as little as possible with slaves. For until they are seven years old they must live at home; and therefore, even at this early age, all that is mean and low should be banished from their sight and hearing. Indeed, there is nothing which the legislator should be more careful to drive away than indecency of speech; for the light utterance of shameful words is akin to shameful actions. The young especially should never be allowed to repeat or hear anything of the sort. A freeman who is fond of saying or doing what is forbidden, if he be too young as yet to have the privilege of a place at the public tables, should be disgraced and beaten, and an elder person degraded as his slavish conduct deserves. And since we do not allow improper language, clearly we should also banish pictures or tales which are indecent. Let the rulers take care that there be no image or picture representing unseemly actions, except in the temples of those Gods at whose festivals the law permits even ribaldry, and whom the law also permits to be worshipped by persons of mature age on behalf of themselves, their children, and their wives. But the legislator should not allow youth to be hearers of satirical Iambic verses or spectators of comedy until they are of an age to sit at the public tables and to drink strong wine; by that time education will have armed them against the evil influences of such representations.

**Should live at home, but not be left to slaves.**

**Care for their morals.**

We have made these remarks in a cursory manner,— they are enough for the present occasion; but hereafter we will return to the subject and after a fuller discussion[1] determine whether such liberty should or should not be granted, and in what way granted, if at all. Theodorus, the tragic actor, was quite right in saying that he would not allow any other actor, not even if he were quite second-rate, to enter before himself, because the spectators grew fond of the voices which they first heard. And the same principle of association applies universally to things as well as persons, for we always like best whatever comes first. And therefore youth should be kept strangers to all that is bad, and especially to things which suggest vice or hate.

**Lasting influence of early associations.**

[1] A promise unfulfilled, or if fulfilled the discussion is not extant.

When the five years have passed away, during the two following years they must look on at the pursuits which they are hereafter to learn. There are two periods of life into which education has to be divided, from seven to the age of puberty, and onwards to the age of one and twenty. (The poets) who divide ages by sevens are not always right: we should rather adhere to the divisions actually made by nature; for the deficiencies of nature are what art and education seek to fill up.

**Periods of life.**

Let us then first enquire if any regulations are to be laid down about children, and secondly, whether the care of them should be the concern of the state or the private individuals, which latter is in our own day the common custom, and in the third place, what these regulations should be.

## BOOK VIII

**Character of education determined by character of the state.**

1. No one will doubt that the legislator should direct his attention above all to the education of youth, or that the neglect of education does harm to states. The citizen should be moulded to suit the form of government under which he lives. For each government has a peculiar character which originally formed and which continues to preserve it. The character of democracy creates democracy, and the character of oligarchy creates oligarchy; and always the better the character, the better the government.

**Education should be public and the same for all, and for the good of all.**

Now for the exercise of any faculty or art a previous training and habituation are required; clearly therefore for the practice of virtue. And since the whole city has one end, it is manifest that education should be one and the same for all, and that it should be public, and not private, — not as at present, when every one looks after his own children separately, and gives them separate instruction of the sort which he thinks best; the training in things which are of common interest should be the same for all. Neither must we suppose that any one of the citizens belongs to himself, for they all belong to the state, and are each of them a part of the state, and the care of each part is inseparable from the care of the whole. In this particular the Lacedæmonians are to be praised, for they take the greatest pains about their children, and make education the business of the state.

Aim of education; liberal or practical.

2. That education should be regulated by law and should be an affair of state is not to be denied, but what should be the character of this public education, and how young persons should be educated, are questions which remain to be considered. For mankind are by no means agreed about the things to be taught, whether we look to virtue or the best life. Neither is it clear whether education is more concerned with intellectual or with moral virtue. The existing practice is perplexing; no one knows on what principle we should proceed — should the useful in life, or should virtue, or should the higher knowledge, be the aim of our training; all three opinions have been entertained. Again, about the means there is no agreement; for different persons, starting with different ideas about the nature of virtue, naturally disagree about the practice of it. There can be no doubt that children should be taught those useful things which are really necessary, but not all things; for occupations are divided into liberal and illiberal; and to young children should be imparted only such kinds of knowledge as will be useful to them without vulgarizing them. And any occupation, art, or science, which makes the body or soul or mind of the freeman less fit for the practice or exercise of virtue, is vulgar; wherefore we call those arts vulgar which tend to deform the body, and likewise all paid employments, for they absorb and degrade the mind. There are also some liberal arts quite proper for a freeman to acquire, but only in a certain degree, and if he attend to them too closely, in order to attain perfection in them, the same evil effects will follow. The object also which a man sets before him makes a great difference; if he does or learns anything for his own sake or for the sake of his friends, or with a view to excellence, the action will not appear illiberal; but if done for the sake of others, the very same action will be thought menial and servile. The received subjects of instruction, as I have already remarked, are partly of a liberal and partly of an illiberal character.

3. The customary branches of education are in number

four; they are—(1) reading and writing, (2) gymnastic exercises, (3) music, to which is sometimes added (4) drawing. Of these, reading and writing and drawing are regarded as useful for the purposes of life in a variety of ways, and gymnastic exercises are thought to infuse courage. Concerning music a doubt may be raised—in our own day most men cultivate it for the sake of pleasure, but originally it was included in education, because nature herself, as has often been said, requires that we should be able, not only to work well, but to use leisure well; for, as I must repeat once and again, the first principle of all action is leisure. Both are required, but leisure is better than occupation; and therefore the question must be asked in good earnest, what ought we to do when at leisure? Clearly we ought not to be amusing ourselves, for then amusement would be the end of life. But if this is inconceivable, and yet amid serious occupations amusement is needed more than at other times (for he who is hard at work has need of relaxation, and amusement gives relaxation, whereas occupation is always accompanied with exertion and effort), at suitable times we should introduce amusements, and they should be our medicines, for the emotion which they create in the soul is a relaxation, and from the pleasure we obtain rest. Leisure of itself gives pleasure and happiness and enjoyment of life, which are experienced, not by the busy man, but by those who have leisure. For he who is occupied has in view some end which he has not attained; but happiness is an end which all men deem to be accompanied with pleasure and not with pain. This pleasure, however, is regarded differently by different persons, and varies according to the habit of individuals; the pleasure of the best man is the best, and springs from the noblest sources. It is clear then that there are branches of learning and education which we must study with a view to the enjoyment of leisure, and these are to be valued for their own sake; whereas those kinds of knowledge which are useful in business are to be deemed necessary, and exist for the sake of other things. And therefore our fathers admitted music into education, not on the ground either of its necessity or utility, for it is not necessary, nor indeed useful in the same manner as

**Subject-matter of education.**

**Purpose of music.**

reading and writing, which are useful in money-making, in the management of a household, in the acquisition of knowledge and in political life, nor like drawing, useful for a more correct judgment of the works of artists, nor again like gymnastic, which gives health and strength; for neither of these is to be gained from music. There remains, then, the use of music for intellectual enjoyment in leisure; which appears to have been the reason of its introduction, this being one of the ways in which it is thought that a freeman should pass his leisure; as Homer says —

> 'How good it is to invite men to the pleasant feast,'

and afterwards he speaks of others whom he describes as inviting

> 'The bard who would delight them all.'[1]

And in another place Odysseus says there is no better way of passing life than when

> 'Men's hearts are merry and the banqueters in the hall, sitting in order, hear the voice of the minstrel.'[2]

It is evident, then, that there is a sort of education in which parents should train their sons, not as being useful or necessary, but because it is liberal or noble. Whether this is of one kind only, or of more than one, and if so, what they are, and how they are to be imparted, must hereafter be determined. Thus much we are now in a position to say that the ancients witness to us; for their opinion may be gathered from the fact that music is one of the received and traditional branches of education. Further, it is clear that children should be instructed in some useful things, — for example, in reading and writing, — not only for their usefulness, but also because many other sorts of knowledge are acquired through them. With a like view they may be taught drawing, not to prevent their making mistakes in their own purchases, or in order that they may not be imposed upon in the buying or selling of articles, but rather because it makes them judges of the beauty of the human form. To be always seeking after the useful does

Reading, writing, and drawing have a liberal purpose.

[1] *Odyssey*, XVII. 385.

[2] *Odyssey*, IX. 7.

not become free and exalted souls. Now it is clear that in education habit must go before reason, and the body before the mind; and therefore boys should be handed over to the trainer, who creates in them the proper habit of body, and to the wrestling-master, who teaches them their exercises.

**Gymnastic.**

4. Of those states which in our own day seem to take the greatest care of children, some aim at producing in them an athletic habit, but they only injure their forms and stunt their growth. Although the Lacedæmonians have not fallen into this mistake, yet they brutalize their children by laborious exercises which they think will make them courageous. But in truth, as we have often repeated, education should not be exclusively directed to this or to any other single end. And even if we suppose the Lacedæmonians to be right in their end, they do not attain it. For among barbarians and among animals courage is found associated, not with the greatest ferocity, but with a gentle and lion-like temper. There are many races who are ready enough to kill and eat men, such as the Achæans and Heniochi, who both live about the Black Sea; and there are other inland tribes, as bad or worse, who all live by plunder, but have no courage. It is notorious that the Lacedæmonians, while they were themselves assiduous in their laborious drill, were superior to others, but now they are beaten both in war and gymnastic exercises. For their ancient superiority did not depend on their mode of training their youth, but only on the circumstance that they trained them at a time when others did not. Hence we may infer that what is noble, not what is brutal, should have the first place; no wolf or other wild animal will face a really noble danger; such dangers are for the brave man. And parents who devote their children to gymnastics while they neglect their necessary education, in reality vulgarize them; for they make them useful to the state in one quality only, and even in this the argument proves them to be inferior to others. We should judge the Lacedæmonians not from what they have been but from what they are; for now they have rivals who compete with their education; formerly they had none.

**Athletic training injurious.**

**Roughness or ferocity is not courage.**

It is an admitted principle, that gymnastic exercises

The young should not be overtaxed.

should be employed in education, and that for children they should be of a lighter kind, avoiding severe regimen or painful toil, lest the growth of the body be impaired. The evil of excessive training in early years is strikingly proved by the example of the Olympic victors; for not more than two or three of them have gained a prize both as boys and as men; their early training and severe gymnastic exercises exhausted their constitutions. When boyhood is over, three years should be spent in other studies; the period of life which follows may then be devoted to hard exercise and strict regimen. Men ought not to labour at the same time with their minds and with their bodies;[1] for the two kinds of labour are opposed to one another, the labour of the body impedes the mind, and the labour of the mind the body.

Why music should be studied: as an amusement; because it affects character; because it contributes to the enjoyment of leisure.

5. Concerning music there are some questions which we have already raised; these we may now resume and carry further; and our remarks will serve as a prelude to this or any other discussion of the subject. It is not easy to determine the nature of music, or why any one should have a knowledge of it. Shall we say, for the sake of amusement and relaxation, like sleep or drinking, which are not good in themselves, but are pleasant, and at the same time 'make care to cease;' as Euripides[2] says? And therefore men rank them with music, and make use of all three, — sleep, drinking, music, — to which some add dancing. Or shall we argue that music conduces to virtue, on the ground that it can form our minds and habituate us to true pleasures as our bodies are made by gymnastic to be of a certain character? Or shall we say that it contributes to the enjoyment of leisure and mental cultivation, which is a third alternative? Now obviously youth are not to be instructed with a view to their amusement, for learning is no pleasure, but is accompanied with pain. Neither is intellectual enjoyment suitable to boys of that age, for it is the end, and that which is imperfect cannot attain the perfect or end. But perhaps it may be said that boys learn music for the sake of the amusement which they will have when

Need we play and sing ourselves?

[1] Cf. Plato, *Republic*, VII. 537; p. 217 of this volume.

[2] Bacchæ, 380.

they are grown up. If so, why should they learn themselves, and not, like the Persian and Median kings, enjoy the pleasure and instruction which is derived from hearing others? (for surely skilled persons who have made music the business and profession of their lives will be better performers than those who practise only to learn). If they must learn music, on the same principle they should learn cookery, which is absurd. And even granting that music may form the character, the objection still holds: why should we learn ourselves? Why cannot we attain true pleasure and form a correct judgment from hearing others, like the Lacedæmonians?—for they, without learning music, nevertheless can correctly judge, as they say, of good and bad melodies. Or again, if music should be used to promote cheerfulness and refined intellectual enjoyment, the objection still remains—why should we learn ourselves instead of enjoying the performance of others? We may illustrate what we are saying by our conception of the Gods; for in the poets Zeus does not himself sing or play on the lyre. Nay, we call professional performers vulgar; no freeman would play or sing unless he were intoxicated or in jest. But these matters may be left for the present.

**Music may be considered, (1) an amusement,**

The first question is whether music is or is not to be a part of education. Of the three things mentioned in our discussion, which is it?—Education or amusement or intellectual enjoyment, for it may be reckoned under all three, and seems to share in the nature of all of them. Amusement is for the sake of relaxation, and relaxation is of necessity sweet, for it is the remedy of pain caused by toil, and intellectual enjoyment is universally acknowledged to contain an element not only of the noble but of the pleasant, for happiness is made up of both. All men agree that music is one of the pleasantest things, whether with or without song; as Musæus says,

> 'Song is to mortals of all things the sweetest.'

Hence and with good reason it is introduced into social gatherings and entertainments, because it makes the hearts of men glad: so that on this ground alone we may assume that the young ought to be trained in it. For innocent pleasures are not only in harmony with the perfect end of life, but they also provide relaxation. And whereas men rarely attain the end, but often rest by the way and amuse themselves, not only with a view to some good, but also for the pleasure's sake, it may be well for them at times to find a refreshment in music. It sometimes happens that men make amusement the end, for the end probably contains some element of pleasure, though not any ordinary or lower pleasure; but they mistake the lower for the higher, and in seeking for the one find the other, since every pleasure has a likeness to the end of action. For the end is not eligible, nor do the pleasures which we have described exist, for the sake of any future good but of the past, that is to say, they are the alleviation of past toils and pains. And we may infer this to be the reason why men seek happiness from common pleasures. But music is pursued, not only as an alleviation of past toil, but also as providing recreation. And who can say whether, having this use, it may not also have a nobler one? In addition to this common pleasure, felt and shared in by all (for the pleasure given by music is natural, and therefore adapted to all ages and characters), may it not have also some influence over the character and the soul? It must have such an influence if characters are affected by it. And that they are so affected is proved by the power which the songs of Olympus and of many others exercise; for beyond question they inspire enthusiasm, and enthusiasm is an emotion of the ethical part of the soul. Besides, when men hear imitations, even unaccompanied by melody or rhythm, their feelings move in sympathy. Since then music is a pleasure, and virtue consists in rejoicing and loving and hating aright, there is clearly nothing which we are so much concerned to acquire and to cultivate as the power of forming right judgments, and of taking delight in good dispositions and noble actions.[1] Rhythm and melody supply imitations of anger and gentleness, and also of courage and temperance and of virtues and vices in general, which hardly fall short of the actual affections, as we know from our own experience,

(2) as having an ethical influence.

[1] Cf. Plato, *Republic*, III. 401–402; p. 161 of this volume, and Plato, *Laws*, II. 658–659; pp. 227–228 of this volume.

for in listening to such strains our souls undergo a change. The habit of feeling pleasure or pain at mere representations is not far removed from the same feeling about realities;[1] for example, if any one delights in the sight of a statue for its beauty only, it necessarily follows that the sight of the original will be pleasant to him. No other sense, such as taste or touch, has any resemblance to moral qualities; in sight only there is a little, for figures are to some extent of a moral character, and (so far) all participate in the feeling about them. Again, figures and colours are not imitations, but signs of moral habits, indications which the body gives of states of feeling. The connection of them with morals is slight, but in so far as there is any, young men should be taught to look, not at the works of Pauson, but at those of Polygnotus, or any other painter or statuary who expresses moral ideas. On the other hand, even in mere melodies there is an imitation of character, for the musical modes differ essentially from one another, and those who hear them are differently affected by each. Some of them make men sad and grave, like the so-called Mixolydian, others enfeeble the mind, like the relaxed harmonies, others, again, produce a moderate and settled temper, which appears to be the peculiar effect of the Dorian; the Phrygian inspires enthusiasm. The whole subject has been well treated by philosophical writers on this branch of education, and they confirm their arguments by facts. The same principles apply to rhythms: some have a character of rest, others of motion, and of these latter again, some have a more vulgar, others a nobler movement. Enough has been said to show that music has a power of forming the character, and should therefore be introduced into the education of the young. The study is suited to the stage of youth, for young persons will not, if they can help, endure anything which is not sweetened by pleasure, and music has a natural sweetness. There seems to be in us a sort of affinity to harmonies and rhythms, which makes some philosophers say that the soul is a harmony, others, that she possesses harmony.

**More than painting and statuary.**

**Various melodies and rhythms have various ethical effects.**

6. And now we have to determine the question which

[1] Cf. Plato, *Republic*, III. 395; pp. 155–156 of this volume.

Children should be taught to sing and play.

has been already raised, whether children should be themselves taught to sing and play or not. Clearly there is a considerable difference made in the character by the actual practice of the art. It is difficult, if not impossible, for those who do not perform to be good judges of the performance of others. Besides, children should have something to do, and the rattle of Archytas, which people give to their children in order to amuse them and prevent them from breaking anything in the house, was a capital invention, for a young thing cannot be quiet. The rattle is a toy suited to the infant mind and (musical) education is a rattle or toy for children of a larger growth. We conclude then that they should be taught music in such a way as to become not only critics but performers.

They must not become professionals.

The question what is or is not suitable for different ages may be easily answered; nor is there any difficulty in meeting the objection of those who say that the study of music is vulgar. We reply (1) in the first place, that they who are to be judges must also be performers, and that they should begin to practise early, although when they are older they may be spared the execution; they must have learned to appreciate what is good and to delight in it, thanks to the knowledge which they acquired in their youth. As to (2) the vulgarizing effect which music is supposed to exercise, this is a question (of degree), which we shall have no difficulty in determining, when we have considered to what extent freemen who are being trained to political virtue should pursue the art, what melodies and what rhythms they should be allowed to use, and what instruments should be employed in teaching them to play, for even the instrument makes a difference. The answer to the objection turns upon these distinctions; for it is quite possible that certain methods of teaching and learning music do really have a degrading effect. It is evident then that the learning of music ought not to impede the business of riper years, or to degrade the body or render it unfit for civil or military duties, whether for the early practice or for the later study of them.

The right measure will be attained if students of music stop short of the arts which are practised in professional contests, and do not seek to acquire those fantastic marvels of execution which are now the fashion in such contests, and from these have passed into education. Let the young pursue their studies until they are able to feel delight in noble melodies and rhythms, and not merely in that common part of music in which every slave or child and even some animals find pleasure.

**What instruments should be used.**

From these principles we may also infer what instruments should be used. The flute, or any other instrument which requires great skill, as for example the harp, ought not to be admitted into education, but only such as will make intelligent students of music or of the other parts of education. Besides, the flute is not an instrument which has a good moral effect; it is too exciting. The proper time for using it is when the performance aims not at instruction, but at the relief of the passions. And there is a further objection; the impediment which the flute presents to the use of the voice detracts from its educational value. The ancients therefore were right in forbidding the flute to youths and freemen, although they had once allowed it. For when their wealth gave them greater leisure, and they had loftier notions of excellence, being also elated with their success, both before and after the Persian War, with more zeal than discernment they pursued every kind of knowledge, and so they introduced the flute into education. At Lacedæmon there was a Choragus who led the Chorus with a flute, and at Athens the instrument became so popular that most freemen could play upon it. The popularity is shown by the tablet which Thrasippus dedicated when he furnished the Chorus to Ecphantides. Later experience enabled men to judge what was or was not really conducive to virtue, and they rejected both the flute and several other old-fashioned instruments, such as the Lydian harp, the many-stringed lyre, the 'heptagon,' 'triangle,' 'sambuca,' and the like—which are intended only to give pleasure to the hearer, and require extraordinary skill of hand.[1] There is a meaning also in the myth of the ancients, which tells how Athene invented the flute and then threw it away. It was not a bad idea of theirs, that the Goddess disliked the instrument because it made the face ugly; but with still more reason

**Not the flute.**

[1] Cf. Plato, *Republic*, III. 399; p. 160 of this volume.

may we say that she rejected it because the acquirement of flute-playing contributes nothing to the mind, since to Athene we ascribe both knowledge and art.

**Professionalism vulgarizes music.** Thus then we reject the professional instruments and also the professional mode of education in music — and by professional we mean that which is adopted in contests, for in this the performer practises the art, not for the sake of his own improvement, but in order to give pleasure, and that of a vulgar sort, to his hearers. For this reason the execution of such music is not the part of a freeman but of a paid performer, and the result is that the performers are vulgarized, for the end at which they aim is bad. The vulgarity of the spectator tends to lower the character of the music and therefore of the performers; they look to him — he makes them what they are, and fashions even their bodies by the movements which he expects them to exhibit.

**Melodies and rhythms.** 7. We have also to consider rhythms and harmonies. Shall we use them all in education or make a distinction? and shall the distinction be that which is made by those who are engaged in education, or shall it be some other? For we see that music is produced by melody and rhythm, and we ought to know what influence these have respectively on education, and whether we should prefer excellence in melody or excellence in rhythm. But as the subject has been very well treated by many musicians of the present day, and also by philosophers who have had considerable experience of musical education, to these we would refer the more exact student of the subject; we shall only speak of it now after the matter of the legislator, having regard to general principles.

**Classification of melodies.** We accept the division of melodies proposed by certain philosophers into ethical melodies, melodies of action, and passionate or inspiring melodies, each having, as they say, a mode or harmony corresponding to it. But we maintain further that music should be studied, not for the sake of one, but of many benefits, that is to say, with a view to (1) education, (2) purification (the word 'purification' we use at present without explanation, but when hereafter we speak of poetry, we will treat the subject with more precision); music may also serve (3) for intellectual enjoyment, for relaxation and for recreation after exertion. It is clear, therefore, that all the harmonies must be employed by us, but not all of them in the same manner. In education ethical melodies are to be preferred, but we may listen to the melodies of action and passion when they are performed by others. For feelings such as pity and fear, or, again, enthusiasm, exist very strongly in some souls, and have more or less influence over all. Some persons fall into a religious frenzy, whom we see disenthralled by the use of mystic melodies, which bring healing and purification to the soul. Those who are influenced by pity or fear and every emotional nature have a like experience, others in their degree are stirred by something which specially affects them, and all are in a manner purified and their souls lightened and delighted. The melodies of purification likewise give an innocent pleasure to mankind. Such are the harmonies and the melodies in which those who perform music at the theatre should be invited to compete. But since the spectators are of two kinds — the one free and educated, the other a vulgar crowd composed of mechanics, labourers, and the like—there ought to be contests and exhibitions instituted for the relaxation of the second class also. And the melodies will correspond to their minds; for as their minds are perverted from the natural state, so there are exaggerated and corrupted harmonies which are in like manner a perversion. A man receives pleasure from what is natural to him, and therefore professional musicians may be allowed to practise this lower sort of music before an audience of a lower type. But, for the purposes of education, as I have already said, those modes and melodies should be employed which are ethical, such as the Dorian ; though we may include any others which are approved by philosophers who have had a musical education. The Socrates of the Republic[1] is wrong in retaining only the Phrygian mode along with the Dorian, and the more so because he rejects the flute; for the Phrygian is to the modes what the flute is to musical instruments — both of them are exciting and emotional. Poetry proves this, for Bacchic frenzy and all similar emotions are most suitably expressed by the flute, and are better set to the Phrygian than to any

**Ethical melodies to be preferred in education.**

**Music for the multitude.**

**The Dorian mode is ethical and educational**

[1] Cf. Plato, *Republic*, III. 399; p. 160 of this volume.

other harmony. The dithyramb, for example, is acknow edged to be Phrygian, a fact of which the connoisseurs ( music offer many proofs, saying, among other things, th: Philoxenus, having attempted to compose his Tales as dithyramb in the Dorian mode, found it impossible, ar fell back into the more appropriate Phrygian. All me agree that the Dorian music is the gravest and manlies And whereas we say that the extremes should be avoide and the mean followed, and whereas the Dorian is a mea between the other harmonies (the Phrygian and tl Lydian), it is evident that our youth should be taught tl Dorian music.

**Principles controlling the use of music in education.**

Two principles have to be kept in view, what is possibl what is becoming: at these every man ought to aim. Bı even these are relative to age; the old, who have lost the powers, cannot very well sing the severe melodies, an nature herself seems to suggest that their songs should t of the more relaxed kind. Wherefore the musicians lik wise blame Socrates, and with justice, for rejecting tl relaxed harmonies in education under the idea that the are intoxicating, not in the ordinary sense of intoxicatio (for wine rather tends to excite men), but because the have no strength in them. And so with a view to a tim of life when men begin to grow old, they ought to practi: the gentler harmonies and melodies as well as the other And if there be any harmony, such as the Lydian abo all others appears to be, which is suited to children ( tender age, and possesses the elements both of order ar of education, clearly (we ought to use it, for) educatic should be based upon three principles — the mean, tl possible, the becoming, these three.[1]

[1] This last selection is the eighth Book complete. Its abrupt termination further evidence that the treatise on education is fragmentary and incomple

## VII. THE LATER COSMOPOLITAN GREEK EDUCATION

**The Period.** — The decline of the national systems of education in Greece was consummated with the loss of political ambition and independent existence at the battle of Chæronea, 338 B.C. Even before this time Greek systems had lost much of their peculiar force. The decay and the attempted revivification of the Spartan system in the third century have been mentioned. The new education at Athens had introduced much greater freedom in Athenian practice, so that the education there was rather cosmopolitan than national. But of this cosmopolitan education Athens remained the centre throughout the Macedonian and Roman periods, though other centres, such as Rhodes, Tarsus, and Alexandria, became strong rivals. Interest now centres in higher education, which has become wholly intellectual in character. The chief characteristics of this period are: first, the organization of the various schools of philosophy finally combined into the University of Athens; second, the systematization of higher education under the control of, and finally with the support of, the state. While there is great emphasis upon the intellectual and philosophical life, education comes to be of minor political and social importance. Comparatively little material is to be found bearing upon the actual organization of Greek education during all this long period, save as its general features are presented in the tendencies of the new education and of the philosophical schools. However, the discussion of Roman education of the Græco-Roman period will supplement the information here given concerning the status of Greek education during much of this period. With the ascendency of the Christian religion a new influential factor is introduced into Greek education, this factor not becoming wholly dominant, however, until the University of Athens is closed by Justinian.

**The Sources.** — The first and second selections given consist of a decree of the Athenian Senate and one of the Assembly, relating to the education of the ephebes for some year about a century previous to the beginning of the Christian era. These selections are taken from the collection of inscriptions by Dumont, given in his *Essai sur L'Éphébie Attique.*

The third selection is an extract from the *Panegyric* of Gregory of Nazianzus on Saint Basil, and dates from the fourth Christian century. Gregory was a student at Athens about 350 to 356 A.D. Among his fellow-students was Basil, with whom he formed an intimate friendship. Both Gregory and Basil were prominent in the conflict with Arianism, and both held prominent places among the early church writers. Both were primarily students, though Basil gave up the student life for one of activity in furthering the practical interests of the church. Basil died in 379, and though Gregory was not present at the funeral, he later delivered the panegyric upon some anniversary of his friend's death. In this panegyric he gives a brief description of student life in Athens as it was during the period of their attendance at the university. The fourth selection consists of the greater part of Plutarch's essay upon the *Training of Children*. This presents the general views of a cosmopolitan Greek at about the opening of the second Christian century. While cosmopolitan, Plutarch was thoroughly Greek in his education and his sympathies. As giving a scientific though extremely practical exposition of the best Grecian educational ideas and practices, this selection from Plutarch might have been classed with that from Aristotle; but placed here, it will serve the additional purpose of illustrating the persistence of these ideas, four centuries later, at a time when Greece yet retained her intellectual leadership.

**The Philosophical Schools.** — The schools of the Sophists were entirely private schools, and for the most part consisted of the group of students gathered around any one instructor. There was no system of beliefs or unity of methods that would lead to the formation of any permanent institution. Socrates did not have any definite place for giving instruction or any definite body of pupils. So long as no fees were exacted, there would be no definite student body. Plato, and very probably Aristotle, followed the example of Socrates in this respect. But Plato's successor, Speusippus, demanded regular fees, as did also the teachers of the other philosophical groups. This gave both definiteness and continuity of administration. A further factor in the development of definite schools was the acquiring of definite locations and names. The leading gymnasia of Athens were the Academy, the Cynosarges, and the Lyceum. These were in the suburbs, and were somewhat of the nature of public parks, being provided with water and gardens as well as exercise grounds. Plato taught chiefly at the Academy, both in the public gymnasium and in private grounds which he acquired near by. This plot of ground, together with the headship of the school, Plato left to his nephew, Speusippus. The small property became the nucleus of a considerable foundation, for it was enriched, not only by fees, but by gifts from wealthy patrons and by the bequests of the heads of the school. In time friends and pupils also made bequests, until a considerable endowment was accumulated. The heads of the school were called *scholarchs*, and received their positions either through the designation of their predecessor or, later, by election. In a similar way Aristotle settled in the Lyceum and Antisthenes in the Cynosarges. Later the pupils of the latter removed to the frescoed portico in Athens, whence they were called Stoics. Epicurus taught in his own private grounds, which he left as the nucleus of an endowment for his school. As with the successors of Plato, each of these groups became definitely organized into a school with an endowment, and with a recognized head, or scholarch.

The attendance on these schools was very large. Theophrastus, the successor of Aristotle in the headship of the Lyceum, is said to have had more than two thousand pupils at one time. The scholarchs were assisted by a staff of assistants who collectively constituted the school. At any rate Lycon, the successor of Theophrastus, bequeathed the school to his pupils, or assistants, collectively, leaving to them the selection or election of a scholarch. Later on the scholarchs for some of the schools were elected by the council, usually after some form of examination. Still later, when these positions became salaried imperial offices, disputed elections were settled, or positions filled, by imperial officers, sometimes by the emperor himself.

Even in the early period, in addition to the immediate group of assistants or favorite pupils, a great number of minor teachers of grammar, rhetoric, dialectic, physics, and mathematics gathered around these four great schools of philosophy. Besides these philosophers and Sophists, there were numerous private tutors who prepared candidates for entrance to these higher schools, helped the younger students in their exercises, and directed them in their reading and note work. The philosophical chairs thus became the centre of the intellectual activity in all Greece.

The character of the work of these schools was very different from that of their founders. From the very first the scholarchs attempted only to set forth the ideas of the respective founders of the schools. This is what distinguishes them from the earlier schools: there was no attempt to apply the ideas of the great teachers in investigation, research, or even in discussion on new topics. For the most part the work became as formal and as artificial as the work of the Sophists, only it was directed toward a different object. The philosophical schools at least had a definite body of doctrine to expound and to comment upon. In the case of the Lyceum the works of the founder were soon removed from Athens, and the ideas of Aristotle were preserved only in fragments, chiefly by means of note-books in the school. Not only did the Lyceum fail to develop new doctrine; it did not even succeed in preserving the old. In all these schools there grew up a reverence for the written word that had great influence, literary and religious as well as educational. So far as the spirit of education was concerned, this later development was distinctly inferior to the earlier conditions.

**The University of Athens** originated in a combination of these philosophical schools with the old Athenian institution for the education of the ephebes. This latter education had originally consisted of the two years' military training and service required of all Athenian youths during their eighteenth and nineteenth years. During the period of the new education the military rigor was so much relaxed that much of the time could be devoted to intellectual ends in the philosophical and sophistic schools. After the Peloponnesian War the term of ephebic service was reduced to one year, and after the Macedonian conquest it was made wholly optional. Coincident with these changes, the literary element of the training grew in importance until finally it dominated. It became customary for the entire corps of ephebes to attend the lectures either of one philosophical school, or of all save that of Epicurus; for it does not appear that during this stage of their education they were allowed to patronize this institution. The term of higher education under state control was reduced to one year, during which period the youth were under the direction of an elective state officer, the rector, who held office for but one year. A change of quite as great importance as that of making this course optional for Athenian youths was the admission of foreign-born youths to the ephebic corps. During the Roman period the foreign youths were quite as numerous as the native. The old military state training had then become a literary university training. This year of study under the direction of the state officer came to be merely introductory. Many remained for a much longer period, and their number was supplemented by the great many adult students drawn from all quarters by the philosophical schools. During the earlier Christian centuries the period of study had extended to four or five years, or even more.

Two further changes brought about an organization of these various educational institutions into one more unified. The military operations of Philip V. of Macedon (200 B.C.) and of the dictator Sulla (86 B.C.) resulted in the injury, if not the destruction, of the gymnasia situated in the suburbs. These schools then followed the Stoics into the city. There, in public gymnasia, especially that of Ptolemy and later that of Hadrian, and also in private theatres, these schools were conducted. The second of these changes was the public support given to these schools of philosophy, and to the chairs of rhetoric, by the Roman Empire from the first Christian century on to the suppression of the University. This was begun by Vespasian, though Hadrian and the Antonines were the emperors especially interested in building up the University of Athens, and in making it the centre of learning for the Empire. These chairs, never more than ten in all, did not constitute all of the University. Their work was supplemented by that of a considerable number of private lecturers, who continued the old practice of lecturing for fees; and by a great number of tutors and pedagogues, who were responsible for the work and conduct of the younger students. During the Christian centuries the University life presents many characteristics of University life in mediæval or modern times. The ephebic organization seems to have degenerated into students' clubs or secret societies. Initiation into such societies, hazing, the wearing of distinctive gowns, and many other customs, present strong resemblances to characteristic features of the mediæval University, some of these being described in the selection from

Gregory. Such similarities have led to the theory that there was a direct connection between the University of Athens of the sixth century, and the mediæval universities of the eleventh. The University of Athens as a centre of classical learning aroused the opposition of the Christian church. This opposition, together with other causes, finally led to the suppression of the University by the Emperor Justinian, 529 A.D. As long previous to this decree the rhetorical and sophistic schools had disappeared, it was only a few of the philosophical teachers, chiefly of the Neoplatonic school, that at the decree of Justinian then fled to Persia.

### *A Decree of the Athenian Senate, from about* 100 *B.C.*[1]

'That whereas the Ephebi of last year sacrificed duly at their matriculation in the Guildhall, by the sacred fire of the City, in the presence of their Rector and the Priests of the People and the Pontiffs, according to the laws and decrees, and conducted the procession in honour of Artemis the Huntress, . . . and took part in others of like kind, and ran in the customary torch-races, and escorted the statue of Pallas to Phalerum, and helped to bring it back again, and light it on its way in perfect order, and carried Dionysus also from his shrine into the theatre in like fashion, and brought a bull worthy of the God at the Dionysiac festival, . . . and took part in all due offerings to our Gods and our Benefactors, as the laws and the decrees ordain; and have been regular in their attendance all the year at the gymnasia, and punctually obeyed their Rector, thinking it of paramount importance to observe discipline, and to study diligently what the People has prescribed; — whereas there has been no ground for complaint, but they have kept all the rules made by their Rec-

[1] Dumont, *Essai sur l'Éphébie Attique*, II. 152. Translation taken from Capes. *University Life in Ancient Athens*, pp. 21 et seq.

tor and their Tutors, and have attended without fail the lectures of Zenodotus in the Ptolemæum and the Lyceum, as also those of all the other Professors of Philosophy in the Lyceum and Academy; and have mounted guard in good order at the popular assemblies, and have gone out to meet our Roman friends and benefactors on their visits; . . . and have given 70 drachmæ, as the law provides to the proper functionaries to provide the goblet for the Mother of the Gods, and offered another also in the temple at Eleusis; and have marched out under arms to the Athenian frontiers, and made themselves acquainted with the country and the roads, . . . and have gone out to Marathon and offered their garlands and said prayers at the shrine of the heroes who died fighting for their country's freedom; . . . and have gone on shipboard to the feast of Aiantæa, and held boat-races and processions there, and earned the praises of the Salaminians, and the present of a golden crown because of their good discipline and orderly behaviour; — and whereas they have lived in friendly harmony all the year without a jar as their Rector wished, and have passed their Examinations in the Senate House as the law requires; and being full of honourable ambition and desire to help their Rector in his public-spirited endeavours to promote the public good as well as their own credit, they have taken in hand one of the old catapults that was out of gear, and repairing it at their own expense, have learnt once more how to use the engine, the practice of which had been disused for years; and in all other matters have conducted themselves with all propriety, and have provided all that was required for the religious services of their own gymnasia — to show the wish of the Senate and the People to honour them for their merits and obedience to the laws and to their Rector, in their first year of adult life, the Senate is agreed to instruct the Presidents of the next assembly following, to lay before the People for approval the Resolution of the Senate to pass an honorary vote in praise of the Ephebi of last year, and to present them with a golden crown for their constant piety and discipline and public spirit, and to compliment their Tutors, their trainer Timon, and the fencing master Satyrus, and the marksman Nicander, and the bowman

Asclepiades, and Calchedon the instructor in the catapults, and the attendants, and to award a crown of leaves to each; and to have the decree engraved by the Secretary for the time being on two pillars of stone, to be placed one in the Market-place, and the second wherever may seem best.'

### *A Decree of the Athenian Assembly from the Same Period*[1]

'Whereas the People always has a hearty interest in the training and discipline of the Ephebi, hoping that the rising generation may grow up to be men able to take good care of their fatherland, and has passed laws to require them to gain a knowledge of the country, of the guard-posts and of the frontiers, and to train themselves as soldiers in the use of arms, thanks to which discipline the City has been decked with many glories and imposing trophies; and whereas on this account the People has always chosen a Rector of unblemished character, and accordingly last year Dionysius the son of Socrates, the Phylasian, had the care of the Ephebi entrusted to him by the People, and duly sacrificed with them at their matriculation, . . . and has trained them worthily, keeping them constantly engaged at the gymnasia, and making them all efficient in their drill, and insisting on decorum, that they should not fail throughout the year in obedience to the Generals, the Tutors and himself; and whereas he has watched over their habits of order and of self-control, taking them with him to the Professor's Lectures, and being present always at their courses of instruction . . . and whereas he has also roused their public spirit by teaching them to be good marksmen with the catapult, and accompanied them in their rounds to the guardposts and the frontiers . . . and has arranged the boat-races in the processions at Munychia . . . and also the footraces in the gymnasia, and the escorts of honour for our Roman friends and allies . . . and reviewed them on parade at the Theseia and Epitaphia . . . and has been vigilant in all cases to maintain their pride, being constant in attendance on

[1] Same sources.

them through the year, and has watched over their studies, and ruled them with impartial justice, keeping them in sound health and friendly intercourse, treating them with a father's care — in return for all of which the Ephebi have presented him with a golden crown and a bronze statue, to show their sense of his character and loving care; and whereas he has passed his accounts as the law requires, the Senate and the People wishing to show due honour to such Rectors as serve with merit and impartiality, Resolve to praise Dionysius, late Rector of the Ephebi of last year and to present him with a golden crown, and have proclamation made thereof in the great festival of Dionysus, and also at the athletic contests of the Panathanaic and Eleusinian feasts.'

### *Selection from the Panegyric on Saint Basil, by Gregory Nazienzen*

15. We were contained by Athens, like two branches of some river-stream, for after leaving the common fountain of our fatherland, we had been separated on our varying pursuits of culture, and were now again united by the impulsion of God no less than by our own agreement. I preceded him by a little, but he soon followed me, to be welcomed with great and brilliant hopes. For he was versed in many languages, before his arrival, and it was a great thing for either of us to outstrip the other in the attainment of some object of our study. And I may well add as a seasoning to my speech, a short narrative, which will be a reminder to those who know it, a source of information to those who do not. Most of the young men at Athens in their folly are mad after rhetorical skill — not only those who are ignobly born and unknown, but even the noble and illustrious, in the general mass of young men difficult to keep under control. They are just like men devoted to horses and exhibitions, as we see, at the horse races; they leap,[1] they shout, raise clouds of dust,

[1] This passage refers to the speculators who unite in sympathy with, and in their excitement, imitate, as far as possible, the actions of those who drive the chariots in the races.

they drive in their seats, they beat the air (instead of the horses) with their fingers as whips, they yoke and unyoke the horses, though they are none of theirs; they readily exchange with one another drivers, horses, positions, leaders; and who are they who do this? Often poor and needy fellows, without the means of support for a single day. This is just how the students feel in regard to their own tutors, and their rivals, in their eagerness to increase their own numbers and thereby enrich them. The matter is absolutely absurd and silly. Cities, roads, harbours, mountain tops, coast lines are seized upon — in short, every part of Attica, or of the rest of Greece, with most of the inhabitants; for even these they have divided between the rival parties.

16. Whenever any newcomer arrives and falls into the hands of those who seize upon him, either by force or willingly, they observe this Attic law, of combined jest and earnest. He is first conducted to the house of one of those who were the first to receive him, or of his friends, or kinsmen, or countrymen, or of those who are eminent in debating power and purveyors of arguments and therefore especially honoured among them; and their reward consists in the gain of adherents. He is next subjected to the raillery of any one who will, with the intention, I suppose, of checking the conceit of the newcomers, and reducing them to subjection at once. The raillery is of a more argumentative or insolent kind, according to the refinement or boorishness of the railer: and the performance which seems very fearful and brutal to those who do not know it, is to those who have experienced it, very pleasant and humane: for its threats are feigned rather than real. Next he is conducted, in procession, from the market place to the bath. The procession is formed by those who are charged with it in the young man's honour, who arrange themselves in two ranks separated by an interval, and precede him to the bath. But when they have approached it, they shout and leap wildly, as if possessed, shouting that they must not advance, but stay, since the bath will not admit them; and at the same time frighten the youth by furiously knocking at the doors; then allowing him to enter, they present him with his

freedom, and receive him after the bath as an equal and one of themselves. This they considered the most pleasant part of the ceremony, as being a speedy change and release from annoyances. On this occasion I not only refused to put to shame my friend, the great Basil, out of respect for the gravity of his character, and the ripeness of his reasoning powers, but also persuaded all the rest of the students to treat him likewise, who happened not to know him. For he was from the first, respected by most of them, his reputation having preceded him. The result was that he was the only one to escape the general rule, and be accorded a greater honour than belongs to a freshman's position.

### *Selections from the Discourse touching the Training of Children, by Plutarch*[1]

1. The course which ought to be taken for the training of free-born children, and the means whereby their manners may be rendered virtuous, will, with the reader's leave, be the subject of our present disquisition.

• • • • • • •

**Three things requisite for virtue: nature, reason, and use.**

4. . . . What we are wont to say of arts and sciences may be said also concerning virtue: that there is a concurrence of three things requisite to the completing thereof in practice, — which are nature, reason, and use. Now by reason here I would be understood to mean learning; and by use, exercise. Now the principles come from instruction, the practice comes from exercise, and perfection from all three combined. And accordingly as either of the three is deficient, virtue must needs be defective. For if nature be not improved by instruction, it is blind; if instruction be not assisted by nature, it is maimed; and if exercise fail of the assistance of both, it is imperfect as to the attainment of its end. And as in husbandry it is first requisite that the soil be fertile, next that the husbandman be skil-

[1] Translation by Simon Ford, D.D., in Professor W. W. Goodwin's edition of Plutarch's *Morals.*

ful, and lastly that the seed he sows be good; so here nature resembles the soil, the instructor of youth the husbandman, and the rational principles and precepts which are taught, the seed. And I would peremptorily affirm that all these met and jointly conspired to the completing of the souls of those universally celebrated men, Pythagoras, Socrates, and Plato, together with all others whose eminent worth hath gotten them immortal glory. And happy is that man certainly, and well-beloved of the Gods, on whom by the bounty of any of them all these are conferred.

And yet if any one thinks that those in whom Nature hath not thoroughly done her part may not in some measure make up her defects, if they be so happy as to light upon good teaching, and withal apply their own industry towards the attainment of virtue, he is to know that he is very much, nay, altogether, mistaken. For as a good natural capacity may be impaired by slothfulness, so dull and heavy natural parts may be improved by instruction; and whereas negligent students arrive not at the capacity of understanding the most easy things, those who are industrious conquer the greatest difficulties. And many instances we may observe, that give us a clear demonstration of the mighty force and successful efficacy of labor and industry. For water continually dropping will wear hard rocks hollow; yea, iron and brass are worn out with constant handling. Nor can we, if we would, reduce the felloes of a cart-wheel to their former straightness, when once they have been bent by force; yea, it is above the power of force to straighten the bended staves sometimes used by actors upon the stage. So far is that which labor effects, though against nature, more potent than what is produced according to it. . . .

The care of children.

5. The next thing that falls under our consideration is the nursing of children, which, in my judgment, the mothers should do themselves. . . . For childhood is a tender thing, and easily wrought into any shape. Yea, and the very souls of children readily receive the impressions of those things that are dropped into them while they are yet but soft; but when they grow older, they will, as all hard things are, be more difficult to be wrought upon. And as soft

wax is apt to take the stamp of the seal, so are the minds of children to receive the instructions imprinted on them at that age. Whence, also, it seems to me good advice which divine Plato[1] gives to nurses, not to tell all sorts of common tales to children in infancy, lest thereby their minds should chance to be filled with foolish and corrupt notions. The like good counsel Phocylides, the poet, seems to give in this verse of his:—

> 'If we'll have virtuous children, we should choose
> Their tenderest age good principles to infuse.'

6. Nor are we to omit taking due care, in the first place, that those children who are appointed to attend upon such young nurslings, and to be bred with them for play-fellows, be well-mannered, and next that they speak plain, natural Greek; lest, being constantly used to converse with persons of a barbarous language and evil manners, they receive corrupt tinctures from them. For it is a true proverb, that if you live with a lame man, you will learn to halt.

**Choice of a pedagogue.**

7. Next, when a child is arrived at such an age as to be put under the care of pedagogues, great care is to be used that we be not deceived in them, and so commit our children to slaves or barbarians or cheating fellows. For it is a course never enough to be laughed at which many men nowadays take in this affair; for if any of their servants be better than the rest, they dispose some of them to follow husbandry, some to navigation, some to merchandise, some to be stewards in their houses, and some, lastly, to put out their money to use for them. But if they find any slave that is a drunkard or a glutton, and unfit for any other business, to him they assign the government of their children; whereas, a good pedagogue ought to be such a one in his disposition as Phœnix, tutor to Achilles, was.

**Choice of teachers.**

And now I come to speak of that which is a greater matter, and of more concern than any that I have said. We are to look after such masters for our children as are blameless in their lives, not justly reprovable for their manners, and of the best experience in teaching. For the very spring and root of honesty and virtue lies in the felicity of

[1] Plato, *Republic*, II. 377; p. 139 of this volume.

lighting on good education. And as husbandmen are wont to set forks to prop up feeble plants, so do honest schoolmasters prop up youth by careful instructions and admonitions, that they may duly bring forth the buds of good manners. But there are certain fathers nowadays who deserve that men should spit on them in contempt, who, before making any proof of those to whom they design to commit the teaching of their children, either through unacquaintance, or, as it sometimes falls out, through unskilfulness, intrust them to men of no good reputation, or, it may be, such as are branded with infamy. Although they are not altogether so ridiculous, if they offend herein through unskilfulness; but it is a thing most extremely absurd, when, as oftentimes it happens, though they know and are told beforehand, by those who understand better than themselves, both of the inability and rascality of certain schoolmasters, they nevertheless commit the charge of their children to them, sometimes overcome by their fair and flattering speeches, and sometimes prevailed on to gratify friends who entreat them. This is an error of like nature with that of the sick man, who, to please his friends, forbears to send for the physician that might save his life by his skill, and employs a mountebank that quickly dispatcheth him out of the world; or of him who refuses a skilful shipmaster, and then, at his friend's entreaty, commits the care of his vessel to one that is therein much his inferior. In the name of Jupiter and all the Gods, tell me how can that man deserve the name of a father, who is more concerned to gratify others in their requests, than to have his children well educated? Or, is not that rather fitly applicable to this case, which Socrates, that ancient philosopher, was wont to say, — that, if he could get up to the highest place in the city, he would lift up his voice and make this proclamation thence: "What mean you, fellow-citizens, that you thus turn every stone to scrape wealth together, and take so little care of your children, to whom, one day, you must relinquish it all?" — to which I would add this, that such parents do like him that is solicitous about his shoe, but neglects the foot that is to wear it. And yet many fathers there are, who so love their money and hate their children, that, lest it should cost them more than they are willing to spare to hire a good schoolmaster for them, they rather choose such persons to instruct their children as are of no worth; thereby beating down the market, that they may purchase ignorance cheap. It was, therefore, a witty and handsome jeer which Aristippus bestowed on a sottish father, who asked him what he would take to teach his child. He answered, A thousand drachms. Whereupon the other cried out: O Hercules, what a price you ask! for I can buy a slave at that rate. Do so, then, said the philosopher, and thou shalt have two slaves instead of one,—thy son for one, and him thou buyest for another. Lastly, how absurd it is, when thou accustomest thy children to take their food with their right hands, and chidest them if they receive it with their left, yet thou takest no care at all that the principles that are infused into them be right and regular. . . .

**Importance of education.**

8. In brief therefore I say (and what I say may justly challenge the repute of an oracle rather than of advice), that the one chief thing in this matter—which compriseth the beginning, middle, and end of all—is good education and regular instruction; and that these two afford great help and assistance towards the attainment of virtue and felicity. For all other good things are but human and of small value, such as will hardly recompense the industy required to the getting of them. It is, indeed, a desirable thing to be well descended; but the glory belongs to our ancestors. Riches are valuable; but they are the goods of Fortune, who frequently takes them from those that have them, and carries them to those that never so much as hoped for them. Yea, the greater they are, the fairer mark are they for those to aim at who design to make our bags their prize; I mean evil servants and accusers. But the weightiest consideration of all is, that riches may be enjoyed by the worst as well as the best of men. Glory is a thing deserving respect, but unstable; beauty is a prize that men fight to obtain, but, when obtained, it is of little continuance; health is a precious enjoyment, but easily impaired; strength is a thing desirable, but apt to be the prey of diseases and old age. And, in general, let any man who values himself upon strength of body know that he makes a great mistake; for what indeed is any

proportion of human strength, if compared to that of other animals, such as elephants and bulls and lions? But learning alone, of all things in our possession, is immortal and divine. And two things there are that are most peculiar to human nature, reason and speech; of which two, reason is the master of speech, and speech is the servant of reason, impregnable against all assaults of fortune, not to be taken away by false accusation, nor impaired by sickness, nor enfeebled by old age. For reason alone grows youthful by age; and time, which decays all other things, increaseth knowledge in us in our decaying years. Yea, war itself, which like a winter torrent bears down all other things before it and carries them away with it, leaves learning alone behind. Whence the answer seems to me very remarkable, which Stilpo, a philosopher of Megara, gave to Demetrius, who, when he levelled that city to the ground and made all the citizens bondmen, asked Stilpo whether he had lost anything. Nothing, said he, for war cannot plunder virtue. To this saying that of Socrates also is very agreeable; who, when Gorgias (as I take it) asked him what his opinion was of the king of Persia, and whether he judged him happy, returned answer, that he could not tell what to think of him, because he knew not how he was furnished with virtue and learning, — as judging human felicity to consist in those endowments, and not in those which are subject to fortune.

**Speak only on proper occasions.**

9. Moreover, as it is my advice to parents that they make the breeding up of their children to learning the chiefest of their care, so I here add, that the learning they ought to train them up unto should be sound and wholesome, and such as is most remote from those trifles which suit the popular humor. For to please the many is to displease the wise. To this saying of mine that of Euripides himself bears witness: —

> I'm better skilled to treat a few, my peers,
> Than in a crowd to tickle vulgar ears;
> Though others have the luck on't, when they babble
> Most to the wise, then most to please the rabble.[1]

* * * * * * *

[1] Euripides, *Hippolytus*, 986.

**Preparation necessary for speech and for action.**

If any one ask what the next thing is wherein I would have children instructed, and to what further good qualities I would have them inured, I answer, that I think it advisable that they neither speak nor do anything rashly; for, according to the proverb, the best things are the most difficult. But extemporary discourses are full of much ordinary and loose stuff, nor do such speakers well know where to begin or where to make an end. And besides other faults which those who speak suddenly are commonly guilty of, they are commonly liable to this great one, that they multiply words without measure; whereas, premeditation will not suffer a man to enlarge his discourse beyond a due proportion. To this purpose it is reported of Pericles, that, being often called upon by the people to speak, he would not, because (as he said) he was unprepared. And Demosthenes also, who imitated him in the managery of public affairs, when the Athenians urged him to give his counsel, refused it with this answer: I have not yet prepared myself. Though it may be that this story is a mere fiction, brought down to us by uncertain tradition, without any credible author. But Demosthenes, in his oration against Midias, clearly sets forth the usefulness of premeditation. For there he says: "I confess, O ye Athenians! that I came hither provided to speak; and I will by no means deny that I have spent my utmost study upon the composing this oration. For it had been a pitiful omission in me, if, having suffered and still suffering such things, I should have neglected that which in this cause was to be spoken by me." But here I would not be understood altogether to condemn all readiness to discourse extempore, nor yet to allow the use of it upon such occasions as do not require it; but we are to use it only as we do physic. Still, before a person arrives at complete manhood, I would not permit him to speak upon any sudden incident occasion; though, after he has attained a radicated faculty of speaking, he may allow himself a greater liberty, as opportunity is offered. For as they who have been a long time in chains, when they are at last set at liberty, are unable to walk, on account of their former continual restraint, and are very apt to trip, so they who have been used to a fettered way of speaking a great while, if upon any occasion they be enforced to speak on a sudden, will hardly be able to express themselves without some tokens of their former confinement. But to permit those that are yet children to speak extemporarily is to give them occasion for extremely idle talk. A wretched painter, they say, showing Apelles a picture, told him withal that he had taken a very little time to paint it. If thou hadst not told me so, said Apelles, I see cause enough to believe it was a hasty draught; but I wonder that in that space of time thou hast not painted many more such pictures.

**Simplicity of speech advised.**

I advise therefore (for I return now to the subject that I have disgressed from) the shunning and avoiding, not merely of a starched, theatrical, and over-tragical form of speaking, but also of that which is too low and mean. For that which is too swelling is not fit for the managery of public affairs; and that, on the other side, which is too thin is very inapt to work any notable impression upon the hearers. For as it is not only requisite that a man's body be healthy, but also that it be of a firm constitution, so ought a discourse to be not only sound, but nervous also. For though such as is composed cautiously may be commended, yet that is all it can arrive at; whereas that which hath some adventurous passages in it is admired also. And my opinion is the same concerning the affections of the speaker's mind. For he must be neither of a too confident nor of a too mean and dejected spirit; for the one is apt to lead to impudence, the other to servility; and much of the orator's art, as well as great circumspection, is required to direct his course skilfully betwixt the two. . . .

10. Wherefore, though we ought not to permit an ingenuous child entirely to neglect any of the common sorts of learning, so far as they may be gotten by lectures or from public shows; yet I would have him to salute these only as in his passage, taking a bare taste of each of them (seeing no man can possibly attain to perfection in all), and

**Philosophy should be the chief pursuit.**

to give philosophy the pre-eminence of them all. I can illustrate my meaning by an example. It is a fine thing to sail round and visit many cities, but it is profitable to fix our dwelling in the best. . . . Whence it follows, that we ought to make philosophy the chief of all our learning.

For though, in order to the welfare of the body, the industry of men hath found out two arts, — medicine, which assists to the recovery of lost health and gymnastics, which help us to attain a sound constitution, — yet there is but one remedy for the distempers and diseases of the mind, and that is philosophy. For by the advice and assistance thereof it is that we come to understand what is honest, and what dishonest; what is just, and what unjust; in a word, what we are to seek, and what to avoid. We learn by it how we are to demean ourselves towards the Gods, towards our parents, our elders, the laws, strangers, governors, friends, wives, children, and servants. That is, we are to worship the Gods, to honor our parents, to reverence our elders, to be subject to the laws, to obey our governors, to love our friends, to use sobriety towards our wives, to be affectionate to our children, and not to treat our servants insolently; and (which is the chiefest lesson of all) not to be overjoyed in prosperity nor too much dejected in adversity; not to be dissolute in our pleasures, nor in our anger to be transported with brutish rage and fury. These things I account the principal advantages which we gain by philosophy. For to use prosperity generously is the part of a man; to manage it so as to decline envy, of a well governed man; to master our pleasures by reason is the property of wise men; and to moderate anger is the attainment only of extraordinary men. But those of all men I count most complete, who know how to mix and temper the managery of civil affairs with philosophy; seeing they are thereby masters of two of the greatest good things that are, — a life of public usefulness as statesmen, and a life of calm tranquillity as students of philosophy. For, whereas there are three sorts of lives, — the life of action, the life of contemplation, and the life of pleasure, — the man who is utterly abandoned and a slave to pleasure is brutish and mean-spirited; he that spends his time in contemplation without action is an unprofitable man; and he that lives in action and is destitute of philosophy is a rustical man, and commits many absurdities. Wherefore we are to apply our utmost endeavor to enable ourselves for both; that is, to manage public employment, and withal, at convenient seasons, to give ourselves to

**Its advantages.**

philosophical studies. Such statesmen were Pericles and Archytas[1] the Tarentine; such were Dion[2] the Syracusan and Epaminondas[3] the Theban, both of whom were of Plato's familiar acquaintance.

Value of literature in education.

I think it not necessary to spend many more words about this point, the instruction of children in learning. Only it may be profitable at least, or even necessary, not to omit procuring for them the writings of ancient authors, but to make such a collection of them as husbandmen are wont to do of all needful tools. For of the same nature is the use of books to scholars, as being the tools and instruments of learning, and withal enabling them to derive knowledge from its proper fountains.

Importance of gymnastic.

11. In the next place, the exercise of the body must not be neglected; but children must be sent to schools of gymnastics, where they may have sufficient employment that way also. This will conduce partly to a more handsome carriage, and partly to the improvement of their strength. For the foundation of a vigorous old age is a good constitution of the body in childhood. Wherefore, as it is expedient to provide those things in fair weather which may be useful to the mariners in a storm, so it is to keep good order and govern ourselves by rules of temperance in youth, as the best provision we can lay in for age. Yet must they husband their strength, so as not to become dried up (as it were) and destitute of strength to follow their studies. For, according to Plato, sleep and weariness are enemies to the arts.

But why do I stand so long on these things? I hasten to speak of that which is of the greatest importance, even beyond all that has been spoken of; namely, I would have boys trained for the contests of wars by practice in the

[1] A famous geometrician and astronomer, who was seven times elected governor of his native city during the fourth century B.C.

[2] A pupil of Plato, and a scholar attached to the court of Dionysius the Elder and Dionysius the Younger of Syracuse. The latter tyrant he overthrew, substituting for his sway the rule of a philosopher. This proved unpopular, and Dion was overthrown and slain, 354 B.C.

[3] The soldier and statesman who raised Thebes to the hegemony of Greece. Killed in the battle of Mantinea, 362 B.C.

throwing of darts, shooting of arrows, and hunting of wild beasts. For we must remember in war the goods of the conquered are proposed as rewards to the conquerors. But war does not agree with a delicate habit of body, used only to the shade; for even one lean soldier that hath been used to military exercises shall overthrow whole troops of mere wrestlers who know nothing of war. But, somebody may say, whilst you profess to give precepts for the education of all free-born children, why do you carry the matter so as to seem only to accommodate those precepts to the rich, and neglect to suit them also to the children of poor men and plebeians? To which objection it is no difficult thing to reply. For it is my desire that all children whatsoever may partake of the benefit of education alike; but if yet any persons, by reason of the narrowness of their estates, cannot make use of my precepts, let them not blame me that give them, but Fortune, which disableth them from making the advantage by them they otherwise might. Though even poor men must use their utmost endeavor to give their children the best education; or, if they cannot, they must bestow upon them the best that their abilities will reach. Thus much I thought fit here to insert in the body of my discourse, that I might the better be enabled to annex what I have yet to add concerning the right training of children.

**Preparation for war.**

12. I say now, that children are to be won to follow liberal studies by exhortations and rational motives, and on no account to be forced thereto by whipping or any other contumelious punishments. I will not urge that such usage seems to be more agreeable to slaves than to ingenuous children; and even slaves, when thus handled, are dulled and discouraged from the performance of their tasks, partly by reason of the smart of their stripes, and partly because of the disgrace thereby inflicted. But praise and reproof are more effectual upon free-born children than any such disgraceful handling; the former to incite them to what is good, and the latter to restrain them from that which is evil. But we must use reprehensions and commendations alternately, and of various kinds according to the occasion; so that when they grow petulant, they may be shamed by reprehension, and again, when

**Use exhortation and not punishment.**

they better deserve it, they may be encouraged by commendations. Wherein we ought to imitate nurses, who, when they have made their infants cry, stop their mouths with the nipple to quiet them again. It is also useful not to give them such large commendations as to puff them up with pride; for this is the ready way to fill them with a vain conceit of themselves, and to enfeeble their minds.

13. Moreover, I have seen some parents whose too much love to their children hath occasioned, in truth, their not loving them at all. I will give light to this assertion by an example to those who ask what it means. It is this: while they are over-hasty to advance their children in all sorts of learning beyond their equals, they set them too hard and laborious tasks, whereby they fall under discouragement; and this, with other inconveniences accompanying it, causeth them in the issue to be ill affected to learning itself. For as plants by moderate watering are nourished, but with over-much moisture are glutted, so is the spirit improved by moderate labors, but overwhelmed by such as are excessive. We ought therefore to give children some time to take breath from their constant labors, considering that all human life is divided betwixt business and relaxation. To which purpose it is that we are inclined by nature not only to wake, but to sleep also; that as we have sometimes wars, so likewise at other times peace; as some foul, so other fair days; and, as we have seasons of important business, so also the vacation times of festivals. And, to contract all in a word, rest is the sauce of labor. Nor it is thus in living creatures only, but in things inanimate too. For even in bows and harps, we loosen their strings, that we may bend and wind them up again. Yea, it is universally seen that, as the body is maintained by repletion and evacuation, so is the mind by employment and relaxation.

Evil of over-training.

Those parents, moreover, are to be blamed who, when they have committed their sons to the care of pedagogues or schoolmasters, never see or hear them perform their tasks; wherein they fail much of their duty. For they ought, ever and anon, after the intermission of some days, to make trial of their children's proficiency; and not intrust their hopes of them to the discretion of a hireling. For even that sort

Parent must coöperate with teacher.

of men will take more care of the children, when they know that they are regularly to be called to account. And here the sayings of the king's groom is very applicable, that nothing made the horse so fat as the king's eye.

But we must most of all exercise and keep in constant employment the memory of children; for that is, as it were, the storehouse of all learning. Wherefore the mythologists have made Mnemosyne, or Memory, the mother of the Muses, plainly intimating thereby that nothing doth so beget or nourish learning as memory. Wherefore we must employ it to both those purposes, whether the children be naturally apt or backward to remember. For so shall we both strengthen it in those to whom Nature in this respect hath been bountiful, and supply that to others wherein she hath been deficient. And as the former sort of boys will thereby come to excel others, so will the latter sort excel themselves. For that of Hesiod was well said, —

**Improve the memory.**

> Oft little add to little, and the account
> Will swell: heapt atoms thus produce a mount.[1]

Neither, therefore, let the parents be ignorant of this, that the exercising of memory in the schools doth not only give the greatest assistance towards the attainment of learning, but also to all the actions of life. For the remembrance of things past affords us examples in our consults about things to come.

14. Children ought to be made to abstain from speaking filthily, seeing, as Democritus said, words are but the shadows of actions. They are, moreover, to be instructed to be affable and courteous in discourse. For as churlish manners are always detestable, so children may be kept from being odious in conversation, if they will not be pertinaciously bent to maintain all they say in dispute. For it is of use to a man to understand not only how to overcome, but also how to give ground when to conquer would turn to his disadvantage. For there is such a thing sometimes as a Cadmean victory; which the wise Euripides attesteth, when he saith, —

**Importance of moderation.**

> Where two discourse, if the one's anger rise,
> The man who lets the contest fall is wise.[2]

[1] Hesiod, *Works and Days*, 371. [2] Euripides, *Protesilaus*, Frag. 656.

Add we now to these things some others of which children ought to have no less, yea, rather greater care; to wit, that they avoid luxurious living, bridle their tongues, subdue anger, and refrain their hands. Of how great moment each of these counsels is, I now come to inquire; and we may best judge of them by examples. To begin with the last: some men there have been, who, by opening their hands to take what they ought not, have lost all the honor they got in the former part of their lives. So Gylippus the Lacedæmonian, for unsewing the public money-bags, was condemned to banishment from Sparta. And to be able also to subdue anger is the part of a wise man. Such a one was Socrates; for when a hectoring and debauched young man rudely kicked him, so that those in his company, being sorely offended, were ready to run after him and call him to account for it, What, said he to them, if an ass had kicked me, would you think it handsomely done to kick him again? And yet the young man himself escaped not unpunished; for when all persons reproached him for so unworthy an act, and gave him the nickname of *Λακτιστής* or the kicker, he hanged himself. The same Socrates, — when Aristophanes, publishing his play which he called the Clouds, therein threw all sorts of the foulest reproaches upon him, and a friend of his, who was present at the acting of it, repeated to him what was there said in the same comical manner, asking him withal, Does not this offend you, Socrates? — replied: Not at all, for I can as well bear with a fool in a play as at a great feast. And something of the same nature is reported to have been done by Archytas of Tarentum and Plato. Archytas, when, upon his return from the war, wherein he had been a general, he was informed that his land had been impaired by his bailiff's negligence, sent for him, and said only thus to him when he came: If I were not very angry with thee, I would severely correct thee. And Plato, being offended with a gluttonous and debauched servant, called to him Speusippus, his sister's son, and said unto him: Go beat thou this fellow; for I am too much offended with him to do it myself.

These things, you will perhaps say, are very difficult to be imitated. I confess it; but yet we must endeavor to the utmost of our power, by setting such examples before us, to repress the extravagancy of our immoderate, furious anger. For neither are we able to rival the experience or virtue of such men in many other matters; but we do, nevertheless, as sacred interpreters of divine mysteries and priests of wisdom, strive to follow these examples, and, as it were, to enrich ourselves with what we can nibble from them.

And as to bridling of the tongue, concerning which also I am obliged to speak, if any man think it a small matter or of mean concernment, he is much mistaken. For it is a point of wisdom to be silent when occasion requires, and better than to speak, though never so well. And, in my judgment, for this reason the ancients instituted mystical rites of initiation in religion, that, being in them accustomed to silence, we might thence transfer the fear we have of the Gods to the fidelity required in human secrets. Yea, indeed, experience shows that no man ever repented of having kept silence; but many that they have not done so. And a man may, when he will, easily utter what he hath by silence concealed; but it is impossible for him to recall what he hath once spoken. And, moreover, I can remember infinite examples that have been told me of those that have procured great damages to themselves by intemperance of the tongue; one or two of which I will give, omitting the rest.

**Truthfulness.**

. . . Besides all these things, we are to accustom children to speak the truth, and to account it, as indeed it is, a matter of religion for them to do so. For lying is a servile quality, deserving the hatred of all mankind; yea, a fault for which we ought not to forgive our meanest servants.

* * * * * * *

**Youthful errors are dangerous.**

16. . . . Thus far have I discoursed concerning the right ordering and decent carriage of children. I will now pass thence, to speak somewhat concerning the next age, that of youth. For I have often blamed the evil custom of some, who commit their boys in childhood to pedagogues and teachers, and then suffer the impetuosity of their youth to range without restraint; whereas boys of that age need to be kept under a stricter guard than chil-

dren. For who does not know that the errors of childhood are small, and perfectly capable of being amended; such as slighting their pedagogues, or disobedience to their teachers' instructions. But when they begin to grow towards maturity, their offences are oftentimes very great and heinous. . . . Wherefore it is expedient that such impetuous heats should with great care be kept under and restrained. For the ripeness of that age admits no bounds in its pleasures, is skittish, and needs a curb to check it; so that those parents who do not hold in their sons with great strength about that time find to their surprise that they are giving their vicious inclinations full swing in the pursuit of the vilest actions. Wherefore it is a duty incumbent upon wise parents, in that age especially, to set a strict watch upon them, and to keep them within the bounds of sobriety by instructions, threatenings, entreaties, counsels, promises, and by laying before them examples of those men (on one side) who by immoderate love of pleasures have brought themselves into great mischief, and of those (on the other) who by abstinence in the pursuit of them have purchased to themselves very great praise and glory. For these two things (hope of honor, and fear of punishment) are, in a sort, the first elements of virtue; the former whereof spurs men on the more eagerly to the pursuit of honest studies, while the latter blunts the edge of their inclinations to vicious courses.

Rules for conduct.

17. And in sum, it is necessary to restrain young men from the conversation of debauched persons, lest they take infection from their evil examples. This was taught by Pythagoras in certain enigmatical sentences, which I shall here relate and expound, as being greatly useful to further virtuous inclinations. Such are these. Taste not of fish that have black tails; that is converse not with men that are smutted with vicious qualities. Stride not over the beam of the scales; wherein he teacheth us the regard we ought to have for justice, so as not to go beyond its measures. Sit not on a chœnix;[1] wherein he forbids sloth, and requires us to take care to provide ourselves with the necessaries of life. Do not strike hands with every man; he means we ought not to be over hasty to make acquaintances

[1] A Greek measure; approximately, a quart cup.

or friendships with others. Wear not a tight ring; that is, we are to labor after a free and independent way of living, and to submit to no fetters. Stir not up the fire with a sword; signifying that we ought not to provoke a man more when he is angry already (since this is a most unseemingly act), but we should rather comply with him while his passion is in its heat. Eat not thy heart; which forbids to afflict our souls, and waste them with vexatious cares. Abstain from beans; that is, keep out of public offices, for anciently the choice of the officers of state was made by beans. Put not food in a pot; wherein he declares that elegant discourse ought not to be put into an impure mind; for discourse is the food of the mind, which is rendered unclean by the foulness of the man who receives it. When men are arrived at the goal, they should not turn back; that is, those who are near the end of their days, and see the period of their lives approaching, ought to entertain it contentedly, and not to be grieved at it.

**Danger of flatterers.**

But to return from this digression—our children, as I have said, are to be debarred the company of all evil men, but especially flatterers. For I would still affirm what I have often said in the presence of divers fathers, that there is not a more pestilent sort of men than these, nor any that more certainly and speedily hurry youth into precipices. Yea, they utterly ruin both fathers and sons, making the old age of the one and the youth of the other full of sorrow, while they cover the hook of their evil counsels with the unavoidable bait of voluptuousness. Parents, when they have good estates to leave their children, exhort them to sobriety, flatterers to drunkenness; parents exhort to continence, these to lasciviousness; parents to good husbandry, these to prodigality; parents to industry, these to slothfulness. And they usually entertain them with such discourses as these: The whole life of man is but a point of time; let us enjoy it therefore while it lasts, and not spend it to no purpose. Why should you so much regard the displeasure of your father?—an old doting fool, with one foot already in the grave, and 'tis to be hoped it will not be long ere we carry him thither altogether. And some of them there are who procure young men foul harlots, yea, prostitute wives to them; and they even make a prey of those things which the careful fathers have provided for the sustenance of their old age. A cursed tribe! True friendship's hypocrites, they have no knowledge of plain dealing and frank speech. They flatter the rich, and despise the poor; and they seduce the young, as by a musical charm. When those who feed them begin to laugh, then they grin and show their teeth. They are mere counterfeits, bastard pretenders to humanity, living at the nod and beck of the rich; free by birth, yet slaves by choice, who always think themselves abused when they are not so, because they are not supported in idleness at others' cost. Wherefore, if fathers have any care for the good breeding of their children, they ought to drive such foul beasts as these out of doors. They ought also to keep them from the companionship of vicious school-fellows, for these are able to corrupt the most ingenuous dispositions.

18. These counsels which I have now given are of great worth and importance; what I now have to add touches certain allowances that are to be made to human nature. Again therefore I would not have fathers of an over-rigid and harsh temper, but so mild as to forgive some slips of youth, remembering that they themselves were once young. But as physicians are wont to mix their bitter medicines with sweet syrups, to make what is pleasant a vehicle for what is wholesome, so should fathers temper the keenness of their reproofs with lenity. They may occasionally loosen the reins, and allow their children to take some liberties they are inclined to, and again, when it is fit, manage them with a straighter bridle. But chiefly should they bear their errors without passion, if it may be; and if they chance to be heated more than ordinary, they ought not to suffer the flame to burn long. For it is better that a father's anger be hasty than severe; because the heaviness of his wrath, joined with unplacableness, is no small argument of hatred towards the child. It is good also not to discover the notice they take of divers faults, and to transfer to such cases that dimness of sight and hardness of hearing that are wont to accompany old age; so as sometimes not to hear what they hear, nor to see what they see, of their children's miscarriages. We use to bear with some failings in our friends, and it is no wonder if we do the like to our children, es-

Danger of over-severity.

pecially when we sometimes overlook drunkenness in our very servants. Thou hast at times been too straight-handed to thy son; make him at other whiles a larger allowance. Thou hast, it may be, been too angry with him; pardon him the next fault to make him amends. He hath made use of a servant's wit to circumvent thee in something; restrain thy anger. He hath made bold to take a yoke of oxen out of the pasture, or he hath come home smelling of his yesterday's drink; take no notice of it; and if of ointments too, say nothing. For by this means the wild colt sometimes is made more tame. . . . I will add a few words more, and put an end to these advices. The chiefest thing that fathers are to look to is, that they themselves become effectual examples to their children, by doing all those things which belong to them and avoiding all vicious practices, that in their lives, as in a glass, their children may see enough to give them an aversion to all ill words and actions. For those that chide children for such faults as they themselves fall into unconsciously accuse themselves, under their children's names. And if they are altogether vicious in their own lives, they lose the right of reprehending their very servants, and much more do they forfeit it towards their sons. Yea, what is more than that, they make themselves even counsellors and instructors to them in wickedness. For where old men are impudent, there of necessity must the young men be so too. Wherefore we are to apply our minds to all such practices as may conduce to the good breeding of our children. And here we may take example from Eurydice of Hierapolis, who, although she was an Illyrian, and so thrice a barbarian, yet applied herself to learning when she was well advanced in years, that she might teach her children. Her love towards her children appears evidently in this Epigram of hers, which she dedicated to the Muses:—

**Teaching by example.**

> Eurydice to the Muses here doth raise
> This monument, her honest love to praise;
> Who her grown sons that she might scholars breed,
> Then well in years, herself first learned to read.

And thus have I finished the precepts which I designed to give concerning this subject. But that they should all be followed by any one reader is rather, I fear, to be wished than hoped. And to follow the greater part of them, though it may not be impossible to human nature, yet will need a concurrence of more than ordinary diligence joined with good fortune.

# PART II

## ROMAN EDUCATION

### I. EARLY ROMAN EDUCATION

**Periods of Roman Education.** — Roman education falls into two general periods of clearly defined characteristics, though the line of demarcation between the two is not distinct. The first of these periods is from the earliest days to the time when Grecian ideas of life, culture, and enjoyment came in and Rome became as cosmopolitan in its ideas and manners as it had already become in arms and government. The second period dates from this change, approximately the middle of the second century B.C., when Macedonia was conquered and Greece became a Roman province, and includes the latter years of the Republic and all of the imperial period. This one contrast between the old Roman and the Græco-Roman period gives that which is fundamental to the understanding of the history of Roman education. Each of these general periods may be again divided into sub-periods, which will be referred to as the first, second, third, and fourth periods, while the term "general" will be used to indicate the more comprehensive divisions. The historic evolution of Roman education can be better understood by grouping the sources under these four periods. The first of these includes the legendary and the early historic period to the beginning of the third century B.C. The second extends to the beginning of the Græco-Roman period, 146 B.C. The third dates to the rather indefinite time in the second and third Christian centuries when Roman society gave general evidence of that moral and cultural decline that previously had become characteristic of the imperial court. The fourth includes the centuries of decadence to the termination of the imperial office in the West. So far as there is anything distinctive about the education of this last period that is not also true of the later portion of the third period, it centres about the opposition between the Christian religion and the pagan culture. Since this opposition is more closely connected with mediæval than with classical education, the source material is not included here; none of the present selections date from later than the middle of the second Christian century. The general features of the education of the later period, so far as they are Roman, are similar to those of the second Christian century.

**Sources of Information for the Old Roman Period.** — What the laws of Moses were to early Hebrew education, the laws of Lycurgus to Spartan education, the laws of Solon and to a certain extent the Homeric poems to the early Athenian education, the Laws of the Twelve Tables were to the early education of the Romans. Not only do these express the ideals of Roman education, but to a large extent they form the subject-matter thereof. Their influence is dominant from the time of their formation, the middle of the fifth century B.C. to the opening of the first century B.C., by which time the Homeric poems and the early Latin literature had largely usurped their place. The fragments of these tables, preserved and given here, form the most important single source for this early period.

A second source, though not presented here, is the biographical and traditional material relating to the early Roman heroes. This material performed the same service for the Romans as did the Homeric poems for the Greeks. It is characteristic of the practical nature of Roman life and education that these stories, whether truth or fiction, should relate to actual men, not to gods or demigods. Such ideals could be imitated, and so appealed to the conscience as well as to the imagination of the child. The Romans, not being a literary people, did not, like the Greeks, put these accounts of their early life into literary form; at least, not during this period. Hence it is not possible to draw upon them directly as sources; yet, since references to the use of such material as the basis of their educational work are abundant, many such are to be found in the selections here given. It cannot be doubted that Plutarch has given in permanent form much of this material, and that his *Lives* represents, both in form and substance, one phase of the education of this extended period. No place has, however, been accorded this material in this collection, for it is not very direct evidence. Plutarch's ideas on education, representing the best cosmopolitan views of the Græco-Roman period have already been given. A third source is found in references to works of this period no longer extant. The most important of such works is the lost treatise, *De liberis educandis*, by Cato the Censor (b. 234 B.C., d. 149 B.C.), which, according to Quintilian, is the earliest Roman work on education. A further source, represented in this collection, is found in extracts from authors of a later period, presenting the ideals, methods, or subject-matter of education of these earlier days. Such references, though brief, are numerous, and are here represented by several selections.

**The Laws of the Twelve Tables.** — These laws were adopted in 451 and 450 B.C. To a large extent they are a formulation of previous usage, but also contain some new elements. These latter were, to some extent, now thought to be slight, provisions borrowed from Grecian states relating to the curbing of the privileges enjoyed by patricians. The tradition runs that in 454 a commission of three men had been sent abroad to study the laws of Athens and other Greek cities. But for the most part in principle and in detail the laws are indigenous, and offer marked contrasts with Grecian laws. In the period preceding the adoption of the tables, there had been great dissatisfaction upon the part of the plebs. The consequent agitation led, in the two years mentioned, to the substitution of the power of ten men, the *decemviri*, for that of all the existing magistrates. The ten tables are the work of the decemvirs of 451; the two supplementary tables are the work of the decemvirs of 450. The decemvirs of the latter year usurped the power for two succeeding years, but by revolution the old form of government was reinstituted upon the basis of the new code. These tables aimed at two results: first, the defining and publication of the laws in order to prevent usurpation and abuse upon the part of the patrician magistrates; and, second, the placing of the plebeians and patricians upon an equality. The latter result was not secured, but the definite and public form, now first given to Roman law, remained the basis of Roman polity until the adoption of the Justinian code almost one thousand years later (about 430 A.D.). The laws were, however, gradually overlaid by the prætorian decisions which adapted the laws to existing needs. In time these edicts came to be of greater importance than the laws themselves.

Publicity and permanency were first given the laws by posting them in the Forum, inscribed on bronze tablets, and by requiring that all Roman boys should learn them by heart. In this way they became the basis of Roman education, so far as it was literary, during all of the two earlier educational periods. This requirement, however, fell into decay by the opening of the first century before Christ, at which time the Grecian education had become dominant. For several centuries, first in the homes, then in the schools (when they were established), the Laws of the Twelve Tables were the basis of the instruction in reading, writing, and literary work. Not only did they form the most important part of the subject-matter of early literary education, but they also expressed the ideals of life that dominated this education.

Neither the order nor the exact wording of the Laws of the Twelve Tables is preserved; but enough has been left in the form of fragments, which preserve the exact wording, and in the form of numerous references throughout Latin literature, which preserve the spirit, to enable scholars to restore the tables. Nor is there any certainty as to their completeness. The reproduction of these fragments here given is taken from Prichard and Nasmith's translation of Ortolan's *Histoire de la Législation Romaine et Généralisation du Droit*, perhaps the best product of modern scholarship on this subject.

**Ideals of Roman Education.** — While these fragments of the Twelve Tables do not give full expression to the ideals which controlled early Roman life and education, they give practical form to many of them. The fact most clearly indicated by the laws is that even at this early date the Romans were a people prone to litigation; that is, to the settlement of conflicts of personal rights according to well-defined principles of justice. To the Roman the rights of the individual as expressed in property relations were more important than to any other early people. Hence there was an emphasis laid on, and a place found for, individuality, which, while limited and well-defined, was more secure than with the Greeks or other early peoples. This emphasis on the individual was of an extremely practical sort, and revealed itself chiefly in economic affairs. In this respect the Tables give expression to the Roman ideal *prudentia*, the prudence of the practical man in the everyday affairs of life, as well as to a further practical ideal, *honestas*, fair dealing in these economic relationships. Though a litigious people, all conflicts of personal rights were to be settled by appeal to general principles, — all were subordinate to the Roman idea of justice. This was not the Platonic or Grecian idea of justice, or of virtue as the resultant of the union of all minor virtues. To the Roman it meant the regulation of private rights by the still more general obligations to the state, or, more immediately, the settlement of conflicting claims of individuals according to custom and the tradition of their ancestors. In either case it is an extremely practical virtue as opposed to the idealism of the Greeks. This supremacy of the state and the complete subordination of the individual to the welfare of the state is expressed in another ideal, *virtus*, that is, courage, fortitude. While this finds expression in the laws only incidentally, it is clearly revealed in every other evidence relating to early Roman life. The educational expression of this ideal is seen in the use of the lives of Roman heroes, and of incidents in Roman history, in the formation of the character of each succeeding generation.

While the laws are very largely devoted to the regulation of personal and property rights, Tables IV. and V. indicate the importance of two other ideals. The first is *pietas*, or obedience, — the performance of duties to the gods, to ancestors, and to parents and fellow-men, — or as expressed positively in the Laws, the absolute supremacy of the *patria potestas*. This ideal again finds expression in Table X. on Sacred Laws. These Tables, especially Table X. also evidence another ideal, largely religious but also affecting every aspect of Roman life, that is, *pudor*, modesty, or reverence. To these ideals must be added two others, of which we find circumstantial, if not direct, evidence in the Twelve Tables, as in every other aspect of Roman history. One is *constantia*, or character, manliness, firmness, which with *virtus* gives the chief characteristic of the Roman soldier; the other is *gravitas*, — or earnestness, seriousness, sedateness. To the possession of those two ideals are attributable certain aspects of the Roman character that are wanting in that of the Greek, and that are of especial importance during the early general period when education centred so largely in the home.

**The Subject-matter, Method, and Organization** of early Roman education are not indicated in the one source available, save so far as the Tables themselves formed the subject-matter. The importance of these laws from this point of view is borne out by a brief selection appended, — the forty-fourth paragraph of Cicero's *De Oratore*. This was written in the year 55 B.C. and indicates the esteem in which the laws were still held from the educational point of view, even though they had ceased to hold first place. Not only were these laws committed to memory, but they were understood and mastered as a source of practical guidance for after life. In fact, with the Romans the subject-matter of education bore directly upon life as it has done with few people. The importance of this study from the intellectual point of view must also be considered. While literature, science, or language made up no part of the subject-matter of education during the early period (for the use of the Greek had not become common until the middle of the third century B.C.), the study of the Twelve Tables formed no mean intellectual discipline. Both from the disciplinary and the practical point of view it would compare favorably with other educational schemes having as their nucleus language, literature, or science. In addition to this it is also to be remembered that no people, either before or since, has made such use of its own history in education. History, including biography and the study of Roman law, comprised the subject-matter of early Roman education. Further evidence on this point will be found in succeeding selections. In the sources contrasting the early with the later Roman education, as well as in those bearing directly upon the later period, the method and the organization of education in this early period will be more accurately indicated. Discussions of these points will be given connection with those periods.

## *Fragments of the Laws of the Twelve Tables*

### TABLE I

The Summons before the Magistrate.

I. "If you summon a man before a magistrate and he refuses to go, take witnesses and arrest him."[1]

[1] Where the exact rendering of the law is possible, quotation marks are used; where the substance is restored from various sources, quotation marks are omitted.

II. "If he attempt evasion or flight, lay hands upon him."

III. "If he be prevented by sickness or old age, let him who summons him before the magistrate provide the means of transport; but not a covered vehicle, unless as an act of benevolence."

IV. "For a rich man, a rich man only can be *vindex*.[1] In the case of a *proletarius*, any one may be vindex."

V. "If the parties agree, that is to say, come to terms, let the suit be stopped and the matter arranged."

VI. "If no arrangement is made between the parties, let the cause be entered before midday, either in the comitium or in the forum, in the presence of both parties."

VII. "After midday let the magistrate grant judgment to the party present."

VIII. "No step shall be taken in an action after sunset."

IX. . . .

TABLE II

Judicial Proceedings.

I. The provisions of the Twelve Tables upon the amount to be deposited, called *sacramentum*, by the litigants respectively.

II. ". . . A serious illness . . . an engagement with a *peregrinus*[2] . . . should either of these circumstances exist in connection with the judge, the arbiter, or one of the litigants, the cause must be adjourned."

III. "Any one who wants a witness must summon him by calling upon him in a loud voice, stating that he will require his attendance on the third day of the market."[3]

[1] A kind of bail or surety.

[2] A stranger or foreigner to the city.

[3] The markets took place every ninth day; the third day of the market would be the twenty-seventh day.

IV. The provision which permitted the compounding of a theft.

## TABLE III

Execution following Confession or Judgment.

I. "In case of debt either upon confession or judgment, the debtor shall have thirty days' grace."

II. "That term having expired, the plaintiff shall have the *manus injectio*[1] to bring the debtor before the magistrate."

III. "If the debt is not paid, or surety provided, the creditor shall take the debtor, put him into chains or into the stocks, the weight of the chains not to exceed fifteen pounds, but less at the creditor's will."

IV. "The debtor shall be at liberty to live as he thinks fit, provided it be at his own expense. In the event of his being unable to provide his own nourishment, the creditor in whose custody he is shall supply him with at least one pound of bread daily."

V. Provision relating to —

1°. The right of compromise.

2°. The debtor's captivity, in default of compromise within sixty days, and of his production during this interval in the comitium on three successive market days, and the public declaration of the amount in which he was condemned.

VI. Provision allowing the creditor after the third market day, he not being paid, either to put his debtor to death or to sell him to any stranger resident beyond the Tiber; and which, in the case of there being several creditors, enacts as follows: "After the third market day, his body may be divided. Any one taking more than his just share shall be held guiltless."

[1] A species of execution of final process.

### TABLE IV

The Rights of the Father.

I. Provision as to the immediate destruction of monstrous or deformed offspring.

II. Provision relating to the control of the father over his children, the right existing during their whole life to imprison, scourge, keep to rustic labour in chains, to sell or slay, even though they may be in the enjoyment of high state offices.

III. "Three consecutive sales of the son by the father releases the former from the *patria potestas.*"

IV. Provision relating to the duration of gestation: no child born more than ten months after the decease of his reputed father to be held legitimate.

### TABLE V

Inheritance and Tutelage.

I. Provision relating to the perpetual tutelage of women. Vestals are free both from their tutelage and from the *patria potestas.*

II. Provision prohibiting the *usucapion*[1] of *res mancipi*[2] belonging to females under the tutelage[3] of their agnates,[4] except in the case where they have been delivered by the woman herself with the authority of her tutor.

III. "The testament of the father shall be law as to all provisions concerning his property and the tutelage thereof."

IV. "In the event of his death intestate and without *suus hæres*, the nearest agnate shall succeed."

[1] Acquisition by use or by possession for a certain period.

[2] Things requiring more than mere delivery to constitute transfer of ownership.

[3] Protection exercised over those who did not have the capacity required by civil law for the accomplishment of legal acts.

[4] Blood relatives on the father's side.

V. "In default of agnates, the gentiles[1] shall succeed."

VI. In the event of no tutor being specified in the will, the agnates are the legitimate tutors.

VII. "The custody of an idiot and of his property, in case there is no curator (custos), belongs to the agnates; in default of agnates to his gentiles."

VIII. A provision by which the inheritance of an enfranchised dying without *hæres suus* was transferred to his patron.

IX. The inheritance is divided as of right among the heirs.

X. Provision from which is derived the *actio familiæ erciscundæ*, that is, the action which must be taken to enforce the division of an inheritance.

XI. The slave enfranchised by will, upon condition of his giving a certain sum to the heir, can, in the event of his being alienated by the heir, secure his freedom by the payment of this sum to the alienee.

### TABLE VI

Dominion and Possession.

I. "The words pronounced in the ceremonies of the *nexum*[2] and the *mancipium* shall be law."

II. Provision enforcing double payment as penalty for denying the declaration of the *nexum* or *mancipium*.

III. "Possession for the period of two years in the case of land, or of one year in connection with other things, vests the property."

IV. Provision relating to the acquisition of the marital power over the woman by the fact of possession of one year, with the faculty given to

[1] Belonging to the same clan or gens.

[2] The general term for alienation or transfer of property, especially *per æs et libram* — by the bronze piece and the balance.

the woman of preventing this effect of possession by absenting herself for three nights consecutively in each year from the house of her husband.

V. "No possession by an alien, however long, can vest in him the property of a citizen."

VI. In the case of the *manuum consertio*,[1] let the magistrate give the provisional possession to whomsoever he may think fit. In the case, however, of a claim to liberty, the magistrate shall always give the provisional possession in favour of liberty.

VII. "Timber attached to a building or the support of a vine shall not be removed."

VIII. But an action to recover the double value lies against the user of the property of another.

IX. "If the material becomes detached, and so long as it remains so . . . (the owner can recover by *vindicatio*[2])."

X. The property in a thing sold and delivered does not pass to the purchaser till payment.

XI. Provision confirming the *cessio*[3] before the magistrate, as likewise the *mancipatio*.

### TABLE VII

The Law Concerning Real Property.

I. Two feet and a half at least must be left between adjoining edifices for the purposes of proper ventilation.

II. Provisions concerning plantations and constructions or excavations upon adjoining plots of ground.

III. "A garden . . . a small inheritance . . . a barn."[4]

[1] A feigned judicial combat for trying the right to property in a given thing.

[2] A legal process of claiming possession.

[3] Alienation or surrendering of property.

[4] Not restored.

IV. A space of five feet must be left between adjoining fields for the purposes of access and the turning of the plough. This space cannot be acquired by usucapio.

V. In the event of there being any dispute about the boundaries, the magistrate is to give three arbiters to the parties, who shall settle the matter.

VI. The breadth of a road is to be eight feet; at the end, where it turns, sixteen feet. If the road is impassable, the owner of a right of way may cross wherever he pleases.

VII. The proprietor whose property is threatened with damage arising from artificial works for the collection of rain-water, or from an aqueduct, has a right to demand a guarantee against this injury.

VIII. The branches of a tree overhanging adjoining property must be pruned all round up to fifteen feet from the ground.

IX. A proprietor may go on to adjoining land to pick up the fruit that has fallen from his tree.

### TABLE VIII

On Torts.

I. Capital punishment is decreed against libellers and public defamers.

II. "Retaliation against him who breaks the limb of another and does not offer compensation."

III. For the fracture of the bone (of the tooth) of a freeman, the penalty is 300 asses;[1] in the case of a slave, 150.

IV. "For any injury whatsoever committed upon another the penalty shall be 25 asses."

V. ". . . For damage unjustly caused . . . (but if by accident) reparation."

[1] A small copper coin, worth in the earlier period about 16⅔ cents; depreciated until by the time of the Second Punic War it was worth about two-thirds of a cent.

VI. For damage caused by a quadruped, reparation or the forfeiture of the animal.

VII. An action shall lie against him who depastures his flock upon a neighbour's land.

VIII. "He who by enchantment shall blight the crops of another, or attract them from one field to another . . ."

IX. He who during the night furtively either cuts or depastures a neighbour's crops, if of the age of puberty, shall be devoted to Ceres and put to death; if under that age, he shall be scourged at the discretion of the magistrate and condemned in the penalty of double the damage done.

X. The incendiary of a house or of a haystack near a house, if acting intentionally and of sound mind, shall be bound, scourged, and put to death by fire. If by negligence, he shall repair the damage; or, if too poor, shall be chastised moderately.

XI. A penalty of 25 asses is to be inflicted upon any one who without right has felled the trees of another.

XII. "Any one committing a robbery by night may be lawfully killed."

XIII. A robber surprised during the day must not be put to death, unless he attempts to defend himself with arms.

XIV. A thief taken in the act, if a free man, shall be scourged and made over by *addictio* to the person robbed; if a slave, shall be scourged and thrown from the Tarpeian rock; but those under the age of puberty shall, at the discretion of the magistrate, be scourged and condemned to repair the damage.

XV. . . .

XVI. . . .

XVII. Provision prohibiting the acquisition by *usucapio*, that is to say, by possession of stolen property.

XVIII. Interest upon money lent must not exceed an ounce. That is to say, one twelfth part of the principal per annum, which is eight and a third per cent per annum, calculating according to the solar year of twelve months, according to the calendar of Numa. The penalty for exceeding this interest is the quadruple.

XIX. For fraud in bailment a double penalty.

XX. Provision giving all citizens the right of action to remove suspected tutors, and imposing a double penalty for the abstracted property of the pupil.

XXI. "The patron who shall commit a fraud upon his client shall be devoted to the gods."

XXII. "He who has been a witness or acted as scale-bearer and refuses to give testimony shall be accounted infamous, and incapable of giving or receiving testimony."

XXIII. Provision ordering false witnesses to be thrown from the Tarpeian rock.

XXIV. Capital punishment for homicide.

XXV. "(Capital punishment decreed against) any one who practises enchantments or uses poisonous drugs."

XXVI. Provision against seditious gatherings by night in the city, awarding capital punishment.

XXVII. *Sodales*, or members of the same college or corporation, are at liberty to make what rules binding upon themselves they may think fit, provided that they do not contravene the law.

### TABLE IX

Public Law.

I. Provision prohibiting the passing of any law concerning a private individual.

II. The great comitia, that is to say, the comitia by centuries, have alone the right to enact laws inflicting capital punishment upon a citizen, that is to say, which could deprive him of life, liberty, or citizenship.

III. The penalty of death is awarded to the judge or arbitrator appointed by the magistrate who accepts a bribe.

IV. Provision relating to the question in the case of homicide; and the right of appeal to the people in the case of any penal sentence.

V. The penalty of death decreed against any one who should excite the enemy against the Roman people; or who should deliver a citizen to the enemy.

TABLE X

Sacred Law.

I. "The dead must not be buried nor burned within the city."

II. "Do no more than this . . . The wood of the funeral pile shall not be smoothed."

III. Restrictions against sumptuous funerals; the dead are not to be buried nor burned in more than three robes; nor in more than three fillets of purple; nor shall the funeral be attended by more than ten flute players.

IV. "Women shall not be allowed to tear their hair nor make immoderate wailings."

V. "The bones of the deceased shall not be collected for the purpose of giving him a subsequent funeral (except in the case of death in battle, or in a foreign country)."

VI. Provision prohibiting the embalming the bodies of slaves, funeral banquets, expensive libations, coronal garlands, and the erection of incense altars.

VII. "But if the deceased has either personally or by his slaves or horses obtained any public trophy, he shall be entitled to the honour it confers."

VIII. Prohibition against more than one funeral, or more than one funeral ceremony, for the same deceased.

IX. "Gold must not be buried with the dead; but if the teeth are fastened with gold, this may be either buried or burned."

X. No funeral pile or sepulchre shall be erected within sixty feet of another man's house, except with his consent.

XI. Neither a sepulchre nor its vestibule can be acquired by *usucapio*.

### TABLE XI

Supplement to the First Five Tables.

I. Prohibiting marriage between patricians and plebeians.

### TABLE XII

Supplement to the Last Five Tables.

I. Provision establishing the *pignoris capio*[1] against the debtor for the payment of the purchase-money of a victim, or the hire of a beast of burden when the hire has been expressly made in order that the sum paid should be devoted to purpose of sacrifice.

II. "If a slave has committed a theft or any other injury . . . the direct action does not lie against the master, but the *actio noxalis*[2] does."

III. "If any one wrongfully acquires the interim possession of a thing, the magistrate shall appoint three arbitrators to determine the question; and if they decide against him, he shall be mulcted in a sum equal to double the profits."

IV. It is forbidden to consecrate anything which is the subject of a suit, and a double penalty is inflicted for doing so.

V. Abrogates all previous and contradictory enactments.

[1] The seizure of the security. [2] An action on account of an injury.

## *From the De Oratore of Cicero*

### BOOK I., CHAPTER XLIV

Though all the world exclaim against me, I will say what I think: that single little book of the Twelve Tables, if any one look at the fountains and sources of laws, seems to me, assuredly, to surpass the libraries of all the philosophers, both in weight of authority, and in plenitude of utility. And if our country has our love, as it ought to have in the highest degree, — our country, I say, of which the force and natural attraction is so strong, that one of the wisest of mankind preferred his Ithaca, fixed, like a little nest, among the roughest of rocks, to immortality itself, — with what affection ought we to be warmed toward such a country as ours, which, preëminently above all other countries, is the seat of virtue, empire, and dignity? Its spirit, customs, and discipline ought to be our first objects of study, both because our country is the parent of us all, and because as much wisdom must be thought to have been employed in framing such laws, as in establishing so vast and powerful an empire. You will receive also this pleasure and delight from the study of the law, that you will then most readily comprehend how far our ancestors excelled other nations in wisdom, if you compare our laws with those of their Lycurgus, Draco, and Solon. It is indeed incredible how undigested and almost ridiculous is all civil law, except our own; on which subject I am accustomed to say much in my daily conversation, when I am praising the wisdom of our countrymen above that of all other men, and especially of the Greeks. For these reasons have I declared, Scævola, that the knowledge of the civil law is indispensable to those who would become accomplished orators.

**Importance of the Twelve Tables in the education of the later period.**

## II. THE SECOND PERIOD OF EARLY ROMAN EDUCATION

**The Period.** — The second period of early Roman education covers the century and a half previous to the conquest of Greece (300–146 B.C.). This is the period during which Rome grew from a small local power into a world dominion, including as it does the Italian, Punic, and Macedonian wars. One result of this long warfare was to bring Rome into intimate contact with the Greeks in Italy, Sicily, and Greece. The educational characteristic of the period is the institutionalizing of education and the gradual growth of the Greek influence. At the opening of the period Rome could not be said to have schools at all. Education was centred in the family, and was largely moral, social, and military in character. It was distinctly a training process, for no instruction save that connected with the Laws of the Twelve Tables was considered necessary. At the close of the period schools were well established; they presented the appearance of a system corresponding to our elementary, secondary, and higher education; and it had become the approved thing for the Roman boy to receive his education from them, though there were many who yet clung to the old education, and though even after this time there were governmental efforts to check the growth of Greek ideas and customs in education.

**The Sources.** — The two selections given narrate the introduction and growth of these secondary and higher educational institutions. They are the introductory portions of the two remaining fragments of the works of Suetonius on the *Lives of Eminent Grammarians* and on the *Lives of Eminent Rhetoricians.* Gaius Suetonius Tranquillus was an historian, born about 79 A.D., and therefore a contemporary of the younger Pliny and Tacitus. He was in high favor with the emperors of that period, until deprived of his office by Hadrian in 121 A.D. In this time of disfavor he wrote his historical works, which are chiefly of a biographical character. The two selections, introductory to numerous biographical accounts of distinguished teachers of the period of the Hellenized Roman education, form a brief sketch of this earlier period.

**The Introduction of Schools and the Process of Hellenization.** — At the beginning of this period there are evidences of the existence of elementary schools. Such a school, the *ludus*, afforded instruction in reading and writing, perhaps also in calculation. Instead of such instruction being imparted in each home by the parent or family slave, it was now given for several families by a slave or, perhaps, by a freeman. Our detailed knowledge of these schools is drawn from the succeeding period. These schools are referred to by Suetonius as the schools of the literators or grammatists (*On Grammarians*, Ch. IV.).

Early in this period a higher type, the school of the grammaticus, was introduced by the Greeks. The earliest of these grammar schools was that established by Livius Andronicus some time about the middle of that century. At the same time he translated the *Odyssey* into Latin, which thereafter became the basis of grammar school work. Ennius was brought to Rome 204 B.C., and afterward gave instruction in Greek and Latin grammar. Plutarch refers to Spurius Carvilius, who established a school

240 B.C. as the first to take fixed fees. Carvilius was twice consul, first in 234, — a notable rise for a schoolmaster. By the middle of the second century B.C. there was quite a body of this early Latin literature, either translated from, or written in imitation of, Grecian works, much of which became the basis of grammar school work. It is about this time (157 B.C.) that Crates established his school, which is referred to by Suetonius as affording the first definite study of grammar. In the same chapter Suetonius refers to nine other grammarians that taught at about this time or a little later. It is evident, therefore, that literary instruction after the Grecian fashion was well established at Rome in grammar schools by the close of the old Roman period.

By this time a third type of school had appeared, — the school of the rhetor or rhetorician. As Suetonius suggests in his *Lives of Grammarians* (Ch. IV.), the offices of the grammaticus and of the rhetor were not at first distinct. The grammarians taught rhetoric as well: secondary education and higher education were not differentiated. Both were of a literary character, both were Grecian imitations. They furnished the instruction and training in declamation and debate. Suetonius states that the early rhetors alternated their work in rhetoric, either on successive days or on mornings and afternoons, with that in grammar. Certain it is that by 161 B.C. such schools have become numerous enough to be considered a menace to Roman institutions and the preservation of the old Roman character, for in that year the Senate approved the proposition of the prætor that the rhetoricians along with the philosophers be expelled from Rome. Of course such methods were ineffective against tendencies so manifestly in accord with the whole movement of the times. Later developments along this line fall into the third special period; but it seems that by seventy years later the Greek rhetoricians had been supplemented by a new type, the Latin rhetoricians, who were considered to be still more pernicious. The charges against these schools sound very much like the charges entered against the schools of the Sophists when they were first introduced at Athens; and, in fact, they indicate a change very similar in character to that indicated in the *Clouds*. The close of the first general period leaves Roman society fully equipped with a frame-work of educational institutions, to be extended and amplified in the succeeding period. The method and content of their work can be best understood when that more detailed evidence is presented.

### *Selections from the Lives of Eminent Grammarians, by Suetonius*

I. The science of grammar was in ancient times far from being in vogue at Rome; indeed, it was of little use in a rude state of society, when the people were engaged in constant wars, and had not much time to bestow on the cultivation of the liberal arts. At the outset, its pretensions were very slender, for the earliest men of learning, who were both poets and orators, may be considered as half-Greek: I speak of Livius[1] and Ennius,[2] who are

[1] Livius Andronicus is regarded as the founder of Roman epic and dramatic poetry. He was by birth a Greek of southern Italy. Upon the conquest of that region by the Romans, he was brought as a slave to Rome in 272 B.C. He was given his liberty and became a teacher in the Greek and Latin languages. During this time he translated the *Odyssey* into Latin. This became the chief text-book of the Roman schools for centuries, in time supplanting the Twelve Tables. In 240 B.C. he produced the first Roman drama, modelled after the Grecian dramas.

[2] Ennius was born in Calabria in 239 B.C. He was brought from Sardinia to Rome by Porcius Cato in 204 B.C. Here he became a teacher of the Greek language, also translating Greek plays for the Roman stage.

acknowledged to have taught both languages as well at Rome as in foreign parts. But they only translated from the Greek, and if they composed anything of their own in Latin, it was only from what they had before read. For although there are those who say that this Ennius published two books, one on "Letters and Syllables," and the other on "Metres," Lucius Cotta has satisfactorily proved that they are not the works of the poet Ennius, but of another writer of the same name,[1] to whom also the treatise on the "Rules of Augury" is attributed.

II. Crates[2] of Mallos,[3] then, was, in our opinion, the first who introduced the study of grammar at Rome. He was cotemporary with Aristarchus,[4] and having been sent by king Attalus[5] as envoy to the senate in the interval between the second and third Punic wars,[6] soon after the death of Ennius, he had the misfortune to fall into an open sewer in the Palatine quarter of the city, and broke his leg. After which, during the whole period of his embassy and convalescence, he gave frequent lectures, taking much pains to instruct his hearers, and he has left us an example well worthy of imitation. It was so far followed, that poems hitherto little known, the works either of deceased friends or other approved writers, were brought to light, and being read and commented on, were explained to others. Thus, Caius Octavius Lampadio edited the Punic War of Nævius,[7] which having been written in one volume without any break in the manuscript, he divided into seven books. After that, Quintus Vargonteius undertook the Annals of Ennius, which he read on certain fixed days to crowded audiences. So Lælius Archelaus, and Vectius Philocomus, read and commented on the Satires of their friend Lucilius,[8] which Lenæus Pompeius, a freedman,

[1] This is all that is known of this writer.

[2] Founded a grammar school in Pergamus, came to Rome as above narrated in 157 B.C.

[3] In Cilicia in Asia Minor.

[4] A celebrated Grecian grammarian, one of the greatest critics of antiquity, especially of the Homeric poems.

[5] Of Pergamus. An ally of the Romans.

[6] 149–146 B.C.

[7] A Roman epic and dramatic poet, born about 270 B.C.

[8] The creator of Roman satire, born 148 B.C., died 109.

tells us he studied under Archelaus; and Valerius Cato, under Philocomus. Two others also taught and promoted grammar in various branches, namely, Lucius Ælius Lanuvinus, the son-in-law of Quintus Ælius, and Servius Claudius, both of whom were Roman knights, and men who rendered great services both to learning and the republic.

* * * * * * *

IV. The appellation of grammarian was borrowed from the Greeks; but at first, the Latins called such persons *literati*. Cornelius Nepos,[1] also, in his book, where he draws a distinction between a literate and a philologist, says that in common phrase, those are properly called *literati* who are skilled in speaking or writing with care or accuracy, and those more especially deserve the name who translated the poets, and were called *grammarians* by the Greeks. It appears that they were named *literators* by Messala Corvinus, in one of his letters, when he says, "that it does not refer to Furius Bibaculus, nor even to Sigida, nor to Cato, the *literator*," meaning, doubtless, that Valerius Cato[2] was both a poet and an eminent grammarian. Some there are who draw a distinction between a *literati* and a *literator*, as the Greeks do between a grammarian and a grammatist, applying the former term to men of real erudition, the latter to those whose pretensions to learning are moderate; and this opinion Orbilius supports by examples. For he says that in old times, when a company of slaves was offered for sale by any person, it was not customary, without good reason, to describe either of them in the catalogue as a literate, but only as a literator, meaning that he was not a proficient in letters, but had a smattering of knowledge.

The early grammarians taught rhetoric also, and we have many of their treatises which include both sciences; whence it arose, I think, that in later times, although the two professions had then become distinct, the old custom was retained, or the grammarians introduced into their teaching some of the elements required for public speaking, such as the problem, the periphrasis, the choice of words, descrip-

[1] A Roman historian, born 100 B.C.

[2] A celebrated grammarian, of the time of the Civil Wars.

tion of character, and the like; in order that they might not transfer their pupils to the rhetoricians no better than ill-taught boys. But I perceive that these lessons are now given up in some cases, on account of the want of application, or the tender years, of the scholar, for I do not believe that it arises from any dislike in the master. I recollect that when I was a boy it was the custom of one of these, whose name was Princeps, to take alternate days for declaiming and disputing; and sometimes he would lecture in the morning, and declaim in the afternoon, when he had his pulpit removed. I heard, also, that even within the memories of our own fathers, some of the pupils of the grammarians passed directly from the schools to the courts, and at once took a high place in the ranks of the most distinguished advocates. The professors at that time were, indeed, men of great eminence, of some of whom I may be able to give an account in the following chapters.

* * * * * * *

### *Selections from the Lives of Eminent Rhetoricians, by Suetonius*

I. Rhetoric, also, as well as Grammar, was not introduced amongst us till a late period, and with still more difficulty, inasmuch as we find that, at times, the practice of it was even prohibited. In order to leave no doubt of this, I will subjoin an ancient decree of the senate, as well as an edict of the censors:— "*In the consulship*[1] *of Caius Fannius Strabo, and Marcus Valerius Messala:* the prætor Marcus Pomponius moved the senate, that an act be passed respecting Philosophers and Rhetoricians. In this matter, they have decreed as follows: 'IT SHALL BE LAWFUL for M. Pomponius, the prætor, to take such measures, and make such provisions, as the good of the Republic, and the duty of his office, require, that no Philosophers or Rhetoricians be suffered at Rome.'

"After some interval, the censor[2] Cnæus Domitius Ænobarbus and Lucius Lucinius Crassus issued the following edict upon the same subject: 'IT IS REPORTED to us that

[1] 592 A.U.C.; 161 B.C. [2] 92 B.C.

certain persons have instituted a new kind of discipline; that our youth resort to their schools; that they have assumed the title of Latin Rhetoricians; and that young men waste their time there for whole days together. Our ancestors have ordained what instruction it is fitting their children should receive, and what schools they should attend. These novelties, contrary to the customs and instructions of our ancestors, we neither approve, nor do they appear to us good. Wherefore it appears to be our duty that we should notify our judgment both to those who keep such schools, and those who are in the practice of frequenting them, that they meet our disapprobation.'"

However, by slow degrees, rhetoric manifested itself to be a useful and honourable study, and many persons devoted themselves to it both, as a means of defence and of acquiring reputation. Cicero declaimed in Greek until his prætorship, but afterwards, as he grew older, in Latin also; and even in the consulship[1] of Hirtius and Pansa, whom he calls "his great and noble disciples." Some historians state that Cneius Pompey[2] resumed the practice of declaiming even during the civil war, in order to be better prepared to argue against Caius Curio, a young man of great talents, to whom the defence of Cæsar was entrusted. They say, likewise, that it was not forgotten by Mark Antony, nor by Augustus, even during the war of Modena. Nero also declaimed even after he became emperor, in the first year of his reign, which he had done before in public but twice. Many speeches of orators were also published. In consequence, public favour was so much attracted to the study of rhetoric, that a vast number of professors and learned men devoted themselves to it; and it flourished to such a degree, that some of them raised themselves by it to the rank of senators and the highest offices.

But the same mode of teaching was not adopted by all, nor, indeed, did individuals always confine themselves to the same system, but each varied his plan of teaching according to circumstances. For they were accustomed, in stating their argument with the utmost clearness, to use figures and apologies, to put cases, as circumstances required, and to relate facts, sometimes briefly and succinctly,

[1] 43 B.C. [2] With Cæsar and Crassus formed the first triumvirate.

and, at other times, more at large and with greater feeling. Nor did they omit, on occasion, to resort to translations from the Greek, and to expatiate in the praise, or to launch their censures on the faults, of illustrious men. They also dealt with matters connected with every-day life, pointing out such as are useful and necessary, and such as are hurtful and needless. They had occasion often to support the authority of fabulous accounts, and to detract from that of historical narratives, which sort the Greeks call "Propositions," "Refutations" and "Corroborations," until by a gradual process they have exhausted these topics, and arrive at the gist of the argument.

Among the ancients, subjects of controversy were drawn either from history, as indeed some are even now, or from actual facts, of recent occurrence. It was, therefore, the custom to state them precisely, with details of the names of places. We certainly so find them collected and published, and it may be well to give one or two of them literally, by way of example:

"A company of young men from the city, having made an excursion to Ostia in the summer season, and going down to the beach, fell in with some fishermen who were casting their nets in the sea. Having bargained with them for the haul, whatever it might turn out to be, for a certain sum, they paid down the money. They waited a long time while the nets were being drawn, and when at last they were dragged on shore, there was no fish in them, but some gold sewn up in a basket. The buyers claim the haul as theirs, the fishermen assert that it belongs to them."

Again: "Some dealers having to land from a ship at Brundusium a cargo of slaves, among which there was a handsome boy of great value, they, in order to deceive the collectors of the customs, smuggled him ashore in the dress of a freeborn youth, with the *bullum* [1] hung about his neck. The fraud easily escaped detection. They proceed to Rome; the affair becomes the subject of judicial inquiry; it is alleged that the boy was entitled to his freedom, because his master had voluntarily treated him as free."

[1] A circular piece of metal, or leather, worn by Roman children, suspended from the neck. It was laid aside at adolescence as a sign of manhood.

## III. CONTRAST BETWEEN EARLIER AND LATER PERIODS OF ROMAN EDUCATION

**The Periods.** — As became a practical, sturdy, severe, and reverential people, with respect for tradition and a genius for originating and preserving institutions, the change in educational ideas and practices came very much more gradually with the Romans than with the Greeks. The contrast here offered is essentially that between the third period (the last century of the Republic and the first two centuries of the Empire) and the first and second periods. While in the second period schools had become common and Grecian educational ideas and practices were being steadily introduced, education for the typical Roman was still essentially a home process, and even so far as it had become institutionalized was not yet literary. The first essentially literary school was that of Spurius Carvilius, opened in 260 B.C. Accordingly to Plutarch, he was the first to take fixed fees for his instruction. Elementary schools, however, undoubtedly existed before this time. Less than a generation later, Livius Andronicus, the founder of Roman epic and dramatic poetry, latinized the *Odyssey*, which soon shared with the Laws of the Twelve Tables the first place in Roman schools. Not until the middle of the second century B.C. does education cease to be essentially Roman. The conquest of Greece led to the free introduction and imitation of Grecian ideas, and soon thereafter Rome becomes, on the intellectual side, thoroughly Hellenized. In this latter connection, a decree of the Senate passed in 161 B.C. may be taken as the epochal mark. This decree called for the expulsion of the philosophers and rhetoricians from Rome. The account of the decree as given by Suetonius has already been presented. Its provisions were non-effective; its significance is rather as an indication of a fact accomplished than of a reform instituted. The contrast presented in this section is not, then, between the decadent education of the late imperial times and the early Roman, but rather that between the Græco-Roman education at its best (the third period of Roman education) and the old Roman education at its best.

**The Sources. Their Interpretation.** — The evidences of this transition, be it development or decline, are abundant, as are also literary references to the change. Yet conscious comparisons with direct reference to the educational changes are rarer than those concerning the similar transition with the Greeks. This is due partly to the fact that the change was less sharp than with the Greeks; partly, to the fact that the Latins did not give full expression to all their life in permanent literary form. As sources, two direct comparisons, of widely different character, are here given. One of these dates from almost two centuries before the Christian era, the other from three-quarters of a century after its beginning. Evidently the same conditions cannot enter into the comparison, though the general characteristics of the old education are substantially the same in each selection. The first is a very brief comparison found in the *Bacchides* of Plautus (Act III., Scene 3), first presented in 189 B.C. The poet begins by presenting the main features of the old Roman education, and then by way of contrast, the changes occurring under the influence of the new ideas and tendencies. This play is written, however, in the latter part of the *old* period, and indicates that these changes have already begun, though the extreme characterization of existing conditions cannot be accepted without qualification. Plautus (254–189 B.C.) was one of the earliest and one of the most free-spoken Roman comic poets, and so the delineations of his times must be interpreted from the point of view of the comic stage. The scene of the *Bacchides* is laid in Greece, and in the play itself Plautus, as was his custom, drew very largely from Grecian sources. Hence the extreme view of the poet may be partially due to the fact that he has Grecian as well as Roman conditions in mind. His characterization of the new education relates to one point only, the relations of the parent, pupil, and tutor. Whatever reservations need be made, we can accept as true the statement of Plautus that much of the old Roman reverence and modesty of action in youth has departed. The selection is given, then, more for its succinct presentations of the characteristics of the early education than for its evidence as to the time of transition to new conditions.

The second selection, taken from the *Dialogus de Oratoribus* of Tacitus, is of very different character, and is accurate evidence from one of the most judicious and observing of Roman historians. This is probably the earliest work of Tacitus (b. about 50 A.D., d. about 117), as it was written about 79 A.D. The entire work is an educational treatise of the same general character as the *De Oratore* of Cicero. It is an essay in the form of a dialogue, giving an account of the decay of oratory under the Empire. As this was the period when oratory expressed the whole aim of education so far as it was represented by schools, the essay presents clearly the condition of education at that time. The passage selected (Chs. XXVIII.–XXXV. inclusive) bears directly upon education in the broader sense of the terms and contains the direct comparison in Chs. XXVIII. and XXXIV., between the old education and the new. In the interpretation of the passage it is well to bear in mind that Tacitus, while a close observer, was quite pessimistic concerning conditions of Roman society. This is shown in his other writings, especially the *Germania*. His contemporary, Pliny the Younger, gives a brighter view of Roman education at that period as he does of Roman society in general (see Ch. V.).

**The Contrast as to Aim, Subject-matter, Method, Organization.** — In the earlier periods education had the general aim of preparation for full Roman citizenship, military, civic, economic, and oratorical. This was no narrow ideal, though toward the latter part of this first general period, upon the basis of the economic and civic training, the Roman youth might specialize on military or legal, that is, oratorical, lines. Oratory as a single aim did not yet exist. Husbandry, the army, public meetings and courts, each demanded of every Roman citizen the performance of certain civic duties. The aim was general; the education, broad. Into it entered little of the literary element, and the little demanded scarcely called for formal training. In the latter period the whole aim of higher education is expressed in the one word, oratory. A full exposition of this conception of education, at its best, is given later in the selections from Cicero's *De Oratore*. The account given by Tacitus is drawn from the same period, but a century later, when oratorical education had become much more formal and artificial. The content of education in the respective periods follows the aim very closely. In the early periods, its essential part was a training in the duties of the householder, the soldier, the member of certain civic assemblies, the defender of one's own rights and ideas before courts of laws. This general training demanded a certain amount of literary instruction, small at first, but of constantly increasing volume. It included reading, writing, calculation, mastering of the Twelve Tables, and the acquisition of national hymns and legends. In the second part of the old Roman period there was added a small amount of literary study centring around the Latinized *Odyssey* and early Latin literature. On this point, however, there is little direct evidence. In the contrast presented by Tacitus, the content of education — at least of higher education — has become wholly literary, and in the hands of the rhetoricians is made extremely artificial. This training in the "rhetorical circus" supplants the earlier training in all-round citizenship. The contrast in methods and institutional organization is even greater. The method of old Roman education is essentially that of the apprentice system; the youth learns by observation and direct imitation of the master, in the army, at the farm, in the courts and the forum. To this training is added a small amount of instruction by the parent or by the master. In the latter period, the school supplants the home and the camp and forum, and this early training gives place to the formal instruction of the rhetorical school. Here the instruction is largely philological instead of literary in the broader sense; and dialectical discussion of fictitious cases replaces the observation of, and practice in, the rendering of justice and the shaping of men's motives and actions.

Such a change could not but be related, both as cause and effect, to a change in spirit — a change in regard to the attitude of parents toward the education of their children; a change in the attitude of pupils toward their teachers, their school work, and their life obligations; and a change in the attitude of teachers toward their profession and their pupils. This change in spirit is indicated in both selections.

### *Selections from the Bacchides*[1] *of Plautus*

Act III., Sc. III.

**Contrast between the old and the new Roman education;**

27. Lydus. I declare that for your first twenty years you had not *even* this *much* liberty, to move your foot out of the house *even* a finger's length away from your tutor. When it did happen *so*, this evil, too, was added to the evil; both pupil and preceptor were esteemed disgraced. Before the rising of the sun had you not come to the school for exercise,[2] no slight punishment would you have had at the hands of the master of the school. There did they exercise themselves rather with running, wrestling, the quoit, the javelin, boxing, the ball, *and* leaping, rather than with harlots or with kissing; there did they prolong their lives, *and* not in secret-lurking holes. Then, when from the hippodrome[3] and school of exercise you had returned home, clad in your belted frock, upon a stool by your master[4] would you sit; *and* there, when you were reading your book, if you made a mistake in a single syllable, your skin would be made as spotted as your nurse's gown.

[1] The scene is laid in Greece. This passage, however, indicates the change that has come over old Roman education with the introduction of Grecian ideas and the degeneracy of old Roman morals.

[2] The palæstra, the school for athletic exercise.

[3] The riding school.

[4] The music or literary school.

MNES. [*aside*]. I'm sorely vexed, to my sorrow, that on my account these things should be said about my friend. In his innocence he incurs this suspicion for my sake.

PHILO. The manners, Lydus, now are altered.

LYD. That, for my part, I know full well. For formerly, a man used to receive *public* honors by the votes of the people, before he ceased to be obedient to one appointed his tutor. But now-a-days, before he is seven years old, if you touch a boy with your hand, at once the child breaks his tutor's head with his tablet. When you go to complain to the father, thus says the father to the child: "Be you my own *dear boy*, since you can defend yourself from an injury." The tutor *then* is called for; "Hallo! you old good-for-nothing,[1] don't you be touching the child for this reason, that he has behaved so boldly;" *and thus* the despised tutor becomes just like a lantern with his oiled linen rags.[2] Judgment pronounced, they go away thence. Can this preceptor then, on these terms, keep up his authority, if he himself is to be beaten the first?

**as to the relation between pupil and teacher.**

## *Tacitus: Dialogue concerning Oratory*[3]

**Decline of education in the early imperial period.**

28. Messala resumed his discourse. The causes of the decay of eloquence are by no means difficult to be traced. They are, I believe, well known to you, Maternus, to Secundus, and even to Aper,[4] though I am now, at your request to expound what we all feel. For is it not obvious that eloquence, with the rest of the polite arts, has lost its former lustre, not for want of men, but through the dissipation of our young men, the inattention of parents, the ignorance of those who pretend to give instruction, and the total neglect of ancient discipline? The mischief began at Rome, it has overrun all Italy, and is now spreading through the provinces. You, however, know more than I of the state

[1] Ordinarily they were slaves.

[2] Commentators suppose this to mean that he is comparing his head, when it has been broken by the tablets and plastered over with oiled linen, to the ordinary Roman lantern made of oiled linen cloth.

[3] The scene of the dialogue is laid in the sixth year of Vespasian, 75 A.D.

[4] Personages of the dialogue.

of your provinces in this respect, and therefore I shall confine myself to those peculiar and indigenous vices of the capital which beset our youth from their birth, and gather more and more upon them through every season of life. But before I enter on the subject, let me premise a few words on the strict discipline of our ancestors, in educating and training up their children. In the first place the son of every family was the legitimate offspring of a virtuous mother. The infant, as soon as born, was not consigned to the mean dwelling of a hireling nurse, but was reared and cherished in the bosom of its mother, whose highest praise it was to take care of her household affairs, and attend to her children. It was customary likewise for each family to choose some elderly female relation of approved conduct, to whose charge the children were committed. In her presence not one indecent word was uttered; nothing was done against propriety and good manners. The hours of study and serious employment were settled by her direction; and not only so, but even the diversions of the children were conducted with modest reserve and sanctity of manners. Thus it was that Cornelia, the mother of the Gracchi, superintended the education of her illustrious issue. It was thus that Aurelia trained up Julius Cæsar; and thus Atia formed the mind of Augustus. The consequence of this regular discipline was, that the young mind, whole and sound, and unwarped by irregular passions, received the elements of the liberal arts with hearty avidity. Whatever was the peculiar bias, whether to the military art, the study of the laws, or the profession of eloquence, that engrossed the whole attention, that was imbibed thoroughly and totally.

Training of the child according to old Roman ideas.

29. In the present age what is our practice? The infant is committed to a Greek chambermaid, and a slave or two, chosen for the purpose, generally the worst of the whole household train, and unfit for any office of trust. From the idle tales and gross absurdities of these people, the tender and uninstructed mind is suffered to receive its earliest impressions. Throughout the house not one servant cares what he says or does in the presence of his young master; and indeed, how should it be otherwise? since the parents themselves are so far from training their

Compared with the training given them in imperial times.

young families to virtue and modesty, that they set them the first examples of luxury and licentiousness. Thus our youth gradually acquire a confirmed habit of impudence, and a total disregard of that reverence they owe both to themselves and to others. To say truth, it seems as if a fondness for horses, actors, and gladiators, the peculiar and distinguishing folly of this our city, was impressed upon them even in the womb: and when once a passion of this contemptible sort has seized and engaged the mind, what opening is there left for the noble arts? Who talks of anything else in our houses? If we enter the schools, what other subjects of conversation do we hear among the boys? The preceptors themselves choose no other topic more frequently to entertain their hearers; for it is not by establishing a strict discipline, or by giving proofs of their genius, that this order of men gain pupils, but by fawning and flattery. Not to mention how ill instructed our youth are in the very elements of literature, sufficient pains are by no means taken in bringing them acquainted with the best authors, or in giving them a proper notion of history, together with a knowledge of men and things. The whole that seems to be considered in their education is, to find out a person for them called a rhetorician. I will presently give you some account of the introduction of this profession at Rome, and show you with what contempt it was received by our ancestors.

**Character of school life no better.**

30. At present, I must advert to that scheme of discipline which the ancient orators practised. Their unwearied diligence, their habits of meditation, and their constant exercises in every branch of study, are amply displayed in their own writings. The treatise of Cicero, called "Brutus," is in all our hands. In the latter part of that work (the former part is employed in commemorating the ancient orators), he gives a sketch of the several progressive steps by which he formed his eloquence. He there acquaints us, that he studied the civil law under Q. Mucius;[1] that he was instructed in the several branches of philosophy by Philo the Academic,[2] and Diodorus the Stoic; that, not

**Education of the orator, according to old ideas.**

[1] Quintus Mucius Scævola, the leading jurist of his time.

[2] A leading philosopher of the Platonic school.

satisfied with attending the lectures of those eminent masters, of whom there were at that time great numbers in Rome, he made a voyage into Greece and Asia, in order to enlarge his knowledge, and embrace the whole circle of the sciences. Accordingly he appears by his writings to have been familiar with geometry, music, grammar, and every liberal art. He was versed in the subtleties of ethics, and the practical lore of moral philosophy. He had studied the operations of nature, and explored the causes of her phenomena. And thus it was, my worthy friends, that from deep learning and the confluence of many arts and universal science, that overflowing and exuberant eloquence derived its strength and fulness. For it is not with the oratorical power and faculty as with others, which are exercised within certain precise and determinate limits: on the contrary, he alone can justly be deemed an orator, who can speak on every subject gracefully, ornately, and persuasively, in a manner suitable to the dignity of his subject, and with pleasure to his hearers.

**Scope of his education.**

31. So thought those renowned orators of old. In order, however, to attain these eminent qualifications, they did not think it necessary to declaim in the schools, and to exercise their tongues and their voices alone upon fictitious controversies, remote from all reality; but rather to fill their minds with such studies as concern life and manners, as treat of moral good and evil, of justice and injustice, of the decent and the unbecoming in actions, because these constitute the subject matter of the orator; for in the courts of law we generally descant on equity; in deliberations, on moral rectitude; whilst yet these two branches are not so absolutely distinct, but that they are frequently blended with each other. Now it is impossible to speak on such topics with fulness, variety, and elegance, unless the orator is perfectly well acquainted with human nature; unless he understands the power and extent of moral duties, the perversity of vice, and other things besides, which do not partake either of vice or virtue.

**Skill gained not from school, but from contact with actual life.**

From the same source, likewise, he must derive his influence over the passions. He who knows the nature of indignation, will be able to kindle or allay that passion in the breast of the judge; and the advocate who has con-

**His training must be broad, both in practical life**

sidered the effect of compassion, and from what secret springs it flows, will best know how to soften the mind, and melt it into tenderness. It is by these secrets of his art that the orator gains his influence. Whether he has to do with the prejudiced, the angry, the envious, the melancholy, or the timid, he can bridle their various passions, and hold the reins in his own hand. According to the disposition of each, he will apply his skill, and modify his speech, having the needful appliances in readiness for every occasion. Some there are who like best that close mode of oratory, which in a laconic manner states the facts, and forms an immediate conclusion: in that case, it is obvious how necessary it is to be a complete master of the rules of logic. Others admire a more diffuse and level style, illustrated by images drawn from common observation: towards moving such hearers the Peripatetic writers will give him some assistance; and indeed they will, in general, supply him with many useful hints in all the different methods of popular address. The Academics will inspire him with a becoming warmth: Plato will give him loftiness, Xenophon suavity. Even the exclamatory manner of Epicurus, or Metrodorus,[1] may be found, in some circumstances, not altogether unserviceable. For take note that I am not laying down rules for building up an imaginary wise man, or a city of the Stoics, but for accomplishing one who ought not to confine his attention to any one sect, but gather freely from all. Accordingly, the ancient orators not only studied the civil laws, but also grammar, poetry, music, and geometry. Indeed, there are few causes (perhaps I might justly say there are none) wherein a skill in the first is not absolutely necessary; and there are many in which an acquaintance with the last-mentioned sciences is highly requisite.

**and in literary studies.**

32. Let no one object to me that "eloquence is the single science requisite for the orator; an occasional recourse to the others will be sufficient for all his purposes;" I answer, in the first place, there will always be a remarkable difference in the manner of applying what we take up, as it were, upon loan, and what we properly possess; so that it will ever be manifest, whether the orator is indebted to

**Eloquence not the result of rhetorical study only.**

[1] The favorite disciple of Epicurus.

others for what he produces, or derives it from his own unborrowed fund. And, in the next, the sciences throw an inexpressible grace over our compositions, even where they are not immediately concerned; as their effects are discernible where we least expect to find them. This powerful charm is not only distinguished by the learned and the judicious, but strikes even the most common and popular class of auditors; insomuch that one may frequently hear them applauding a speaker of this approved kind, as a man of genuine erudition; as enriched with the whole treasures of eloquence; and, in one word, a complete orator. But no man, I affirm, ever did, or ever can, maintain that exalted character, unless, like the soldier marching to battle, armed at all points, he enters the forum equipped with the whole panoply of knowledge. So much, however, is this principle neglected by our modern professors of oratory, that their pleadings are debased by the vilest colloquial barbarisms; they are ignorant of the laws, unacquainted with the acts of the senate; the common law of Rome they professedly ridicule, and philosophy they seem to regard as something that ought to be shunned and dreaded. Thus eloquence, like a dethroned potentate, is banished her rightful dominions, and confined to barren points and low conceits: and she who was once mistress of the whole circle of sciences, and charmed every beholder with the goodly appearance of her glorious train, is now shorn and curtailed, stripped of all her honours, all her attendants, (I had almost said of all her genius,) and is taken up as one of the meanest of the mechanic arts. This, therefore, I consider as the first, and the principal reason of our having so greatly declined from the spirit of the ancients.

**Decline of oratory due to this narrow view of education.**

If I were called upon to support my opinion by authorities, might I not justly name, among the Grecians, Demosthenes? who, we are informed, constantly attended the lectures of Plato: so also, among our own countrymen, Cicero himself assures us, (and in these very words, if I rightly remember,) that he owed whatever advances he had made in eloquence, not to the rhetoricians, but to the Academic philosophers.

Other and very considerable reasons might be produced

for the decay of eloquence. But I leave them, my friends, as it is proper I should, to be mentioned by you; having performed my share in the examination of this question, and with a freedom which will give, I imagine, as usual, much offence. I am sure, at least, if certain of our contemporaries were to be informed of what I have here maintained, I should be told, that in laying it down as a maxim, that a knowledge both of law and philosophy are essential qualifications in an orator, I have been fondly pursuing a phantom of my own imagination.

33. I am so far from thinking, replied Maternus, that you have completed the part you undertook, that I should rather imagine you had only given us the first general sketch of your design. You have marked out to us, indeed, those sciences wherein the ancient orators were instructed, and have placed in strong contrast their successful industry with our sloth and ignorance. But something further still remains; and as you have shown us what was the vastness of their knowledge, and the littleness of our own, I would have you acquaint us also with the particular exercises by which the youth of those earlier days were wont to strengthen and improve their genius. For I think you will not deny that oratory is acquired by practice far better than by precept: and our friends here seem, by their countenances, to imply as much.

Aper and Secundus having signified their assent, Messala, resumed his discourse as follows:

**The methods of the old education.**

Having then, as it should seem, disclosed to your satisfaction the seeds and first principles of ancient eloquence, by specifying the several studies in which the ancient orators were trained; I shall now lay before you the practical exercises they pursued, in order to gain a facility in the exertion of eloquence. Note, however, that the very act of studying implies practice; for it is impossible to acquire knowledge so various and recondite, without knowledge leading to reflection, reflection to grasp and command of thought, and this to ready power of utterance. Thus it appears that to learn what you shall deliver, and to be able to deliver what you have learned, are in principle one and the same. But if in this I appear to any one to speculate too abstrusely; if any one insist on separating knowledge from practice, at least he will not deny that a mind filled with manifold instruction will enter with so much the more advantage upon those exercises peculiar to the oratorical circus.

Education by apprenticeship.

34. The practice of our ancestors was agreeable to this theory. The youth who was intended for public declamation, was introduced by his father, or some near relation, with all the advantages of home discipline and a mind furnished with useful knowledge, to the most eminent orator of the time, whom thenceforth he attended upon all occasions; he listened with attention to his patron's pleadings in the tribunals of justice, and his public harangues before the people; he heard him in the warmth of argument; he noted his sudden replies; and thus, in the field of battle, if I may so express myself, he learned the first rudiments of rhetorical warfare. The advantages of this method are obvious: the young candidate gained courage, and improved his judgment; he studied in open day, amidst the heat of the conflict, where nothing weak or idle could be said with impunity; where everything absurd was instantly rebuked by the judge, exposed to ridicule by the adversary, and condemned by the whole body of advocates. In this way they imbibed at once the pure and uncorrupted streams of genuine eloquence. But though they chiefly attached themselves to one particular orator, they heard likewise all the rest of their contemporary pleaders, in many of their respective debates; and they had an opportunity of acquainting themselves with the various sentiments of the people, and of observing what pleased or disgusted them most in the several orators of the forum. Thus they were supplied with an instructor of the best and most improving kind, exhibiting, not the feigned semblance of Eloquence, but her real and lively manifestation: not a pretended, but a genuine adversary, armed in earnest for the combat; an audience, ever full and ever new, composed of foes as well as friends, and where not a single expression could fall uncensured, or unapplauded. For you are aware that a solid and lasting reputation of eloquence must be acquired by the censure of our enemies, as well as by the applause of our friends; or rather, indeed, it is from the former that it

derives its surest and most unquestioned strength and firmness. Under such a schooling, the youth of whom we are speaking, a disciple of all the orators; an attentive hearer of all judicial proceedings; instructed by the experience of others; daily conversant with the laws of his country; familiar with the faces of the judges, and the aspect of a full audience; and well acquainted with the popular taste, — might be called on to conduct a prosecution or a defence, and was equal to cope, single handed, with the difficulties of his task. Crassus, at the age of nineteen, Cæsar at twenty-one, Pollio at twenty-two, and Calvus when he was but a few years older, pronounced those several speeches againt Carbo, Dolabella, Cato, and Vatinius, which we read to this hour with admiration.

**Modern methods place instruction before practice. This instruction is artificial.**

35. On the other hand, our modern youth are sent to the mountebank schools of certain declaimers called rhetoricians: a set of men who made their first appearance in Rome a little before the time of Cicero. And that they were by no means approved by our ancestors, plainly appears from their being enjoined, under the censorship[1] of Crassus and Domitius, to shut up their *schools of impudence*, as Cicero expresses it. But I was going to say, our youths are sent to certain academies, where it is hard to determine whether the place, the company, or the method of instruction is most likely to infect the minds of young people, and produce a wrong turn of thought. There can be nothing to inspire respect in a place where all who enter it are of the same low degree of understanding; nor any advantage to be received from their fellow-students, where a parcel of boys and raw youths of unripe judgments harangue before each other, without the least fear or danger of criticism.

**Formal character of the rhetorical schools.**

And as for their exercises, they are ridiculous in their very nature. They consist of two kinds, and are either persuasive or controversial. The first, as being easier and requiring less skill, is assigned to the younger lads; the other is the task of more mature years. But, good gods! with what incredible absurdity are they composed! And this as a matter of course, for the style of the declamations must needs accord with the preposterous nature of the subjects. Thus being taught

[1] 92 A.D.; 662 A.U.C.

to harangue in a most pompous diction, on the rewards due to tyrannicides, on the election to be made by deflowered virgins, on the licentiousness of married women, on the ceremonies to be observed in times of pestilence, with other topics,[1] which are daily debated in the schools, and scarce ever in the forum; when they come before the real judges. . . .

[1] These are specimen topics of themes debated in the rhetorical schools.

## IV. SURVIVAL OF EARLY ROMAN EDUCATIONAL IDEALS IN THE LATER PERIOD

**The Sources** bearing on this topic are minor selections from historians relative to the education of historic characters, and the first chapter from the *Thoughts* of the Emperor Marcus Aurelius. The education of the four youths therein described falls in the third period of Roman education. Each of the four attended to some extent the Hellenized school, and in this respect these selections should be classified with those of the succeeding group. But while they throw light upon the education of that period, they are not typical of it. They represent the preservation of the old Roman educational traditions in the Hellenized period, modified necessarily by the dominant influences; but in spirit and method, and, to a certain extent in organization, though not in content, they represent the education of the earlier period. The earliest of the four quotations is the brief description of the early education of Titus Pomponius Atticus, born 109 B.C. The description is taken from the *Lives of Eminent Commanders* of Cornelius Nepos. Here is given the bare outlines of the education at home of a youth of equestrian rank. When twenty-one years of age, this youth removed to Athens, thereafter devoting many years to study, though of this Nepos tells little.

The second quotation dates from almost a century later, and relates to the education given by the first emperor,

Cæsar Augustus, to his daughter and grandchildren. The importance of the evidence is due to the light it throws on the method and content of education in the imperial family, as such education is clearly a survival of that of the earlier period. Unfortunately, there is no parallel in results, for the later career of these children was quite in accord with the degeneracy of the upper classes of society at that time; but even here we find an evidence of the validity of old Roman educational methods, for the children did but imitate the example of father and grandfather.

The third reference is indicative of the survival of the old ideas in the provinces, and relates to the education of Cnæus Julius Agricola (37–93 A. D.). It is taken from the biography by the historian Tacitus, and bears evidence of the importance of parental influence in education and of the method of apprenticeship in military training.

The fourth selection gives in great detail the education of a noble youth according to old custom, for the most part long since fallen into decay. It is the autobiographical chapter of the *Thoughts* of the philosopher emperor, and belongs to the second Christian century. Marcus Aurelius Antoninus (b. 121 A.D., d. 180) was the adopted son of the Emperor Antoninus Pius, and associated with him for many years in the imperial office. At the death of Pius, in 161, Marcus became emperor, in turn associating with him Lucius Verus. After the death of Verus, Marcus ruled alone for the remainder of his life, a reign of nineteen years. His early education was cared for by his paternal grandfather and by his foster-father, who was one of the best Roman emperors of any period. In spirit and method it represents the continuation of the old Roman traditions; in its content, it was much more literary, — not literary, however, after the prevailing notions, for Marcus Aurelius early turned to the study of philosophy instead of the popular study of rhetoric. The type of philosophy pursued was the Stoic, which formed a continuation of old Roman ideals in a literary age and in a philosophical form. His practical education was directed in the same manner. In fact, the Stoic philosophy at that period was little more than the practical wisdom of old Roman life put in Grecian literary form. The life of the emperor was one of practical military duties, revealing throughout the effects of his early education. The one blot on his character was his persecutions of the Christians, the new religious sect which he did not understand, and which at that time was causing so much disturbance throughout the empire. His *Thoughts* were written while on a campaign against the Marcomanni, and are dated at the various camps along the Danube. The first chapter gives the account of the formation of his character and the outline of his early education. The remaining eleven chapters, or books, are a collection of maxims, or thoughts, — one of the best practical expositions of the Stoic philosophy.

**The Stoic Philosophy** represented the continuance of old Roman ideas and practices in the later imperial period. Its introduction into Rome was coincident with the change to the Hellenized Roman education. In its origin, two centuries earlier, it had represented the early influence of the West on Grecian thought, and had never found popular acceptance until transplanted to Rome. There it became dominant, not so much as a school of philosophical discussion, as was the case in Greece, but rather as a school of thought and a type of life. In the imperial period, however, Eclecticism and Epicureanism, rather than Stoicism, were more in line with the tendencies of the times. In the last century and a half of the Republic, Stoicism became popular as a systematization of old Roman ideas of life, and it continued in imperial periods only so far as the old ideals commanded respect. Hence even the literary education as described by Marcus Aurelius is not typical, but represents the only possible survival of the old in an age of culture and intellectual refinement. Even at best, the Stoic philosophy was so bound up with the old, especially the old religion, that it could not command full sympathy in quarters of independent thought. Hence, opposed by the Cynics and Eclectics on the one hand, by the Epicureans and the indifferent or scoffing public on the other, these survivals of the old commanded neither the following nor the respect that their character would seem to justify.

**Summary of Survivals.** — The most patent of these relates to the organization of education. Training, instruction, centre in the home; the parent retains the interest, the sense of responsibility, and the character that made for the results of earlier times. Where the parent cannot give the higher instruction, tutors are employed under the direct supervision of the parent. As to purpose, education is still largely moral and relates to conduct rather than to acquisition of knowledge or of oratorical power. The enumeration by Aurelius of the influences to which were due the formation of his character, are, in this respect, most suggestive. So far as instruction is literary, it has for its aim the acquisition of practical wisdom rather than of dialectic skill or forensic verbosity. A large part of the content of education is to learn by experience and observation the duties of the householder, of the military commander, of the public administrator. This method, which makes education a training and not a process of instruction, is essentially the old Roman method. Formation of character and the development of the power to do through direct experience in the observation and imitation of others, are its essential characteristics.

### *Selection from the Life of T. Pomponius Atticus, by Cornelius Nepos*

CHAPTER I

**Early education and talents of a Roman youth of highest rank.**

Pomponius Atticus, descended of an ancient Roman family, kept the equestrian dignity, received by uninterrupted succession from his ancestors. He had a diligent and indulgent father, and, as the times were then, rich, and above all things, a lover of learning. As he loved learning himself, he instructed his son in all that sort of literature that youth ought to be acquainted with. There was in him when a boy, besides a docility of wit, a mighty sweetness of mouth and voice, that he not only quickly took in what was taught him, but also pronounced excellently; upon which account he was reckoned famous amongst his fellows in his childhood, and shone out more brightly than his noble school-fellows were able to bear with a patient mind; wherefore he pushed them all forward by his great application, in which number was L. Torquatus, C. Marius the son, M. Cicero, whom he so engaged to him by his acquaintance with them, that nobody was all along all more dear to them.

### *Selection from the Lives of the First Twelve Cæsars by C. Suetonius Tranquillus—Life of Cæsar Augustus*

LXIV

He had three grandsons by Agrippa and Julia, Caius, Lucius, and Agrippa; and two grand-daughters, Julia and

**Education of children of highest rank in the home.**

Agrippina. Julia he married to Lucius Paullus, the Censor's son, and Agrippina to Germanicus, his sister's grandson. Caius and Lucius he adopted at home, by the ceremony of purchase from their father; advanced them, whilst yet but very young, to posts in the government; and after he had procured them to be chosen Consuls, sent them upon a tour through the provinces of the empire and the several armies. In the breeding of his daughter and grand-daughters, he accustomed them to domestic employments, and obliged them to speak and act everything openly before the family, that it might be put down in the diary. He so strictly prohibited them from all converse with strangers, that he once wrote a letter to Lucius Vinicius, a handsome young man of a good family, in which he told him, "You have not behaved very modestly, in making a visit to my daughter at Baiæ." He usually instructed his grandsons himself in reading, swimming, and other rudiments of knowledge; and he labored at nothing more than to perfect them in the imitation of his handwriting. He never supped but he had them sitting at the foot of his bed; nor ever travelled but with them in a chariot before him, or riding beside him.

## *Selection from the Agricola of Tacitus*

**The influence of a Roman mother in the education of her son.**

4. CNÆUS JULIUS AGRICOLA was born at the ancient and illustrious colony of Forumjulii.[1] . . . His mother was Julia Procilla, a lady of exemplary chastity. Educated with tenderness in her bosom, he passed his childhood and youth in the attainment of every liberal art. He was preserved from the allurements of vice, not only by a naturally good disposition, but by being sent very early to pursue his studies at Massilia;[2] a place where Grecian politeness and provincial frugality are happily united. I remember he was used to relate, that in his early youth

[1] Probably in Narbonnensian Gaul, though there was another colony of the same name in Umbria.

[2] Marseilles. It was a Grecian colony, and Grecian characteristics remained during the Roman control.

he should have engaged with more ardour in philosophical speculation than was suitable to a Roman and a senator, had not the prudence of his mother restrained the warmth and vehemence of his disposition: for his lofty and upright spirit, inflamed by the charms of glory and exalted reputation, led him to the pursuit with more eagerness than discretion. Reason and riper years tempered his warmth; and from the study of wisdom, he retained what is most difficult to compass, — moderation.

5. He learned the rudiments of war in Britain, under Suetonius Paullinus, an active and prudent commander, who chose him for his tent companion, in order to form an estimate of his merit. Nor did Agricola, like many young men, who convert military service into wanton pastime, avail himself licentiously or slothfully of his tribunitial title, or his inexperience, to spend his time in pleasures and absences from duty; but he employed himself in gaining a knowledge of the country, making himself known to the army, learning from the experienced, and imitating the best; neither pressing to be employed through vainglory, nor declining it through timidity; and performing his duty with equal solicitude and spirit.

**Military education by apprenticeship.**

## *Selections from the Thoughts of the Emperor Marcus Aurelius Antoninus*[1]

### CHAPTER I

1. From my grandfather Verus (I learned) good morals and the government of my temper.

2. From the reputation and remembrance of my father,[2] modesty and a manly character.

3. From my mother,[3] piety and beneficence, and abstinence, not only from evil deeds, but even from evil thoughts; and further, simplicity in my way of living, far removed from habits of the rich.

**Early influence of his parents and tutors.**

[1] From the translation by Long.

[2] Bearing the same name as his grandfather, Annius Verus.

[3] Domitia Calvilla.

4. From my great-grandfather,[1] not to have frequented public schools, and to have had good teachers at home, and to know that on such things a man should spend liberally.

5. From my governor, to be neither of the green nor of the blue party at the games in the Circus,[2] nor a partisan either of the Parmularius or the Scutarius,[3] at the gladiators' fights; from him too I learned endurance of labor, and to want little, and to work with my own hands, and not to meddle with other people's affairs, and not to be ready to listen to slander.

6. From Diognetus, not to busy myself about trifling things, and not to give credit to what was said by miracle-workers and jugglers about incantations and the driving away of dæmons and such things; and not to breed quails (for fighting), nor to give myself up passionately to such things; and to endure freedom of speech; and to have become intimate with philosophy; and to have been a hearer, first of Bacchius, then of Tandasis and Marcianus; and to have written dialogues in my youth; to have desired a plank bed and skin, and whatever else of the kind belongs to the Grecian discipline.

Influence of the teachings of the Stoics.

7. From Rusticus[4] I received the impression that my character required improvement and discipline; and from him I learned not to be led astray to sophistic emulation, nor to writing on speculative matters, nor to delivering little hortatory orations, nor to showing myself off as a man who practises much discipline, or does benevolent

[1] It is suggested that his mother's grandfather, Catilius Severus, is here referred to.

[2] The factions were originally companies of contractors who provided horses, drivers, and all other requisites for the games. These factions were distinguished by colors, — originally two, — red and white; later, in the time of Augustus, blue and green were added; still later, purple and gold. In time each faction was organized into a collegium or union. The rivalry between these became intense, the populace taking sides. Even at Rome factional fights took place; later at Constantinople these became very serious, one during the reign of Justinian causing the loss of thirty thousand lives.

[3] The parmularius carried the parma, a small round shield; the scutarius carried the scutum, a large oblong shield.

[4] A Stoic philosopher.

acts in order to make a display; and to abstain from rhetoric, and poetry, and fine writing; and not to walk about in the house in my outdoor dress, nor to do other things of the kind; and to write my letters with simplicity, like the letter which Rusticus wrote from Sinuessa to my mother; and with respect to those who have offended me by words, or done me wrong, to be easily disposed to be pacified and reconciled, as soon as they have shown a readiness to be reconciled; and to read carefully, and not to be satisfied with a superficial understanding of a book; nor hastily to give my assent to those who talk over-much; and I am indebted to him for being acquainted with the discourses of Epictetus, which he communicated to me out of his own recollection.

8. From Apollonius[1] I learned freedom of will and undeviating steadiness of purpose; and to look to nothing else, not even for a moment, except to reason; and to be always the same, in sharp pains, on the occasion of the loss of a child, and in long illness; and to see clearly in a living example that the same man can be most resolute and yielding, and not peevish in giving his instruction; and to have had before my eyes a man who clearly considered his experience and his skill in expounding philosophical principles as to the smallest of his merits; and from him I learned how to receive from friends what are esteemed favors, without being either humbled by them or letting them pass unnoticed.

9. From Sextus,[2] a benevolent disposition, and the example of a family governed in a fatherly manner, and the idea of living conformably to nature; and gravity without affectation, and to look carefully after the interests of friends, and to tolerate ignorant persons, and those who form opinions without consideration: he had the power of readily accommodating himself to all, so that intercourse with him was more agreeable than any flattery; and at the same time he was most highly venerated by those who associated with him; and he had the faculty both of discovering and ordering, in an intelligent and methodical

[1] A Stoic philosopher, preceptor to Antoninus.

[2] A grandson of Plutarch.

way, the principles necessary for life; and he never showed anger or any other passion, but was entirely free from passion, and also most affectionate; and he could express approbation without noisy display, and he possessed much knowledge without ostentation.

Influence of the grammatical and rhetorical teachers.

10. From Alexander,[1] the grammarian, to refrain from fault-finding, and not in a reproachful way to chide those who uttered any barbarous or solecistic or strange-sounding expression; but dexterously to introduce the very expression which ought to have been used, and in the way of answer or giving confirmation, or joining in an inquiry about the thing itself, not about the word, or by some other fit suggestion.

11. From Fronto[2] I learned to observe what envy and duplicity, and hypocrisy are in a tyrant, and that generally those among us who are called Patricians are rather deficient in paternal affection.

12. From Alexander the Platonic, not frequently nor without necessity to say to any one, or to write in a letter, that I have no leisure; nor continually to excuse the neglect of duties required by our relation to those with whom we live, by alleging urgent occupations.

13. From Catulus,[3] not to be indifferent when a friend finds fault, even if he should find fault without reason, but to try to restore him to his usual disposition; and to be ready to speak well of teachers, as it is reported of Domitius and Athenodotus; and to love my children truly.

His apprenticeship in Politus.

14. From my brother Severus,[4] to love my kin, and to love truth, and to love justice; and through him I learned to know Thrasea, Helvidius, Cato, Dion, Brutus;[5] and from him I received the idea of a polity in which there is the same law for all, a polity administered with regard to equal rights and equal freedom of speech, and the idea of a kingly government which respects most of all the freedom

[1] A grammaticus, a native of Phrygia.

[2] Cornelius Fronto, a rhetorician and teacher and friend of Antoninus.

[3] A Stoic philosopher.

[4] Antoninus has no brother. It may mean cousin, or the word brother may not be genuine.

[5] See Plutarch's *Lives* for the latter three.

of the governed; I learned from him also consistency and undeviating steadiness in my regard for philosophy; and a disposition to do good, and to give to others readily, and to cherish good hopes, and to believe that I am loved by my friends; and in him I observed no concealment of his opinions with respect to those whom he condemned, and that his friends had no need to conjecture what he wished or did not wish, but it was quite plain.

15. From Maximus[1] I learned self-government, and not to be led aside by anything; and cheerfulness in all circumstances, as well as in illness; and a just admixture in the moral character of sweetness and dignity, and to do what was set before me without complaining. I observed that everybody believed that he thought as he spoke, and that in all that he did he never had any bad intention; and he never showed amazement and surprise, and was never in a hurry, and never put off doing a thing, nor was perplexed nor dejected, nor did he ever laugh to disguise his vexation, nor, on the other hand, was he ever passionate or suspicious. He was accustomed to do acts of beneficence, and was ready to forgive, and was free from all falsehood; and he presented the appearance of a man who could not be diverted from right rather than of a man who had been improved. I observed, too, that no man could ever think that he was despised by Maximus, or ever venture to think himself a better man. He had also the art of being humorous in an agreeable way.

**Education at home through imitation.**

16. In my father[2] I observed mildness of temper, and unchangeable resolution in the things which he had determined after due deliberation, and no vain-glory in those things which men call honors, and a love of labor and perseverance, and a readiness to listen to those who had anything to propose for the common weal, and undeviating firmness in giving to every man according to his deserts and a knowledge derived from experience of the occasions for vigorous action and for remission. And I observed that he had overcome all passion for boys; and he considered himself no more than any other citizen, and

[1] A Stoic philosopher.

[2] His foster-father and predecessor, the Emperor Antoninus Pius.

he released his friends from all obligation to sup with him or to attend him of necessity when he went abroad, and those who had failed to accompany him, by reason of any great circumstances, always found him the same. I observed too his habit of careful inquiry in all matters of deliberation, and his persistency, and that he never stopped his investigation through being satisfied with appearances which first present themselves; and that his disposition was to keep his friends, and not to be soon tired of them, nor yet to be extravagant in his affection; and to be satisfied on all occasions, and cheerful; and to foresee things a long way off, and to provide for the smallest without display; and to check immediately popular applause and all flattery; and to be ever watchful over the things which were necessary for the administration of the empire, and to be a good manager of the expenditure, and patiently to endure the blame which he got for such conduct; and he was neither superstitious with respect to the gods, nor did he court men by gifts or by trying to please them, or by flattering the populace; but he showed sobriety in all things and firmness, and never any mean thoughts or action, nor love of novelty. And the things which conduce in any way to the commodity of life, and of which fortune gives an abundant supply, he used without arrogance and without excusing himself, so that when he had them he enjoyed them without affectation, and when he had them not he did not want them. No one could ever say of him that he was either a sophist, or a (home-bred) flippant slave, or a pedant; but every one acknowledged him to be a man ripe, perfect, above flattery, able to manage his own and other men's affairs. Besides this, he honored those who were true philosophers, and he did not reproach those who pretended to be philosophers, nor yet was he easily led by them. He was also easy in conversation, and he made himself agreeable without any offensive affectation. He took a reasonable care of his body's health, not as one who was greatly attached to life, nor out of regard to personal appearance, nor yet in a careless way, but so that through his own attention he very seldom stood in need of the physician's art or of medicine or external applications. He was most ready to give way without envy to those who possessed any particular faculty, such as that of eloquence or knowledge of the law or of morals, or of anything else; and he gave them his help, that each might enjoy reputation according to his deserts; and he always acted comformably to the institutions of his country, without showing any affectation of doing so. Further, he was not fond of change, nor unsteady, but he loved to stay in the same places, and to employ himself about the same things; and after his paroxysms of headache he came immediately fresh and vigorous to his usual occupations. His secrets were not many, but very few and very rare, and these only about public matters; and he showed prudence and economy in the exhibition of the public spectacles and the construction of public buildings, his donations to the people, and in such things, for he was a man who looked to what ought to be done, not to the reputation which is got by a man's acts. He did not take the bath at unseasonable hours; he was not fond of building houses, nor curious about what he ate, nor about the texture and color of his clothes, nor about the beauty of his slaves. His dress came from Lorium, his villa on the coast, and from Lanuvium [1] generally. We know how he behaved to the toll-collector at Tusculum who asked his pardon; and such was all his behavior. There was in him nothing harsh, nor implacable, nor violent, nor, as one may say, anything carried to the sweating point; but he examined all things severally, as if he had abundance of time, and without confusion, in an orderly way, vigorously and consistently. And that might be applied to him which is recorded of Socrates,[2] that he was able both to abstain from and to enjoy those things which many are too weak to abstain from and cannot enjoy without excess. But to be strong enough both to bear the one and to be sober in the other is the mark of a man who has a perfect and invincible soul, such as he showed in the illness of Maximus.

**Religious and moral training.**

17. To the gods I am indebted for having good grandfathers, good parents, a good sister, good teachers, good associates, good kinsmen and friends, nearly every thing good. Further, I owe it to the gods that I was not hurried

[1] A villa on the coast north of Rome. Antoninus was brought up there.

[2] Xenophon, *Memorabilia*, I., 3, 15.

into any offence against any of them, though I had a disposition which, if opportunity had offered, might have led me to do something of this kind; but through their favor there never was such a concurrence of circumstances as put me to the trial. Further, I am thankful to the gods that I was not longer brought up with my grandfather's concubine, . . . and that I was subjected to a ruler and a father who was able to take away all pride from me, and to bring me to the knowledge that it is possible for a man to live in a palace without wanting either guards or embroidered dresses, or torches and statues, and such-like show; but that it is in such a man's power to bring himself very near to the fashion of a private person, without being for this reason either meaner in thought or more remiss in action with respect to the things which must be done for the public interest in a manner that befits a ruler. I thank the gods for giving me such a brother, who was able by his moral character to rouse me to vigilance over myself, and who at the same time pleased me by his respect and affection; that my children have not been stupid nor deformed in body; that I did not make more proficiency in rhetoric, poetry, and the other studies, in which I should perhaps have been completely engaged if I had seen that I was making progress in them; that I made haste to place those who brought me up in the station of honor which they seemed to desire, without putting them off with hope of my doing it some time after, because they were then still young; that I knew Apollonius, Rusticus, Maximus; that I received clear and frequent impressions about living according to nature, and what kind of a life that is, so that so far as depended on the gods, and their gifts, and help, and inspirations, nothing hindered me from forthwith living according to nature, though I still fall short of it through my own fault and through not observing the admonitions of the gods, and I may almost say, their direct instructions; that my body has held out so long in such kind of life; that I never touched either Benedicta or Theodotus, and that after having fallen into amatory passions I was cured; and, though I was often out of humor with Rusticus, I never did any thing of which I had occasion to repent; that though it was my mother's

His gratitude for the blessings conferred by the gods.

fate to die young, she spent the last years of her life with me; that whenever I wished to help any man in his need, or on any other occasion, I was never told that I had not the means of doing it; and that to myself the same necessity never happened to receive any thing from another; that I have such a wife, so obedient, and so affectionate, and so simple; that I had abundance of good masters for my children; and that remedies have been shown to me by dreams, both others, and against bloodspitting and giddiness;[1] . . . and that when I had an inclination to philosophy I did not fall into the hands of any sophists, and that I did not waste my time on writers (of histories), or in the resolution of syllogisms, or occupy myself about the investigation of appearances in the heavens; for all these things require the help of the gods and fortune.

**Escape from a literary education.**

Among the Quadi at the Granua.[2]

[1] Probably written during the war with the Quadi. They lived in what is now the southern part of Bohemia. The Granua flows into the Danube.

[2] Text is corrupt.

## V. THE THIRD PERIOD: THE HELLENIZED ROMAN EDUCATION

**The Period** in which the Hellenized education dominated without causing a complete extinction of the old Roman virility, includes the last century of the Republic and the first century and a half or two centuries of the Empire. Within that period profound changes occurred, though education had not yet become a purely artificial and lifeless affair, nor Roman stability and morality, a thing of the past. This period comprises the Ciceronian, the Augustan, and the "Silver Age" of Latin literature. During this period the Romans attained to whatever merits they possessed of literary and artistic character. It covers that time wherein their great genius for assimilation and organization was directed into purely intellectual channels. During this time Grecian educational ideas and practices were modified to fit Roman conditions, and a characteristic education resulted. This differed in content from the Grecian, for the Romans were too practical to be able to obtain liberalizing results from music and gymnastic, and too sedate to tolerate much that was thoroughly characteristic of the Greek. Education though much better organized and systematized than with the Greek, was in its method less thoroughly rationalized; for with the Romans education remained essentially a training process. The sources given in this section are all drawn from the literature of the early imperial period, and, with the exception of the selection from the *Satires* of Horace, refer to the education of this portion of the third period.

**The Sources and their Authors.** — The first selections given are several brief excerpts from the *Satires*, *Epistles*, and *Ars Poetica* of Horace. They relate to the ideals, subject-matter, method, and organization of education during the period of his boyhood. Horace was born 65 B.C. at Venusia, where he received his early education. Dissatisfied with the work of the provincial schools, his father removed to the capital for the express purpose of improving his son's educational opportunities. Hence the testimony of Horace concerning the schooling of his time is especially valuable; for although given incidentally, the educational conditions referred to were of epoch-making importance in his life. At Rome he attended the school of Orbilius, whose life is given by Suetonius in his *Eminent Grammarians*. Horace became practically the laureate of the Augustan Age. The *Epistles* and *Satires*, from which these selections are made, were written between the years 35 B.C. and 8 B.C., the year of the poet's death. Both because they give a most intimate view of everyday Roman life, and also because they soon came to be an established text-book in Roman schools, the writings of Horace are valuable to the student of education.

The two *Epigrams* of Martial relate to the Roman schools, and give intimate views of their practical workings. M. Valerius Martialis was born in Spain 43 A.D., came to Rome during the reign of Nero, and for thirty-five years remained in the favor of successive emperors. His fifteen hundred *Epigrams* form an important source of information concerning the social customs of the first century of the empire. The two books from which the two selections are made were written between 90 and 99 A.D.

One brief selection, given from the *Lives of the Twelve Cæsars*, by Suetonius, relates to the grant of imperial support to education. It has been previously noted that the literary work of Suetonius followed his fall from favor, 121 A.D. The reign of Vespasian, to whom was due the beginning of this most important custom, extended from 70 to 79 A.D.

The fragments of the writings of Gaius Musonius Rufus furnish the next selection. Musonius lived during the last half of the first Christian century, and was especially in favor with Vespasian. While the discussion directly concerns the education of women, it relates at the same time to the methods and character of education in general, since Musonius held that it should be essentially the same as that of men.

Aside from the work of Quintilian, the most extensive references to the educational conditions of the times are to be found in the correspondence of the younger Pliny. Gaius Plinius Cæcilius Secundus was born 62 A.D., and died about 114. His life was spent in the service of the state, where he held many important offices, including those of consul and of provincial governor. He was a pupil of Quintilian and a friend of Martial, Suetonius, and Tacitus. As is evidenced by his *Epistles*, he is interested in almost every aspect of the public, social, and intellectual life of his times, and is one of the best types of the broad-minded Roman citizen. The collection of letters from which these selections are made dates from 97 to 108 A.D. The chief importance of the letters selected is their bearing upon the educational institutions of the times, though they also refer to the method and content of the approved type of education. By reason of his broad experience, his cultivated taste, keen insight, and liberal views and disposition, Pliny is competent to speak on these subjects. He is touched neither by the pessimism of the righteous nor the prevalent corruption of the masses of the times. Upright both in public and private life, when the examples set in high places and frequently followed in inferior ones were the reverse, he gave his wealth and best efforts to the improvement of his fellows. He gives one aspect of the times, while the selections from Juvenal give quite another.

Little definite is known concerning the life of Juvenal, but it is certain that the *Satires* belong to the first two decades of the second Christian century. He speaks with full authority on the education and the customs of his times, since he had the benefit of the liberal education of his times, and seems to have devoted the first forty years of his life to the study and practices of oratory, though rather in following his own inclinations than in preparation for activity in schools or courts. It is only after his fortieth year that he devotes himself to writing. While some allowance must be made for the license of a satirist, we may at least be sure that he speaks with a full knowledge of the state of the education of that period. One of the satires, the seventh, is devoted to a discussion of the status of the literary profession, including teaching; the other, the fourteenth, to the influence of the home in the moral education of the child. The whole of this satire is significant, treating as it does of the decadence of the times, but most of it must be omitted in deference to the standards of modern taste.

**Purpose and Content of Education of this Period.** — This topic is treated in detail in the two chapters following; yet there are side-lights of importance to be found in the selections just referred to. Education, so far as it commands popular interest, has become wholly literary, and is comprehended in the work of the grammatical and rhetorical schools of the day, of which oratory is the sole aim. Nevertheless, while there is little formal change, save by way of improvement, between the age of Cicero and that of Pliny and Juvenal, there is a profound change in the spirit. Education is still wholly rhetorical, but it has now become artificial, critical, affected, imitative, and marked by a pedantry and self-consciousness not found in the last age of the Republic. In these respects, education simply participates in the characteristic changes that have come about in society.

In several of these selections interesting side-lights are thrown on the accepted purpose of education. Horace, in the *Ars Poetica*, objects to the materialistic character of Roman education; Musonius, as becomes a Stoic, insists that philosophy should have an important place in the education of both women and men; Pliny, in the ninth Epistle of the seventh Book, holds that oratory should not be the sole aim of education. Still he does not broaden it beyond literary lines, and his argument is but another evidence of the artificiality of the age as compared with the centuries of the Republic.

**The Organization of Education.** — Both Horace and Martial give pictures of the ordinary school in Rome and in the provincial cities. It is the *ludus* that is referred to by both, though Horace also makes reference to the grammatical school of Orbilius. Of the *ludus* we see the early and long hours; the harsh discipline; the unamiable and inefficient teachers; the simple curriculum, consisting of reading, writing, and arithmetic. Horace, to be sure, speaks quite definitely of the use of literature as the basis of elementary school work, but evidently the *ludus* that he attended was of exceptional character. These schools continue to be tuition schools, the customs as to the time and method of payment being indicated in both Horace and Martial. During this period the *ludi* practically supplant the home as institutions for early instruction; and, if we accept the evidences of the protests of Juvenal, Tacitus, and others of the imperial period, as institutions for moral training as well. The burden of these moralists, whether satirists or philosophers, is insistence upon the responsibility of the parents in this latter respect; and this insistence is good evidence that the old customs have fallen into desuetude.

After a few years in the *ludus*, the boy began attendance upon the secondary school, the school of the *grammaticus*. Here the instruction was wholly grammatical and literary, including both the Latin and Greek languages. To a considerable extent the Greek grammar schools and Latin grammar schools were distinct; the approved plan was to send the boy to the Greek school first. The instruction in grammar continues to be given in many cases, perhaps in most cases, by tutors in the family. The care involved in the selection of these teachers as well as their rewards is indicated in the letters of Pliny and in the seventh Satire of Juvenal. Like the *ludi*, these schools are also private, though late in the second century of the Empire they are the recipients of government aid. Many of these schools trench upon the work of the rhetorical schools in giving instruction in declamation and disputation, as is evidenced in the comments of Suetonius given in the previous chapter and in some of the selections here given.

During this period the higher or rhetorical education is definitely systematized. Despite the action of the Senate during the period of the Republic, and a similar action of the Emperor Domitian, 95 A.D., banishing philosophers and the higher teachers in Rome, this type of education flourished, and the schools of the *rhetors* represented the dominant education. Philosophical schools existed, but were never popular. The schools of the rhetors prepared the great majority for Roman life. While to some extent this rhetorical education was also given by tutors, as is indicated by the third Epistle of the third Book of Pliny; the school was the dominant type, as is demonstrated by the facts of the life of Quintilian and Suetonius' *Lives of Eminent Rhetoricians*, as well as by such descriptions as those of the seventh Satire of Juvenal and of Epistle viii., Book I., and Epistle xiii., Book IV., of Pliny.

To Vespasian, the father of Domitian, who took the hostile attitude just indicated, is due the first public support of education, a fact shown in the account of his life by Suetonius. Moreover, the letters of Pliny indicate that higher education in the provincial cities was still private; and his acts, that, in some cases at least, private munificence came to the assistance of such local schools and that there existed schools supported in part by the civic community. The imperial support of higher education begun by Vespasian was continued by Hadrian (117–138 A.D.) and by the Antonines (138–180 A.D.). To Antoninus Pius is due the conferment of privileges upon the teaching profession, which were afterward granted to the Christian clergy. These privileges were extended to a limited number of grammarians, rhetoricians, and physicians in every civic community, — a custom equivalent to the imperial indorsement of education throughout the Empire. The later emperors, especially Gratian, made this system of support more definite.

An additional feature of education during this period should be borne in mind. This is the custom, then prevalent, of sending Roman youths to Athens and other Eastern educational centres to complete their schooling, and of sending provincial youths to Rome for like reason. As mentioned in the selections, such was the case with Cicero, Pliny, and perhaps Juvenal, on the one hand; and with Horace and Quintilian, on the other. During this period, Athens and the Grecian East are still looked upon as the intellectual and educational centre, the Roman culture being, after all, but an imitation.

**The Method of Education** during this period is also indicated in these selections. The dominant principle of Roman education during all periods was simple; since education was dominantly moral and practical, the method was chiefly that of direct imitation. Hence the great importance of the influence of the parent in the moral training of the child and the great use of biography in his instruction. This principle of method was carried over into his literary education, and as the higher types of schools were introduced, it brought about material modifications in Grecian methods. The Roman attitude toward method is expressed in the very brief quotation from the *Epistles* of Seneca and in the quotations from Horace, Juvenal, and Pliny. The methods of instruction in the rhetorical schools are indicated in the seventh Satire of

Juvenal, and also described in the ninth Epistle, Book VII., of Pliny. This subject is treated in great detail in the selections from Quintilian given later.

**The Education of Women** is treated in the selections from Musonius, which, however, must be taken as an abstract discussion rather than a statement of practical conditions. But the education of women at Rome was on a higher plane than at Athens, for in this, as in other respects, they were more nearly upon an equality with men. The iufluence of cultured women upon the education of their children is seen in the references to the mother of the Gracchi and the mother of Agricola, as well as in the Epistle of Pliny to Correllia Hispulla. While much greater freedom was allowed to married women in Rome than in Greece, and while they were more nearly on an equality with their husbands, their education was essentially a home training. There are evidences that it was nothing uncommon for girls to attend the *ludus;* but if they aspired to the literary or higher education as was possible without loss of reputation and of influence of the home as in Greece, they obtained it through the employment of tutors. There is no definite place for the education of women in the higher education of the times.

**The Decadence of Roman Education** is a question of relativity. Tacitus and Juvenal discuss its decline, the former on the intellectual side, the latter especially on the moral. By the close of the first Christian century there is, to be sure, decline in some respects, but certainly there are advances in others. Both decline and advance are indicated briefly in these sources. Oratory has lost its great inspiration with the change to the Empire, and hence has become much more formal and artificial; the literature of the period is great on account of its form, not on account of its originality or its power of inspiration; and in a similar way, education becomes formal and in time artificial. There is also a marked change in the character of Roman society. While the change in moral standards, together with luxury and debauchery in the higher classes, has become permanent, the fatal weaknesses of Roman society do not appear until later. This decline from the high intellectual and moral status of the earlier period occurs at the time of an extension of the privileges of education and an increased interest in the support of education on the part of the government and public-spirited citizens. This is probably but another evidence of the general decline in virility and morality, for it is in order to combat these tendencies that education is encouraged. There is not only a multiplication of schools and the development of the educational system, but also a similar development in the method and workings of the schools. This again is taken by some to be but a further evidence of the artificiality of the times. At the same time it cannot be doubted that, with the loss of opportunities for intellectual activities in connection with the affairs of state, there was an increase of interest in purely intellectual pursuits along more scholastic lines. Hence it was that the decline in the character, motive, and moral results of education was coincident with a development of educational institutions, the multiplication of libraries, and an increased attendance upon the higher schools. Now the pursuit of the intellectual life, or the scholastic ideals, became a type of life distinct in itself, resembling more the Greek school of the philosophic period than any approved Roman customs. The decline in morality and spirit and purpose, marked by Juvenal and Tacitus, was followed in time by a decline in every other respect. With the Christianization of the Empire and the invasion of the barbarians, education, which had previously become wholly formal and artificial, ceased to arouse any enthusiasm and finally to command any support. This final stage of Roman education is not represented in these selections.

## *Selections from the Satires of Horace*

### BOOK I. 4 (103–129)

Education by example, through the influence of the father.

If my language is ever too free, too playful, such an amount of liberty you will grant me in your courtesy: for to this my good father trained me, to avoid each vice by setting a mark on it by examples. Whenever he would exhort me to live a thrifty, frugal life, contented with what he had saved for me, he would say, "Do you not see how hard it is for the son of Albius to live, and how needy Barrus is, a signal warning, to prevent any one from wasting his inheritance." If he would deter me from dishonourable love, he would say, "Do not be like Sectanus:" to save me from an adulterous passion, when I might enjoy an unforbidden love, he used to say, "Trebonius' exposure was not creditable. A philosopher will give you the right reasons for shunning or choosing things; I am contented,[1] if I can maintain the custom handed down from our ancestors, and, so long as you need a guardian, preserve your life and character from ruin; when mature age has strengthened your body and soul, then you will swim without a cork." Thus he moulded my boyhood by these words, and if he advised me to any course of conduct, he would say, "You have an authority for so acting," and put before me one of the select judges;[2] or if he would

[1] The poet's father was of mean rank, and hence not acquainted with philosophical teachings. He was content to bring up his son according to the ideas of the earlier days.

[2] These judges were selected from the most distinguished men of the senatorial or equestrian rank, in the city by the prætors, in the province by the governors.

forbid me, then said he, "Can you possibly doubt, whether this is disreputable and injurious, when this man and that man are notorious for an evil report. As the funeral of a neighbour frightens to death the intemperate when sick, and, through dread of their own end, makes them careful, so minds still docile are often deterred from vice by the disgrace of others."

I. 6 (65–88)

A father's care and sacrifice for the education of his son.

And yet, if the faults and defects of my nature are moderate ones, and with their exception my life is upright, (just as if one were to censure blemishes found here and there on a handsome body,) if no one can truly lay to my charge avarice, meanness, or frequenting vicious haunts, if (that I may praise myself) my life is pure and innocent, and my friends love me, I owe it all to my father; he, though not rich, for his farm was a poor one, would not send me to the school of Flavius,[1] to which the first youths of the town, the sons of the centurions, the great men there, used to go, with their bags[2] and slates[3] on their left arm, taking the teacher's fee on the Ides of eight months in the year; but he had the spirit[4] to carry me, when a boy, to Rome, there to learn the liberal arts which any knight or senator would have his own sons taught. Had any one seen my dress, and the attendant servants, so far as would be observed in a populous city, he would have thought that such expense was defrayed from an old hereditary estate. He himself was ever present,[5] a guardian incorruptible, at all my studies. Why say more? My modesty, that first grain of virtue, he preserved untainted, not only by an actual stain, but by the very rumour of it;

[1] A schoolmaster at Venusia, the poet's native place.

[2] Bags of counters for arithmetical calculations, more frequently performed in this way than with characters as with us.

[3] Ciphering tables. These were covered with sand or dust, thus permitting characters to be made.

[4] A bold proceeding for a poor farmer, when the rich centurions were content with provincial schools.

[5] Instead of assigning him, as was the custom, to the care of a pedagogue, usually a family slave.

not fearing that any one hereafter should make this a reproach, if as auctioneer,[1] or collector, like himself, I should follow a trade of petty gains; nor should I have grumbled at my lot; but as the case is now, to him more praise is due, I owe him greater thanks.

## *Selections from the Epistles of Horace*

### II. I (70–75)

Character of early education.

When I was little,[2] Orbilius, my master, dictated to me the poems of Livius;[3] he was fond of flogging me, but I am not dead set against those poems, nor think they ought to be destroyed; but that they should be considered faultless and beautiful and almost perfect, does astonish me.

### II. I (126–138)

Poetry the substance of early literary education.

The tender lisping mouth of a child the poet forms; even in their early days he turns the ears of the young from evil words; presently he fashions the heart by kindly precepts, he is the corrector of roughness, of malice, of anger; he tells of virtuous deeds, the dawn of life he furnishes with illustrious examples; the helpless and sad of soul he comforts. Whence could the pious boys and virgins learn their hymns of prayer, had not the Muse granted us a bard? The chorus prays for aid, and Heaven's presence feels, and in set form of persuasive prayer implores rain from above, averts disease, drives away dreaded dangers, obtains peace, and a season rich with its crops: appeased by hymns are gods above, and gods below.[4]

[1] The father of Horace became at Rome either a tax-gatherer or an officer attendant upon sales at auction, whose duty it was to collect the purchase money.

[2] Orbilius Puppillus, a native of Beneventum, came to teach at Rome in the consulship of Cicero. He was noted for his severity.

[3] Livius Andronicus.

[4] The poet in the passage is enumerating the advantages that result from his art.

## *Selections from the Ars Poetica of Horace*

(323–333.) The Greeks had genius, the Greeks could speak with well-rounded mouth: this was the Muse's gift to them; they coveted nought but renown. But the Roman boys are taught to divide the as by long calculations into a hundred parts. Supposing the son of Albinus says: "If from five ounces be subtracted one, what is the remainder?" At once you can answer, "A third of an as."[1] "Good, you will be able to keep your property. If an ounce be added, what does it make?" "The half of an as." Ah! when this rust of copper, this slavish love of saving money has once imbued the soul, can we hope for the composition of verses worthy to be rubbed with oil of cedar, or to be kept in cases of polished cypress? Materialistic ideals of later Roman education.

## *Selections from the Epigrams of Martial*

### BOOK IX. — LXVIII. TO THE MASTER OF A NOISY SCHOOL IN HIS NEIGHBOURHOOD

What right have you to disturb me, abominable schoolmaster, object abhorred alike by boys and girls? Before the crested cocks have broken silence, you begin to roar out your savage scoldings and blows. Not with louder noise does the metal resound on the struck anvil, when the workman is fitting a lawyer on his horse;[2] nor is the noise so great in the large amphitheatre, when the conquering gladiator is applauded by his partisans. We, your neighbours, do not ask you to allow us to sleep for the whole night, for it is but a small matter to be occasionally awakened; but to be kept awake all night is a heavy affliction. Dismiss your scholars, brawler, and take as much for keeping quiet as you receive for making a noise.

[1] Originally a pound of copper, of the value of 16⅔ cents. It was the Roman unit of monetary value.

[2] A sneer at the equestrian statues of lawyers.

### BOOK X. — LXII. TO A SCHOOLMASTER

Schoolmaster, be indulgent to your simple scholars; if you would have many a long-haired youth resort to your lectures, and the class seated round your critical table love you. So may no teacher of arithmetic, or of swift writing, be surrounded by a greater ring of pupils. The days are bright, and glow under the flaming constellation of the Lion, and fervid July is ripening the teeming harvest. Let the Scythian scourge with its formidable thongs, such as flogged Marsyas of Celænae,[1] and the terrible cane, the schoolmaster's sceptre, be laid aside, and sleep until the Ides of October.[2] In summer, if boys preserve their health, they do enough.

## *Selection from the Epistles of Seneca*

### EPISTLES XCIV. 51

Method of education by direct imitation.

He must therefore be governed till he begin to be able to govern himself. Children are taught to form their letters, their fingers are held and their hands directed and led, to teach them to fashion and counterfeit letters; then are they commanded to follow such and such examples, and by them to remodel their writings. So is our mind strengthened, if it be instructed by setting up some example after which it may pattern.

## *Selection from the Lives of the First Twelve Cæsars, by C. Suetonius Tranquillus*

### LIFE OF VESPASIAN

First imperial support of public education.

XVIII. He was a great encourager of learning and learned men. He first appointed the Latin and Greek professors of rhetoric the yearly stipend of a hundred thousand sesterces[3]

[1] Reference to a legend concerning a Phrygian god, of the river Marsyas. Becoming skilful upon the flute, Marsyas challenged Apollo, god of the lyre, to a contest. The Muses declared Marsyas vanquished, and the gods flayed him.

[2] The usual time for the opening of the school term.

[3] At this time a sestertius was worth about five cents of our money.

each out of the exchequer. He was likewise extremely generous to such as excelled in poetry, or even the mechanic arts, and particularly to one that brushed up the picture of Venus at Cos, and another who repaired the Colossus. A mechanic offering to convey some huge pillars into the Capitol at a small expense, he rewarded him very handsomely for his invention, but would not accept of his service, saying, "You must allow me to take care of the poor people."

## *Selections from Musonius,*[1] *on the Education of Women*

XIX. The conversation having turned on the question whether people's sons and daughters should receive the same education, the philosopher (after referring to the analogy furnished by the identical training received by both the males and the females of two of the species of animals employed by men to render them active service, horses and dogs) asks whether men ought to receive any special education and training superior to those allowed to women, as if both alike should not acquire the same virtues, or if it is possible for the two sexes to attain to the same virtues otherwise than by the same education. But it is easy to learn that a man has not different virtues from a woman. For, first, the one should have good sense as well as the other; for of what use would either a foolish man or a foolish woman be? Then the man could not be a good citizen if he were unjust. And the woman could not carry on the concerns of the household virtuously if not being just, but the contrary, she should first wrong her husband, as they say Eriphyle[2] did. It is also good that the woman as well as the man should be self-controlled. . . . Perhaps some one would say that courage is a quality befitting men alone; but even this is not so, for the best woman also should be

**Should women have the same education as men?**

**The same virtues are required of each.**

[1] I am indebted to Professor Laurie's *Historical Survey of Pre-Christian Education* for this reference. The translation is by Professor Muir of the University of Edinburgh.

[2] Of Greek mythology. Bribed by the gift of a necklace, she persuaded her husband to take part in the war of the Seven against Thebes, in which he lost his life. In revenge for this, she was slain by her son.

courageous, and be free from weakness, so that she may not be overcome either by toil or by fear. Otherwise how can she continue virtuous, if any one either by terror or by imposing toil can force her to submit to anything disgraceful? Women ought also to repel assaults, for if not they will show themselves weaker than hens, and the females of other birds, which fight for their young against animals much bigger than themselves. How, then, should woman not stand in need of courage? And that they share a certain martial vigour was proved by the race of the Amazons, who subdued many nations by force of arms. So that if other women are deficient in courage, this must be laid to the account of want of training rather than to (weakness of) nature. If, then, the same virtues must pertain to men and women, it follows necessarily that the same training and education must be suitable for both. For in the case of all animals and plants, the application of the proper treatment ought to impart to each the excellence belonging to it. Or, if both men and women should have to possess equal skill in playing the flute, or in performing on the harp, and if this were necessary for their livelihood, we should impart to both equally the requisite instruction. But if both ought to excel in the virtue proper to mankind, and to be in an equal measure wise and temperate, and to partake in courage and righteousness the one no less than the other, shall we not educate them both in the same manner, and teach both equally the art by which a human being may become good? Yes, we must act thus and no otherwise. What then? Some one will perhaps say, Would you think it right to teach men to spin wool just as you do women? and women equally with men to addict themselves to gymnastic exercises? No, this I will never approve. But I say that as in the human race men have a stronger and women a weaker nature, each of these natures should have the tasks which are most suited to it, assigned to it, and that the heavier should be allotted to the stronger, and the lighter to the weaker. Spinning, as well as housekeeping, would therefore be more suitable for women than for men, while gymnastics, as well as out of door work, would be fitter for men than for women: though sometimes some men might properly

Then the same education must be suitable to both.

Each should have tasks suited to his nature.

undertake some of the lighter tasks and such as seem to belong to women; and women again might engage in the harder tasks, and those which appear more appropriate for men, in cases where either bodily qualities, or necessity, or particular occasions, might lead to such action. For perhaps all human tasks are open to all, and common both to men and women, and nothing is necessarily appointed exclusively for either; not that some things may not be more suitable for the one, and others for the other nature; so that some are called men's and others women's occupations. But whatever things have reference to virtue, these one may rightly affirm to be equally appropriate for both natures, since we say that virtues do not belong more to the one than to the other. Wherefore I think it is reasonable that both males and females should be similarly instructed in matters relating to virtue; and they should be taught from their infancy that such and such a thing is good, and such and such a thing is bad (the same thing bad for both) and that one thing is profitable and another injurious, and that this is to be done and that not; from which wisdom is acquired by those who learn, by boys and girls equally, and in no way differently by each; then they are to be inspired with a feeling of shame in regard to everything base. These qualities being implanted in them, it necessarily follows that both men and women will become virtuous. And those who are rightly instructed, whether males or females, are to be accustomed to endure toil, not to fear death, not to be crushed by any calamity, so that they may become courageous (or manly); for it has been shown above that women too should partake in the character of courage (or manliness). Then again, it is an excellent thing to teach them to avoid selfishness and to honour equality, and, as human beings, to seek to benefit and not to injure mankind; and such instruction renders those who receive it just. But why should a man learn these things more than a woman? For if it is fitting that women should be just, then both sexes should be taught these things which are most seasonable and most important. For if the man should know some little matter connected with some artist's department, and the woman not, or conversely, this will not prove the education of each to

**Hence women should have the lighter tasks.**

**But the virtues belong equally to both.**

**Early education should be the same for both.**

be different. Only, as regards any of the most important matters let not the one be taught differently from the other. If anyone asks me what science is to preside over this instruction I shall reply that as without philosophy no man can be rightly instructed, so neither can any woman. But I do not mean to say that if women are to philosophise they ought properly to possess fluency and extraordinary cleverness in discussion; for I do not praise this very much even in men; but I mean that women should acquire a virtuous character and nobleness, since philosophy is the pursuit of a noble character, and nothing else.

**Should be chiefly moral.**

. . . And when one asked him if women too should study philosophy, he began, somewhat in this way, to teach that they should. Women, he said, have received from the gods the same reason as men, the reason which we use in dealing with each other, and by which we discern, in regard to each act, whether it is good or bad, noble or base. So, too, the female has the same perceptions as the male — seeing, hearing, smelling, and so forth. . . . So, too, not only men, but women also, have by nature the desire and the adaptation for virtue; for the latter, no less than the former, are so formed as to be pleased with noble and righteous actions and to disapprove the contraries of these. This being the case, why should it belong to men principally to inquire and consider how they shall live nobly — which is the province of philosophy — and not principally to women? Is it because it is fitting for men to be good, and not for women? But let us inquire in regard to every particular quality suitable for a woman who shall be good; for it will appear that she will derive each of these characteristics principally from philosophy. First, a woman ought to be a good housekeeper, and capable of judging what things are expedient for the house, and qualified to rule the domestics. Now, I say that such qualities would belong most to a woman who studied philosophy, since each of these things is a part of life, and the science of matters regarding life is nothing else than philosophy, and the philosopher, as Socrates said, continues inquiring "what things, good or bad, are done in the house." But the woman should further be self-controlled, so as to keep herself pure . . . not to be the slave of desires, nor

**Have the same reason; hence women should study philosophy.**

**Practical aspect of the philosophical education.**

quarrelsome, nor extravagant, nor fond of dress. These are the works of a virtuous woman; and, in addition, she should control anger, not give way to grief, be superior to all passion. These things philosophy enjoins, and it appears to me that anyone, whether man or woman, who should learn and practise them, would be a most correct person. What then? These things are so. Is not, therefore, a woman justified in studying philosophy, in being a blameless partner of (her husband's) life, a good helpmeet in housekeeping, a careful guardian of her husband and children, and in every way free from the love of gain and from selfishness? And what woman would possess this character more than the student of philosophy, who would be bound, if philosophy is uniform (? in its effects) to esteem the doing worse than the suffering of injustice—insomuch as it is more disgraceful—and to regard being worsted as better than gaining an advantage, and to love her children more than (her own) life? And what woman would be juster than she who possessed such a character? And it befits the educated woman to be more courageous than the uneducated, and the student of philosophy than she who is untrained in it, so that she would neither submit to anything disgraceful from the fear of death, or through shrinking from toil, nor succumb to anyone because he was well born, or powerful, or rich, or even a tyrant. For it is her fortune to have studied to be high-minded, and to regard death as not an evil, and life as not a good, and similarly not to turn away from toil, or at all to indulge in indolence. Whence it is to be expected that such a woman would work with her own hands, and submit to toil, should be able herself to suckle the infants to whom she gave birth, and minister to her husband with her own hands, and fulfil without reluctance tasks which some consider as work only fit for slaves. Would not, now, such a woman be a great treasure for her husband, an ornament to her relatives, and a good example to those of her own sex who knew her?

**The higher aspects of the philosophical education**

But some will say that the women who visit philosophers must generally become bold and presuming when, leaving their household occupations, they live surrounded by men, and practise discussions, and argue subtly, and analyse syllogisms, while they ought to be sitting at home spinning.

**Such education does not destroy womanhood.**

But I am so far from approving of women who are studying philosophy leaving their proper avocations and devoting themselves solely to discussions, that I should not even think it fit for men to do this. But I say that they ought to engage in all the reasonings with which they occupy themselves for the sake of their avocations. For as medical speculations are useless unless they conduce to the health of the human body, so if a philosopher holds or inculcates any doctrine, it is of no value unless it promote the virtue of the human soul. But, above all things, we ought to weigh the principles which we think that women studying philosophy should follow, so as to form a judgment whether the doctrine that teaches that modesty is the greatest good can make women bold, or whether that which inculcates the greatest composure can accustom them to live recklessly (or impudently), or that which shows vice to be the greatest evil does not teach virtuous self-restraint, or that which represents housekeeping as a virtue, and exhorts a woman to be satisfied with it and to work with her own hands, does not dispose a woman to practise household occupations.

Depends upon the kind of philosophy.

## *Selections from the Epistles of Pliny the Younger*

### BOOK I., EPISTLE VIII. TO POMPEIUS SATURNINUS

The occasion for the letter.

Your letters, in which you importuned me to send some of my writings to you, came very seasonably. For, I was just then fully determined in that point:[1] you have therefore given the spur to a very willing racer, and have at once saved yourself the excuse of refusing such a trouble, and me the awkward bashfulness of asking it. I think, I may now confidently use the offer, that is made me; neither can you for shame shrink back from your own proposal: however expect not anything new from a man so indolent as I am. What I am going to ask you, is to pass your judgment once more upon that speech, which I made to my fellow-citizens, when I dedicated a public

[1] Pliny made a practice of securing the critical examination of each piece of literary work by his friends before its publication.

library to their use.[1] I remember, you then gave me some criticisms upon it in general; but my present request is, that you would not only give a strict attention to the whole, but that you will not let a single syllable escape your most minute correction; for even after your emendations, I shall still be at liberty, either to publish, or suppress. However, your corrections may possibly determine me; and your pen, by frequently going over the work, may either find it unworthy and unfit for the public, or, by the same means, give it another turn, and make it fit to appear. But I must own, that the motives of my delays and apprehensions arise not so much from the speech itself, as from the subject of it; for certainly it is too full of vanity; because I must inevitably wound my modesty (be my expressions never so condescending and humble) when I am obliged to set forth, not only the munificence of my ancestors, but my own generosity also. The path is dangerous and slippery, even although a man were seduced into it by the most urging necessity. For, if an unwilling ear is lent to the praises we bestow upon others, how much more difficult will it be to obtain a patient hearing, when our whole discourse is about ourselves and our relations? If virtue, when naked, is envied, it will be more so, when set off in any ostentatious manner. In short, good deeds can only escape censure, by being buried in obscurity and silence. For which reason, I have often asked my own conscience, Is this composition of mine merely for my own vanity; or is it not as much for the use of the public in general, as for myself?[2]

**Its educational significance found in the private foundation of a public library.**

Another reflection, that occurs to me, is, that many things, which are necessary whilst we are performing an

[1] The occasion spoken of gives the educational significance of the letter. Pliny had given to the people of Comum, his native city, a public library, which was to be open at all times to all classes. The gift was accompanied by a speech setting forth the advantages to be gained from the use of a library. It is to this speech that the letter refers.

[2] The modesty of the letter is supported by his calling his generosity an imitation of his ancestors, though this is hardly a Roman custom; and by the character of the presentation speech at the time of the gift, being made, as it was, to the decurions alone.

Its chief topic the character of true generosity.

action, must lose their usefulness and their grace, the moment that action is performed. And not to go farther for examples, what could be more useful than to explain the grounds and motives of my liberality, and even to make it the subject of a discourse? From whence these advantages resulted; first our attention was for some time engaged in a series of virtuous and liberal thoughts; and then again, by dwelling long upon them, we became thoroughly acquainted with their beauties; and lastly, we were secured from the uneasiness of that repentance, which is the certain consequence of a rash and overhasty munificence. Hence too we were in a manner brought to a habit of despising money; for as nature has instilled into all men a desire of keeping what they have, we, whose love of liberality proceeded from having long and well weighed that virtue in the equal balance of judgment and reflection, released ourselves from those chains, common as they are to the rest of mankind; and our generosity was likely to appear the more to our honour, as it was the effect of reason, and not the sallies of whim and passion. To these arguments may be farther added, that I did not exhibit games or gladiators;[1] but, in their stead, established an annual income for the maintenance of young persons of good families and small fortunes. Pleasures, that are merely for the entertainment of the eyes and ears, are so far from wanting commendation, that they ought rather to be restrained than to be encouraged by public speeches. To induce a man to undergo the irksomeness and fatigue of education, not only gifts, but the most enticing eloquence is necessary: for if physicians, by kind and gentle language, persuade their patients to swallow down their nauseous, yet wholesome medicines; how much more ought a true lover of the public, to use all the soft bewitching arts of oratory, when he exhibits an entertainment not so acceptable as useful to the people? especially, when it was my business to endeavour, that what was given to those, who

The foundation of scholarships replaces public games and shows.

[1] On all such public occasions it was customary to institute games and exhibit shows in order to increase the solemnity of the public benefaction. Pliny departed from this custom and devoted the money as above indicated, thus giving the second educational significance to this letter.

had children, should be approved of by those, who had none; and that the many others, who must be excluded from an honour, which could be enjoyed only by few, should patiently wait in expectation of that honour, and try to deserve it.

But, as at the time I spoke this speech, I studied more the public advantage, than my own private reputation, in showing how desirous I was, that the full intention and design of my benefaction should be thoroughly understood and take effect accordingly; so now I am afraid, by sending it into the world, I shall appear to have my own glory more in view, than any advantage that can accrue to other people. Besides all this, I cannot forget, that the consciousness of virtue gives more real pleasure, than the fame of it.

Glory should follow, not be pursued: and though merit may not always be crowned with glory, her charms are not the less from that misfortune. But the persons, who do public benefits, and afterwards set them off by public speeches, seem to have done them, that they might be spoken of, not to speak of them, because they had been done. By which means a performance, that might appear highly magnificent, when related by another, vanishes to nothing, when set forth by the author himself. For when people cannot destroy the action, they immediately attack the vanity of it: so that if you do a thing, that ought to be concealed, the action is blamed; and if you do a thing, that ought to be praised, you are blamed for not concealing it.

There is yet another very particular reason, which deters me from making this oration public: for I did not speak it to the people, but I spoke it to the Decurions,[1] nor to them openly, and in the sight of the world, but privately in their own court.[2] I fear therefore it will seem

[1] Senators of the corporate cities of Italy. They had a share in the election of Roman magistrates, and thus these cities participated in the government of the Republic and Empire. Comum had been made a Roman colony by Scipio.

[2] As Pliny's bounty has been intended for the public benefit, it was necessary for him to register the act before the decurions.

inconsistent, that at the time I spoke it I should fly from the applauses and acclamations of the multitude, and should now run after those applauses and acclamations by publishing the work: and that I should then keep out the people, for whom it was designed, even from the walls of the court, merely to avoid the least show of ambition, and should now, as it were by a voluntary piece of ostentation, try to gain those very people, who can really reap no other benefit from my gift, than what may arise from the example of it.

You are now told the causes of my delay: however, I will follow your advice, be it what it will; and your authority shall be a sufficient reason for my actions. Farewell.

### BOOK III., EPISTLE III. TO CORRELLIA HISPULLA

On the selection of a teacher.

It is not easy to determine whether my love or esteem were greater, for that wise and excellent man your father, while from the respect I bear to his memory and your virtues, you are exceedingly dear to me. Can I fail then to wish (as I shall, by every means in my power, endeavour) that your son may resemble his grandfather? Myself, I should prefer his being like his grandfather on the mother's side, though the one on the father's as well was a man of mark and worth, his father and his uncle too will furnish him with illustrious examples. Now the surest way of training him up in the steps of such men is to give him a good, sound, liberal education, and it is of the utmost importance from whom he receives this. Hitherto, owing to his early years, he has been brought up under your eye, and in your house, where he is exposed to few, I should rather say to no, wrong impressions. But he is now of an age to be sent from home, and it is time to place him with some professor of rhetoric; of whose discipline and method, modesty, but, above all, purity and uprightness, you may be well satisfied. Amongst the many advantages for which our young man is indebted to nature and fortune, he has that of a most beautiful person: it is necessary therefore, in this loose and slippery age, to find out one who will not only be his tutor, but guardian and governor as well. I will venture to recommend Julius Genitor to you under that character. I am fond of him, it is true: but my affection by no means prejudices my judgment; on the contrary, it is, actually, the effect of it. His behaviour is grave, and his morals are irreproachable; perhaps somewhat too severe and rigid for the libertine manners of these times. His professional qualifications you may learn from many others, for the gift of eloquence, as it is open to all the world, is soon perceived: but the qualities of the heart lie in deeper recesses, more out of the reach of common observation; and it is on *that* side I undertake to answer for my friend. Your son will hear nothing from this worthy man but what will be to his advantage to know, nor will he learn anything of which it would be better he were ignorant. He will remind him as often, and with as much zeal as you or I should, of the virtues of his ancestors, and what a glorious weight of illustrious characters he has to support. You will not hesitate then to place him with a tutor whose first care will be to form his morals and after that to instruct him in eloquence; an attainment ill acquired if to the neglect of his moral culture. Farewell.

### BOOK IV., EPISTLE XIII. TO CORNELIUS TACITUS [1]

I am extremely glad to hear you are come safe to town. Your arrival, though always desirable, is at this time more particularly welcome. I shall still stay some few days in Tusculum, that I may finish a small work which I have in hand; for I am afraid, if I should now break off my pursuit, just when I have brought it near an end, I should find a difficulty in taking it up again. In the mean while, that I may lose no time, I write this precursory letter, to intimate a request, which I must urge personally when we meet. But first hear the reason of my asking, and then what it is I ask.

When I was last in my own country,[2] a son of one of my fellow-citizens came to see me. I asked him, "Do you

[1] The historian; a contemporary of Pliny. The exact date of his birth is unknown, though he was a few days older than Pliny, who was born 61 A.D.

[2] Comum.

Local schools to be supported by endowments from private benefactions instead of by tuition alone.

study?" He answered: "Yes." "Where?" "At Mediolanum."[1] "Why not here?" To which his father answered (for his father was with him, and had introduced the youth to me), "Because we have no preceptors here."[2] "Why have you not? for it much concerns you who are fathers" (and many parents happened luckily to be present), "to have your sons educated here, preferably to any other place. For where can they reside more to their satisfaction, than in their native country? Where can they be bred up more virtuously, than under the eye of their parents? or with less expense, than at home? Upon what easy conditions might you have preceptors brought hither? What a small additional expense must you be at, above what it already costs you in your children's lodgings, diet, and other necessaries, which are now all bought abroad? For my part, I, who have no children, but consider my country as my child or my parent, am ready to contribute a third part of the sum, which you shall think proper to establish upon this occasion. I would even promise to be at the whole expense, did I not fear that such a donation might be corrupted, and made to serve private interests: Which I see happen in many places, where preceptors are chosen by the public. There is but this one remedy to obviate the evil. If the right of choice be left entirely to the parents, their care, in that choice, will be still augmented, by the necessity they are under of contributing towards it: For those, who perhaps would be negligent in other people's expenses, will certainly be careful in their own: and will use their utmost endeavours, that the person, who is to receive his salary from me, shall be worthy of it, because their own share is likewise to be paid. Therefore consult, and come to some determination among yourselves, and let my example inspire you, and be assured, that the larger my part of the contribution shall be, the better I shall be pleased. You can do nothing more honourable for your

[1] Milan.

[2] The custom of giving imperial support to provincial schools did not grow up until late in the second Christian century, under the Antonines. At the time of Pliny (110 A.D.) such schools were supported either by the municipality or by tuition. Municipal support, however, was not common.

children; nothing more grateful to your country. Let those, who are born here, be educated here; that from their infancy they may love their native soil, by living on it. And I wish you could draw hither such eminent masters, as should make the studies here sought after by neighbouring cities; so that, as your children are now sent to other places, other people's children may, hereafter, resort to this."

**Public interest to be aroused.** I thought it necessary to repeat this conversation circumstantially, and from the beginning; that you may the better judge how grateful it would be to me, if you will undertake what I enjoin. For the importance of the affair makes me both enjoin, and entreat you, that out of the numerous concourse of learned men, who assemble about you, from an admiration of your great abilities, you would look out some masters worth soliciting: With this reserve however, that I shall not be tied down to any particular man: for I leave the parents at full liberty: let them judge; let them choose; I lay claim to nothing but the care and expense. Therefore if one should be found, who relies on his own genius, sufficiently for the task, let him go thither, under this restriction, that he builds upon no certainty, but his own abilities. Farewell.

**Choice of teachers.**

### BOOK VII., EPISTLE IX. TO CORNELIUS FUSCUS

**Approved methods of literary education.** You wish to know from me, in what method you ought to pursue your studies, while you remain, as you have long been, retired in the country. The most useful method, and as many think, the most preferable, is translation either from Greek into Latin, or from Latin into Greek. By this kind of exercise are to be acquired the propriety and beauty of expression, the extent of figures, the power of explanation, besides a facility of imitating the best authors, so as to fall into the same turn of thought. Those circumstances, which may not strike a reader, cannot possibly escape a translator. Knowledge and judgment are both acquired by translation. As soon as you have read a book, by way of emulation, you may undertake the same argument, and subject matter; comparing and carefully weighing your own performance with the book, which you have read:

from hence you will find out in each the several superiorities. It will be great honour to you, if sometimes the advantage appears on your side: It will be great shame, if you are always inferior. It may be proper for you now and then, both to choose out the most distinguished parts, and to vie with those particular passages when chosen; such a contest is rather bold than rash, because it is secret. Although, in this sort of race, I have seen many persons acquire great applause, by out-running such authors, whom they thought it would have been sufficient honour to have followed.

After your work has lain by long enough to be out of your memory, you should review the whole; should retain many things, throw away more; interline some, write others over again. This is an irksome and laborious task, but the difficulty is productive of good consequences; as by it you grow warm afresh, and resume a strength, which had been broken, and was become languid. Lastly, you add, as it were, new limbs to a body already well constituted, without molesting those of the original formation.

Oratory not the sole aim of education.

I know your principal study at present is oratory; but I am far from persuading you to be perpetually pursuing that controversial, and, if I may say so, that warlike style: for, as our lands are sowed with variety of seeds, and those seeds are often changed; so our minds must be employed, sometimes in one, then in another kind of application. I am desirous, that you should comment upon remarkable points of history: I am desirous, that you should be particularly careful in writing letters. I am desirous, that you should make verses; because, in speeches, an absolute necessity often happens for description, not only in an historical, but in a poetical manner. A closer and more delicate vein is adapted to epistles. You should sometimes refresh yourself with poetry. I do not say, that such an exercise should be constant, or that your poems should be long (those circumstances can only be the effect of leisure), but rather witty, and short, fit interludes between all kinds of care and business. Such poems are called amusements; but they often produce as great a share of reputation, as more serious performances. And therefore, why should I not tempt you to versification, by verses themselves?

I

When yielding wax, with pressure warm,
The artist's hand receives,
Each new creation takes its form,
And every figure lives:

II

Mars seems to knit his warlike brow;
Minerva seems to move;
Here, Cupid bends his magic bow;
There, smiles the queen of love.

III

As bursting flames are taught to know
The force of water's power;
As currents, when through meads they flow,
Refresh each field and flower.

IV

So shall the mind, by art impressed,
Like wax, new forms impart,
Or stand like torrent's force confessed,
Or flow from art to art.

In this manner the greatest orators, and even the greatest men, have exercised or amused themselves. Indeed it is wonderful, how much the mind is displayed, and delighted by those trifling performances. For they admit of love, hatred, anger, pity, mirth, in a word, all circumstances that pass in life; even the business in the forum, and the causes at the bar. In such sort of verses we find also the same usefulness as in all other poetry: we take pleasure in the freedom of a prose oration, as soon as we are loosed from the chains of metre. Comparison shows us, which is the easiest, and there we write with the greater willingness. I have now sent you more particulars than you desired; but there is still one point, which I have omitted. I have not told you what books you ought to read, although perhaps I expressed my meaning, by telling you what you ought to write. You will remember to choose the best authors of every kind. The saying

Value of versifying as a method.

As to reading, read much, not many books.

runs, We should read much, not many books. Who those authors are, is a point too well known, and too universally proved, to need any particular description: and besides, I have stretched out my letter so immoderately, that while I am persuading you in what manner to study, I am breaking in upon your time of studying. However, resume your table-books, and either write upon the subjects, which I have mentioned, or continue the particular work you had begun. Adieu.

## *Selection from Satire VII.*[1] *of Juvenal*

Formal character of the work of the schools of the rhetors.

. . . Do you teach declamation?[2] Oh what a heart of steel must Vectius have, when his numerous class kills cruel tyrants![3] For all that the boy has just conned over at his seat, he will then stand up and spout — the same stale theme in the same sing-song. It is the reproduction of the cabbage[4] that wears out the master's life. What is the plea to be urged: what the character of the cause; where the main point of the case hinges; what shafts may issue from the opposing party; — this all are anxious to know; but not one is anxious to pay! "*Pay* do you ask for? why, what do I know?"[5] The blame, forsooth, is laid at the teacher's door, because there is not a spark of energy in the breast of this scion of Arcadia,[6] who dins his awful Hannibal into my ears regularly every sixth day.[7]

[1] This satire gives an account of the general discouragement under which literature labored at Rome. This is shown in regard to the various departments of learning; those discussed previous to the selection given are history, law, and oratory. In the passages given the author shows that even worse conditions exist for the teachers of rhetoric and of grammar.

[2] This was the chief work of the rhetorical schools.

[3] The theme given by Vectius, who stands for any teacher of rhetoric, is supposed to be on the suppression of tyrants.

[4] Refers to the old Greek proverb, "Cabbage heated several times is death," a progenitor of the modern jokes concerning hash.

[5] These are the words of the dull and inattentive scholar to his master.

[6] The Arcadians were proverbially stupid.

[7] The adventures of Hannibal formed a most common theme in the Roman schools.

Whatever the theme be that is to be the subject of his deliberation; whether he shall march at once from Cannæ on Rome; or whether, rendered circumspect after the storms and thunderbolts, he shall lead his cohorts, drenched with the tempest, by a circuitous route.[1] Bargain for any sum you please, and I will at once place it in your hands, on condition that his father should hear him his lesson as often as I have to do it! But six or more sophists [2] are all giving tongue at once; and, debating in good earnest, have abandoned all fictitious declamations about the ravisher.[3] No more is heard of the poison infused,[4] or the vile ungrateful husband,[5] or the drugs that can restore the aged blind to youth.[6] He therefore that quits the shadowy conflicts of rhetoric for the arena of real debate,[7] will superannuate himself, if my advice has any weight with him, and enter on a different path of life; that he may not lose even the paltry sum that will purchase that miserable ticket for corn.[8] Since this is the most splendid reward you can expect. Just inquire what Chrysogonus receives, or Pollio,[9] for teaching the sons of these fine gentlemen, and going into all the details of Theodorus' [10] treatise.

[1] When Hannibal had encamped within three miles of Rome, he was twice assailed by violent storms, at times when both armies were prepared for battle. This was considered an unfavorable omen, and the Carthaginians withdrew from Rome.

[2] Rhetors.

[3] These references are all to fictitious subjects of debates in these schools. This refers to the rape of Helen.

[4] Refers to Medea, of Grecian mythology, celebrated for her skill in magic. The instance referred to is her murder of the daughter of Creon, the king of Corinth, for whom Jason, Medea's husband, had deserted her.

[5] Æneas, who abandoned Dido.

[6] The question for debate was, what drugs restored sight and youth to Æson.

[7] To practice in the law courts.

[8] The poorer Romans received every month tickets, entitling them to certain quantities of corn from the public granaries, either free or at least at a lower than market price.

[9] Rhetorical teachers.

[10] A famous rhetorician.

Little attention paid to education by the wealthy.

The baths will cost six hundred sestertia, and the colonnade still more, in which the great man rides whenever it rains. Is he to wait, forsooth, for fair weather? or bespatter his horses with fresh mud? Nay, far better here! for here the mule's hoof shines unsullied. On the other side must rise a spacious dining-room, supported on stately columns of Numidian marble, and catch the cool sun. However much the house may have cost, he will have besides an artiste who can arrange his table scientifically; another, who can season made-dishes. Yet amid all this lavish expenditure, two poor sestertia will be deemed an ample remuneration for Quintilian. Nothing will cost a father less than his son's education.

Teachers receive little esteem and little reward.

"Then where did Quintilian get the money to pay for so many estates?" Pass by the instances of good fortune that are but rare indeed. It is good *luck* that makes a man handsome and active; good luck that makes him wise, and noble, and well-bred, and attaches the crescent of the senator to his black shoe.[1] Good luck too that makes him the best of orators and debaters, and, though he has a vile cold, sing well! For it makes all the difference what planets welcome you when you first begin to utter your infant cry, and are still red from your mother. If fortune so wills it, you will become consul instead of rhetorician; or, if she will, instead of rhetorician, consul! What was Ventidius[2] or Tullius[3] aught else than a lucky planet, and the strange potency of hidden fate? Fate, that gives kingdoms to slaves, and triumphs to captives. Yes! Quintilian was indeed lucky, but he is a greater rarity even than a white crow. But many a man has repented of this fruitless and barren employment, as the sad end of Thrasymachus[4] proves, and that of Secundus

[1] The senators and patricians wore a black shoe of the finest leather, fastened by a silver or ivory clasp of crescent shape. This is supposed to have indicated the original number of the senators.

[2] A son of a bondwoman, at first a muleteer, was afterward made prætor and consul.

[3] Servius Tullius, sixth king, was son of a captive.

[4] A pupil of Plato and of Isocrates. Was a teacher at Athens. Meeting with no success, he hanged himself.

Carrinas.[1] And you, too, Athens, were witness to the poverty of him on whom you had the heart to bestow nothing save the hemlock that chilled his life-blood!

* * * * * * *

But do you, parents, impose severe exactions on him that is to teach your boys; that he be perfect in the rules of grammar for each word — read all histories — know all authors as well as his own finger-ends; that if questioned at hazard, while on his way to the Thermæ or the baths of Phœbus, he should be able to tell the name of Anchises' nurse, and the name and native land of the stepmother of Anchemolus — tell off-hand how many years Acestes lived — how many flagons of wine the Sicilian king gave to the Phrygians. Require of him that he mould their youthful morals as one models a face in wax. Require of him that he be the reverend father of the company, and check every approach to immorality. **Of teachers much required, with but slight return.**

It is no light task to keep watch over so many boyish hands, so many little twinkling eyes. "This," says the father, "be the object of your care!" — and when the year comes round again, Receive for your pay as much gold as the people demand for the victorious Charioteer![2]

* * * * * * *

## *Selections from Satire XIV. of Juvenal*[3]

. . . The greatest reverence is due to a child! If you are contemplating a disgraceful act, despise not your **The moral education of a child through the home.**

[1] A teacher driven by poverty from Athens and Rome. From thence he was banished by Caligula for political offence.

[2] The charioteer would receive for an hour's work as much as the teacher for a year's.

[3] The entire satire is devoted to this subject: the duty of giving children examples of domestic purity and virtue. This is shown for the most part by indicating the facility with which children copy the vices of their parents. These have some value as an index of the corruption of Roman society that had occurred even at this early portion of the imperial period. Juvenal wrote in the first half of the second century of this era. The vices he dwells upon in this satire are gluttony, cruelty, debauchery, avarice, etc.

child's tender years, but let your infant son act as a check upon your purpose of sinning. For if, at some future time, he shall have done anything to deserve the censor's wrath, and show himself like you, not in person only and in face, but also the true son of your morals, and one who, by following your footsteps, adds deeper guilt to your crimes — then, forsooth! you will reprove and chastise him with clamorous bitterness, and then set about altering your will. Yet how dare you assume the front severe, and license of a parent's speech; you, who yourself, though old, do worse than this; and the exhausted cupping-glass is long ago looking out for your brainless head?[1]

If a friend is coming to pay you a visit, your whole household is in a bustle. "Sweep the floor, display the pillars in all their brilliancy, let the dry spider come down with all her web; let one clean the silver, another polish the embossed plate —" the master's voice thunders out, as he stands over the work, and brandishes his whip.

Importance of example.

You are alarmed then, wretched man, lest your entrance-hall, befouled by dogs, should offend the eye of your friend who is coming, or your corridor be spattered with mud; and yet one little slave could clean all this with half a bushel of saw-dust. And yet, will you not bestir yourself that your own son may see your house immaculate and free from foul spot or crime? It deserves our gratitude that you have presented a citizen to your country and people, if you take care that he prove useful to the state — of service to her lands; useful in transacting the affairs both of war and peace. For it will be a matter of the highest moment in what pursuits and moral discipline you train him.

Child's character formed by imitation of parent's.

The stork feeds her young on snakes and lizards which she has discovered in the trackless fields. They too, when fledged, go in quest of the same animals. The vulture, quitting the cattle, dogs, and gibbets, hastens to her callow brood, and bears to them a portion of the carcass. Therefore this is the food of the vulture too when grown up, and able to feed itself and build a nest in a tree of its own. . . .

[1] The operation of cupping was a common remedy in diseases of the brain, to relieve the pressure of the blood.

## VI. THE ORATOR AS THE IDEAL OF ROMAN EDUCATION

**The Period and the Authority.** — The *De Oratore* was published in 55 B.C., though the ostensible scene of the dialogue was laid in 91 B.C. The conception of a liberal education here presented is the ideal of this third period of Roman educational development. It was written at the close of the most flourishing period of Roman oratory, by the consummate master of that art, then at the fulness of his experience and at the height of his influence. Since the *De Oratore* is also considered to be the best expression of Ciceronian style, we find here in every respect the most authoritative, though very general, expression of this rhetorical conception of education.

Cicero's life covered the period from 106 to 43 B.C., the period of the decline of the Republic. With the transition to the Empire, oratory lost its chief incentive, liberty; but its loss in intent was made up for a time by increase in extent, representing as it did the accomplishment of every educated Roman. Oratorical education gained also in becoming more systematic and better defined. On the educational side there was development for more than a century after the death of its leading exponent. The expression of the ideal here given is true for the last century of the Republic and the first century of the Empire. Cicero was not an educator, and does not write from the educational point of view, hence there is a lack of definiteness and detail in this respect; on the contrary, he writes as a publicist would now write, not from a knowledge of educational processes, but from a knowledge of its results and of the demands made by society upon educated men.

In the early life of Cicero, no less than in his writings, is found an exposition of the Roman education of his time. He attended the ordinary Roman schools, one of which at least was under the care of Aulus Licinius Archias, a distinguished Greek rhetorician, who in after years was defended in a lawsuit by his former pupil. This defence, the *Pro Archia*, forms an additional source of information for the educational history of this period. In accordance with the old educational customs, Cicero was placed, after the theoretical training in rhetoric, under the direction or tutorship of the distinguished lawyer, Scævola, one of the characters in the *De Oratore*. Still later he received a similar training from Diodotus the Stoic and in the school of the rhetorician Molo. The old customs are further represented in his education in military science, which he received through actual service under direction of one of the generals in the campaign of the Consul, Pompeius Strabo. On the other hand, the later Roman educational customs are illustrated by his two years of travel and sojourn in the philosophical school of Athens.

In his accomplishments, as well, Cicero typifies the education, whose ideals he here sets forth. As an orator, he ranks next to Demosthenes as the greatest of ancient orators, and there are yet preserved, either in whole or in part, seventy-seven of his orations, all masterpieces of that art. As a philosopher, he is the author of several treatises; as a rhetorician, he created Latin prose as a literary language; as a soldier, he justified his claim to a triumph, denied him only because of the civil strife incident to the formation of the first triumvirate; as a statesman, he ranks with the great of that century, which was the most productive of great men in Roman history; as a patriot, he ranks among the foremost, though his actions are marred by the indecision and timidity that has given basis in recent times to a view the opposite of this; as a historian, his reputation can hardly be tested by extant works, though he has a claim to rank as such. As a poet, however, he does not rank so high, his reputation in this respect depending upon his youthful productions. All these activities are summed up in the one term "orator," which presents the educational ideal of the period and the achievements of such a career.

**The Source.** — In the *De Oratore*, Cicero sets forth in a completed form his opinions concerning oratory and incidentally concerning education, since the orator is identified with the educated man. This Cicero had already done in earlier years, but now, after his long experience in public life, he returns to the task. These dialogues form a very extensive work, summarizing in popular rhetorical form all that is important in the rhetorical treatises of Aristotle, Isocrates, and other previous writers on oratory. The persons of the dialogue are Lucius Licinius Crassus and Marcus Antonius, the two most eminent orators of their day; Quintus Mucius Scævola, a former teacher of Cicero, who was celebrated for his knowledge of the civil law; and two young men, Caius Amelius Cotta and Publius Sulpicius Rufus, who were anxious to distinguish themselves in oratory and for whose benefit the dialogues are supposed to have been delivered. The views of Cicero are expressed by Crassus, who contends that the complete orator must be acquainted with the whole circle of the arts and sciences. Antonius maintains that universal knowledge is unattainable; that the attempt to acquire too much will result in dissipation of energy and distraction of thought; that much less is required of the successful orator; and that one will accomplish more by concentration of attention upon more practical and immediate improvement of the natural powers. The ideas of Cicero, as given by Crassus, express the ideal of the last century of the Republic and the first century of the Empire. But more than that, his ideas have had a vogue unparalleled, running as they did through many centuries and revived as they were in the Ciceronianism of the fifteenth and sixteenth centuries, again to dominate education as an ideal. This dominion is due quite as much to his style as to his ideas. It is because Cicero made of Latin prose a universal language that his ideas came to have the same validity as did his form of expression. These educational ideals—both as to form and content—were handed down by Quintilian of the first century, the "Christian Cicero," Lactantius, of the fourth century, John of Salisbury of the twelfth, Petrarch of the fourteenth, and Erasmus of the sixteenth, until they again dominated in the later period mentioned.

In the selections given from the *De Oratore* no attempt has been made to preserve the continuity of the discussion. The few paragraphs given lose the proportion of the extended dialogues, for they constitute less than one-sixteenth of the entire work. The passages quoted present Cicero's exposition of the consummation of all education as found in the orator; second, the content of that education, identical with our conception of the "humanities";

third, the notable account, in paragraphs 31 to 35, of his own education. These selections are all taken from the first of the three books.

**Summary of Contents of the Source.** — To the Roman, oratory was of much broader connotation than to the modern. The orator included the teacher, the publicist, the religious teacher, of the present, as well as the man devoted to legal, judicial, or legislative activities: the orator was the educated man participating in public affairs. In the absence of the modern pulpit, of the press, of the university and scientific organization, the orator combined the functions of these with the functions of the bar and forum. The spoken word then accomplished what both the spoken and written word does now. Oratory meant efficient public interest and activity. The only rival to the orator as the type of the educated man was the Grecian ideal of the philosopher, — an ideal foreign to the Roman genius, for it had no relation to practical life or the needs of the Roman state. The philosopher was interested either in knowledge for its own sake or in experience for his own satisfaction. Whether the philosophical ideal was Academician or Epicurean, it was a narrow one to the Roman. With his practical instinct the Roman avoided that individualism — cast though it might be in the highest form — which had brought destruction to the Grecian state at the same time that it made the influence of Greece cosmopolitan.

Cicero presents both sides of the question: the philosopher as viewed by the orator, and the orator as viewed by the philosopher. In his conception, the orator should have the knowledge of the philosopher in respect both of things and human nature, but in addition he should have the power to make such knowledge of practical value in influencing his fellows through his power of speech. To the Roman this power of speech stood for the various ways in which the modern educated man can make his knowledge effective in the service of his fellows. It is not that this conception of education was narrow, but rather that the social organization of the times gave but few facilities for bringing intellect to bear upon practical interests. Even the great warriors of the period were no less great orators: oratory was not separated from practical efficiency. In fact, Cicero offers the first example of a man who won his way to prominence and influence primarily as a speaker. To Cicero and the Romans philosophy, whatever might be its character, was deficient, because it was self-centred; and it is a fact that the decline of public and patriotic interest was coincident with the growth of philosophic interest, and was partly due to it. From this point of view, oratory was a broader as well as a higher aim than philosophy, — it was inclusive of philosophy. If there were many who failed to reach this ideal, if there was much public speaking that was not eloquence, it was at least easily detected, was, in fact, self-evident. On the other hand, philosophy, though only a partial aim at best, was easily imitated, and the imitation was with difficulty detected. In fact, there were more delinquents in the latter field than defectives in the former; for philosophy as it became popular at a later time was simply the theory of the individualized and self-centred life, while oratory set high standards, even though its actual accomplishment might be far below its ideals.

The argument of the philosopher against the orator is fourfold: first, the orator obtains all his knowledge concerning "the immortal gods, the discipline of youth, justice, patience, temperance, moderation in everything, and other matters," only from philosophy; second, the books of the rhetoricians are filled not with these large affairs, but with rules and petty details; third, even if this literature should be of a higher grade and rhetoricians more intelligent teachers, eloquence is a natural gift and not an acquired art; fourth, no writer on the art of rhetoric was even moderately eloquent in speech. The diffuse reply to those arguments cannot be included in the selections given on account of its length. The reply, however, has been substantially presented in the previously expressed view of Cicero: eloquence presupposes the knowledge of the philosopher,— oratory is based both upon a knowledge of philosophy and a knowledge of rhetoric.

In addition to this general discussion of the oratorical conception of education, Cicero gives a general outline of the content and the method of his own education. Both, however, refer to the work of the rhetorical schools previously described. This narrower view is to be supplemented by the general tenor of his entire discussion, which insists that the whole realm of knowledge is the proper subject-matter of oratorical education. This broader view is stated at least in the earlier paragraphs of the selection. The entire subject is further treated in detail in the dialogue *On Brutus*. This extensive work is a concrete demonstration and defence of the oratorical conception of education, and forms an epitome of Roman history in the lives of its eminent orators. Views therein given corroborate in numerous details, though not in direct exposition, statements made in the *De Oratore*. The systematic exposition of the orator as an educational type is given by Quintilian a century and a half later.

## *Selections from the De Oratore of Cicero*

### BOOK I

III. . . . "The whole art of speaking lies before us, and is concerned with common usage and the custom and language of all men; so that while in other things that is most excellent which is most remote from the knowledge and understanding of the illiterate, it is in speaking even the greatest of faults to vary from the ordinary kind of language, and the practice sanctioned by universal reason.

**Oratory becomes the aim of education at Rome.**

IV. Yet it cannot be said with truth, either that more are devoted to the other arts, or that they are excited by greater pleasure, more abundant hope, or more ample rewards; for to say nothing of Greece, which was always desirous to hold the first place in eloquence, and Athens, that inventress of all literature, in which the utmost power of oratory was both discovered and brought to perfection, in this very city of ours, assuredly, no studies were ever pursued with more earnestness than those tending to the acquisition of eloquence. For when our empire over all nations was established, and after a period of peace had secured tranquillity, there was scarcely a youth ambitious of praise who did not think that he must strive, with all his endeavours, to attain the art of speaking. For a time, indeed, as being ignorant of all method, and as thinking there was no course of exercise for them, or any precepts of art, they attained what they could by the single force of genius and thought. But afterwards, having heard the Greek orators, and gained an acquaintance with Greek literature, and procured instructors, our countrymen were inflamed with an incredible passion for eloquence. The magnitude, the variety, the multitude of all kind of causes, excited them to such a degree, that to that learning which each had acquired by his individual study, frequent practice, which was superior to the precepts of all masters, was at once added. There were then, as there are also now, the highest inducements offered for the cultivation of this study, in regard to public favour, wealth, and dignity. The abilities of our countrymen (as we may judge from many particulars), far excelled those of the men of every other nation. For which reasons, who would not justly wonder that in the records of all ages, times, and states, so small a number of orators should be found?

But the art of eloquence is something greater, and collected from more sciences and studies, than people imagine. V. For who can suppose that, amid the greatest multitude of students, the utmost abundance of masters, the most eminent geniuses among men, the infinite variety of causes, the most ample rewards offered to eloquence, there is any other reason to be found for the small number of orators than the incredible magnitude and difficulty of the art? A knowledge of a vast number of things is necessary, without which volubility of words is empty and ridiculous; speech itself is to be formed, not merely by choice, but by careful construction of words; and all the emotions of the mind, which nature has given to man, must be intimately known; for all the force and art of speaking must be employed in allaying or exciting the feelings of those who listen. To this must be added a certain portion of grace and wit, learning worthy of a well-bred man, and quickness and brevity in replying as well as attacking, accompanied with a refined decorum and urbanity. Besides, the whole of antiquity and a multitude of examples is to be kept in the memory; nor is the knowledge of laws in general, or of the civil law in particular, to be neglected. And why need I add any remarks on delivery itself, which is to be ordered by action of body, by gesture, by look, and by modulation and variation of the voice, the great power of which, alone and in itself, the comparatively trivial art of actors and the stage proves, on which though all bestow their utmost labour to form their look, voice, and gesture, who knows not how few there are, and have ever been, to whom we can attend with patience? What can I say of that repository for all things, the memory, which, unless it be made the keeper of the matter and words that are the fruits of thought and invention, all the talents of the orator, we see, though they be of the highest degree of excellence, will be of no avail? Let us then cease to wonder what is the cause of the scarcity of good speakers, since eloquence results from all those qualifications, in each of which singly it is a great

**Essential qualifications of an orator.**

merit to labour successfully; and let us rather exhort our children, and others whose glory and honour is dear to us, to contemplate in their minds the full magnitude of the object, and not to trust that they can reach the height at which they aim, by the aid of the precepts, masters, and exercises, that they are all now following, but to understand that they must adopt others of a different character.

**Breadth of knowledge essential.**

VI. In my opinion, indeed, no man can be an orator possessed of every praiseworthy accomplishment, unless he has attained the knowledge of everything important, and of all liberal arts, for his language must be ornate and copious from knowledge, since, unless there be beneath the surface matter understood and felt by the speaker, oratory becomes an empty and almost puerile flow of words. Yet I will not lay so great a burden upon orators, especially our own, amid so many occupations of public and private life, as to think it allowable for them to be ignorant of nothing; although the qualifications of an orator, and his very profession of speaking well, seem to undertake and promise that he can discourse gracefully and copiously on whatever subject is proposed to him. But because this, I doubt now, will appear to most people an immense and infinite undertaking, and because I see that the Greeks, men amply endowed not only with genius and learning, but also with leisure and application, have made a kind of partition of the arts, and have not singly laboured in the whole circle of oratory, but have separated from the other parts of rhetoric that department of eloquence which is used in the forum on trials or in deliberations, and have left this species only to the orator; I shall not embrace in these books more than has been attributed to this kind of speaking by the almost unanimous consent of the greatest men, after much examination and discussion of the subject; and I shall repeat, not a series of precepts drawn from the infancy of our old and boyish learning, but matters which I have heard were formerly argued in a discussion among some of our countrymen who were of the highest eloquence, and of the first rank in every kind of dignity. Not that I contemn the instructions which the Greek rhetoricians and teachers have left us, but, as they are already public, and within the reach of all, and can

**Only certain types of oratory discussed.**

neither be set forth more elegantly, nor explained more clearly by my interpretation, you will, I think, excuse me, my brother, if I prefer to the Greeks the authority of those to whom the utmost merit in eloquence has been allowed by our own countrymen.

* * * * * * *

**Even with these limitations, a vast range of knowledge necessary.**

XI. . . . "A controversy indeed on the word Orator has long disturbed the minute Grecians, who are fonder of argument than of truth. For if any one pronounces him to be an orator who can speak fluently only on law in general, or on judicial questions, or before the people, or in the senate, he must yet necessarily grant and allow him a variety of talents; for he cannot treat even of these matters with sufficient skill and accuracy without great attention to all public affairs, nor without a knowledge of laws, customs, and equity, nor without understanding the nature and manners of mankind; and to him who knows these things, without which no one can maintain even the most minute points in judicial pleadings, how much is wanting of the knowledge even of the most important affairs? But if you allow nothing to belong to the orator but to speak aptly, ornately, and copiously, how can he even attain these qualities without that knowledge which you do not allow him? for there can be no true merit in speaking, unless what is said is thoroughly understood by him who says it.

**Eloquence essential to every type of educated man.**

If, therefore, the natural philosopher Democritus spoke with elegance, as he is reported to have spoken, and as it appears to me that he did speak, the matter on which he spoke belonged to the philosopher, but the graceful array of words is to be ascribed to the orator. And if Plato spoke divinely upon subjects most remote from civil controversies, as I grant that he did; if also Aristotle, and Theophrastus, and Carneades, were eloquent, and spoke with sweetness and grace on those matters which they discussed; let the subjects on which they spoke belong to other studies, but their speech itself, surely, is the peculiar offspring of that art of which we are now discoursing and inquiring. For we see that some have reasoned on the same subjects jejunely and drily, as Chrysippus, whom they celebrate as the acutest of philosophers; nor is he on this account to be thought to have been deficient in philosophy, because he did not gain the talent of speaking from an art which is foreign to philosophy.

Oratory depends upon mastery of subject as well as copiousness of speech.

XII. "Where then lies the difference? Or by what term will you discriminate the fertility and copiousness of speech in those whom I have named, from the barrenness of those who use not this variety and elegance of phrase? One thing there will certainly be, which those who speak well will exhibit as their own; a graceful and elegant style, distinguished by a peculiar artifice and polish. But this kind of diction, if there be not matter beneath it clear and intelligible to the speaker, must either amount to nothing, or be received with ridicule by all who hear it. For what savours so much of madness, as the empty sound of words, even the choicest and most elegant, when there is no sense or knowledge contained in them? Whatever be the subject of a speech, therefore, in whatever art or branch of science, the orator, if he has made himself master of it, as of his client's cause, will speak on it better and more elegantly than even the very originator and author of it can. If indeed any one shall say that there are certain trains of thought and reasoning properly belonging to orators, and a knowledge of certain things circumscribed within the limits of the forum, I will confess that our common speech is employed about these matters chiefly; but yet there are many things, in these very topics, which those masters of rhetoric, as they are called, neither teach nor understand.

To the knowledge of the subject of the philosopher, the orator adds a knowledge of human nature and the ability to make his knowledge effective.

For who is ignorant that the highest power of an orator consists in exciting the minds of men to anger, or to hatred, or to grief, or in recalling them from these more violent emotions to gentleness and compassion? which power will never be able to effect its object by eloquence, unless in him who has obtained a thorough insight into the nature of mankind, and all the passions of humanity, and those causes by which our minds are either impelled or restrained. But all these are thought to belong to the philosophers, nor will the orator, at least with my consent, ever deny that such is the case; but when he has conceded to them the knowledge of things, since they are willing to exhaust their labours of that alone, he will assume to himself the treatment of oratory, which without that knowledge is nothing. For the proper concern of an orator, as I have already often said, is language of power and elegance accommodated to the feelings and understandings of mankind.

XIII. "On these matters I confess that Aristotle and Theophrastus have written. But consider, Scævola, whether this is not wholly in my favour. For I do not borrow from them what the orator possesses in common with them; but they allow that what they say on these subjects belongs to oratory. Their other treatises, accordingly, they distinguish by the name of the science on which each is written; their treatises on oratory they entitle and designate as books of rhetoric. For when, in their discussions, (as often happens,) such topics present themselves as require them to speak of the immortal gods, of piety, of concord, of friendship, of the common rights of their fellow-citizens, or those of all mankind, of the law of nations, of equity, of temperance, of greatness of mind, of every kind of virtue, all the academies and schools of philosophy, I imagine, will cry out that all these subjects are their property, and that no particle of them belongs to the orator. But when I have given them liberty to reason on all these subjects in corners to amuse their leisure, I shall give and assign to the orator his part, which is, to set forth with full power and attraction the very same topics which they discuss in such tame and bloodless phraseology. These points I then discussed with the philosophers in person at Athens, for Marcus Marcellus, our countryman, who is now curule ædile, obliged me to do so, and he would certainly have taken part in our present conversation, were he not now celebrating the public games; for he was then a youth marvellously given to these studies.

**Subject-matter of the philosopher and the orator the same; differ in form of presentation and purpose.**

Of the institution of laws, of war, of peace, of alliances, of tributes, of the civil law as relating to various ranks and ages respectively, let the Greeks say, if they will, that Lycurgus or Solon (although I think that these should be enrolled in the number of the eloquent) had more knowledge than Hypereides or Demosthenes, men of the highest accomplishments and refinement in oratory; or let our countrymen prefer, in this sort of knowledge, the Decemviri who wrote the Twelve Tables, and who must have

**Cicero's definition of an orator.**

been wise men, to Servius Galba, and your father-in-law Lælius, who are allowed to have excelled in the glorious art of speaking. I, indeed, shall never deny that there are some sciences peculiarly well understood by those who have applied their whole study to the knowledge and consideration of them; but the accomplished and complete orator I shall call him who can speak on all subjects with variety and copiousness.

Necessity for a general knowledge demonstrated.

XIV. For often in those causes which all acknowledge properly to belong to orators, there is something to be drawn forth and adopted, not from the routine of the Forum, which is the only knowledge that you grant to the orator, but from some of the more obscure sciences. I ask whether a speech can be made for or against a general, without an acquaintance with military affairs, or often without a knowledge of certain inland and maritime countries? whether a speech can be made to the people about passing or rejecting laws, or in the senate on any kind of public transactions, without the greatest knowledge and judgment in political matters? whether a speech can be adapted to excite or calm the thoughts and passions (which alone is a great business of the orator) without a most diligent examination of all those doctrines which are set forth on the nature and manners of men by the philosophers? I do not know whether I may not be less successful in maintaining what I am going to say; but I shall not hesitate to speak that which I think. Physics, and mathematics, and those other things which you just now decided to belong to other sciences, belong to the peculiar knowledge of those who profess them; but if any one would illustrate those arts by eloquence, he must have recourse to the power of oratory. Nor, if, as is said, Philo, the famous architect, who built an arsenal for the Athenians, gave that people an eloquent account of his work, is it to be imagined that his eloquence proceeded from the art of the architect, but from that of the orator. Or, if our friend Marcus Antonius had had to speak for Hermodorus on the subject of dock-building, he would have spoken, when he had learned the case from Hermodorus, with elegance and copiousness, drawn from an art quite unconnected with dock-building. And Asclepiades, whom we knew as a phy-

.sician and a friend, did not, when he excelled others of his profession in eloquence, employ, in his graceful elocution, the art of physic, but that of oratory. What Socrates used to say, that *all men are sufficiently eloquent in that which they understand*, is very plausible, but not true. It would have been nearer truth to say, that no man can be eloquent on a subject that he does not understand; and that, if he understands a subject ever so well, but is ignorant how to form and polish his speech, he cannot express himself eloquently even about what he does understand.

**But knowledge without power of effective speech is not oratory.**

XV. "If, therefore, any one desires to define and comprehend the whole and peculiar power of an orator, that man, in my opinion, will be an orator, worthy of so great a name, who, whatever subject comes before him, and requires rhetorical elucidation, can speak on it judiciously, in set form, elegantly, and from memory, and with a certain dignity of action. But if the phrase which I have used, 'on whatever subject,' is thought by any one too comprehensive, let him retrench and curtail as much of it as he pleases; but this I will maintain, that though the orator be ignorant of what belongs to other arts and pursuits, and understands only what concerns the discussions and practice of the Forum, yet if he has to speak on those arts, he will, when he has learned what pertains to any of them from persons who understand them, discourse upon them much better than the very persons of whom those arts form the peculiar province. Thus, if our friend Sulpicius have to speak on military affairs, he will inquire about them of my kinsman Caius Marius, and when he has received information, will speak upon them in such a manner, that he shall seem to Marius to understand them better than himself. Or if he has to speak on the civil law, he will consult with you, and will excel you, though eminently wise and learned in it, in speaking on those very points which he shall have learned from yourself. Or if any subject presents itself, requiring him to speak on the nature and vices of men, on desire, on moderation, on continence, on grief, on death, perhaps, if he thinks proper (though the orator ought to have a knowledge of these things), he will consult with Sextus Pompeius, a man learned in philosophy. But this he will certainly accomplish, that, of

**Further definition of the orator, and of his attainments.**

whatever matter he gains a knowledge, or from whomsoever, he will speak upon it much more elegantly than the very person from whom he gained the knowledge. But, since philosophy is distinguished into three parts, inquiries into the obscurities of physics, the subtleties of logic, and the knowledge of life and manners, let us, if Sulpicius will listen to me, leave the two former, and consult our ease; but unless we have a knowledge of the third, which has always been the province of the orator, we shall leave him nothing in which he can distinguish himself. The part of philosophy, therefore, regarding life and manners, must be thoroughly mastered by the orator; other subjects, even if he has not learned them, he will be able, whenever there is occasion, to adorn by his eloquence, if they are brought before him and made known to him.

Relation of philosophy and oratory.

Further illustration of the wide learning and the general power of the orator.

XVI. "For if it is allowed amongst the learned that Aratus, a man ignorant of astronomy, has treated of heaven and the constellations in extremely polished and excellent verses; if Nicander, of Colophon, a man totally unconnected with the country, has written well on rural affairs, with the aid of poetical talent, and not from understanding husbandry, what reason is there why an orator should not speak most eloquently on those matters of which he shall have gained a knowledge for a certain purpose and occasion? For the poet is nearly allied to the orator; being somewhat more restricted in numbers, but less restrained in the choice of words, yet in many kinds of embellishment his rival and almost equal; in one respect, assuredly, nearly the same, that he circumscribes or bounds his jurisdiction by no limits, but reserves to himself full right to range wherever he pleases with the same ease and liberty. For why did you say, Scævola, that you would not endure, unless you were in my domain, my assertion, that the orator ought to be accomplished in every style of speaking, and in every part of polite learning? I should certainly not have said this if I had thought myself to be the orator whom I conceive in my imagination. But, as Caius Lucilius used frequently to say (a man not very friendly to you, and on that account less familiar with me than he could wish, but a man of learning and good breeding), I am of this opinion, that no one is to be numbered among orators who is not thoroughly accomplished in all branches of knowledge requisite for a man of good breeding; and though we may not put forward such knowledge in conversation, yet it is apparent, and indeed evident, whether we are destitute of it, or have acquired it; as those who play at tennis do not exhibit, in playing, the gestures of the palæstra, but their movements indicate whether they have learned those exercises or are unacquainted with them; and as those who shape out anything, though they do not then exercise the art of painting, yet make it clear whether they can paint or not; so in orations to courts of justice, before the people, and in the senate, although other sciences have no peculiar place in them, yet is it easily proved whether he who speaks has only been exercised in the parade of declamation, or has devoted himself to oratory after having been instructed in all liberal knowledge."

* * * * * * *

**The argument that philosophy is the end of education.**

XIX. "Certain men of eloquence at Athens, versed in public affairs and judicial pleadings, disputed on the other side; among whom was Menedemus, lately my guest at Rome; but when he had observed that there is a sort of wisdom which is employed in inquiring into the methods of settling and managing governments, he, though a ready speaker, was promptly attacked by the other, a man of abundant learning, and of an almost incredible variety and copiousness of argument; who maintained that every portion of such wisdom must be derived from philosophy, and that whatever was established in a state concerning the immortal gods, the discipline of youth, justice, patience, temperance, moderation in everything, and other matters, without which states would either not subsist at all, or be corrupt in morals, was nowhere to be found in the petty treatises of the rhetoricians. For if those teachers of rhetoric included in their art such a multitude of the most important subjects, why, he asked, were their books crammed with rules about proems and perorations, and such trifles (for so he called them), while about the model-

**How oratory is viewed by the philosopher.**

ling of states, the composition of laws, about equity, justice, integrity, about mastering the appetites, and forming the morals of mankind, not one single syllable was to be found in their pages? Their precept she ridiculed in such a manner, as to show that the teachers were not only destitute of the knowledge which they arrogated to themselves, but that they did not even know the proper art and method of speaking; for he thought that the principal business of an orator was, that he might appear to those to whom he spoke to be such as he would wish to appear (that this was to be attained by a life of good reputation, on which those teachers of rhetoric had laid down nothing in their precepts); and that the minds of the audience should be affected in such a manner as the orator would have them to be affected, an object, also, which could by no means be attained, unless the speaker understood by what methods, by what arguments, and by what sort of language the minds of men are moved in any particular direction; but that these matters were involved and concealed in the profoundest doctrines of philosophy, which these rhetoricians had not touched even with the extremity of their lips. These assertions Menedemus endeavoured to refute, but rather by *authorities* than by *arguments;* for, repeating from memory many noble passages from the orations of Demosthenes, he showed that that orator, while he swayed the minds of judges or of the people by his eloquence, was not ignorant by what means he attained his end, which Charmadas denied that any one could know without philosophy.

**In their view eloquence is due to philosophical knowledge and natural ability.**

XX. "To this Charmadas replied, that he did not deny that Demosthenes was possessed of consummate ability and the utmost energy of eloquence; but whether he had these powers from natural genius, or because he was, as was acknowledged, a diligent hearer of Plato, it was not what Demosthenes could do, but what the rhetoricians taught, that was the subject of inquiry. Sometimes too he was carried so far by the drift of his discourse, as to maintain that there was no art at all in speaking; and having shown by various arguments that we are so formed by nature as to be able to flatter, and to insinuate ourselves, as suppliants, into the favour of those from whom we wish to obtain anything, as well as to terrify our enemies by menaces, to relate matters of fact, to confirm what we assert, to refute what is said against us, and, finally, to use entreaty or lamentation; particulars in which the whole faculties of the orator are employed; and that practice and exercise sharpened the understanding, and produced fluency of speech, he rested his cause, in conclusion, on a multitude of examples that he adduced; for first, as if stating an indisputable fact, he affirmed that no writer on the art of rhetoric was ever even moderately eloquent, going back as far as I know not what Corax and Tisias, who, he said, appeared to be the inventors and first authors of rhetorical science; and then named a vast number of the most eloquent men who had neither learned, nor cared to understand the rules of art, and amongst whom, (whether in jest, or because he thought, or had heard something to that effect,) he instanced me as one who had received none of their instructions, and yet, as he said, had some abilities as a speaker; of which two observations I readily granted the truth of one, that I had never been instructed, but thought that in the other he was either joking with me, or was under some mistake. But he denied there was any art, except such as lay in things that were known and thoroughly understood, things tending to the same object, and never misleading; but that everything treated by the orators was doubtful and uncertain; as it was uttered by those who did not fully understand it, and was heard by them to whom knowledge was not meant to be communicated, but merely false, or at least obscure notions, intended to live in their minds only for a short time. In short, he seemed bent on convincing me that there was no art of speaking, and that no one could speak skilfully, or so as fully to illustrate a subject, but one who had attained that knowledge which is delivered by the most learned of the philosophers. On which occasions Charmadas used to say, with a passionate admiration of your genius, Crassus, that I appeared to him very easy in listening, and you most pertinacious in disputation.

**Cicero's earlier distinction between the good speaker and the orator.**

XXI. "Then it was that I, swayed by this opinion, remarked in a little treatise which got abroad, and into people's hands without my knowledge and against my will, that I had known many good speakers, but never yet any one that was truly eloquent; for I accounted him *a good speaker*, who could express his thoughts with accuracy and perspicuity, according to the ordinary judgment of mankind, before an audience of moderate capacity; but I considered him alone *eloquent*, who could in a more admirable and noble manner amplify and adorn whatever subjects he chose, and who embraced in thought and memory all the principles of everything relating to oratory.

* * * * * * *

Cicero describes his own education.

XXXI. . . . "In the first place, I will not deny that, as becomes a man well born and liberally educated, I learned those trite and common precepts of teachers in general; first, that it is the business of an orator to speak in a manner adapted to persuade; next, that every speech is either upon a question concerning a matter in general, without specification of persons or times, or concerning a matter referring to certain persons and times. But that, in either case, whatever falls under controversy, the question with regard to it is usually, whether such a thing has been done, or, if it has been done, of what nature it is, or by what name it should be called; or, as some add, whether it seems to have been done rightly or not. That controversies arise also on the interpretation of writing, in which anything has been expressed ambiguously, or contradictorily, or so that what is written is at variance with the writer's evident intention; and that there are certain lines of argument adapted to all these cases. But that of such subjects as are distinct from general questions, part come under the head of judicial proceedings, part under that of deliberations; and that there is a third kind which is employed in praising or censuring particular persons. That there are also certain commonplaces on which we may insist in judicial proceedings, in which equity is the object; others, which we may adopt in deliberations, all which are to be directed to the advantage of those to whom we give counsel; others in panegyric, in which all must be referred to the dignity of the persons commended. That since all the business and art of an orator is divided into five parts, he ought first to find out what he should say; next, to dispose and arrange his matter, not only in a certain order, but with a sort of power and judgment; then to clothe and deck his thoughts with language; then to secure them in his memory; and lastly, to deliver

First the commonplaces of rhetorical teaching.

them with dignity and grace. I had learned and understood also, that before we enter upon the main subject, the minds of the audience should be conciliated by an exordium; next, that the case should be clearly stated; then, that the point in controversy should be established; then, that what we maintain should be supported by proof, and that whatever was said on the other side should be refuted; and that, in the conclusion of our speech, whatever was in our favour should be amplified and enforced, and whatever made "for our adversaries should be weakened and invalidated."

XXXII. "I had heard also what is taught about the costume of a speech; in regard to which it is first directed that we should speak correctly and in pure Latin; next, intelligibly and with perspicuity; then gracefully; then suitably to the dignity of the subject, and as it were becomingly; and I had made myself acquainted with the rules relating to every particular. Moreover, I had seen art applied to those things which are properly endowments of nature; for I had gone over some precepts concerning action, and some concerning artificial memory, which were short indeed, but requiring much exercise; matters on which almost all the learning of those artificial orators is employed; and if I should say that it is of no assistance, I should say what is not true; for it conveys some hints to admonish the orator, as it were, to what he should refer each part of his speech, and to what points he may direct his view, so as not to wander from the object which he has proposed to himself. But I consider that with regard to all precepts the case is this, not that orators by adhering to them have obtained distinction in eloquence; but that certain persons have noticed what men of eloquence practised of their own accord, and formed rules accordingly; so that eloquence has not sprung from art, but art from eloquence; not that, as I said before, I entirely reject art, for it is, though not essentially necessary to oratory, yet proper for a man of liberal education to learn. And by you, my young friends, some preliminary exercise must be undergone; though indeed you are already on the course; but those who are to enter upon a race, and those who are preparing for what is to be done in the forum, as their field of battle, may alike

**Accepted precepts concerning rhetorical study.**

previously learn, and try their powers, by practising in sport." "That sort of exercise," said Sulpicius, "is just what we wanted to understand; but we desire to hear more at large what you have briefly and cursorily delivered concerning art; though such matters are not strange even to us. Of that subject, however, we shall inquire hereafter; at present we wish to know your sentiments on exercise."

Methods of rhetorical instruction approved.

XXXIII. "I like that method," replied Crassus, "which you are accustomed to practise, namely, to lay down a case similar to those which are brought on in the forum, and to speak upon it, as nearly as possible, as if it were a real case. But in such efforts the generality of students exercise only their voice (and not even that skilfully), and try their strength of lungs, and volubility of tongue, and please themselves with a torrent of their own words; in which exercise what they have heard deceives them, *that men by speaking succeed in becoming speakers*. For it is truly said also, *That men by speaking badly make sure of becoming bad speakers*. In those exercises, therefore, although it be useful even frequently to speak on the sudden, yet it is more advantageous, after taking time to consider, to speak with greater preparation and accuracy. But the chief point of all is that which (to say the truth) we hardly ever practise (for it requires great labour, which most of us avoid); I mean, to write as much as possible. *Writing* is said to be *the best and most excellent modeller and teacher of oratory;* and not without reason; for if what is meditated and considered easily surpasses sudden and extemporary speech, a constant and diligent habit of writing will surely be of more effect than meditation and consideration itself; since all the arguments relating to the subject on which we write, whether they are suggested by art, or by a certain power of genius and understanding, will present themselves, and occur to us, while we examine and contemplate it in the full light of our intellect; and all the thoughts and words, which are the most expressive of their kind, must of necessity come under and submit to the keenness of our judgment while writing; and a fair arrangement and collocation of the words is effected by writing, in a certain rhythm and measure, not poetical, but oratorical. Such are the qualities which bring applause and admiration to good orators; nor will any man ever attain them, unless after long and great practice in writing, however resolutely he may have exercised himself in extemporary speeches; and he who comes to speak after practice in writing brings this advantage with him, that though he speak at the call of the moment, yet what he says will bear a resemblance to something written; and if ever, when he comes to speak, he brings anything with him in writing, the rest of his speech, when he departs from what is written, will flow on in a similar strain. As, when a boat has once been impelled forward, though the rowers suspend their efforts, the vessel herself still keeps her motion and course during the intermission of the impulse and force of the oars; so, in a continued stream of oratory, when written matter fails, the rest of the speech maintains a similar flow, being impelled by the resemblance and force acquired from what was written.

**Relative merits of declamation and translation.**

XXXIV. "But in my daily exercises I used, when a youth, to adopt chiefly that method which I knew that Caius Carbo, my adversary, generally practised; which was, that, having selected some nervous piece of poetry, or read over such a portion of a speech as I could retain in my memory, I used to declaim upon what I had been reading in other words, chosen with all the judgment that I possessed. But at length I perceived that in that method there was this inconvenience, that Ennius, if I exercised myself on his verses, or Gracchus, if I laid one of his orations before me, had forestalled such words as were peculiarly appropriate to the subject, and such as were the most elegant and altogether the best; so that, if I used the same words, it profited nothing; if others, it was even prejudicial to me, as I habituated myself to use such as were less eligible. Afterwards I thought proper, and continued the practice at a rather more advanced age, to translate the orations of the best Greek orators; by fixing upon which I gained this advantage, that while I rendered into Latin what I had read in Greek, I not only used the best words, and yet such as were of common occurrence, but also formed some words by imitation, which would be new to our countrymen, taking care, however, that they were unobjectionable.

Subject-matter of study.

"As to the exertion and exercise of the voice, of the breath, of the whole body, and of the tongue itself, they do not so much require art as labour; but in those matters we ought to be particularly careful whom we imitate and whom we would wish to resemble. Not only orators are to be observed by us, but even actors, lest by vicious habits we contract any awkwardness or ungracefulness. The memory is also to be exercised, by learning accurately by heart as many of our own writings, and those of others, as we can. In exercising the memory, too, I shall not object if you accustom yourself to adopt that plan of referring to places and figures which is taught in treatises on the art. Your language must then be brought forth from this domestic and retired exercise, into the midst of the field, into the dust and clamour, into the camp and military array of the forum; you must acquire practice in everything; you must try the strength of your understanding; and your retired lucubrations must be exposed to the light of reality. The poets must also be studied; an acquaintance must be formed with history; the writers and teachers in all the liberal arts and sciences must be read, and turned over, and must, for the sake of exercise, be praised, interpreted, corrected, censured, refuted; you must dispute on both sides of every question; and whatever may seem maintainable on any point, must be brought forward and illustrated. The civil law must be thoroughly studied; laws in general must be understood; all antiquity must be known; the usages of the senate, the nature of our government, the rights of our allies, our treaties and conventions, and whatever concerns the interests of the state, must be learned. A certain intellectual grace must also be extracted from every kind of refinement, with which, as with salt, every oration must be seasoned. I have poured forth to you all I had to say, and perhaps any citizen whom you had laid hold of in any company whatever, would have replied to your inquiries on these subjects equally well."

## VII. SCIENTIFIC EXPOSITION OF ROMAN EDUCATION

**Period and Author.** — The *De Institutione Oratoria* was published in the year 96 A.D. It is a systematic summary of the views of education accepted during the last century of the Republic and the first century of the Empire. The former period is included because many of the views of the *Institutes* are avowedly not original, but represent the consensus of opinion for the entire period, Cicero especially being accepted as the authority. Quintilian's experience as a teacher extended from 59 A.D. to the publication of the work, — not an unbroken experience, for portions of that time were devoted to the work of the advocate, and several years to the study and labor incident to the preparation of the *Institutes*. The period represented is, then, practically the third, that of the Hellenized Roman education in its prime.

Marcus Fabius Quintilianus was born at Calagurris in Spain about 35 A.D. He was educated as an orator in Rome, but returned in 59 A.D. to practice in the provinces. After ten years he returned to the capital in the suite of the Emperor Galba. Here he practised as an advocate, and in the reign of Vespasian opened a public school, being the first to receive state support through the practice instituted by that emperor. Among his contemporaries Quintilian was noted for having acquired a large fortune by teaching. He was finally rewarded with a consulship by the Emperor Domitian for his great success as a teacher and for his influence on his times. He was the most cultured as well as the most successful of Roman teachers. His death occurred at about the close of the century. Besides the *Institutes,* there is extant a collection of school exercises or declamations, many of them the work of Quintilian, the remainder the work of his pupils.

**The Source.** — Cicero's exposition of Roman education is from the viewpoint of the orator and practical man of the world; Quintilian's is from the viewpoint of an educator. In the *De Oratore* we have the ideas of an educated man concerning the purpose and methods of a system of education through which he himself has gone and the results of which he has tested by years of experience; in the *Institutes* we have the view of a most successful educator of twenty years' experience who has made himself familiar with the literature of his country and of his subject, whether presented from the Roman or the Grecian point of view. The very purpose of the work was to bring into harmony the conflicting views of previous writers and to systematize accepted views and approved or common practices. While the view of education of this period and of this work is somewhat narrow, yet every phase of education receives some attention, and every problem some consideration. There is to be found in the study of the *Institutes* little of such inspiration as results from consideration of almost any of the similar works of the Greeks. It is a very practical, prosaic presentation of the education of a matter-of-fact people that had borrowed the form without imbibing the spirit of Grecian culture. Both as to form and content, it is most typically Roman; and in its constructive literary form at least it is superior to the Greek.

The *Institutes* consists of twelve books, from the first, second, and last of which the selections have been made. The first book relates to the elements of instruction under the teachers of grammar and of rhetoric, and to the nature of rhetoric itself; that is, to secondary and higher education. The great bulk of the work is a technical treatise on rhetoric itself as constituting the whole scope of secondary and higher education, the purpose of which was the production of the orator. Books III. to VII. inclusive are devoted to the study of invention; Books VIII. to XI. inclusive, to the discussion of elocution, including memory and pronunciation. The twelfth book is devoted to the consideration of the orator himself, — "what his morals ought to be; what should be his practice in understanding, studying, and pleading causes; what should be his style of eloquence; what termination there should be to his pleading and what may be his employments after its termination." This work became the final and standard treatise on the theory and practice of Roman oratory, and is the most elaborate and complete treatise on Roman education ever written. The selections given include all passages that bear upon education in general, omitting such portions as have to do merely with the technique of grammar and rhetoric.

**General Character of the Educational Content of the *Institutes*.** — The general conception of education is the same as that of Cicero: the aim of education is to produce the orator. This term is of much wider significance than at the present day, being then identical with the cultivated man. Quintilian's definition of the orator is "the good man skilled in speaking." The Romans draw a definite contrast between the orator and the philosopher, the only rival of the orator as the type of the educated man. The philosopher cannot be the Roman ideal, for he is not interested in the practical affairs of life. He is not "*the good man*," however skilled in speaking he may be. Moreover, philosophers are rejected because they withdraw themselves from public occupations. It is by insisting upon this distinction that the Romans avoid the disintegrating effects of the individualizing tendencies of such a period in social and educational evolution as characterized the Greeks in a similar period. Another objection urged by Quintilian against making philosophy the aim of education is that philosophy could be simulated while eloquence could not. It is this breadth of view that gives to the teachings of Quintilian much of their educational significance. In contrast with the extremely technical and narrow discussions on rhetoric and the art of oratory which so abounded at this time, and on the other hand with the very general and individualistic views of the popular philosophies of the times, whether Stoic, Cynic, Epicurean, or Eclectic, was this very definite view of Quintilian that education is something which acts upon the whole intellectual and moral nature, and something the object of which is the production of the effective moral man in practical life.

Such an education as that described by Quintilian is a formal institutionalized process; it is the work of instruction given in schools, preferably public schools. It is wholly different from the old Roman education. Yet this presupposition of his should be kept in mind: "It is to be stated, however, in the first place, that precepts and treatises on art are of no avail without the assistance of nature; and these instructions, therefore, are not written for him to whom talent is wanting, any more than treatises on agriculture for barren ground." As with the Greeks, then, education depends upon the three factors, nature, training, and instruction. The treatise is almost wholly devoted to the last, with incidental reference to the second.

The content of such an education was largely grammatical and rhetorical. Hence the larger part of this educational treatise has no longer vital interest, since the conception of education has changed so radically. But the general treatment is yet of interest, and the spirit is independent of either content or purpose, being that of a liberal education of any age. In addition to the grammatical and rhetorical training and instruction, a broad literary education is, according to Quintilian, essential. The tenth book of the *Institutes*, devoted to a discussion of the Greek and Latin literature, is a critique which has few equals. The spirit and the breadth of this aspect of education required by Quintilian is of the best. The grammatical and rhetorical instruction is to be supplemented by a brief study of music, astronomy, geometry, and philosophy. Such studies, however, are incidental, and are recommended because contributory to success as an orator. In the same manner the prospective orator must have a general knowledge of all subjects — must be a well-informed, though not necessarily an erudite, man. Here, however, there is no approach to the Grecian conception of the value of music and the mathematical sciences in the development of the mind.

In the first and second books, Quintilian deals in detail with the methods, subject-matter, and organization of elementary and secondary education. Many of his points of view are essentially modern. All are marked by the same judicious spirit. He would have the work of the school fitted to the disposition and ability of the child; he calls upon teachers to study the characteristics of their pupils; he opposes corporal punishment, and advises attractive rather than compulsory methods; he approves of education in public schools, rather than in the home — a preference due largely to the moral corruption of the times, but also to the inability of the parent to rival the work of a successful teacher, even in the supervision and selection of tutors.

Though Roman education after the time of Quintilian did not remain upon the high plane upon which he placed it, there was probably no marked decay for at least a century or even two centuries later. Some of the material presented bears upon this point. Both Pliny the Younger and Tacitus were pupils of Quintilian, and their testimony refers to about this time. The form, methods, and content of education remained about the same throughout the imperial period, or at least until the imperial interests were centred in the East. But in the spirit and purpose of education there was a marked and immediate decline. In fact, if we may accept the testimony of Tacitus, Quintilian was rather stemming the tide in this respect. The *Institutes* may be taken as descriptive of education throughout the imperial period so far as general aim, form, and method are concerned; and, in addition, as representative of the general conception and spirit of Hellenized education at its best. It forms the most thorough, systematic and scientific treatment of education to be found in classical literature, whether Greek or Roman.

## *Selections from the Institutes of Oratory, by Quintilian*[1]

### BOOK I., CHAPTER I

**General capacity of children.**

1. Let a father, then, as soon as his son is born, conceive, first of all, the best possible hopes of him; for he will thus grow the more solicitous about his improvement from the very beginning; since it is a complaint without foundation that "to very few people is granted the faculty of comprehending what is imparted to them, and that most, through dulness of understanding, lose their labour and their time." For, on the contrary, you will find the greater number of men both ready in conceiving and quick in learning; since such quickness is natural to man; and as birds are born to fly, horses to run, and wild beasts to show fierceness, so to us peculiarly belong activity and sagacity of understanding; whence the origin of the mind is thought to be from heaven. 2. But dull and unteachable persons are no more produced in the course of nature than are persons marked by monstrosity and deformities; such are certainly but few. It will be a proof of this assertion, that, among boys, good promise is shown in the far greater number; and, if it passes off in the progress of time, it is manifest that it was not natural ability, but care, that was wanting. 3. But one surpasses another, you will say, in ability. I grant that this is true; but only so far as to accomplish more or less; whereas there is no one who has not gained something by study. Let him who is convinced of this truth, bestow, as soon as he becomes a parent, the most vigilant possible care on cherishing the hopes of a future orator.

**Importance of early training by nurses,**

4. Before all things, let the talk of the child's nurses not be ungrammatical. Chrysippus[2] wished them, if possible, to be women of some knowledge; at any rate he would have the best, as far as circumstances would allow, chosen. To their morals, doubtless, attention is first to be paid; but let them also speak with propriety.

[1] These selections are made from the *Watson* translation of the *Bohn Library Series*, by special permission of Messers. Bell and Sons.

[2] A Greek philosopher of the Stoic school who lived 282–206 B.C. A few fragments of his writings yet remain.

5. It is they that the child will hear first; it is their words that he will try to form by imitation. We are by nature most tenacious of what we have imbibed in our infant years; as the flavour, with which you scent vessels when new, remains in them; nor can the colours of wool, for which its plain whiteness has been exchanged, be effaced; and those very habits, which are of a more objectionable nature, adhere with the greater tenacity; for good ones are easily changed for the worse, but when will you change bad ones into good? Let the child not be accustomed, therefore, even while he is yet an infant, to phraseology which must be unlearned.

parents, 6. In parents I should wish that there should be as much learning as possible. Nor do I speak, indeed, merely of fathers; for we have heard that Cornelia, the mother of the Gracchi (whose very learned writing in her letters has come down to posterity), contributed greatly to their eloquence; the daughter of Lælius [1] is said to have exhibited her father's elegance in her conversation; and the oration of the daughter of Quintus Hortensius,[2] delivered before the Triumviri, is read not merely as an honour to her sex. 7. Nor let those parents, who have not had the fortune to get learning themselves, bestow the less care on the instruction of their children, but let them, on this very account, be more solicitous as to other particulars.

Of the boys, among whom he who is destined to this prospect is to be educated, the same may be said as concerning nurses.

pedagogues. 8. Of *pædagogi* this further may be said, that they should either be men of acknowledged learning, which I should wish to be the first object, or that they should be conscious of their want of learning; for none are more pernicious than those who, having gone some little beyond the first elements, clothe themselves in a mistaken persua-

[1] Surnamed Sapiens, was born 186 B.C. He had two daughters, one of whom was married to Caius Fannius, and the other to Mucius Scævola. Quintilian evidently refers to the latter.

[2] Quintus Hortensius was a distinguished Roman orator who lived 114-50 B.C. The reference here is to a plea made by his daughter, Hortensia, before the triumviri, Octavianus, Antony, and Lepidus, for a remission of part of the tax laid on matrons.

sion of their own knowledge; since they disdain to yield to those who are skilled in teaching, and, growing imperious, and sometimes fierce, in a certain right, as it were, of exercising their authority (with which that sort of men are generally puffed up), they teach only their own folly. 9. Nor is their misconduct less prejudicial to the manners of their pupils; for Leonidas,[1] the tutor of Alexander, as is related by Diogenes[2] of Babylon, tinctured him with certain bad habits, which adhered to him, from his childish education, even when he was grown up and become the greatest of kings.

10. If I seem to my reader to require a great deal, let him consider that it is an orator that is to be educated; an arduous task, even when nothing is deficient for the formation of his character; and that more and more difficult labours yet remain; for there is need of constant study, the most excellent teachers, and a variety of mental exercises. 11. The best of rules, therefore, are to be laid down; and if any one shall refuse to observe them, the fault will lie, not in the method, but in the man.

If however it should not be the good fortune of children to have such nurses as I should wish, let them at least have one attentive *pædagogus*, not unskilled in language, who, if anything is spoken incorrectly by the nurse in the presence of his pupil, may at once correct it, and not let it settle in his mind. But let it be understood that what I prescribed at first is the right course, and this only a remedy.

Study of Greek and Latin.

12. I prefer that a boy should begin with the Greek language, because he will acquire Latin, which is in general use, even though we tried to prevent him, and because, at the same time, he ought first to be instructed in Greek learning, from which ours is derived. 13. Yet I should not wish this rule to be so superstitiously observed that he should for a long time speak or learn only Greek, as is

[1] Leonidas was kinsman of Olympias, the mother of Alexander the Great. He was instructor to the latter previous to the arrival of Aristotle, and was noted for his severity.

[2] A native of Seleucia, Babylon, who flourished about 240–152 B.C. None of his books are extant.

the custom with most people; for hence arise many faults of pronunciation, which is viciously adapted to foreign sounds, and also of language, in which when Greek idioms have become inherent by constant usage, they keep their place most pertinaciously even when we speak a different tongue. 14. The study of Latin ought therefore to follow at no long interval, and soon after to keep pace with the Greek; and thus it will happen, that, when we have begun to attend to both tongues with equal care, neither will impede the other.

Proper age for beginning to learn.

15. Some have thought that boys, as long as they are under seven years of age, should not be set to learn, because that is the earliest age that can understand what is taught, and endure the labour of learning. Of which opinion a great many writers say that Hesiod[1] was, at least such writers as lived before Aristophanes[2] the grammarian, for he was the first to deny that the *Hupothækai*,[3] in which this opinion is found, was the work of that poet. 16. But other writers likewise, among whom is Eratosthenes,[4] have given the same advice. Those, however, advise better, who, like Chrysippus[5] think that no part of a child's life should be exempt from tuition; for Chrysippus, though he has allowed three years to the nurses, yet is of opinion that the minds of children may be imbued with excellent instruction even by them. 17. And why should not that age be under the influence of learning, which is now confessedly subject to moral influences? I am not indeed ignorant that, during the whole time of which I am speaking, scarcely as much can be done as one year may afterwards accomplish, yet those who are of

[1] The earliest epic poet, Homer excepted, whose writings have come down to us. He was born at Ascra in Bœotia, about the beginning of the eighth century B.C.

[2] A native of Byzantium (about) 260–183 B.C. He has come down to us as one of the ablest grammarians and critics of antiquity.

[3] *Hupothækai* (counsel), a poem now lost, but generally ascribed to Hesiod.

[4] The keeper of the Alexandrian library in the time of Ptolemy Euergetes and the author of several works, which are all lost save a few fragments. ( –222 B.C.)

[5] See note p. 451.

the opinion which I have mentioned, appear with regard to this part of life to have spared not so much the learners as the teachers. 18. What else, after they are able to speak, will children do better, for they must do something? Or why should we despise the gain, how little soever it be, previous to the age of seven years? For certainly, small as may be the proficiency which an earlier age exhibits, the child will yet learn something greater during the very year in which he would have been learning something less. 19. This advancement extended through each year, is a profit on the whole; and whatever is gained in infancy is an acquisition to youth. The same rule should be prescribed as to the following years, so that what every boy has to learn, he may not be too late in beginning to learn. Let us not then lose even the earliest period of life, and so much the less, as the elements of learning depend on the memory alone, which not only exists in children, but is at that time of life even most tenacious.

**Proper methods of early instruction**

20. Yet I am not so unacquainted with differences of age, as to think that we should urge those of tender years severely, or exact a full complement of work from them; for it will be necessary, above all things, to take care lest the child should conceive a dislike to the application which he cannot yet love, and continue to dread the bitterness which he has once tasted, even beyond the years of infancy. Let his instruction be an amusement to him; let him be questioned, and praised; and let him never feel pleased that he does not know a thing; and sometimes, if he is unwilling to learn, let another be taught before him, of whom he may be envious. Let him strive for victory now and then, and generally suppose that he gains it; and let his powers be called forth by rewards, such as that age prizes.

21. We are giving small instructions, while professing to educate an orator; but even studies have their infancy; and as the rearing of the very strongest bodies commenced with milk and the cradle, so he, who was to be the most eloquent of men, once uttered cries, tried to speak at first with a stuttering voice, and hesitated at the shapes of the letters. Nor, if it is impossible to learn a thing completely, is it therefore unnecessary to learn it at all. 22. If no

one blames a father, who thinks that these matters are not to be neglected in regard to his son, why should he be blamed who communicates to the public what he would practise to advantage in his own house? And this is so much the more the case, as younger minds more easily take in small things; and as bodies cannot be formed to certain flexures of the limbs unless while they are tender, so even strength itself makes our minds likewise more unyielding to most things. 23. Would Philip, king of Macedonia, have wished the first principles of learning to be communicated to his son Alexander by Aristotle, the greatest philosopher of that age, or would Aristotle have undertaken that office, if they had not both thought that the first rudiments of instruction are best treated by the most accomplished teacher, and have an influence on the whole course? 24. Let us suppose, then, that Alexander were committed to me, and laid in my lap, an infant worthy of so much solicitude (though every man thinks his own son worthy of similar solicitude), should I be ashamed, even in teaching him his very letters, to point out some compendious methods of instruction?

**Of learning the alphabet,**

For that at least, which I see practised in regard to most children, by no means pleases me, namely, that they learn the names and order of the letters before they learn their shapes. 25. This method hinders their recognition of them, as, while they follow their memory that takes the lead, they do not fix their attention on the forms of the letters. This is the reason why teachers, even when they appear to have fixed them sufficiently in the minds of children, in the straight order in which they are usually first written, make them go over them again the contrary way, and confuse them by variously changing the arrangement, until their pupils know them by their shape, not by their place. It will be best for children, therefore, to be taught the appearances and names of the letters at once, as they are taught those of men. 26. But that which is hurtful with regard to letters, will be no impediment with regard to syllables. I do not disapprove, however, the practice, which is well known, of giving children, for the sake of stimulating them to learn, ivory figures of letters to play with, or whatever else can be invented, in which that infantine age may take delight, and which may be pleasing to handle, look at, or name.

27. But as soon as the child shall have begun to trace the forms of the letters, it will not be improper that they should be cut for him, as exactly as possible, on a board, that his style[1] may be guided along them as along grooves, for he will then make no mistakes, as on wax (since he will be kept in by the edge on each side, and will be unable to stray beyond the boundary); and, by following these sure traces rapidly and frequently, he will form his hand, and not require the assistance of a person to guide his hand with his own hand placed over it. 28. The accomplishment of writing well and expeditiously, which is commonly disregarded by people of quality, is by no means an indifferent matter; for as writing itself is the principal thing in our studies, and that by which alone sure proficiency, resting on the deepest roots, is secured, a too slow way of writing retards thought, a rude and confused hand cannot be read; and hence follows another task, that of reading off what is to be copied from the writing. 29. At all times, therefore, and in all places, and especially in writing private and familiar letters, it will be a source of pleasure to us, not to have neglected even this acquirement.

**and of writing.**

30. For learning syllables there is no short way; they must all be learned throughout; nor are the most difficult of them, as is the general practice, to be postponed, that children may be at a loss, forsooth, in writing words. 31. Moreover, we must not even trust to the first learning by heart; it will be better to have syllables repeated, and to impress them long upon the memory; and in reading too, not to hurry on, in order to make it continuous or quick, until the clear and certain connexion of the letters become familiar, without at least any necessity to stop for recollection. Let the pupil then begin to form words from syllables, and to join phrases together from words. 32. It is incredible how much retardation is caused to reading by haste; for hence arise hesitation, interruption, and repetition, as children attempt more than they can manage; and then, after making mistakes, they become distrustful even of what they know. 33. Let reading, therefore, be at

**Of learning to read.**

[1] The iron pencil used for writing on waxen tablets.

first sure, then continuous, and for a long time slow, until, by exercise, a correct quickness is gained. 34. For to look to the right, as everybody teaches, and to look forward, depends not merely on rule, but on habit, since, while the child is looking to what follows, he has to pronounce what goes before, and, what is very difficult, the direction of his thoughts must be divided, so that one duty may be discharged with his voice, and another with his eyes.

When the child shall have begun, as is the practice, to write words, it will cause no regret if we take care that he may not waste his efforts on common words, and such as perpetually occur. 35. For he may readily learn the explanations of obscure terms, which the Greeks call *glossai*,[1] while some other occupation is before him, and acquire, amidst his first rudiments, a knowledge of that which would afterwards demand a special time for it. Since, too, we are still attending to small matters, I would express a wish that even the lines, which are set him for his imitation in writing, should not contain useless sentences, but such as convey some moral instruction. 36.

**Learning by heart.**

The remembrance of such admonitions will attend him to old age, and will be of use even for the formation of his character. It is possible for him, also, to learn the sayings of eminent men, and select passages, chiefly from the poets (for the reading of poets is more pleasing to the young), in his play-time; since memory (as I shall show in its proper place) is most necessary to an orator, and is eminently strengthened and nourished by exercise; and, at the age of which we are now speaking, and which cannot, as yet, produce anything of itself, it is almost the only faculty that can be improved by the aid of teachers. 37. It

**Importance of pronunciation.**

will not be improper, however, to require of boys of this age (in order that their pronunciation may be fuller and their speech more distinct) to roll forth, as rapidly as possible, certain words and lines of studied difficulty, composed of several syllables, and those roughly clashing together, and, as it were, rugged-sounding; the Greeks

[1] *Glossai* was the term the Greeks applied to a foreign or obsolete word that required explanation.

call them *Chalepoi.*[1] This may seem a trifling matter to mention, but when it is neglected, many faults of pronunciation, unless they are removed in the years of youth, are fixed by incorrigible ill habit for the rest of life.

## CHAPTER II

**Public education to be preferred to private.**

1. But let us suppose that the child now gradually increases in size, and leaves the lap, and applies himself to learning in earnest. In this place, accordingly, must be considered the question, whether it be more advantageous to confine the learner at home, and within the walls of a private house, or to commit him to the large numbers of a school, and, as it were, to public teachers. 2. The latter mode, I observe, has had the sanction of those by whom the polity of the most eminent states were settled, as well as that of the most illustrious authors.

Yet it is not to be concealed, that there are some who, from certain notions of their own, disapprove of this almost public mode of instruction. These persons appear to be swayed chiefly by two reasons: one, that they take better precautions for the morals of the young, by avoiding a concourse of human beings of that age which is most prone to vice (from which cause I wish it were falsely asserted that provocations to immoral conduct arise); the other, that whoever may be the teacher, he is likely to bestow his time more liberally on one pupil, than if he has to divide it among several. 3. The first reason indeed deserves great consideration; for if it were certain that schools, though advantageous to studies, are pernicious to morals, a virtuous course of life would seem to me preferable to one even of the most distinguished eloquence. But in my opinion, the two are combined and inseparable; for I am convinced that no one can be an orator who is not a good man; and, even if any one could, I should be unwilling that he should be. On this point, therefore, I shall speak first.

4. People think that morals are corrupted in schools; for indeed they are at times corrupted; but such may be

[1] *Chalepoi* was the term the Greeks applied to words and phrases difficult to pronounce.

**Public schools no more immoral than homes.**

the case even at home. Many proofs of this fact may be adduced; proofs of character having been vitiated, as well as preserved with the utmost purity, under both modes of education. It is the disposition of the individual pupil, and the care taken of him, that make the whole difference. Suppose that his mind be prone to vice, suppose that there be neglect in forming and guarding his morals in early youth, seclusion would afford no less opportunity for immorality than publicity; for the private tutor may be himself of bad character; nor is intercourse with vicious slaves at all safer than that with immodest free-born youths. 5. But if his disposition be good, and if there be not a blind and indolent negligence on the part of his parents, it will be possible for them to select a tutor of irreproachable character, (a matter to which the utmost attention is paid by sensible parents,) and to fix on a course of instruction of the very strictest kind; while they may at the same time place at the elbow of their son some influential friend or faithful freedman, whose constant attendance may improve even those of whom apprehensions may be entertained.

**Moral weakness begins with early home training.**

6. The remedy for this object of fear is easy. Would that we ourselves did not corrupt the morals of our children! We enervate their very infancy with luxuries. That delicacy of education, which we call fondness, weakens all the powers, both of body and mind. What luxury will he not covet in his manhood, who crawls about on purple! He cannot yet articulate his first words, when he already distinguishes scarlet, and wants his purple. 7. We form the palate of children before we form their pronunciation. They grow up in sedan chairs; if they touch the ground, they hang by the hands of attendants supporting them on each side. We are delighted if they utter anything immodest. Expressions which would not be tolerated even from the effeminate youths of Alexandria, we hear from them with a smile and a kiss. Nor is this wonderful; we have taught them; they have heard such language from ourselves. 8. They see our mistresses, our male objects of affection; every dining room rings with impure songs; things shameful to be told are objects of sight. From such practices springs habit, and afterwards nature. The unfortunate children learn these vices before they know that

they are vices; and hence, rendered effeminate and luxurious, they do not imbibe immorality from schools, but carry it themselves into schools.

Reply to the objection that a pupil receives less attention from a schoolmaster than from a domestic tutor.

9. But, it is said, one tutor will have more time for one pupil. First of all, however, nothing prevents that one pupil, whoever he may be, from being the same with him who is taught in the school. But if the two objects cannot be united, I should still prefer the day-light of an honourable seminary to darkness and solitude; for every eminent teacher delights in a large concourse of pupils, and thinks himself worthy of a still more numerous auditory. 10. But inferior teachers, from a consciousness of their inability, do not disdain to fasten on single pupils, and to discharge the duty as it were of *pædagogi.* 11. But supposing that either interest, or friendship, or money, should secure to any parent a domestic tutor of the highest learning, and in every respect unrivalled, will he however spend the whole day on one pupil? Or can the application of any pupil be so constant as not to be sometimes wearied, like the sight of the eyes, by continued direction to one object, especially as study requires the far greater portion of time to be solitary? 12. For the tutor does not stand by the pupil while he is writing, or learning by heart, or thinking; and when he is engaged in any of those exercises, the company of any person whatsoever is a hindrance to him. Nor does every kind of reading require at all times a prælector or interpreter; for when, if such were the case, would the knowledge of so many authors be gained? The time, therefore, during which the work as it were for the whole day may be laid out, is but short. 13. Thus the instructions which are to be given to each may reach to many. Most of them, indeed, are of such a nature that they may be communicated to all at once with the same exertion of the voice. I say nothing of the topics and declamations of the rhetoricians, at which, certainly, whatever be the number of the audience, each will still carry off the whole. 14. For the voice of the teacher is not like a meal, which will not suffice for more than a certain number, but like the sun, which diffuses the same portion of light and heat to all. If a grammarian, too, discourses on the art of speaking, solves questions, explains matters of history, or illustrates poems,

as many as shall hear him will profit by his instructions. 15. But, it may be said, number is an obstacle to correction and explanation. Suppose that this be a disadvantage in a number (for what in general satisfies us in every respect?) we will soon compare that disadvantage with other advantages.

Yet I would not wish a boy to be sent to a place where he will be neglected. Nor should a good master encumber himself with a greater number of scholars than he can manage; and it is to be a chief object with us, also, that the master may be in every way our kind friend, and may have regard in his teaching, not so much to duty, as to affection. Thus we shall never be confounded with the multitude. 16. Nor will any master, who is in the slightest degree tinctured with literature, fail particularly to cherish that pupil in whom he shall observe application and genius, even for his own honour. But even if great schools ought to be avoided (a position to which I cannot assent, if numbers flock to a master on account of his merit), the rule is not to be carried so far that schools should be avoided altogether. It is one thing to shun schools, another to choose from them.

**Advantages of a public school education:** 17. If I have now refuted the objections which are made to schools, let me next state what opinions I myself entertain. 18. First of all, let him who is to be an orator, and who must live amidst the greatest publicity, and in the full daylight of public affairs, accustom himself, from his boyhood, not to be abashed at the sight of men, nor pine in a solitary and as it were recluse way of life. The mind requires to be constantly excited and roused, while in such retirement it either languishes, and contracts rust, as it were, in the shade, or on the other hand, becomes swollen with empty conceit, since he who compares himself to no one else, will necessarily attribute too much to his own powers. 19. Besides, when his acquirements are to be displayed in public, he is blinded at the light of the sun, and stumbles at every new object, as having learned in solitude that which is to be done in public. 20. I say nothing of friendships formed at school, which remain in full force even to old age, as if cemented with a certain religious obligation; for to have been initiated in the same

**emulation,**

**friendships,**

studies is a not less sacred bond than to have been initiated in the same sacred rites. That sense, too, which is called common sense, where shall a young man learn when he has separated himself from society, which is natural not to men only, but even to dumb animals? 21. Add to this, that, at home, he can learn only what is taught himself; at school, even what is taught others. 22. He will daily hear many things commended, many things corrected; the idleness of a fellow student, when reproved, will be a warning to him; the industry of any one, when commended, will be a stimulus; emulation will be excited by praise; and he will think it a disgrace to yield to his equals in age, and an honour to surpass his seniors. All these matters excite the mind; and though ambition itself be a vice, yet it is often the parent of virtues.

**profit from advances and error of others,**

23. I remember a practice that was observed by my masters, not without advantage. Having divided the boys into classes, they assigned them their order in speaking in conformity to the abilities of each; and thus each stood in the higher place to declaim according as he appeared to excel in proficiency. 24. Judgments were pronounced on the performances; and great was the strife among us for distinction; but to take the lead of the class was by far the greatest honour. Nor was sentence given on our merits only once; the thirtieth day brought the vanquished an opportunity of contending again. Thus he who was most successful, did not relax his efforts, while uneasiness incited the unsuccessful to retrieve his honour. 25. I should be inclined to maintain, as far as I can form a judgment from what I conceive in my own mind, that this method furnished stronger incitements to the study of eloquence, than the exhortations of preceptors, the watchfulness of *pædagogi*, or the wishes of parents.

**incitement to the study of eloquence,**

26. But as emulation is of use to those who have made some advancement in learning, so, to those who are but beginning, and are still of tender age, to imitate their schoolfellows is more pleasant than to imitate their master, for the very reason that it is more easy; for they who are learning the first rudiments will scarcely dare to exalt themselves to the hope of attaining that eloquence which they regard as the highest; they will rather fix on what is near-

**imitation of those more advanced,**

est to them, as vines attached to tree gain the top by taking hold of the lower branches first. 27. This is an observation of such truth, that it is the care even of the master himself, when he has to instruct minds that are still unformed, not (if he prefer at least the useful to the showy) to overburden the weakness of his scholars, but to moderate his strength, and to let himself down to the capacity of the learner. 28. For as narrow-necked vessels reject a great quantity of the liquid that is poured upon them, but are filled by that which flows or is poured into them by degrees, so it is for us to ascertain how much the minds of boys can receive, since what is too much for their grasp of intellect will not enter their minds, as not being sufficiently expanded to admit it. 29. It is of advantage therefore for a boy to have school-fellows whom he may first imitate, and afterwards try to surpass. Thus will he gradually conceive hope of higher excellence.

greater incentive to masters.

To these observations I shall add, that masters themselves, when they have but one pupil at a time with them, cannot feel the same degree of energy and spirit in addressing him, as when they are excited by a large number of hearers. 30. Eloquence depends in a great degree on the state of the mind, which must conceive images of objects, and transform itself, so to speak, to the nature of the things of which we discourse. Besides, the more noble and lofty a mind is, by the more powerful springs, as it were, is it moved, and accordingly is both strengthened by praise, and enlarged by effort, and is filled with joy at achieving something great. 31. But a certain secret disdain is felt at lowering the power of eloquence, acquired by so much labour, to one auditor; and the teacher is ashamed to raise his style above the level of ordinary conversation. Let any one imagine, indeed, the air of a man haranguing, or the voice of one entreating, the gesture, the pronunciation, the agitation of mind and body, the exertion, and, to mention nothing else, the fatigue, while he has but one auditor; would not he seem to be affected with something like madness? There would be no eloquence in the world, if we were to speak only with one person at a time.

## CHAPTER III

**Dispositions and abilities of pupils to be ascertained.**

1. Let him that is skilled in teaching, ascertain first of all, when a boy is entrusted to him, his ability and disposition. The chief symptom of ability in children is memory, of which the excellence is two-fold, to receive with ease and retain with fidelity. The next symptom is imitation; for that is an indication of a teachable disposition, but with this provision, that it express merely what it is taught, and not a person's manner or walk, for instance, or whatever may be remarkable for deformity. 2. The boy who shall make it his aim to raise a laugh by his love of mimicry, will afford me no hope of good capacity; for he who is possessed of great talent will be well disposed; else I should think it not at all worse to be of a dull, than of a bad, disposition; but he who is honourably inclined will be very different from the stupid or idle. 3. Such a pupil as I would have, will easily learn what is taught him, and will ask questions about some things, but will still rather follow than run on before. That precocious sort of talent scarcely ever comes to good fruit. 4. Such are those who do little things easily, and, impelled by impudence, show at once all that they can accomplish in such matters. But they succeed only in what is ready to their hand; they string words together, uttering them with an intrepid countenance, not in the least discouraged by bashfulness; and do little but do it readily. 5. There is no real power behind, or any that rests on deeply fixed roots; but they are like seeds which have been scattered on the surface of the ground and shoot up prematurely, and like grass that resembles corn, and grows yellow, with empty ears, before the time of harvest. Their efforts give pleasure, as compared with their years; but their progress comes to a stand and our wonder diminishes.

**Precociousness not desirable.**

**Management of pupils.**

6. When a tutor has observed these indications, let him next consider how the mind of his pupil is to be managed. Some boys are indolent, unless you stimulate them; some are indignant at being commanded; fear restrains some, and unnerves others; continued labour forms some; with others, hasty efforts succeed better. 7. Let the boy be given to me, whom praise stimulates, whom honour delights,

who weeps when he is unsuccessful. His powers must be cultivated under the influence of ambition; reproach will sting him to the quick; honour will incite him; and in such a boy I shall never be apprehensive of indifference.

**Relaxation and play.**

8. Yet some relaxation is to be allowed to all; not only because there is nothing that can bear perpetual labour, (and even those things that are without sense and life are unbent by alternate rest, as it were, in order that they may preserve their vigour), but because application to learning depends on the will, which cannot be forced. 9. Boys, accordingly, when re-invigorated and refreshed, bring more sprightliness to their learning, and a more determined spirit, which for the most part spurns compulsion. 10. Nor will play in boys displease me; it is also a sign of vivacity; and I cannot expect that he who is always dull and spiritless will be of an eager disposition in his studies, when he is indifferent even to that excitement which is natural to his age. 11. There must however be bounds set to relaxation, lest the refusal of it beget an aversion to study, or too much indulgence in it a habit of idleness. There are some kinds of amusement, too, not unserviceable for sharpening the wits of boys, as when they contend with each other by proposing all sorts of questions in turn. 12. In their plays, also, their moral dispositions show themselves more plainly, supposing that there is no age so tender that it may not readily learn what is right and wrong; and the tender age may best be formed at a time when it is ignorant of dissimulation, and most willingly submits to instructors; for you may break, sooner than mend, that which has hardened into deformity. 13. A child is as early as possible, therefore, to be admonished that he must do nothing too eagerly, nothing dishonestly, nothing without self-control; and we must always keep in mind the maxim of Virgil, *Adeo in teneris consuescere multum est*, "of so much importance is the acquirement of habit in the young."

Corporal punishment.

14. But that boys should suffer corporal punishment, though it be a received custom, and Chrysippus makes no objection to it, I by no means approve; first, because it is a disgrace, and a punishment for slaves, and in reality (as will be evident if you imagine the age changed) an affront;

secondly, because, if a boy's disposition be so abject as not to be amended by reproof, he will be hardened, like the worst of slaves, even to stripes; and lastly, because, if one who regularly exacts his tasks be with him, there will not be the least need of any such chastisement. 15. At present, the negligence of *pædagogi* seems to be made amends for in such a way that boys are not obliged to do what is right, but are punished whenever they have not done it. Besides, after you have coerced a boy with stripes, how will you treat him when he becomes a young man, to whom such terror cannot be held out, and by whom more difficult studies must be pursued? 16. Add to these considerations, that many things unpleasant to be mentioned, and likely afterwards to cause shame, often happen to boys while being whipped, under the influence of pain or fear; and such shame enervates and depresses the mind, and makes them shun people's sight and feel a constant uneasiness. 17. If, moreover, there has been too little care in choosing governors and tutors of reputable character, I am ashamed to say how scandalously unworthy men may abuse their privilege of punishing, and what opportunity also the terror of the unhappy children may sometimes afford to others. I will not dwell upon this point; what is already understood is more than enough. It will be sufficient therefore to intimate, that no man should be allowed too much authority over an age so weak and so unable to resist ill-treatment.

18. I will now proceed to show in what studies he who is to be so trained that he may become an orator, must be instructed, and which of them must be commenced at each particular period of youth.

## CHAPTER IV

**Grammatical studies the foundation.**

1. In regard to the boy who has attained facility in reading and writing, the next object is instruction from the grammarians. Nor is it of importance whether I speak of the Greek or Latin grammarian, though I am inclined to think that the Greek should take the precedence. 2. Both have the same method. This profession, then, distinguished as it is, most compendiously, into two parts,

the art *of speaking correctly*, and the *illustration of the poets*, carries more beneath the surface than it shows on its front. 3. For not only is the *art of writing* combined with that of speaking, but *correct reading* also precedes illustration, and with all these is joined the exercise of *judgment*, which the old grammarians, indeed, used with such severity, that they not only allowed themselves to distinguish certain verses with a particular mark of censure, and to remove, as spurious, certain books which had been inscribed with false titles, from their sets, but even brought some authors within their canon, and excluded others altogether from classification. 4. Nor is it sufficient to have read the poets only; every class of writers must be studied, not simply for matter, but for words, which often receive their authority from writers. Nor can grammar be complete without a knowledge of music, since the grammarian has to speak of metre and rhythm; nor if he is ignorant of astronomy, can he understand the poets, who, to say nothing of other matters, so often allude to the rising and setting of the stars in marking the seasons; nor must he be unacquainted with philosophy, both on account of numbers of passages, in almost all poems, drawn from the most abstruse subtleties of physical investigation, and also on account of Empedocles[1] among the Greeks, and Varro[2] and Lucretius[3] among the Latins, who have committed the precepts of philosophy to verse. 5. The grammarian has also need of no small portion of eloquence, that he may speak aptly and fluently on each of those subjects which are here mentioned. Those therefore are by no means to be regarded who deride this science as trifling and empty, for unless it lays a sure foundation for the future orator, whatever superstructure you raise will fall;

[1] A Greek philosopher and poet, born at Agrigentum in Sicily about 490 B.C. He is supposed to have died in Greece about 430 B.C. His philosophy is grounded upon the assumption of four unchangeable elements, fire, air, earth, and water, and two opposing forces, Love and Hate.

[2] A Roman poet (82–36 B.C.), of whose works we have a few fragments. His fame rests in the domain of narrative epic poetry.

[3] A Roman poet, born at Rome about 98 B.C. and died by his own hand in 55 B.C. His chief work is a didactic poem in hexameter verse of six books concerning the nature of things (*De Rerum Natura*).

it is a science which is necessary to the young, pleasing to the old, and an agreeable companion in retirement, and which alone, of all departments of learning, has in it more service than show.

## CHAPTER VIII

1. Reading remains to be considered; in which how a boy may know when to take breath, where to divide a verse, where the sense is concluded, where it begins, when the voice is to be raised or lowered, what is to be uttered with any particular inflexion of sound, or what is to be pronounced with greater slowness or rapidity, with greater animation or gentleness than other passages, can be taught only in practice. 2. There is but one direction, therefore, which I have to give in this part of my work, namely, *that he may be able to do all this successfully, let him understand what he reads.* On reading.

* * * * * * *

4. Other points demand much admonition to be given on them; and care is to be taken, above all things, that tender minds, which will imbibe deeply whatever has entered them while rude and ignorant of everything, may learn, not only what is eloquent, but, still more, what is morally good. 5. It has accordingly been an excellent custom, that reading should commence with *Homer* and *Virgil*, although, to understand their merits, there is need of maturer judgment; but for the acquisition of judgment there is abundance of time; for they will not be read once only. In the meantime, let the mind of the pupil be exalted with the sublimity of the heroic verse, conceive ardour from the magnitude of the subjects, and be imbued with the noblest sentiments. 6. The reading of *tragedies* is beneficial; the *lyric poets* nourish the mind, provided that you select from them, not merely authors, but portions of their works; for the Greeks are licentious in many of their writings, and I should be loath to interpret Horace in certain passages. As to *elegy*, at least that which treats of love, and *hendecasyllables*,[1] and poems in Authors to be read.

[1] A line of eleven syllables. This refers chiefly to the Phalæcian verse, such as Catullus wrote.

which there are portions of Sotadic[1] verses, (for concerning Sotadic verses themselves no precept need even be mentioned,) let them be altogether kept away, if it be possible; if not, let them at least be reserved for the greater strength of mature age. 7. Of *comedy*, which may contribute very much to eloquence, as it extends to all sorts of characters and passions, I will state a little further on, in the proper place, the good which I think it may do to boys; when their morals are out of danger, it will be among the subjects to be chiefly read. It is of *Menander*[2] that I speak, though I would not set aside other comic writers; for the Latin authors, too, will confer some benefit. 8. But those writings should be the subjects of lectures for boys, which may best nourish the mind and enlarge the thinking powers; for reading other books, which relate merely to erudition, advanced life will afford sufficient time.

The old Latin authors, however, will be of great use, though most of them, indeed, were stronger in genius than in art. Above all they will supply a *copia verborum*; while in their tragedies may be found a weightiness of thought, and in their comedies elegance, and something as it were of *Atticism*. 9. There will be seen in them, too, a more careful regard to regularity of structure than in most of the moderns, who have considered that the merit of every kind of composition lies solely in the thoughts. Purity, certainly, and, that I may so express myself, manliness, is to be gained from them; since we ourselves have fallen into all the vices of refinement, even in our manner of speaking. 10. Let us, moreover, trust to the practice of the greatest orators, who have recourse to the poems of the ancients, as well for the support of their arguments, as for the adornment of their eloquence. 11. For in Cicero, most of all, and frequently, also, in Asinius,[3] and others

[1] A peculiar metre originated by Sotades, a Greek poet of the third century B.C., which was much imitated. It was chiefly used for malicious satires, generally on indelicate subjects.

[2] The chief representative of the Later Attic Comedy. He was born at Athens and lived 342–290 B.C. Fragments of his works are extant.

[3] A celebrated Roman poet, orator, and historian, who lived 75 B.C.–4 A.D. He wrote many works, but not one has survived.

nearest to his times, we see verses of *Ennius*,[1] *Accius*,[2] *Pacuvius*,[3] *Lucilius*,[4] *Terence*,[5] *Cæcilius*,[6] and other poets, introduced, with the best effect, not only for showing the learning of the speakers, but for giving pleasure to the hearers, whose ears find in the charms of poetry a relief from the want of elegance in forensic pleading. 12. To this is to be added no mean advantage, as the speakers confirm what they have stated by the sentiments of the poets, as by so many testimonies. But those first observations of mine have reference rather to boys, the latter to more advanced students, for the love of letters, and the benefit of reading, are bounded, not by the time spent at school, but by the extent of life.

* * * * * * *

## CHAPTER X

1. These remarks I have made, as briefly as I could, upon grammar, not so as to examine and speak of every thing, which would be an infinite task, but merely of the most essential points. I shall now add some concise observations on the other departments of study, in which I think that boys should be initiated before they are committed to the teacher of rhetoric, in order that that circle of instruction, which the Greeks call ἐγκύκλιος παιδεία[7] may be completed.

[1] Born at Rudiæ in Calabria in 239 B.C., and died in 170 B.C. He was the founder of the Hellenized type of Latin poetry. His greatest work was the *Annales*, a chronological narrative of Roman history in verse.

[2] The most highly esteemed as well as prolific of the tragic poets under the Republic. He was born at Pisaurum in Umbria 170 B.C., and died about 90 B.C.

[3] Born about 220 B.C. at Brundisium, and died about 130 B.C. He is the first Roman dramatist who confined himself to the composing of tragedies.

[4] The founder of Roman satire; born about 180 B.C. at Suessa Aurunca in Campania, and died at Naples 103 B.C.

[5] The celebrated Roman comic poet who lived 185–159 B.C. Some of his works have come down to us.

[6] A writer of Latin comedy. He was a Gaul, and came to Rome about 194 B.C., as a prisoner of war. He died 166 B.C.

[7] The circle of those arts and sciences which every freeborn youth was obliged to go through before applying to any professional studies.

Studies preliminary to that of rhetoric.

2. For about the same age the study of other accomplishments must be commenced; concerning which, as they are themselves arts, and cannot be complete without the art of oratory, but are nevertheless insufficient of themselves to form an orator, it is made a question whether they are necessary to this art. 3. Of what service is it, say some people, for pleading a cause, or pronouncing a legal opinion, to know how equilateral triangles may be erected upon a given line? Or how will he, who has marked the sounds of the lyre by their names and intervals, defend an accused person, or direct consultations, the better on that account? 4. They may perhaps reckon, also, many speakers, effective in every way in the forum, who have never attended a geometrician, and who know nothing of musicians except by the common pleasure of listening to them. To these observers I answer in the first place (what Cicero also frequently remarks in his book addressed to Brutus), that it is not such an orator as is or has been, that is to be formed by us, but that we have conceived in our mind an idea of *the perfect orator*, an orator deficient in no point whatever. 5. For when the philosophers would form their *wise man*, who is to be perfect in every respect, and, as they say, a kind of mortal god, they not only believe that he should be instructed, in a general knowledge of divine and human things, but conduct him through a course of questions which are certainly little, if you consider them merely in themselves, (as, sometimes, through studied subtleties of argument,) not because questions about *horns*[1] or *crocodiles*[2] can form a wise man, but because a wise man ought never to be in error even in the least matters. 6. In like manner, it is not the geometrician, or the musician, or the other studies which I shall add to theirs, that will make the perfect orator (who ought to be a wise man), yet these accomplishments will contribute to his perfection. We see

[1] Puzzling questions which appear to have had their name from the following syllogism: "You have what you have not lost; but you have not lost horns; therefore you have horns."

[2] Named from the following question: "A crocodile, having seized a woman's son, said he would restore him to her if she would tell the truth. She replied: 'You will not restore him.' Ought the crocodile to have restored the child or not?"

an antidote, for example, and other medicines to heal diseases and wounds, compounded of many and sometimes opposite ingredients, from the various qualities of which results that single compound, which resembles none of them, yet takes its peculiar virtues from them all; 7. mute insects, too, compose the exquisite flavour of honey, inimitable by human reason, of various sorts of flowers and juices; and shall we wonder that eloquence, than which the providence of the gods has given nothing more excellent to men, requires the aid of many arts, which, even though they may not appear, or put themselves forward, in the course of a speech, yet contribute to it a secret power, and are silently felt? 8. "People have been eloquent," some one may say, "without these arts;" but I want a perfect orator. "They contribute little assistance," another may observe; but that, to which even little shall be wanting, will not be a whole; and it will be agreed that perfection is a whole, of which though the hope may be on a distant height as it were, yet it is for us to suggest every means of attaining it, that something more, at least, may thus be done. But why should our courage fail us? Nature does not forbid the formation of a perfect orator; and it is disgraceful to despair of what is possible.

**As to music; authority for its use.**

9. For myself, I could be quite satisfied with the judgment of the ancients; for who is ignorant that music (to speak of that science first) enjoyed, in the days of antiquity, so much, not only of cultivation, but of reverence, that those who were musicians were deemed also prophets and sages, as, not to mention others, *Orpheus*[1] and *Linus*,[2] both of whom are transmitted to the memory of posterity as having been descended from the gods, and the one, because he soothed the rude and barbarous minds of men by the wonderful effect of his strains, as having drawn after him not only wild beasts, but even rocks and woods. 10. Tima-

[1] The famous mythical poet, son of Œagrus and the muse Calliope. Such was his power in song that he could move trees and rocks, and even tame wild beasts.

[2] A hero representing probably a god of the old Greek nature-worship. His death was commemorated in widely known laments. Tradition says he was the son of Apollo and the princess Psamathe.

genes[1] declares that music was the most ancient of sciences connected with literature; an opinion to which the most celebrated poets give their support, according to whom the praises of gods and heroes used to be sung to the lyre at royal banquets. Does not Virgil's Iopas,[2] too, sing *errantem lunam solisque labores*, "the wandering moon, and labours of the sun;" the illustrious poet thus plainly asserting that music is united with the knowledge of divine things? If this position be granted, music will be necessary also for the orator; for, as I observed, this part of learning, which, after being neglected by orators, has been taken up by the philosophers, was a portion of our business, and, without the knowledge of such subjects, there can be no perfect eloquence.

* * * * * * *

Utility of music.

22. But let us consider what peculiar advantage he who is to be an orator may expect from music. Music has two kinds of measures, the one in the *sounds of the voice*, the other in the *motions of the body;* for in both a certain due regulation is required. Aristoxenus[3] the musician divides all that belongs to the voice into ῥυθμός,[4] "rhythm," and μέλος ἔμμετρον,[5] "melody in measure;" of which the one consists in *modulation*, the other in *singing* and tunes. Are not all these qualifications, then, necessary to the orator, the one of which relates to gesture, the second to the collocation of words, and the third to the inflections of the voice, which in speaking are extremely numerous? 23. Such is undoubtedly the case, unless we suppose, perchance, that a regular structure and smooth combination of words is requisite only in poems and songs, and is superfluous in making a speech; or that composition and modulation are not to be varied in speaking, as in music, according to the nature of the subject. 24. Music, however, by means of

[1] A rhetorician and native of Alexandria. In 55 B.C. he was brought captive to Rome and practised his art in that city. He was disliked by Augustus for his freedom of speech.

[2] A harper at Carthage.

[3] A Greek philosopher and musician, a native of Tarentum, who lived about 330 B.C. He was a pupil of Aristotle.

[4] Ruthmos.

[5] Melos emmetron.

the tone and modulation of the voice, expresses sublime thoughts with grandeur, pleasant ones with sweetness, and ordinary ones with calmness, and sympathises in its whole art with the feelings attendant on what is expressed. 25. In oratory, accordingly, the raising, lowering, or other inflexion of the voice, tends to move the feelings of the hearers; and we try to excite the indignation of the judges in one modulation of phrase and voice, (that I may again use the same term,) and their pity in another; for we see that minds are affected in different ways even by musical instruments, though no words can be uttered by them.

26. A graceful, and becoming motion of the body, also, which the Greeks call *εὐρυθμία*,[1] is necessary, and cannot be sought from any other art than music; a qualification on which no small part of oratory depends, and for treating on which a peculiar portion of our work is set apart. If an orator shall pay extreme attention to his voice, what is so properly the business of music? But neither is this department of my work to be anticipated; so that we must confine ourselves, in the mean time, to the single example of Caius Gracchus, the most eminent orator of his time, behind whom, when he spoke in public, a musician used to stand, and to give, with a pitch-pipe, which the Greeks call *τονάριον*,[2] the tones in which his voice was to be exerted. 28. To this he attended even in his most turbulent harangues, both when he frightened the patricians, and after he began to fear them.

**Necessary for the understanding of literature.**

For the sake of the less learned, and those, as they say, "of a duller muse," I would wish to remove all doubt of the utility of music. 29. They will allow, assuredly, that the poets should be read by him who would be an orator; but are they, then, to be read without a knowledge of music? If any one is so blind of intellect, however, as to hesitate about the reading of other poets, he will doubtless admit that those should be read who have written poems for the lyre. 30. On these matters I should have to en-

[1] The term applied by the Greeks to grace either in music or physical exercise.

[2] The term applied by the Greeks to a tuning-pipe, which was to give the pitch to the speakers or singers.

large more fully, if I recommended this as a new study; but since it has been perpetuated from the most ancient times, even from those of Chiron[1] and Achilles to our own (among all, at least, who have not been averse to a regular course of mental discipline), I must not proceed to make the point doubtful by anxiety to defend it.

* * * * * * *

Utility of geometry.

34. As to *geometry*, people admit that some attention to it is of advantage in tender years; for they allow that the thinking powers are excited, and the intellect sharpened by it, and that a quickness of perception is thence produced; but they fancy that it is not, like other sciences, profitable after it has been acquired, but only whilst it is being studied. 35. Such is the common opinion respecting it. But it is not without reason that the greatest men have bestowed extreme attention on this science; for as geometry is divided between numbers and figures, the knowledge of *numbers*, assuredly, is necessary not only to an orator, but to every one who has been initiated even in the rudiments of learning. In pleading causes, it is very often in request; when the speaker, if he hesitates, I do not say about the amount of a calculation, but if he even betray, by any uncertain or awkward movement of his fingers, a want of confidence in his calculations, is thought to be but imperfectly accomplished in his art. 36. The knowledge of *linear figures*, too, is frequently required in causes; for law-suits occur concerning boundaries and measures. But geometry has a still greater connexion with the art of oratory.

37. Order, in the first place, is necessary in geometry; and is it not also necessary in eloquence? Geometry proves what follows from what precedes, what is unknown from what is known; and do we not draw similar conclusions in speaking? Does not the well known mode of deduction from a number of proposed questions consist almost wholly in syllogisms? Accordingly you may find more persons to say that geometry is allied to logic, than that it is allied to rhetoric. 38. But even an orator, though

[1] Chiron was the son of Cronus and the ocean nymph Philyra. He alone of the Centaurs is represented as wise and just, and was the master and instructor of many Grecian heroes.

rarely, will yet at times prove logically, for he will use syllogisms if his subject shall require them, and will of necessity use the enthymem, which is a rhetorical syllogism. Besides, of all proofs, the strongest are what are called geometrical demonstrations; and what does oratory make its object more indisputably than proof?

**Character of geometry.**

39. Geometry often, moreover, by demonstration, proves what is apparently true to be false. This is also done with respect to numbers, by means of certain figures which they call *ψευδογραφίαι*,[1] and at which we were accustomed to play when we were boys. But there are other questions of a higher nature. For who would not believe the asserter of the following proposition: "Of whatever places the boundary lines measure the same length, of those places the areas also, which are contained by those lines, must necessarily be equal?" 40. But this proposition is fallacious; for it makes a vast difference what figure the boundary lines may form; and historians, who have thought that the dimensions of islands are sufficiently indicated by the space traversed in sailing round them, have been justly censured by geometricians. 41. For the nearer to perfection any figure is, the greater is its capacity; and if the boundary line, accordingly, shall form a circle, which of all plane figures is the most perfect, it will embrace a larger area than if it shall form a square of equal circumference. Squares, again, contain more than triangles of equal circuit, and triangles themselves contain more when their sides are equal than when they are unequal. . . .

**Astronomy; its utility.**

46. Need I add that geometry raises itself still higher, so as even to ascertain the system of the world? When it demonstrates, by calculations, the regular and appointed movements of the celestial bodies, we learn that, in that system, there is nothing unordained or fortuitous; a branch of knowledge which may be sometimes of use to the orator. 47. When Pericles freed the Athenians from fear, at the time that they were alarmed by an eclipse of the sun, by explaining to them the causes of the phænome-

[1] The term used by the Greeks with reference to the drawing of false geometric proofs. Of these, no example is to be found.

non; or when Sulpicius Gallus,[1] in the army of Paulus Æmilius,[2] made a speech on an eclipse of the moon, that the minds of the soldiers might not be terrified as by a supernatural prodigy, do they not, respectively, appear to have discharged the duty of an orator? 48. Had Nicias[3] been possessed of such knowledge in Sicily, he would not have been confounded with similar terror, and have given over to destruction the finest of the Athenian armies; as Dion,[4] we know, when he went to overthrow the tyranny of Dionysius, was not deterred by a similar phænomenon. 49. Though the utility of geometry in war, however, be put out of the question, though we do not dwell upon the fact that Archimedes[5] alone protracted the siege of Syracuse to a great extent, it is sufficient, assuredly, to establish what I assert, that numbers of questions, which it is difficult to solve by any other method, as those about the mode of dividing, about division to infinity, and about the rate of progressions, are accustomed to be solved by those geometrical demonstrations; so that if an orator has to speak (as the next book will show) on all subjects, no man, assuredly, can become a perfect orator without a knowledge of geometry.

## CHAPTER XII

Is there danger of too many studies?

1. It is a common question whether, supposing all these things are to be learned, they can all be taught and acquired at the same time; for some deny that this is possible, as the mind must be confused and wearied by so many studies of different tendency for which neither the

[1] In 168 B.C. he served as tribune of the soldiers in the army of Paulus Æmilius in the war against Macedonia. By foretelling an eclipse, he gained the confidence of the people and was made consul 166 B.C.

[2] Born about 230 B.C., and died 160 B.C. He was one of the best specimens of the high Roman nobles. He received the surname Macedonicus because of his brilliant victory at Pydna in 168 B.C.

[3] One of the most celebrated of the Athenian generals engaged during the Peloponnesian War.

[4] A native of Syracuse who lived about 408–353 B.C.

[5] One of the greatest mathematicians of antiquity. He was born at Syracuse 287 B.C., and was killed by a soldier 212 B.C.

understanding, nor the body, nor time itself, can suffice; and even though mature age may endure such labour, yet that of childhood ought not to be thus burdened.

**Power of the human mind to attend to many things.**

2. But these reasoners do not understand how great the power of the human mind is; that mind which is so busy and active, and which directs its attention, so to speak, to every quarter, so that it cannot even confine itself to do only one thing, but bestows its force upon several, not merely in the same day, but at the same moment. 3. Do not players on the harp, for example, exert their memory, and attend to the sound of their voice, and the various inflexions of it, while, at the same time, they strike part of the strings with their right hand, and pull, stop, or let loose others with their left, while not even their foot is idle, but beats time to their playing, all these acts being done simultaneously? 4. Do not we advocates, when surprised by a sudden necessity to plead, say one thing while we are thinking of what is to follow, and while, at the very same moment, the invention of arguments, the choice of words, the arrangement of matter, gesture, delivery, look, and attitude, are necessarily objects of our attention? If all these considerations, of so varied a nature, are forced, as by a single effort, before our mental vision, why may we not divide the hours of the day among different kinds of study, especially as variety itself refreshes and recruits the mind, while, on the contrary, nothing is more annoying than to continue at one uniform labour? Accordingly writing is relieved by reading, and the tedium of reading itself is relieved by changes of subject. 5. However many things we may have done, we are yet to a certain degree fresh for that which we are going to begin. Who, on the contrary, would not be stupefied, if he were to listen to the same teacher of any art, whatever it might be, through the whole day? But by change a person will be recruited; as is the case with respect to food, by varieties of which the stomach is re-invigorated, and is fed with several sorts less unsatisfactory than with one. Or let those objectors tell me what other mode there is of learning. Ought we to attend to the teacher of grammar only, and then to the teacher of geometry only, and cease to think, during the second course, of what we learned in the

first? Should we then transfer ourselves to the musician, our previous studies being still allowed to escape us? Or while we are studying Latin, ought we to pay no attention to Greek? Or, to make an end of my questions at once, ought we to do nothing but what comes last before us? 7. Why, then, do we not give similar counsel to husbandmen, that they should not cultivate at the same time their fields and their vineyards, their olives and other trees, and that they should not bestow attention at once on their meadows, their cattle, their gardens, and their bee-hives? Why do we ourselves devote some portion of our time to our public business, some to the wants of our friends, some to our domestic accounts, some to the care of our persons, and some to our pleasures, any one of which occupations would weary us, if we pursued it without intermission? So much more easy is it to do many things one after the other, than to do one thing for a long time.

Boys can endure much study.

8. That boys will be unable to bear the fatigue of many studies, is by no means to be apprehended; for no age suffers less from fatigue. This may perhaps appear strange; but we may prove it by experience. 9. For minds, before they are hardened, are more ready to learn; as is proved by the fact that children, within two years after they can fairly pronounce words, speak almost the whole language, though no one incites them to learn; but for how many years does the Latin tongue resist the efforts of our purchased slaves! You may well understand, if you attempt to teach a grown up person to read, that those who do everything in their own art with excellence, are not without reason called *παιδομαθεῖς*, that is, "instructed from boyhood." 10. The temper of boys is better able to bear labour than that of men; for, as neither the falls of children, with which they are so often thrown on the ground, nor their crawling on hands and knees, nor, soon after, constant play, and running all day hither and thither, inconvenience their bodies so much as those of adults, because they are of little weight, and no burden to themselves, so their minds likewise, I conceive, suffer less from fatigue, because they exert themselves with less effort, and do not apply to study by putting any force upon themselves, but merely yield themselves to others to be

formed. 11. Moreover, in addition to the other pliancy of that age, they follow their teachers, as it were, with greater confidence, and do not set themselves to measure what they have already done. Consideration about labour is as yet unknown to them; and, as we ourselves have frequently experienced, toil has less effect upon the powers than thought.

**Abundance of time for all necessary acquirements.**

12. Nor will they ever, indeed, have more disposable time; because all improvement at this age is from hearing. When the pupil shall retire by himself to write, when he shall produce and compose from his own mind, he will then either not have leisure, or will want inclination, to commence such exercises as I have specified. 13. Since the teacher of grammar, therefore, cannot occupy the whole day, and indeed ought not to do so, lest he should disgust the mind of his pupil, to what studies can we better devote his fragmentary intervals, so to term them, of time? 14. For I would not wish the pupil to be worn out in these exercises; nor do I desire that he should sing, or accompany songs with musical notes, or descend to the minutest investigations of geometry. Nor would I make him like an actor in delivery, or like a dancing-master in gesture; though, if I did require all such qualifications, there would still be abundance of time; for the immature part of life, which is devoted to learning, is long; and I am not speaking of slow intellects. 15. Why did Plato, let me ask, excel in all these branches of knowledge which I think necessary to be acquired by him who would be an orator? He did so, because, not being satisfied with the instruction which Athens could afford, or with the science of the Pythagoreans,[1] to whom he had sailed in Italy, he went also to the priests of Egypt, and learned their mysteries.

**Unreasonable pretexts for not pursuing studies.**

16. We shroud our own indolence under the pretext of difficulty; for we have no real love of our work; nor is eloquence ever sought by us, because it is the most honourable and noble of attainments, or for its own sake; but we apply ourselves to labour only with mean views and for

[1] One of the most important of the ancient systems of philosophy. It was founded by Pythagoras (580–504 B.C.).

sordid gain. 17. Plenty of orators may speak in the forum, with my permission, and acquire riches also, without such accomplishments as I recommend; only may every trader in contemptible merchandise be richer than they, and may the public crier make greater profit by his voice! I would not wish to have even for a reader of this work a man who would compute what returns his studies will bring him. 18. But he who shall have conceived, as with a divine power of imagination, the very idea itself of genuine oratory, and who shall keep before his eyes true eloquence, *the queen*, as an eminent poet calls her, *of the world*, and shall seek his gain, not from the pay that he receives for his pleadings, but from his own mind, and from contemplation and knowledge, a gain which is enduring and independent of fortune, will easily prevail upon himself to devote the time, which others spend at shows, in the Campus Martius,[1] at dice, or in idle talk, to say nothing of sleep and the prolongation of banquets, to the studies of geometry and music; and how much more pleasure will he secure from such pursuits than from unintellectual gratifications! 19. For divine providence has granted this favour to mankind, that the more honourable occupations are also the more pleasing. But the very pleasure of these reflections has carried me too far. Let what I have said, therefore, suffice concerning the studies in which a boy is to be instructed before he enters on more important occupations; the next book will commence, as it were, a new subject, and enter on the duties of the teacher of rhetoric.

## BOOK II., CHAPTER I

**Boys should receive instruction from the professor of rhetoric at an early age.**

1. It has been a prevalent custom (which daily gains ground more and more) for pupils to be sent to the teachers of eloquence, to the Latin teachers always, and to the Greeks sometimes, at a more advanced age than reason requires. Of this practice there are

[1] A plain lying to the north of Rome, part of which served as an exercise ground for the Roman youths, and part of which served as meeting-place for the popular assemblies.

two causes: that the rhetoricians, especially our own, have relinquished a part of their duties, and that the grammarians have appropriated what does not belong to them. 2. The rhetoricians think it their business merely to declaim, and to teach the art and practice of declaiming, confining themselves, too, to deliberative and judicial subjects, (for others they despise as beneath their profession,) while the grammarians, on their part, do not deem it sufficient to have taken what has been left them, (on which account also gratitude should be accorded them,) but encroach even upon prosopopeiæ[1] and suasory[2] speeches, in which even the very greatest efforts of eloquence are displayed. 3. Hence, accordingly, it has happened, that what was the first business of the one art has become the last of the other, and that boys of an age to be employed in higher departments of study remain sunk in the lower school, and practise rhetoric under the grammarian. Thus, what is eminently ridiculous, a youth seems unfit to be sent to a teacher of declamation until he already knows how to declaim.

**The profession of the grammarian and of the teacher of rhetoric should be in some degree united.**

4. Let us assign each of these professions its due limits. Let *grammar* (which, turning it into a Latin word, they have called *literatura*, "literature") know its own boundaries, especially as it is so far advanced beyond the humility indicated by its name, to which humility the early grammarians restricted themselves; for, though but weak at its source, yet, having gained strength from the poets and historians, it now flows on in a full channel; since, besides the art of speaking correctly, which would otherwise be far from a comprehensive art, it has engrossed the study of almost all the highest departments of learning; 5. and let not *rhetoric*, to which the power of eloquence has given its name, decline its own duties, or rejoice that the task belonging to itself is appropriated by another; for while it neglects its duties, it is almost expelled from its domain. 6. I would not deny, indeed, that some of those who profess grammar, may make such progress in

[1] Speeches which are suited to the character of the persons by whom they are supposed to have been spoken.

[2] Speeches of a kind which are termed deliberative.

knowledge as to be able to teach the principles of oratory; but, when they do so, they will be discharging the duties of a rhetorician, and not their own.

7. We make it also a subject of inquiry, when a boy may be considered ripe for learning what rhetoric teaches. In which inquiry it is not to be considered of what age a boy is, but what progress he has already made in his studies. That I may not make a long discussion, I think that the question *when a boy ought to be sent to the teacher of rhetoric*, is best decided by the answer, *when he shall be qualified*. 8. But this very point depends upon the preceding subject of consideration; for if the office of the grammarian is extended even to suasory speeches, the necessity for the rhetorician will come later. If the rhetorician, however, does not shrink from the earliest duties of his profession, his attention is required even from the time when the pupil begins narrations, and produces his little exercises in praising and blaming. 9. Do we not know that it was a kind of exercise among the ancients, suitable for improvement in eloquence, for pupils to speak on *theses*,[1] *common places*,[2] and other questions, (without embracing particular circumstances or persons,) on which causes, as well real as imaginary, depend? Hence it is evident how dishonourably the profession of rhetoric has abandoned that department which it held originally, and for a long time solely. 10. But what is there among those exercises, of which I have just now spoken, that does not relate both to other matters peculiar to rhetoricians, and, indisputably, to the sort of causes pleaded in courts of justice? Have we not to make statements of facts in the forum? I know not whether that department of rhetoric is not most of all in request there. 11. Are not eulogy and invective often introduced in those disputations? Do not common places, as well those which are levelled against vice, (such as were composed, we read, by Cicero,) as those

Character of the rhetorical study.

[1] By this term is meant such questions on either side of which a rhetorician may speak with plausibility.

[2] By this Quintilian refers to general disquisitions on points of morality, or questions on points of law, as, for example, what credit should be given to written documents.

in which questions are discussed generally, (such as were published by Quintus Hortensius,[1] as *Ought we to trust to light proofs?* and *for witnesses* and *against witnesses,*) mix themselves with the inmost substance of causes? 12. These weapons are in some degree to be prepared, that we may use them whenever circumstances require. He who shall suppose that these matters do not concern the orator, will think that a statue is not begun when its limbs are cast. Nor let any one blame this haste of mine (as some will consider it) on the supposition that I think the pupil who is to be committed to the professor of rhetoric is to be altogether withdrawn from the teachers of grammar. 13. To these also their proper time shall be allowed, nor need there be any fear that the boy will be overburdened with the lessons of two masters. His labour will not be increased, but that which was confounded under one master will be divided; and each tutor will thus be more efficient in his own province. This method, to which the Greeks still adhere, has been disregarded by the Latin rhetoricians, and, indeed, with some appearance of excuse, as there have been others to take their duty.

## CHAPTER II

1. As soon therefore as a boy shall have attained such proficiency in his studies, as to be able to comprehend what we have called the first precepts of the teachers of rhetoric, he must be put under the professors of that art. Choice of a teacher.

2. Of these professors the morals must first be ascertained; a point of which I proceed to treat in this part of my work, not because I do not think that the same examination is to be made, and with the utmost care, in regard also to other teachers, (as indeed I have shown in the preceding book,) but because the very age of the pupils makes attention to the matter still more necessary. 3. For boys are consigned to these professors when almost grown up, and continue their studies under them even after they are become men; and greater care must in consequence be adopted with regard to them, in order that the purity

[1] See Book I., Ch. I., sec. 6.

of the master may secure their more tender years from corruption, and his authority deter their bolder age from licentiousness. 4. Nor is it enough that he give, in himself, an example of the strictest morality, unless he regulate, also, by severity of discipline, the conduct of those who come to receive his instructions.

Attitude of teacher toward pupils.

Let him adopt, then, above all things, the feelings of a parent towards his pupils, and consider that he succeeds to the place of those by whom the children were entrusted to him. 5. Let him neither have vices in himself, nor tolerate them in others. Let his austerity not be stern, nor his affability too easy, lest dislike arise from the one, or contempt from the other. Let him discourse frequently on what is honourable and good, for the oftener he admonishes, the more seldom will he have to chastise. Let him not be of an angry temper, and yet not a conniver at what ought to be corrected. Let him be plain in his mode of teaching, and patient of labour, but rather diligent in exacting tasks than fond of giving them of excessive length. 6. Let him reply readily to those who put questions to him, and question of his own accord those who do not. In commending the exercises of his pupils, let him be neither niggardly nor lavish; for the one quality begets dislike of labour, and the other self-complacency. 7. In amending what requires correction, let him not be harsh, and, least of all, not reproachful; for that very circumstance, that some tutors blame as if they hated, deters many young men from their proposed course of study. 8. Let him every day say something, and even much, which, when the pupils hear, they may carry away with them, for though he may point out to them, in their course of reading, plenty of examples for their imitation, yet *the living voice*, as it is called, feeds the mind more nutritiously, and especially the voice of the teacher, whom his pupils, if they are but rightly instructed, both love and reverence. How much more readily we imitate those whom we like, can scarcely be expressed.

Attitude of pupils.

9. The liberty of standing up and showing exultation in giving applause, as is done under most teachers, is by no means to be allowed to boys; for the approbation even of young men, when they listen to others, ought to be but

temperate. Hence it will result that the pupil will depend on the judgment of the master, and will think that he has expressed properly whatever shall have been approved by him. 10. But that most mischievous *politeness*, as it is now termed, which is shown by students in their praise of each other's compositions, whatever be their merits, is not only unbecoming and theatrical, and foreign to strictly regulated schools, but even a most destructive enemy to study, for care and toil may well appear superfluous, when praise is ready for whatever the pupils have produced. 11. Those therefore who listen, as well as he who speaks, ought to watch the countenance of the master, for they will thus discern what is to be approved and what to be condemned; and thus power will be gained from composition, and judgment from being heard. 12. But now, eager and ready, they not only start up at every period, but dart forward, and cry out with indecorous transports. The compliment is repaid in kind, and upon such applause depends the fortune of a declamation; and hence result vanity and self-conceit, insomuch that, being elated with the tumultuous approbation of their class-fellows, they are inclined, if they receive but little praise from the master, to form an ill opinion of him. 13. But let masters, also, desire to be heard themselves with attention and modesty; for the master ought not to speak to suit the taste of his pupils, but the pupils to suit that of the master. If possible, moreover, his attention should be directed to observe what each pupil commends in his speeches, and for what reason; and he may then rejoice that what he says will give pleasure, not more on his own account than on that of his pupils who judge with correctness.

**Importance of moral qualifications.**

14. That mere boys should sit mixed with young men, I do not approve; for though such a man as ought to preside over their studies and conduct, may keep even the eldest of his pupils under control, yet the more tender ought to be separate from the more mature, and they should all be kept free, not merely from the guilt of licentiousness, but even from the suspicion of it. 15. This point I thought proper briefly to notice; that the master and his school should be clear of gross vice, I do not suppose it necessary to intimate. And if there is any father

who would not shrink from flagrant vice in choosing a tutor for his son, let him be assured that all other rules, which I am endeavouring to lay down for the benefit of youth, are, when this consideration is disregarded, useless to him.

CHAPTER III

Earlier teachers to be well qualified.

1. Nor is the opinion of those to be passed in silence, who, even when they think boys fit for the professor of rhetoric, imagine that he is not at once to be consigned to the most eminent, but detain him for some time under inferior teachers, with the notion that moderate ability in a master is not only better adapted for beginning instruction in art, but easier for comprehension and imitation, as well as less disdainful of undertaking the trouble of the elements. 2. On this head I think no long labour necessary to show how much better it is to be imbued with the best instructions, and how much difficulty is attendant on eradicating faults which have once gained ground, as double duty falls on succeeding masters, and the task indeed of unteaching is heavier and more important than that of teaching at first. 3. Accordingly they say that Timotheus,[1] a famous instructor in playing the flute, was accustomed to ask as much more pay from those whom another had taught as from those who presented themselves to him in a state of ignorance. 4. The mistakes committed in the matter, however, are two; one, that people think inferior teachers sufficient for a time, and, from having an easily satisfied appetite, are content with their instructions; (such supineness, though deserving of reprehension, would yet be in some degree endurable, if teachers of that class taught only worse, and not less;) the other, which is even more common, that people imagine that those who have attained eminent qualifications for speaking will not descend to inferior matters, and that this is sometimes the case because they disdain to bestow attention on minuter points, and sometimes because they cannot give instruction in them. 5. For my part, I do not consider

Mistakes commonly made on this point.

[1] A famous flute player of Thebes, who flourished under Alexander the Great.

him, who is unwilling to teach little things, in the number of preceptors; but I argue that the ablest teachers can teach little things best, if they will; first, because it is likely that he who excels others in eloquence, has gained the most accurate knowledge of the means by which men attain eloquence; 6. secondly, because method, which, with the best qualified instructors, is always plainest, is of great efficacy in teaching; and lastly, because no man rises to such a height in greater things that lesser fade entirely from his view. Unless indeed we believe that though Phidias[1] made a Jupiter well, another might have wrought, in better style than he, the accessories to the decoration of the work; or that an orator may not know how to speak; or that an eminent physician may be unable to cure trifling ailments.

**Best teachers are best in small things as well as best in great.**

7. Is there not then, it may be asked, a certain height of eloquence too elevated for the immaturity of boyhood to comprehend it? I readily confess that there is; but the eloquent professor must also be a man of sense, not ignorant of teaching, and lowering himself to the capacity of the learner; as any fast walker, if he should happen to walk with a child, would give him his hand, relax his pace, and not go on quicker than his companion could follow. 8. What shall be said, too, if it generally happens that instructions given by the most learned are far more easy to be understood, and more perspicuous than those of others? For perspicuity is the chief virtue of eloquence, and the less ability a man has, the more he tries to raise and swell himself out, as those of short stature exalt themselves on tip-toe, and the weak use most threats. 9. As to those whose style is inflated, displaying a vitiated taste, and who are fond of sounding words, or faulty from any other mode of vicious affectation, I am convinced that they labour under the fault, not of strength, but of weakness, as bodies are swollen, not with health, but with disease, and as men who have erred from the straight road generally make stoppages. Accordingly, the less able a teacher is, the more obscure will he be.

[1] The famous Greek artist; was born at Athens about 500 B.C., and died in 432 B.C.

Better teachers will have better pupils.

Their influence reciprocal.

10. It has not escaped my memory, that I said in the preceding book, (when I observed that education in schools was preferable to that at home,) that pupils commencing their studies, or but little advanced in them, devote themselves more readily to imitate their school-fellows than their master, such imitation being more easy to them. This remark may be understood by some in such a sense, that the opinion which I now advocate may appear inconsistent with that which I advanced before. 11. But such inconsistency will be far from me; for what I then said is the very best of reasons why a boy should be consigned to the best possible instructor, because even the pupils under him, being better taught than those under inferior masters, will either speak in such a manner as it may not be objectionable to imitate, or, if they commit any faults, will be immediately corrected, whereas the less learned teacher will perhaps praise even what is wrong, and cause it, by his judgment, to recommend itself to those who listen to it. 12. Let a master therefore be excellent as well in eloquence as in morals; one who, like Homer's Phœnix,[1] may teach his pupil at once to speak and to act.

## CHAPTER VIII

Variety of capacity and disposition requires variety of treatment.

1. It is generally, and not without reason, regarded as an excellent quality in a master to observe accurately the differences of ability in those whom he has undertaken to instruct, and to ascertain in what direction the nature of each particularly inclines him; for there is in talent an incredible variety; nor are the forms of the mind fewer than those of the body. 2. This may be understood even from orators themselves, who differ so much from each other in their style of speaking, that no one is like another, though most of them have set themselves to imitate those whom they admired. 3. It has also been thought advantageous by most teachers to instruct each pupil in such a manner as to cherish by learning the good qualities inherited from nature, so that the powers may be assisted in their progress towards the object to which they chiefly

[1] *Iliad*, IX. 432.

direct themselves. As a master of palæstric exercises, when he enters a gymnasium full of boys, is able, after trying their strength and comprehension in every possible way, to decide for what kind of exercise each ought to be trained; 4. so a teacher of eloquence, they say, when he has clearly observed which boy's genius delights most in a concise and polished manner of speaking, and which in a spirited, or grave, or smooth, or rough, or brilliant, or elegant one, will so accommodate his instructions to each, that he will be advanced in that department in which he shows most ability; 5. because nature attains far greater power when seconded by culture; and he that is led contrary to nature, cannot make due progress in the studies for which he is unfit, and makes those talents, for the exercise of which he seemed born, weaker by neglecting to cultivate them.

**How far this individual talent or disposition should be encouraged and cultivated.**

6. This opinion seems to me (for to him that follows reason there is free exercise of judgment even in opposition to received persuasions) just only in part. To distinguish peculiarities of talent is absolutely necessary; and to make choice of particular studies to suit them, is what no man would discountenance. 7. For one youth will be fitter for the study of history than another; one will be qualified for writing poetry, another for the study of law, and some perhaps fit only to be sent into the fields. The teacher of rhetoric will decide in accordance with these peculiarities, just as the master of the *palæstra* will make one of his pupils a runner, another a boxer, another a wrestler, or fit him for any other of the exercises that are practised at the sacred games.

8. But he who is destined for public speaking must strive to excel, not merely in one accomplishment, but in all the accomplishments that are requisite for that art, even though some of them may seem too difficult for him when he is learning them; for instruction would be altogether superfluous if the natural state of the mind were sufficient. 9. If a pupil that is vitiated in taste, and turgid in his style, as many are, is put under our care, shall we allow him to go on in his own way? Him that is dry and jejune in his manner, shall we not nourish, and, as it were, clothe? For if it be necessary to prune something away

from certain pupils, why should it not be allowable to add something to others? 10. Yet I would not fight against nature; for I do not think that any good quality, which is innate, should be detracted, but that whatever is inactive or deficient should be invigorated or supplied. 11. Was that famous teacher Isocrates, whose writings are not stronger proofs that he spoke well, than his scholars that he taught well, inclined, when he formed such an opinion of Ephorus[1] and Theopompus[1] as to say that "*the one wanted the rein and the other the spur,*" to think that the slowness in the duller, and the ardour in the more impetuous, were to be fostered by education? On the contrary, he thought that the qualities of each ought to be mixed with those of the other. 12. We must so far accommodate ourselves, however, to feeble intellects, that they may be trained only to that to which nature invites them; for thus they will do with more success the only thing which they can do. But if richer material fall into our hands, from which we justly conceive hopes of a true orator, no rhetorical excellence must be left unstudied. 13. For though such a genius be more inclined, as indeed it must be, to the exercise of certain powers, yet it will not be averse to that of others, and will render them, by study, equal to those in which it naturally excelled; just as the skilful trainer in bodily exercise, (that I may adhere to my former illustration,) will not, if he undertakes to form a pancratiast,[2] teach him to strike with his fist or his heel only, or instruct him merely in wrestling, or only in certain artifices of wrestling, but will practise him in everything pertaining to the pancratiastic art.

The general training preferable.

There may perhaps be some pupil unequal to some of these exercises. He must then apply chiefly to that in which he can succeed. 14. For two things are especially to be avoided; one, to attempt what cannot be accomplished; and the other, to divert a pupil from what he does well to something else for which he is less qualified.

[1] Two Greek historians of the fourth century B.C. Both were pupils of Isocrates.

[2] A youth who trained for the pancratium, where the athletes contested in wrestling and boxing.

But if he be capable of instruction, the tutor, like Nicostratus[1] whom we, when young, knew at an advanced age, will bring to bear upon him every art of instruction alike, and render him invincible, as Nicostratus was in wrestling and boxing, for success in both of which contests he was crowned on the same day. 15. How much more must such training, indeed, be pursued by the teacher of the future orator! For it is not enough that he should speak concisely, or artfully, or vehemently, any more than for a singing master to excel in acute, or middle, or grave tones only, or even in particular subdivisions of them: since eloquence is, like a harp, not perfect, unless, with all its strings stretched, it be in unison from the highest to the lowest note.

## CHAPTER IX

**Pupils should regard their instructors as intellectual parents.**

1. Having spoken thus fully concerning the duties of teachers, I give pupils, for the present, only this one admonition, that they are to love their tutors not less than their studies, and to regard them as parents, not indeed of their bodies, but of their minds. 2. Such affection contributes greatly to improvement, for pupils, under its influence, will not only listen with pleasure, but will believe what is taught them, and will desire to resemble their instructors. They will come together, in assembling for school, with pleasure and cheerfulness; they will not be angry when corrected, and will be delighted when praised; and they will strive, by their devotion to study, to become as dear as possible to the master. 3. For as it is the duty of preceptors to teach, so it is that of pupils to show themselves teachable; neither of these duties, else, will be of avail without the other. And as the generation of man is effected by both parents, and as you will in vain scatter seed, unless the furrowed ground, previously softened, cherish it, so neither can eloquence come to its growth unless by mutual agreement between him who communicates and him who receives.

[1] A native of Cilicia, and renowned for his strength and prowess.

## CHAPTER XIX

Nature contributes more than art in students of moderate ability.

1. I am aware that it is also a question whether *nature* or *learning* contributes most to oratory. This inquiry, however, has no concern with the subject of my work; for a perfect orator can be formed only with the aid of both; but I think it of great importance how far we consider that there is a question on the point. 2. If you suppose either to be independent of the other, nature will be able to do much without learning, but learning will be of no avail without the assistance of nature. But if they be united in equal parts, I shall be inclined to think that, when both are but moderate, the influence of nature is nevertheless the greater; but finished orators, I consider, owe more to learning than to nature. Thus the best husbandman cannot improve soil of no fertility, while from fertile ground something good will be produced even without the aid of the husbandman; yet if the husbandman bestows his labour on rich land, he will produce more effect than the goodness of the soil of itself. 3. Had Praxiteles[1] attempted to hew a statue out of a millstone, I should have preferred to it an unhewn block of Parian[2] marble; but if that statuary had fashioned the marble, more value would have accrued to it from his workmanship than was in the marble itself. In a word, nature is the material for learning; the one forms, and the other is formed. Art can do nothing without material; material has its value even independent of art; but perfection of art is of more consequence than perfection of material.

In those of greater talent, art is more important.

## CHAPTER XXI

Opinions of authorities on subject of rhetoric.

1. As to the *material* of oratory, some have said that it is *speech;* an opinion which Gorgias in Plato[3] is represented as holding. If this be understood in such a way that a discourse, composed on any subject, is to be termed

[1] One of the most famous Greek sculptors, who was born at Athens about 390 B.C.

[2] Marble from Paros, an island in the Ægean Sea.

[3] Plato, *Gorgias*, 449.

a *speech*, it is not the material, but the work; as the statue is the work of a statuary; for speeches, like statues, are produced by art. But if by this term we understand mere words, words are of no effect without matter. 2. Some have said that the material of oratory is *persuasive arguments;* which indeed are part of its business, and are the produce of art, but require material for their composition. Others say that its material is *questions of civil administration;* an opinion which is wrong, not as to the quality of the matter, but in the restriction attached; for such questions are the subject of oratory, but not the only subject. 3. Some, as oratory is a *virtue*, say that the subject of it is *the whole of human life.* Others, as no part of human life is affected by every virtue, but most virtues are concerned only with particular portions of life, (as *justice, fortitude, temperance*, are regarded as confined to their proper duties and their own limits,) say that oratory is to be restricted to one special part, and assign to it the *pragmatic* department of ethics, or *that which relates to the transactions of civil life.*

4. For my part, I consider, and not without authorities to support me, that the material of oratory is *everything that may come before an orator for discussion.* For Socrates in Plato [1] seems to say to Gorgias that *the matter of oratory is not in words but in things.* In the Phædrus [2] he plainly shows that oratory has place, not only in judicial proceedings and political deliberations, but also in private and domestic matters. Hence it is manifest that this was the opinion of Plato himself. 5. Cicero, too, in one passage,[3] calls the material of oratory the topics which are submitted to it for discussion, but supposes that particular topics only are submitted to it. But in another passage [4] he gives his opinion that an orator has to speak upon all subjects, expressing himself in the following words: "The art of the orator, however, and his very profession of speaking well, seems to undertake and promise that he will speak elegantly and copiously on whatever subject may be proposed to him." 6. In a third passage,[5] also, he says:

That of Quintilian agrees with those of Plato and Cicero.

[1] Plato, *Gorgias*, 450–457. [2] Plato, *Phædrus*, 261.
[3] Cicero, *De Oratore*, I. 15; *De Invectione*, I. 4.
[4] Cicero, *De Oratore*, I. 6 [5] Cicero, *De Oratore*, III. 14.

"But by an orator, whatever occurs in human life (since it is on human life that an orator's attention is to be fixed, as the matter that comes under his consideration) ought to have been examined, heard of, read, discussed, handled, and managed.

* * * * * * *

No conflict between rhetoric and philosophy.

12. As to the objection which some make, that it is the business of *philosophy* to discourse of what is good, useful, and just, it makes nothing against me; for when they say a philosopher, they mean a good man; and why then should I be surprised that an orator, whom I consider to be also a good man, should discourse upon the same subjects? 13. especially when I have shown, in the preceding book, that philosophers have taken possession of this province because it was abandoned by the orators, a province which had always belonged to oratory, so that the philosophers are rather trespassing upon our ground. Since it is the business of logic, too, to discuss whatever comes before it, and logic is uncontinuous oratory, why may not the business of continuous oratory be thought the same?

14. It is a remark constantly made by some, that *an orator must be skilled in all arts if he is to speak upon all subjects.* I might reply to this in the words of Cicero, in whom I find this passage:[1] "In my opinion no man can become a thoroughly accomplished orator, unless he shall have attained a knowledge of every subject of importance, and of all the liberal arts;" but for my argument it is sufficient that an orator be acquainted with the subject on which he has to speak. 15. He has not a knowledge of all causes, and yet he ought to be able to speak upon all. On what causes, then, will he speak? On such as he has learned. The same will be the case also with regard to the arts and sciences; those on which he shall have to speak he will study for the occasion, and on those which he has studied he will speak.

* * * * * * *

Scope of oratory.

18. Do subjects of this kind never come to be mentioned in *panegyrical*, or *deliberative*, or *judicial* oratory? When

[1] Cicero, *De Oratore*, I. 6.

it was under deliberation, whether a harbour should be constructed at Ostia,[1] were not orators called to deliver opinions on the subject? yet what was wanted was the professional knowledge of the architect. 19. Does not the orator enter on the question, whether discolorations and tumors of the body are symptoms of ill health or of poison? yet such inquiries belong to the profession of medicine? Will an orator never have to speak of dimensions and numbers? yet we may say that such matters belong to mathematics; for my part, I believe that any subject whatever may, by some chance, come under the cognizance of the orator. If a matter does not come under his cognizance, he will have no concern with it.

Opinion of Quintilian supported by those of other authors.

20. Thus I have justly said, that *the material of oratory is everything that is brought under its notice for discussion*, an assertion which even our daily conversation supports, for whenever we have any subject on which to speak, we often signify by some prefatory remark, that the matter is laid before us. 21. So much was Gorgias[2] of opinion that an orator must speak of everything, that he allowed himself to be questioned by the people in his lecture-room, upon any subject on which any one of them chose to interrogate him. Hermagoras[3] also, by saying, that "the matter of oratory lies in the cause and the questions connected with it," comprehends under it every subject that can possibly come before it for discussion. 22. If indeed he supposed that *the questions* do not belong to oratory, he is of a different opinion from me; but if they do belong to oratory, I am supported by his authority, for there is no subject that may not form part of a cause or the questions connected with it. 23. Aristotle,[4] too, by making three kinds of oratory, the *judicial*, the *deliberative*, and the *demonstrative*, has put almost everything into the

[1] A city of Latium, situated at the mouth of the Tiber, sixteen miles from Rome.

[2] Plato, *Gorgias*, 474.

[3] A native of Temnos (about 120 B.C.). He introduced a most noteworthy system of oratory, which supplied the chief foundation for the theoretical studies of the Romans at the beginning of the first century B.C.

[4] *Rhetoric*, I. 3, 3.

hands of the orator, for there is no subject that may not enter into one of the three kinds.

24. An inquiry has been also started, though by a very few writers, concerning the *instrument* of oratory. The instrument I call *that without which material cannot be fashioned and adapted to the object which we wish to effect.* But I consider that it is not the art that requires the instrument, but the artificer. Professional knowledge needs no tool, as it may be complete though it produces nothing, but the artist must have his tool, as the engraver his graving-instrument, and the painter his pencils. I shall therefore reserve the consideration of this point for that part of my work in which I intend to speak of the *orator.*

### BOOK XII., CHAPTER I

Oratory as the aim of education.

1. Let the orator, then, whom I propose to form, be such a one as is characterized by the definition of Marcus Cato,[1] *a good man skilled in speaking.*[2]

Moral qualities of the educated man.

But the requisite which Cato has placed first in this definition, that an orator should be *a good man*, is naturally of more estimation and importance than the other. It is of importance that an orator should be good, because, should the power of speaking be a support to evil, nothing would be more pernicious than eloquence alike to public concerns and private, and I myself, who, as far as is in my power, strive to contribute something to the faculty of the orator, should deserve very ill of the world, since I should furnish arms, not for soldiers, but for robbers. 2. May I not draw an argument from the condition of mankind? Nature herself, in bestowing on man that which she seems to have granted him preëminently, and by which she appears to have distinguished us from all other animals, would have acted, not as a parent, but as a step-mother, if she had designed the faculty of speech to be the promoter of crime, the oppressor of innocence, and the enemy of truth; for it would have been better for us

[1] Cato, the Censor, born 234 B.C.

[2] Given in his *De Oratore*, as appears from the reference made by Seneca and by Cicero.

to have been born dumb, and to have been left destitute of reasoning powers, than to have received endowments from providence only to turn them to the destruction of one another.

3. My judgment carries me still further; for I not only say that he who would answer my idea of an orator, must be a good man, but that no man, unless he be good, can ever be an orator. To an orator discernment and prudence are necessary; but we can certainly not allow discernment to those, who, when the ways of virtue and vice are set before them, prefer to follow that of vice; nor can we allow them prudence, since they subject themselves, by the unforseen consequences of their actions, often to the heaviest penalty of the law, and always to that of an evil conscience. 4. But if it be not only truly said by the wise, but always justly believed by the vulgar, that no man is vicious who is not also foolish, a fool, assuredly, will never become an orator.

It is to be further considered that the mind cannot be in a condition for pursuing the most noble of studies, unless it be entirely free from vice; not only because there can be no communion of good and evil in the same breast, and to meditate at once on the best things and the worst is no more in the power of the same mind than it is possible for the same man to be at once virtuous and vicious; 5. but also, because a mind intent on so arduous a study should be exempt from all other cares, even such as are unconnected with vice; for then, and then only, when it is free and master of itself, and when no other object harasses and distracts its attention, will it be able to keep in view the end to which it is devoted. 6. But if an inordinate attention to an estate, a too anxious pursuit of wealth, indulgence in the pleasures of the chase, and the devotion of our days to public spectacles, rob our studies of much of our time, (for whatever time is given to one thing is lost to another,) what effect must we suppose that ambition, avarice, and envy will produce, whose excitements are so violent as even to disturb our sleep and our dreams? 7. Nothing indeed is so pre-occupied, so unsettled, so torn and lacerated with such numerous and various passions, as a bad mind; for when it intends evil, it is agitated with

**Why a bad man cannot be a successful orator.**

hope, care, and anxiety, and when it has attained the object of its wickedness, it is tormented with uneasiness, repentance, and the dread of every kind of punishment. Among such disquietudes, what place is there for study, or any rational pursuit? No more certainly than there is for corn in a field overrun with thorns and brambles.

**Objections to this opinion answered.**

8. To enable us to sustain the toil of study, is not temperance necessary? What expectations are to be formed, then, from him who is abandoned to licentiousness and luxury? Is not the love of praise one of the greatest incitements to the pursuit of literature? But can we suppose that the love of praise is an object of regard with the unprincipled? Who does not know that a principal part of oratory consists in discoursing on justice and virtue? But will the unjust man and the vicious treat of such subjects with the respect that is due to them?

9. But though we should even concede a great part of the question, and grant, what can by no means be the case, that there is the same portion of ability, diligence, and attainments, in the worst man as in the best, which of the two, even under that supposition, will prove the better orator? He, doubtless, who is the better man. The same person, therefore, can never be a bad man and a perfect orator, for that cannot be perfect to which something else is superior.

10. That I may not seem, however, like the writers of Socratic dialogues, to frame answers to suit my own purpose, let us admit that there exists a person so unmoved by the force of truth, as boldly to maintain that a bad man, possessed of the same portion of ability, application, and learning, as a good man, will be an equally good orator, and let us convince even such a person of his folly.

11. No man, certainly, will doubt, that it is the object of all oratory, that what is stated to the judge may appear to him to be true and just; and which of the two, let me ask, will produce such a conviction with the greater ease, the good man or the bad? 12. A good man, doubtless, will speak of what is true and honest with greater frequency; but even if, from being influenced by some call of duty, he endeavours to support what is fallacious, (a case which, as I shall show, may sometimes occur,) he must still be heard

with greater credit than a bad man. 13. But with bad men, on the other hand, dissimulation sometimes fails, as well through their contempt for the opinion of mankind, as through their ignorance of what is right; hence they assert without modesty, and maintain their assertions without shame; and, in attempting what evidently cannot be accomplished, there appears in them a repulsive obstinacy and useless perseverance; for bad men, as well in their pleadings as in their lives, entertain dishonest expectations; and it often happens, that even when they speak the truth, belief is not accorded them, and the employment of advocates of such a character is regarded as a proof of the badness of a cause.

* * * * * * *

**A bad man may speak with great force, but does not approach to perfect eloquence.**

23. Let us grant, however, what nature herself by no means brings to pass, that a bad man has been found endowed with consummate eloquence, I should nevertheless refuse to concede to him the name of orator, as I should not allow the merit of fortitude to all who have been active in the field, because fortitude cannot be conceived as unaccompanied with virtue. 24. Has not he who is employed to defend causes need of integrity which covetousness cannot pervert, or partiality corrupt, or terror abash, and shall we honour the traitor, the renegade, the prevaricator, with the sacred name of orator? And if that quality, which is commonly called *goodness*, is found even in moderate pleaders, why should not that great orator, who has not yet appeared, but who may hereafter appear, be as consummate in goodness as in eloquence? 25. It is not a plodder in the forum, or a mercenary pleader, or, to use no stronger term, a not unprofitable advocate, (such as he whom they generally term a *causidicus*,) that I desire to form, but a man who, being possessed of the highest natural genius, stores his mind thoroughly with the most valuable kinds of knowledge; a man sent by the gods to do honour to the world, and such as no preceding age has known; a man in every way eminent and excellent, a thinker of the best thoughts and a speaker of the best language. 26. For such a man's ability how small a scope will there be in the defence of innocence or the repression of guilt in the forum, or in supporting truth against falsehood in litigations about

money? He will appear great, indeed, even in such inferior employments, but his powers will shine with the highest lustre on greater occasions, when the counsels of the senate are to be directed, and the people to be guided from error into rectitude. 27. Is it not such an orator that Virgil appears to have imagined, representing him as a calmer of the populace in a sedition, when they were hurling firebrands and stones?

> Then if perchance a sage they see, rever'd
> For piety and worth, they hush their noise,
> And stand with ears attentive.[1]

We see that he first makes him a good man, and then adds that he is skilled in speaking:

> With words
> He rules their passions and their breasts controls.

28. Would not the orator whom I am trying to form, too, if he were in the field of battle, and his soldiers required to be encouraged to engage, draw the materials for an exhortation from the most profound precepts of philosophy? for how could all the terrors of toil, pain, and even death, be banished from their breasts, unless vivid feelings of piety, fortitude, and honour, be substituted in their place? 29. He, doubtless, will best implant such feelings in the breasts of others who has first implanted them in his own; for simulation, however guarded it be, always betrays itself, nor was there ever such power of eloquence in any man that he would not falter and hesitate whenever his words were at variance with his thoughts. 30. But a bad man must of necessity utter words at variance with his thoughts; while to good men, on the contrary, a virtuous sincerity of language will never be wanting, nor (for good men will also be wise) a power of producing the most excellent thoughts, which, though they may be destitute of showy charms, will be sufficiently adorned by their own natural qualities, since whatever is said with honest feeling will also be said with eloquence.

* * * * * * *

[1] *Æneid*, I. 148.

## CHAPTER II

Orator must study to maintain a high moral character.

1. Since an orator, then, is a good man, and a good man cannot be conceived to exist without virtuous inclinations, and virtue, though it receives certain impulses from nature, requires notwithstanding to be brought to maturity by instruction, the orator must above all things study *morality*, and must obtain a thorough knowledge of all that is just and honourable, without which no one can either be a good, man or an able speaker. 2. Unless, indeed, we feel inclined to adopt the opinion of those who think that the moral character is formed by nature, and is not at all influenced by discipline; and who forsooth, acknowledge that manual operations, and even the meanest of them, cannot be acquired without the aid of teachers, but say that we possess virtue, (than which nothing has been given to man that raises him nearer to the immortal gods,) unsought and without labour, simply because we are born what we are. 3. But will that man be temperate, who does not know even what temperance is? Or will that man be possessed of fortitude, who has used no means to free his mind from the terrors of pain, death, and superstition? Or will that man be just, who has entered into no examination of what is equitable and good, and who has never ascertained from any dissertation of the least learning, the principles either of the laws which are by nature prescribed to all men, or of those which are instituted among particular people and nations? Of how little consequence do they think all this, to whom it appears so easy! 4. But I shall say no more on this point, on which I think that no man, who *has tasted of learning*, as they say, *with but the slightest touch of his lips*, will entertain the least doubt.

Education must reënforce nature in tendencies to virtue.

I pass on to my second proposition, that no man will ever be thoroughly accomplished in eloquence, who has not gained a deep insight into the impulses of human nature, and formed his moral character on the precepts of others and on his own reflection. 5. It is not without reason that Lucius Crassus, in the third book De Oratore,[1] asserts that everything that can come under discussion re-

[1] Cicero's *De Oratore.* Lucius Licinius Crassus, a leading orator of his times, was one of the characters in the dialogue.

specting equity, justice, truth, goodness, and whatever is of an opposite nature, are the proper concerns of the orator; and that the philosophers, when they inculcate those virtues with the force of eloquence, use the arms of the orator and not their own. Yet he admits that the knowledge of these subjects must now be sought from philosophy, because philosophy, apparently, seems to him to be more fully in possession of them. 6. Hence also it is that Cicero remarks, in many passages both of his books and of his letters, that the power of eloquence is to be derived from the deepest sources of wisdom, and that accordingly the same persons were for a considerable time the teachers at once of eloquence and of morality.

This exhortation of mine, however, is not designed to intimate that I should wish the orator to be a philosopher, since no other mode of life has withdrawn itself further from the duties of civil society, and all that concerns the orator. 7. Which of the philosophers, indeed, ever frequented courts of justice, or distinguished himself in public assemblies? Which of them ever engaged even in the management of political affairs, on which most of them have given such earnest precepts? But I should desire the orator, whom I am trying to form, to be a kind of *Roman wise man*, who may prove himself a true statesman, not by discussions in retirement, but by personal experience and exertions in public life. 8. But because the pursuits of philosophy have been deserted by those who have devoted their minds to eloquence, and because they no longer display themselves in their proper field of action, and in the open light of the forum, but have retreated, at first into the porticoes and gymnasia, and since into the assemblies of the schools, the orator must seek that which is necessary for him, and which is not taught by the masters of eloquence, among those with whom it has remained, by perusing with the most diligent application the authors that give instruction in virtue, that his life may be in conformity with a thorough knowledge of divine and human things; and how much more important and noble would these things appear, if those were to teach them who could discourse on them with the highest eloquence? 9. Would that there may some day come a time, when some orator, perfect as we wish him to be, may vindicate to himself the study of philosophy, (which has been rendered odious as well by the arrogant assumptions, as by the vices, of those who have disgraced its excellent nature,) and, by a re-conquest as it were, annex it again to the domain of eloquence!

10. As philosophy is divided into three parts, *physics*, *ethics*, and *dialectics*, by which of the three is it not allied with the business of the orator? **Divisions of philosophy.**

To consider them in the order contrary to that in which I have named them, no man can surely doubt whether the last, which is wholly employed about words, concerns the orator, if it be his business to know the exact significations of terms, to clear ambiguities, to disentangle perplexities, to distinguish falsehood from truth, and to establish or refute what he may desire; 11. though, indeed, we shall not have to use these arts with such exactness and preciseness in pleadings in the forum, as is observed in the disputations of the schools; because the orator must not only instruct his audience, but must move and delight them, and to effect that object there is need of energy, animation, and grace; the difference between the orator and the dialectician being as great as that in the courses of rivers of an opposite character; for the force of streams that flow between high banks, and with a full flood, is far greater than that of shallow brooks, with water struggling against the obstructions of pebbles. 12. And as the teachers of wrestling do not instruct their pupils in all the *attitudes*, as they call them, that they may use all that they have learned in an actual struggle with an adversary, (for more may be effected by weight, and firmness, and ardour,) but that they may have a large number of artifices, of which they may adopt one or other as occasion may require; 13. so the art of logic, or of *disputation*, if we had rather give it that name, though it is often of the greatest use in definitions and deductions, in marking differences and in explaining ambiguities, in distinguishing and dividing, in perplexing and entangling, yet, if it assumes to itself the whole conduct of a cause in the forum, will prove but a hindrance to what is better than itself, and will waste, by its very subtilty, the strength that is divided to suit its **Dialectics.**

niceties. 14. We may accordingly see that some people, extremely acute in disputations, are, when they are drawn beyond the sphere of cavilling, no more able to support any important exertion of eloquence, than certain little animals, which are active enough to escape being caught in a small space, can prevent themselves from being seized in an open field.

Ethics. 15. As to that part of philosophy which is called *moral*, the study of it is certainly wholly suited to the orator; for in such a variety of causes, (as I have remarked in the preceding books,) in which some points are ascertained by conjecture, others are settled by definition, others are set aside by the law, others fall under the state of exception, others are determined by syllogism, others depend on a comparison of different laws, others on explanations of ambiguous terms, scarcely a single cause can occur in some part of which considerations of equity and morality are not concerned. Who does not know, also, that there are numbers of cases which depend entirely on the estimation of the quality of an act, a question purely moral? 16. In deliberative oratory, also, what means would there be of exhortation unconnected with questions of honesty? As to the third kind of oratory, too, which consists in the duties of praising and censuring, what shall be said of it? It is assuredly engaged about considerations of right and wrong. 17. Will not an orator have to speak much of justice, fortitude, abstinence, temperance, piety? Yet the good man, who has a knowledge of these virtues, not by sound and name only, not as heard merely by the ear to be repeated by the tongue, but who has embraced them in his heart, and thinks in conformity with them, will have no difficulty in conceiving proper notions about them, and will express sincerely what he thinks.

18. Again, as every general question is more comprehensive than a particular one, as a part is contained in the whole while the whole is not included in a part, no one will doubt that general questions are intimately connected with that kind of studies of which we are speaking. 19. As there are many points also which require to be settled by appropriate and brief definitions, whence *one state* of causes is called the *definitive*, ought not the orator

to be prepared for giving such definitions by those who have given most attention to that department of study? Does not every question of equity depend either on an exact determination of the sense of words, or on the consideration of what is right, or on conjecture respecting the intention of the author of something written? and of all such questions part will rest on logical and part on ethical science. 20. All oratory, therefore, naturally partakes of these two departments of philosophy: I mean all oratory that truly deserves the name; for mere loquacity, which is ignorant of all such learning, must necessarily go astray, as having either no guides, or guides that are deceitful.

**Natural philosophy.**

But the department of *natural* philosophy, besides that it affords so much wider a field for exercise in speaking than other subjects, inasmuch as we must treat of divine in a more elevated style than of human things, embraces also the whole of moral science, without which, as I have just shown, there can be no real oratory. 21. For if the world is governed by a providence, the state ought surely to be ruled by the superintendence of good men. If our souls are of divine origin, we ought to devote ourselves to virtue, and not to be slaves to a body of terrestrial nature. Will not the orator frequently have to treat of such subjects as these? Will he not have to speak of auguries, oracles, and of everything pertaining to religion, on which the most important deliberations in the senate often depend, at least if he is to be, as I think that he ought to be, a well qualified statesman? What sort of eloquence can be imagined, indeed, to proceed from a man who is ignorant of the noblest subjects of human contemplation?

* * * * * * *

**The orator need not ally himself with any sect.**

27. But an orator has no need to bind himself to the laws of any particular sect; for the office to which he devotes himself, and for which he is as it were a candidate, is of a loftier and better nature, since he is to be distinguished as well by excellence of moral conduct as by merit in eloquence. He will accordingly select the most eloquent orators for imitation in oratory, and for forming his moral character will fix upon the most honourable precepts and the most direct road to virtue. 28. He will indeed

exercise himself on all subjects, but he will attach himself most to those of the highest and noblest nature; for what more fertile subjects can be found, indeed, for grave and copious eloquence, than dissertations on virtue, on government, on providence, on the origin of the human mind, and on friendship? These are the topics by which the mind and the language are alike elevated; *what is really good; what allays fear, restrains cupidity, frees us from the prejudices of the vulgar, and raises the mind towards the heaven from which it sprung.*

Should learn the good of all.

29. Nor will it be proper to understand those matters only which are comprehended in the sciences of which I have been speaking, but still more to know, and to bear continually in mind, the noble deeds and sayings which are recorded of the great men of antiquity, and which certainly are nowhere found in greater number or excellence than in the annals of our own commonwealth. 30. Will men of any other nation give better lessons of fortitude, justice, honour, temperance, frugality, contempt of pain and death, than a Fabricius,[1] a Curius,[2] a Regulus,[3] a Decius,[4] a Mucius,[5] and others without number? for highly as the Greeks abound in precepts, the Romans, what is of far more importance, abound quite as much as in examples; 31. and that man will feel himself in a manner impelled by the biography of his country to a similar course of conduct, who does not think it sufficient

[1] Roman consul, first in 283 B.C., again in 279. Refused bribe from Pyrrhus. Later returned in chains the ambassador of Pyrrhus, who offered to poison his master.

[2] Roman consul, first in 290 B.C. Noted for his simplicity of life.

[3] Roman consul made prisoner by the Carthaginians, 255 B.C. When returned to Rome on an embassy to make peace, he advised against it, and returned as a prisoner to Carthage, to a martyr's death.

[4] A Roman consul who gave his life for the safety of his country in the war against the Latins, 337 B.C.

[5] Mucius Scævola entered the enemy's camp for the purpose of killing King Porsena, but by mistake killed the king's secretary. On being brought to execution by fire, he placed his right hand in the flame until consumed. The king ordered him released on account of his bravery. Mucius then informed Porsena of the purpose of three hundred youths to attempt his death. This so terrified the king that he withdrew.

to regard merely the present age, and the passing day, but considers that any honourable remembrance among posterity is but the just sequel to a life of virtue, and the completion of a career of merit. From this source let the orator whom I would form derive strong encouragements to the observance of justice, and let him show a sense of liberty drawn from hence in his pleadings in the forum and in his addresses to the senate. Nor will he indeed ever be a consummate orator who has not both knowledge and boldness to speak with sincerity. . . .

# INDEX

## THE MEANING OF EDUCATION, WITH OTHER ESSAYS AND ADDRESSES

By **Nicholas Murray Butler**, Columbia University. Cloth, 12mo. $1.00.

### HAMILTON W. MABIE

"I do not recall any recent discussion of educational questions which has seemed to me so adequate in knowledge and so full of genuine insight."

### REVIEW OF REVIEWS

"We are sure that the teachers of the country will be glad to have these articles and addresses brought together in a single volume. On all that pertains to the science of education no writer more readily commands assent than Dr. Butler."

## SOCIAL PHASES OF EDUCATION IN THE SCHOOL AND THE HOME

By **Samuel T. Dutton**, Superintendent of Schools, Brookline, Mass. Cloth, 12mo. $1.25.

## EDUCATIONAL AIMS AND EDUCATIONAL VALUES

By **Paul H. Hanus**, Assistant Professor of the History and Art of Teaching, Harvard University. Cloth, 12mo. $1.00.

## THE DEVELOPMENT OF THE CHILD

By **Nathan Oppenheim**, Attending Physician to the Children's Department of Mt. Sinai Hospital. Cloth, 12mo. $1.25, *net*.

## THE PHYSICAL NATURE OF THE CHILD, AND HOW TO STUDY IT

By **Stuart H. Rowe**, Supervising Principal of the Lovell District, New Haven, Conn. Cloth, 12mo. $1.00.

## THE STUDY OF CHILDREN AND THEIR SCHOOL TRAINING

By **Francis Warner**, M.D. Cloth, 12mo. $1.00, *net*.

---

THE MACMILLAN COMPANY

**66 FIFTH AVENUE, NEW YORK**